SOUL EATER

5

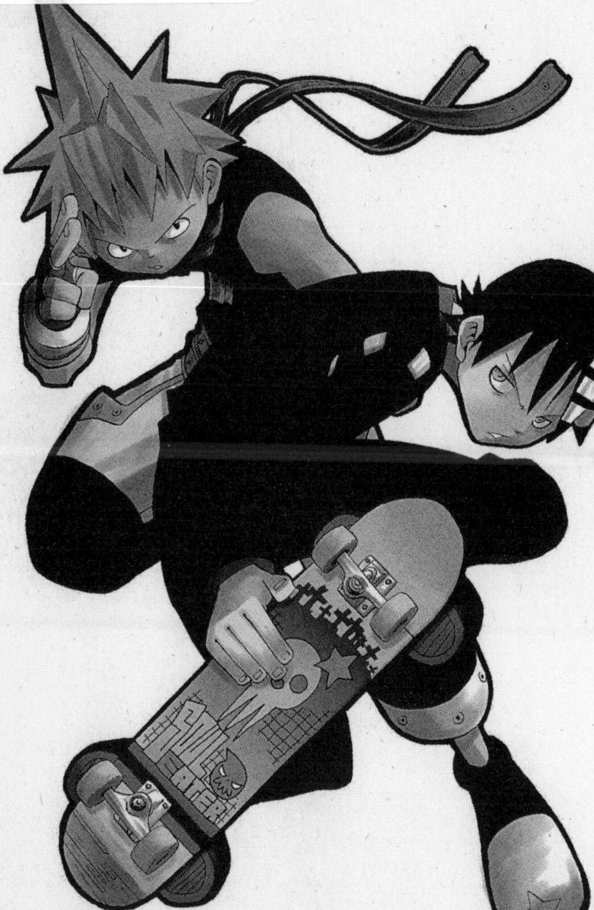

ATSUSHI OHKUBO

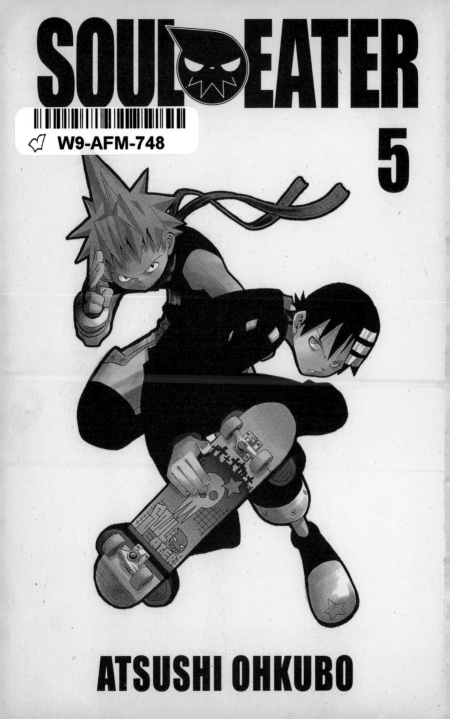

SOUL EAT

vol. 5

by ATSUSHI OHKUBO

While our SOUL lasts till the limit

SOUL EATER 5

CONTENTS

Chapter 15: The Anniversary Celebration 005

Chapter 16: A Fight to the Death at the Anniversary Celebration (Part 1) ..050

Chapter 17: A Fight to the Death at the Anniversary Celebration (Part 2) ..095

Chapter 18: A Fight to the Death at the Anniversary Celebration (Part 3) ..135

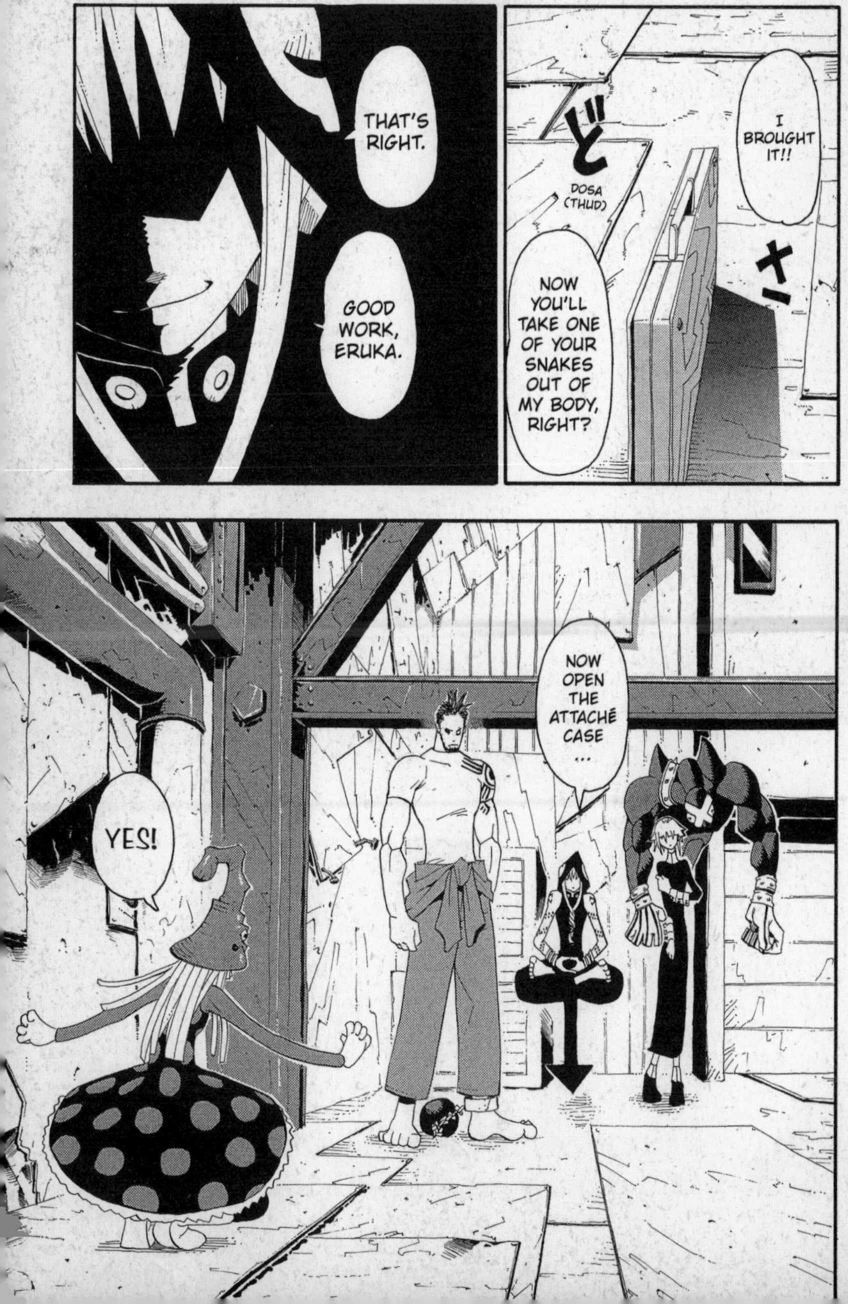
I BROUGHT IT!!
DOSA (THUD)
NOW YOU'LL TAKE ONE OF YOUR SNAKES OUT OF MY BODY, RIGHT?
THAT'S RIGHT.
GOOD WORK, ERUKA.
NOW OPEN THE ATTACHÉ CASE ...
YES!

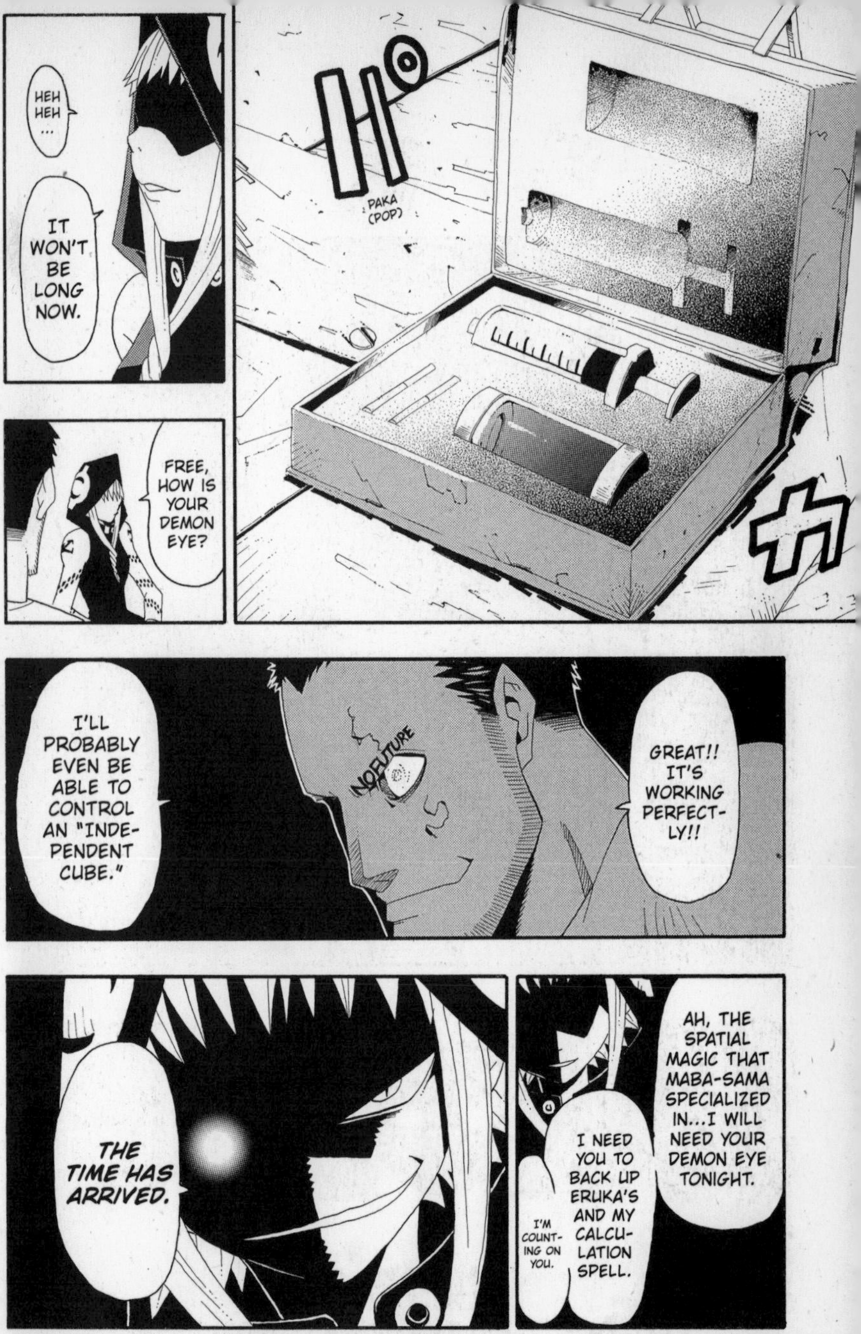
PAKA (POP)
HEH HEH ...
IT WON'T BE LONG NOW.
FREE, HOW IS YOUR DEMON EYE?
GREAT!! IT'S WORKING PERFECTLY!!
NO FUTURE
I'LL PROBABLY EVEN BE ABLE TO CONTROL AN "INDEPENDENT CUBE."
AH, THE SPATIAL MAGIC THAT MABA-SAMA SPECIALIZED IN...I WILL NEED YOUR DEMON EYE TONIGHT.
I NEED YOU TO BACK UP ERUKA'S AND MY CALCULATION SPELL.
I'M COUNTING ON YOU.
THE TIME HAS ARRIVED.

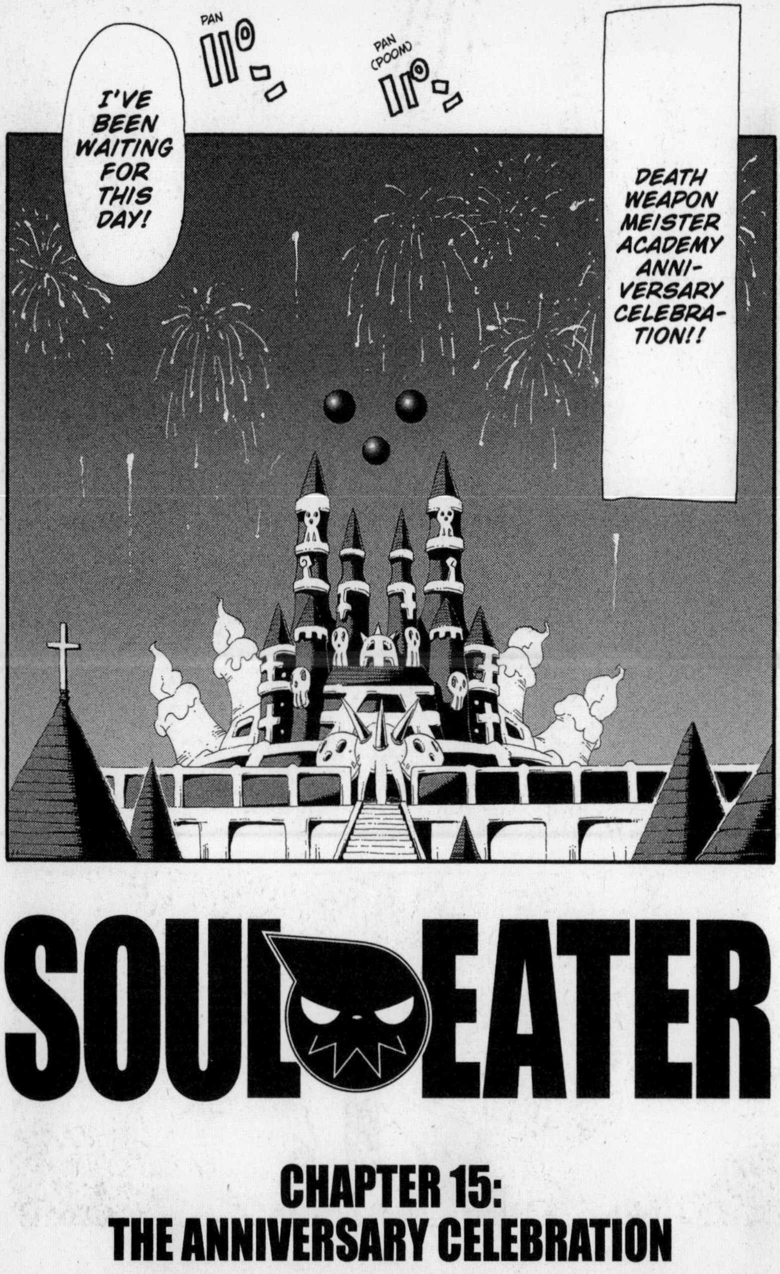
DEATH WEAPON MEISTER ACADEMY ANNIVERSARY CELEBRATION!!
PAN (POOM)
PAN
I'VE BEEN WAITING FOR THIS DAY!

SOUL EATER

CHAPTER 15: THE ANNIVERSARY CELEBRATION

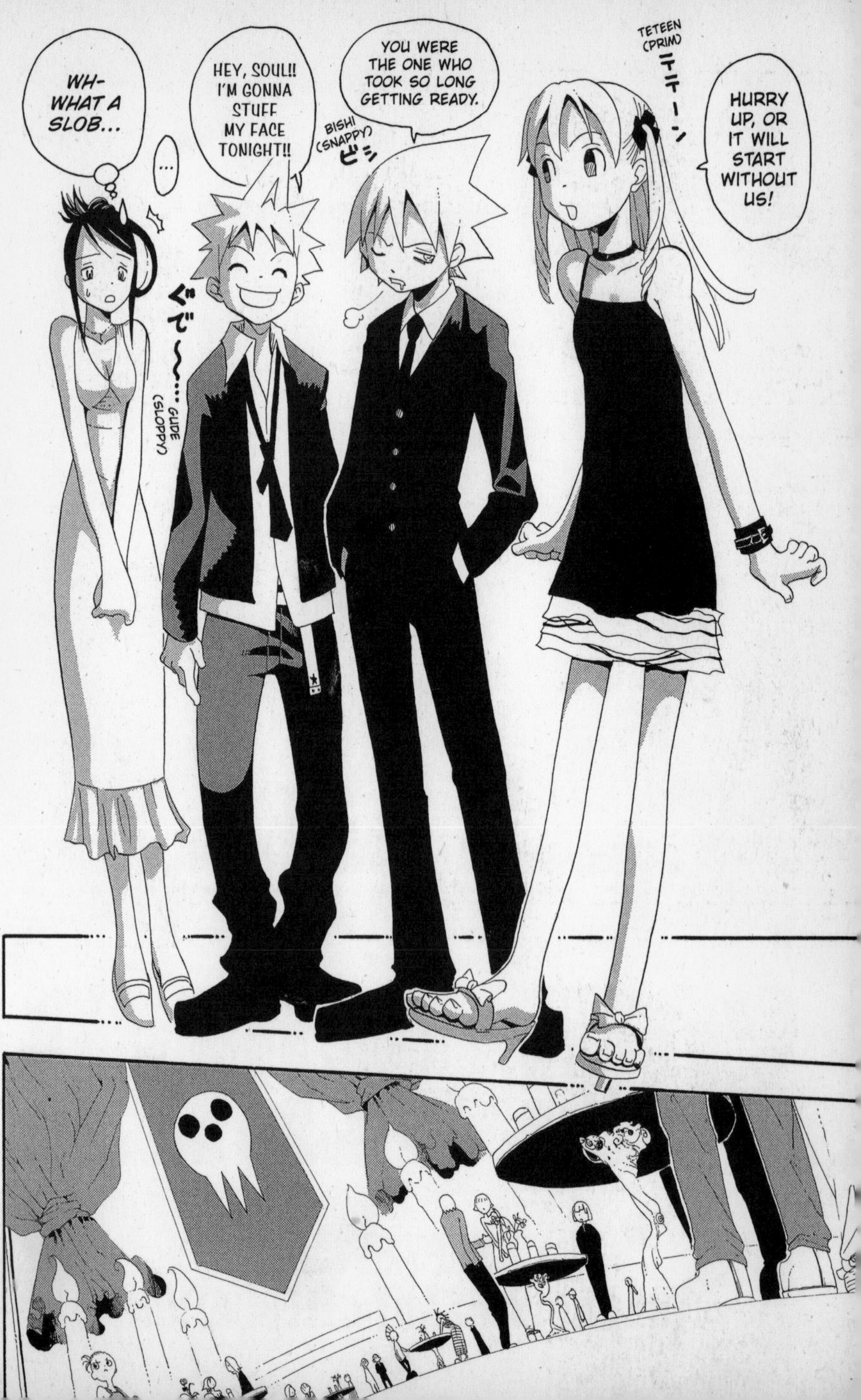
TETEEN (PRIM)
テテーン
HURRY UP, OR IT WILL START WITHOUT US!
YOU WERE THE ONE WHO TOOK SO LONG GETTING READY.
BISHI (SNAPPY)
ビシ
HEY, SOUL!! I'M GONNA STUFF MY FACE TONIGHT!!
ぐで〜…
GUDE (SLOPPY)
...
WH- WHAT A SLOB...

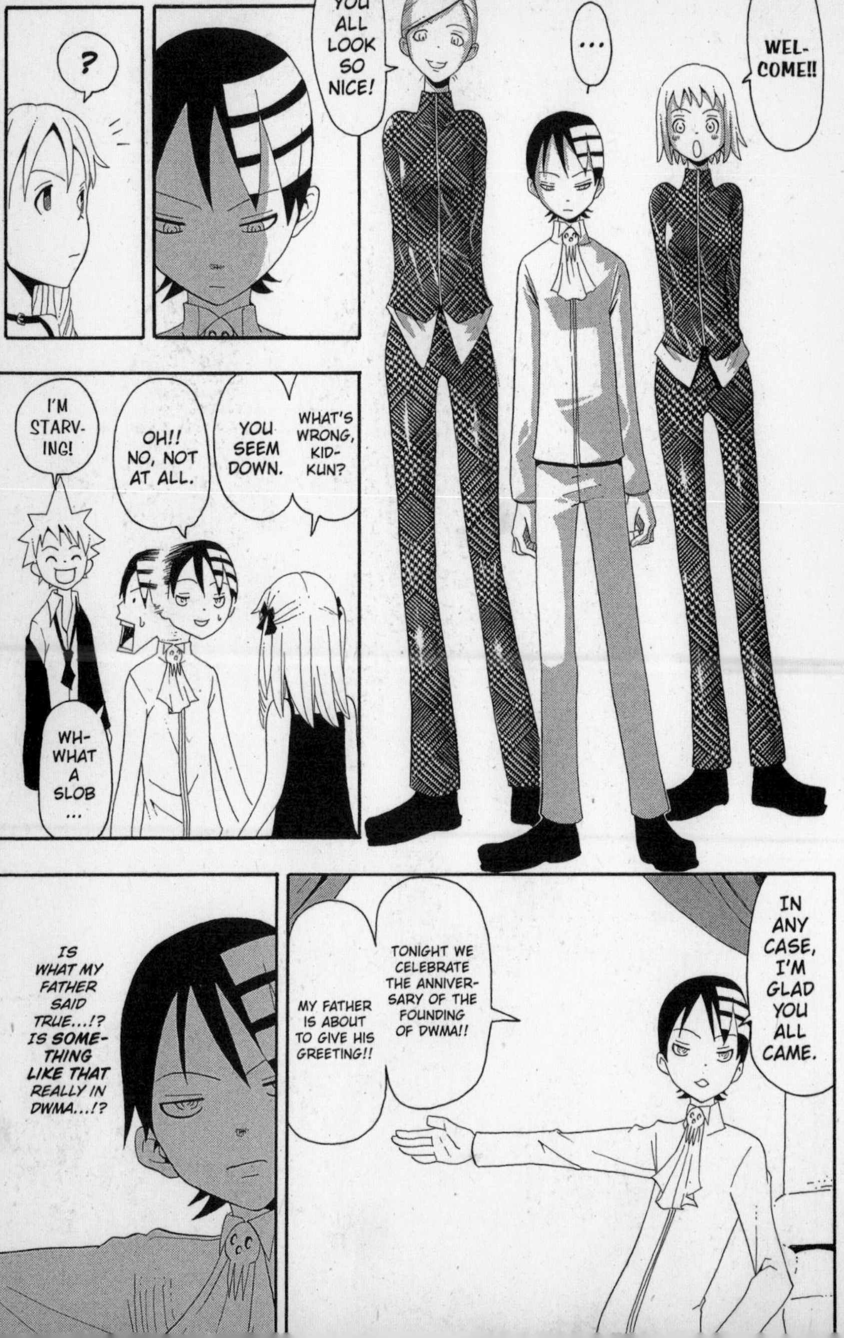
WEL-COME!!
...
YOU ALL LOOK SO NICE!
?
WHAT'S WRONG, KID-KUN?
YOU SEEM DOWN.
OH!! NO, NOT AT ALL.
I'M STARV-ING!
WH-WHAT A SLOB...
IN ANY CASE, I'M GLAD YOU ALL CAME.
TONIGHT WE CELEBRATE THE ANNIVER-SARY OF THE FOUNDING OF DWMA!!
MY FATHER IS ABOUT TO GIVE HIS GREETING!!
IS WHAT MY FATHER SAID TRUE...!? IS SOME-THING LIKE THAT REALLY IN DWMA...!?

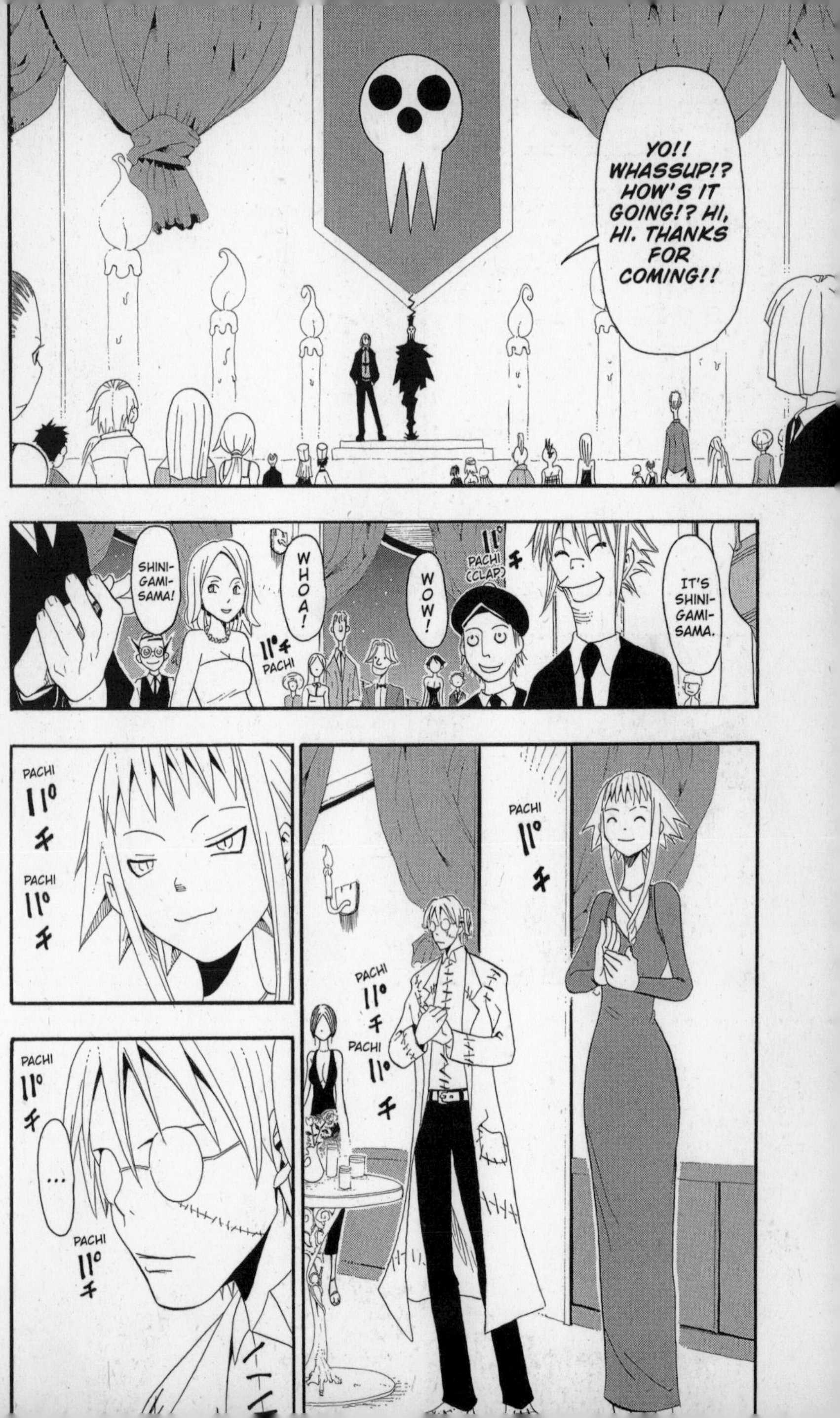
YO!! WHASSUP!? HOW'S IT GOING!? HI, HI. THANKS FOR COMING!!
IT'S SHINIGAMI-SAMA.
PACHI (CLAP)
WOW!
WHOA!
PACHI
SHINIGAMI-SAMA!
PACHI
PACHI
PACHI
PACHI
PACHI
PACHI
...
PACHI

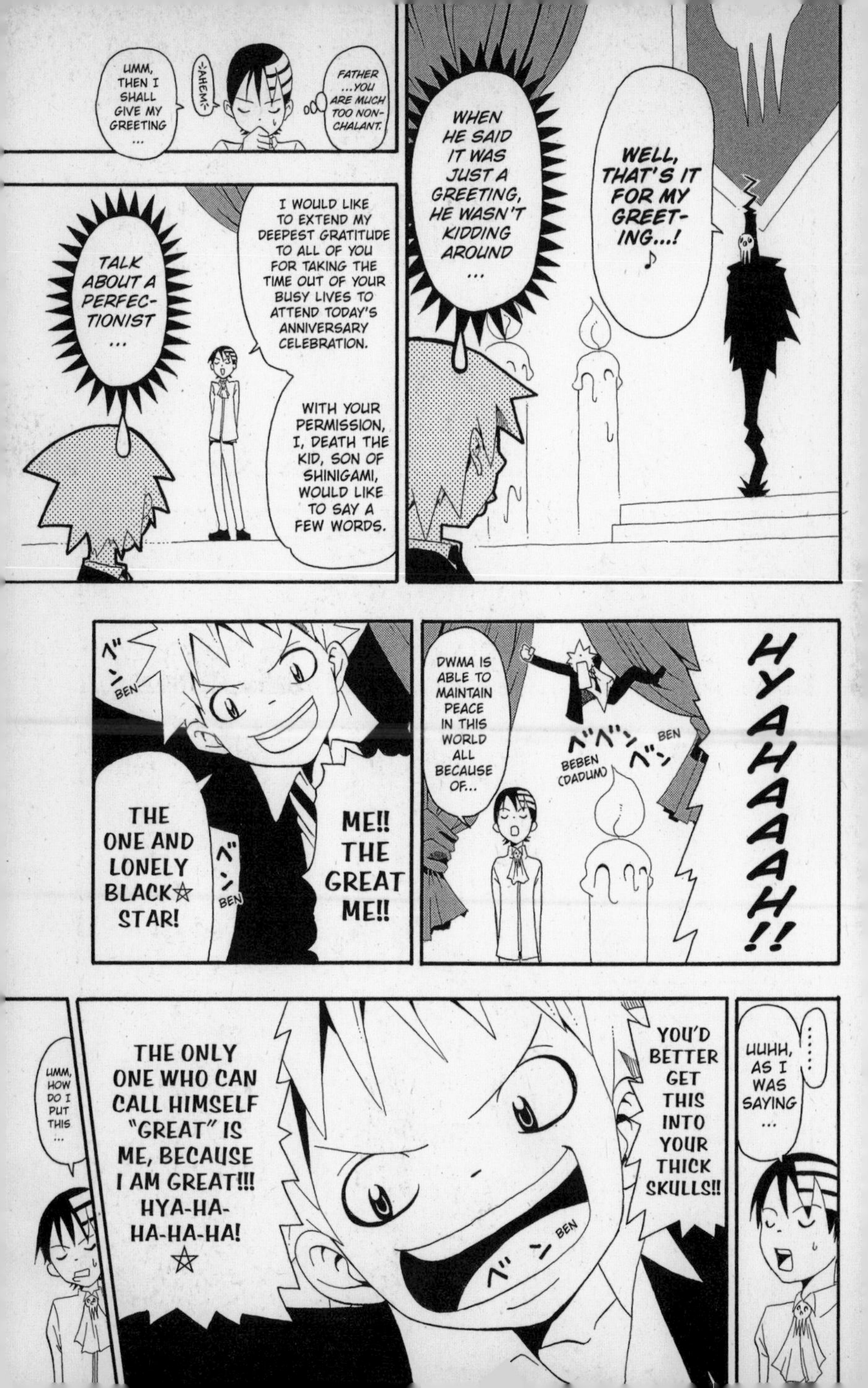
WELL, THAT'S IT FOR MY GREETING...! ♪
WHEN HE SAID IT WAS JUST A GREETING, HE WASN'T KIDDING AROUND...
FATHER ...YOU ARE MUCH TOO NONCHALANT.
-AHEM-
UMM, THEN I SHALL GIVE MY GREETING...
I WOULD LIKE TO EXTEND MY DEEPEST GRATITUDE TO ALL OF YOU FOR TAKING THE TIME OUT OF YOUR BUSY LIVES TO ATTEND TODAY'S ANNIVERSARY CELEBRATION.
WITH YOUR PERMISSION, I, DEATH THE KID, SON OF SHINIGAMI, WOULD LIKE TO SAY A FEW WORDS.
TALK ABOUT A PERFECTIONIST...
HYAHAAAAH!!
DWMA IS ABLE TO MAINTAIN PEACE IN THIS WORLD ALL BECAUSE OF...
BEN
BEBEN (DADUM)
ME!! THE GREAT ME!!
BEN
THE ONE AND LONELY BLACK☆STAR!
BEN
......
UUHH, AS I WAS SAYING...
YOU'D BETTER GET THIS INTO YOUR THICK SKULLS!!
THE ONLY ONE WHO CAN CALL HIMSELF "GREAT" IS ME, BECAUSE I AM GREAT!!! HYA-HA-HA-HA-HA! ☆
BEN
UMM, HOW DO I PUT THIS...

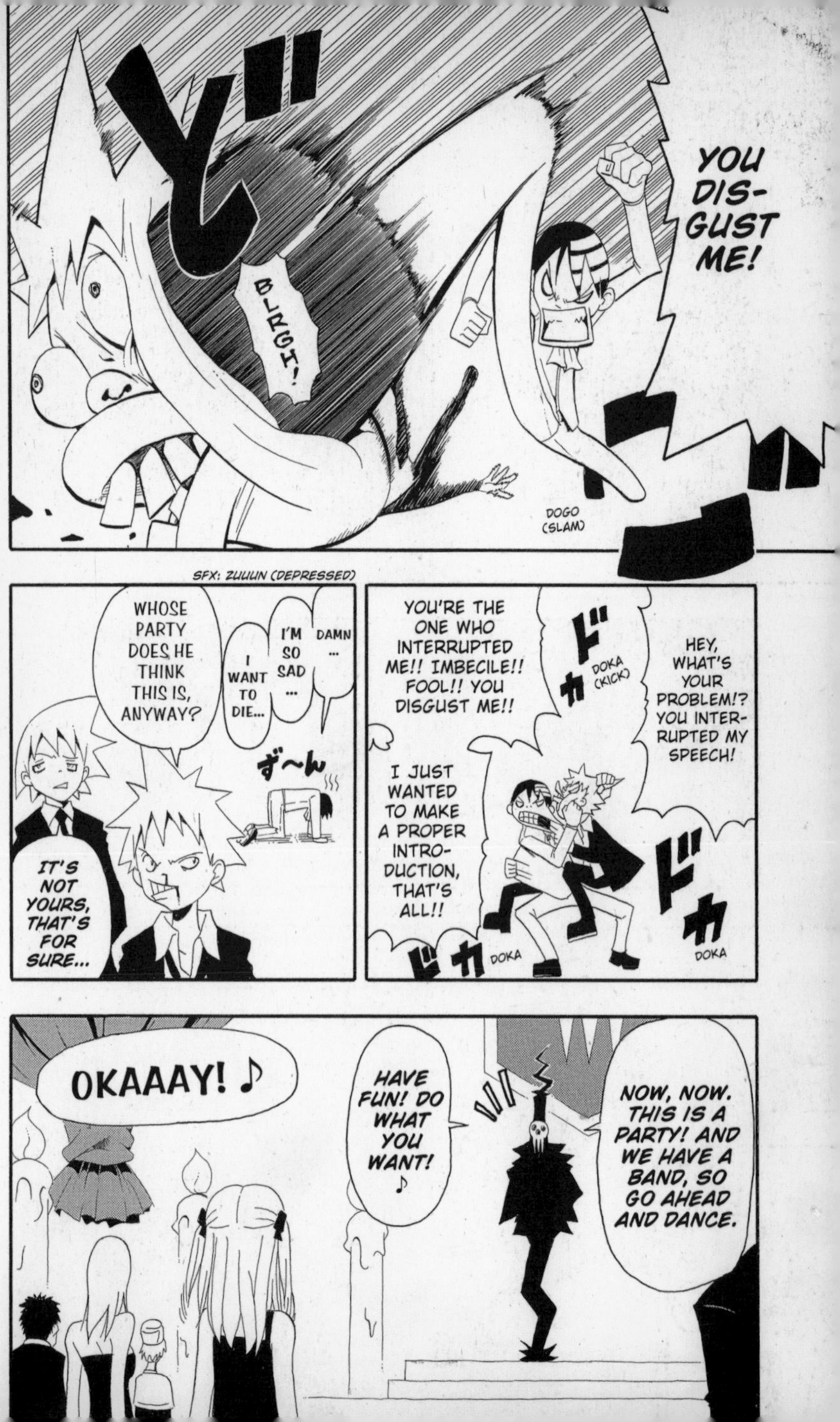
YOU DIS-GUST ME!
BLRGH!
DOGO (SLAM)
SFX: ZUUUN (DEPRESSED)
HEY, WHAT'S YOUR PROBLEM!? YOU INTER-RUPTED MY SPEECH!
ドカ
DOKA (KICK)
YOU'RE THE ONE WHO INTERRUPTED ME!! IMBECILE!! FOOL!! YOU DISGUST ME!!
I JUST WANTED TO MAKE A PROPER INTRO-DUCTION, THAT'S ALL!!
ドカ
DOKA
ドカ
DOKA
DAMN ...
I'M SO SAD ...
I WANT TO DIE...
ず～ん
WHOSE PARTY DOES HE THINK THIS IS, ANYWAY?
IT'S NOT YOURS, THAT'S FOR SURE...
NOW, NOW. THIS IS A PARTY! AND WE HAVE A BAND, SO GO AHEAD AND DANCE.
HAVE FUN! DO WHAT YOU WANT! ♪
OKAAAY! ♪

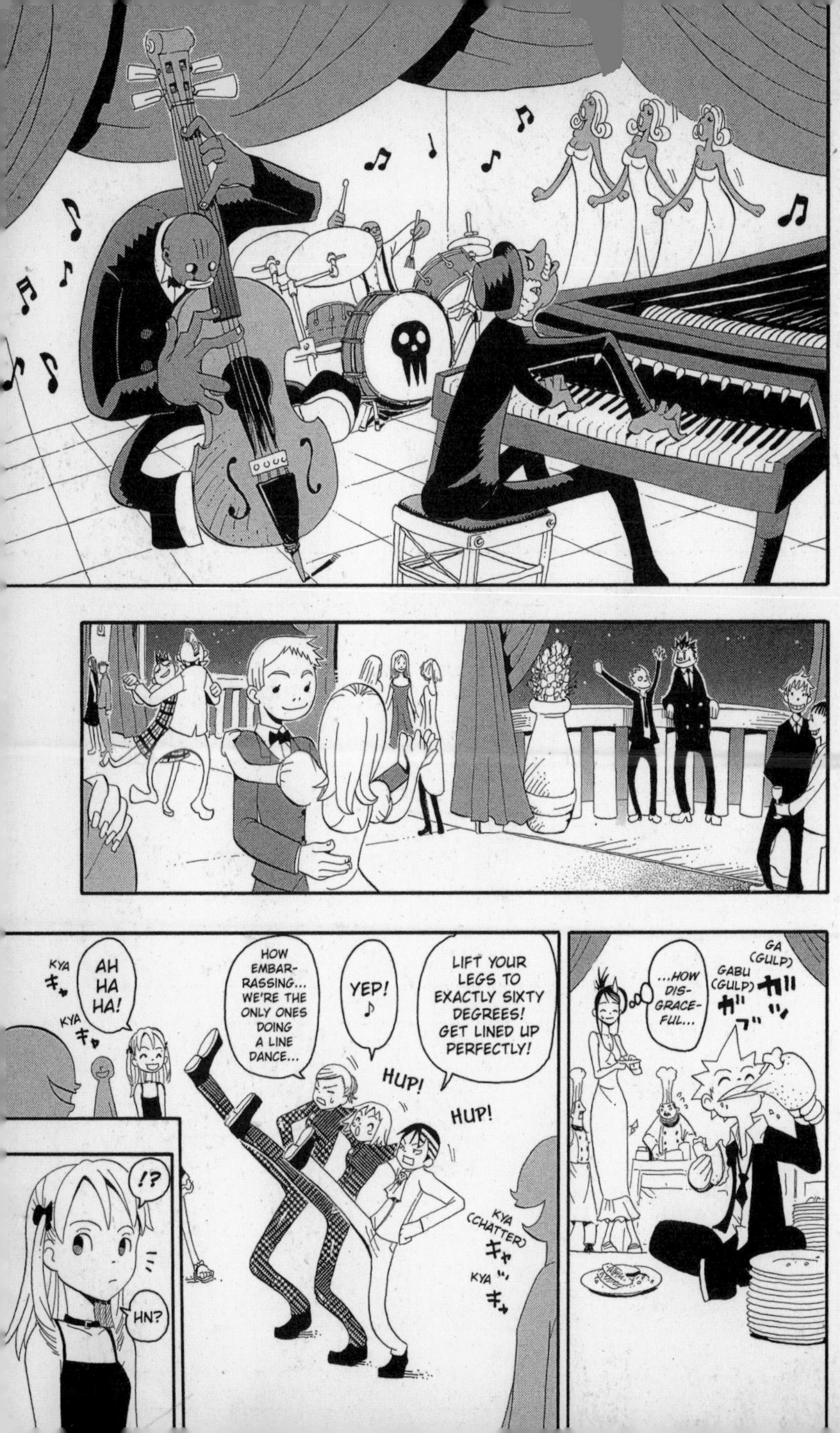
GA (GULP)
GABU (GULP)
...HOW DIS-GRACE-FUL...
LIFT YOUR LEGS TO EXACTLY SIXTY DEGREES! GET LINED UP PERFECTLY!
HUP!
HUP!
YEP! ♪
HOW EMBAR-RASSING... WE'RE THE ONLY ONES DOING A LINE DANCE...
AH HA HA!
KYA キャ
KYA キャ
KYA (CHATTER) キャッ
KYA キャ
!?
HN?

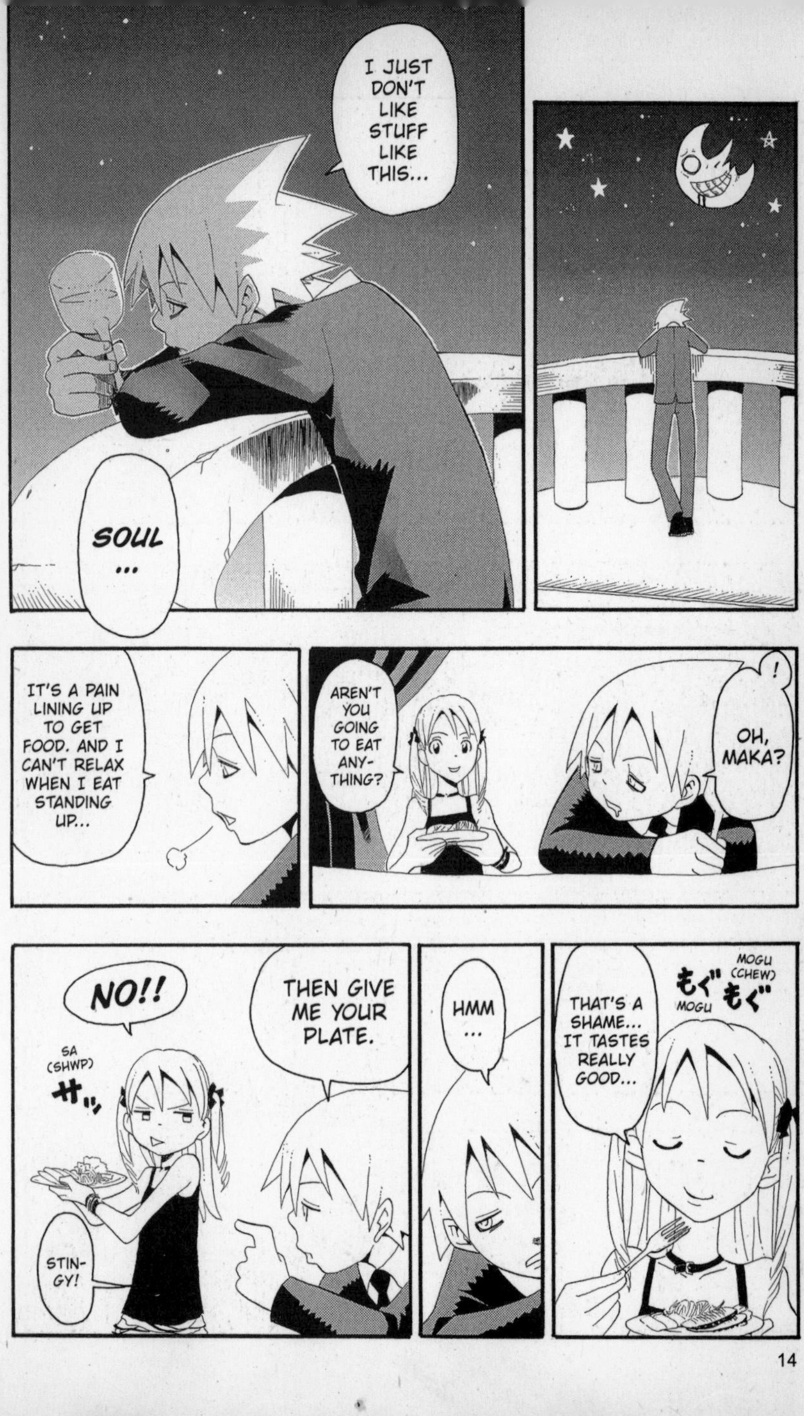
I JUST DON'T LIKE STUFF LIKE THIS...
SOUL ...
!
OH, MAKA?
AREN'T YOU GOING TO EAT ANY-THING?
IT'S A PAIN LINING UP TO GET FOOD. AND I CAN'T RELAX WHEN I EAT STANDING UP...
MOGU (CHEW)
もぐ
MOGU
もぐ
THAT'S A SHAME... IT TASTES REALLY GOOD...
HMM ...
THEN GIVE ME YOUR PLATE.
NO!!
SA (SHWP)
サッ
STIN-GY!

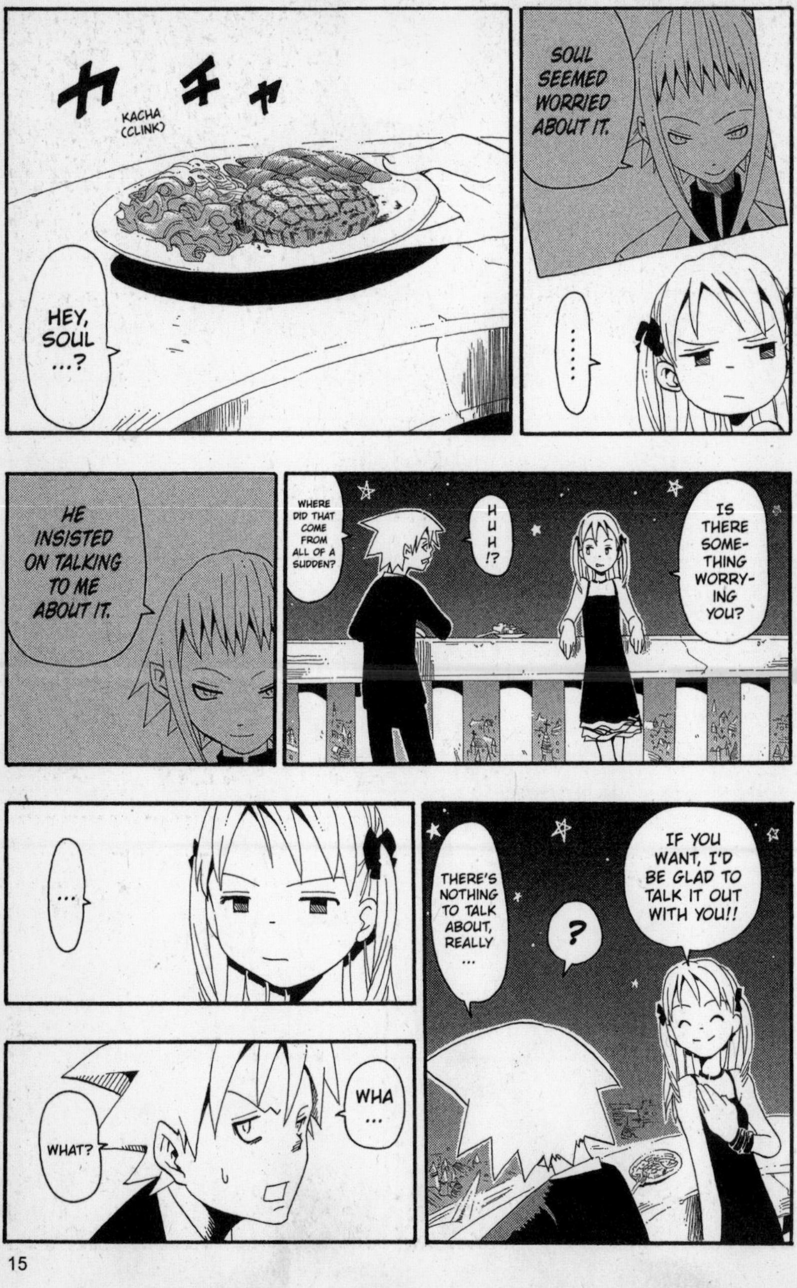
SOUL SEEMED WORRIED ABOUT IT.
......
カチャ
KACHA (CLINK)
HEY, SOUL ...?
IS THERE SOME-THING WORRY-ING YOU?
HUH!?
WHERE DID THAT COME FROM ALL OF A SUDDEN?
HE INSISTED ON TALKING TO ME ABOUT IT.
IF YOU WANT, I'D BE GLAD TO TALK IT OUT WITH YOU!!
?
THERE'S NOTHING TO TALK ABOUT, REALLY ...
...
WHA ...
WHAT?

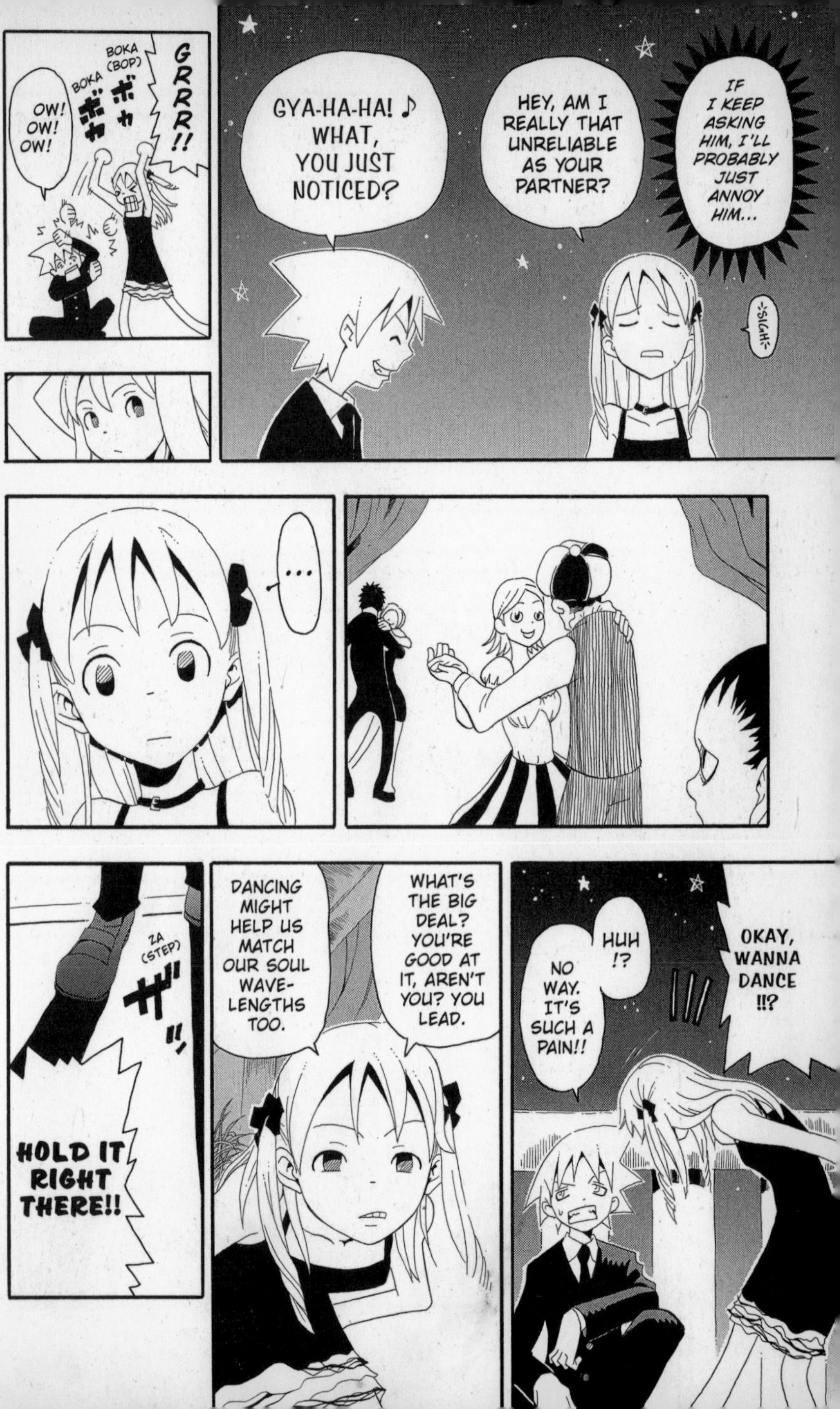
IF I KEEP ASKING HIM, I'LL PROBABLY JUST ANNOY HIM...
SIGH
HEY, AM I REALLY THAT UNRELIABLE AS YOUR PARTNER?
GYA-HA-HA! ♪ WHAT, YOU JUST NOTICED?
GRRR!!
BOKA (BOP)
ボカ
BOKA
ボカ
OW! OW! OW!
...
OKAY, WANNA DANCE!!?
HUH!?
NO WAY. IT'S SUCH A PAIN!!
WHAT'S THE BIG DEAL? YOU'RE GOOD AT IT, AREN'T YOU? YOU LEAD.
DANCING MIGHT HELP US MATCH OUR SOUL WAVE-LENGTHS TOO.
ZA (STEP)
ザ!!
HOLD IT RIGHT THERE!!

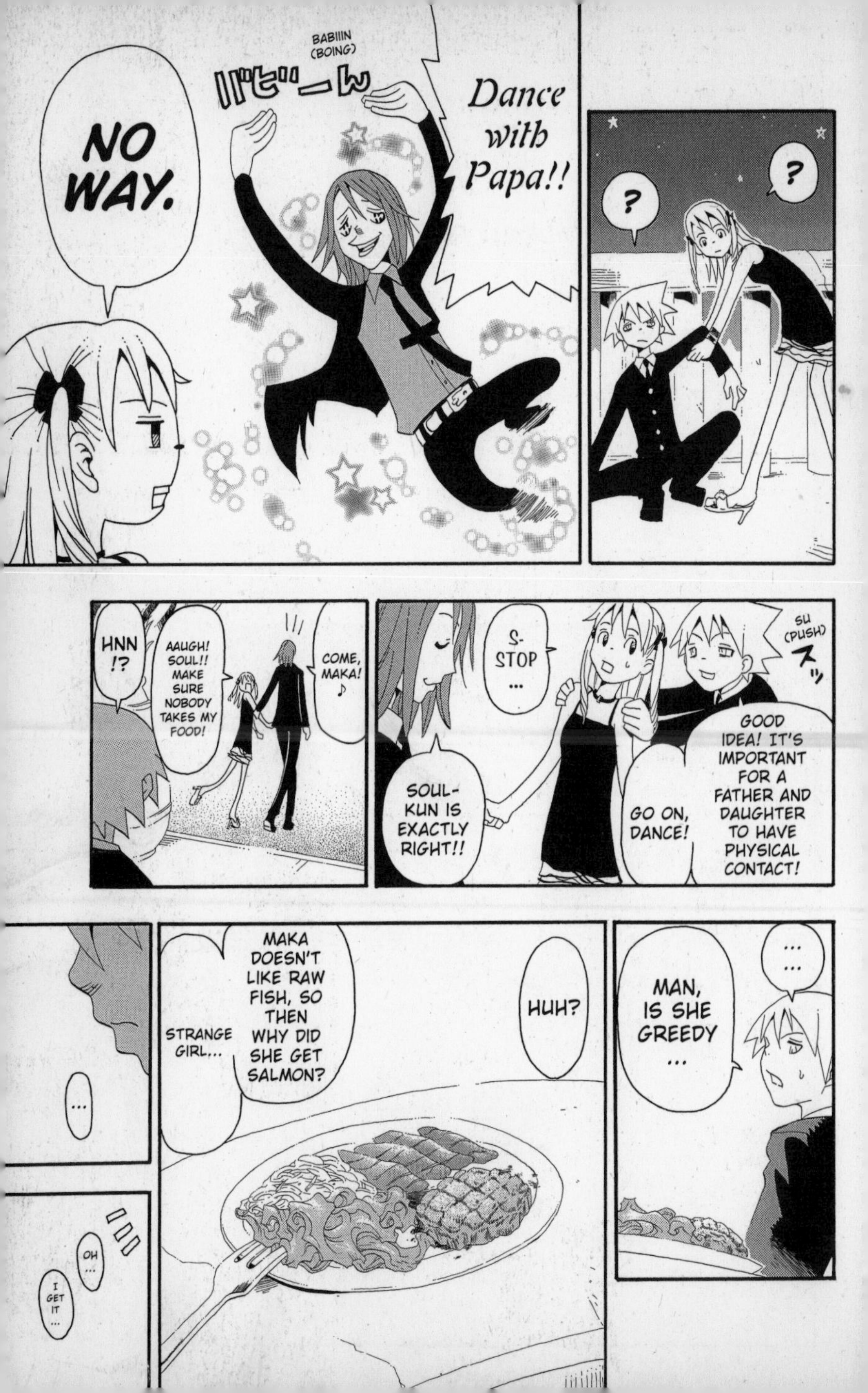
?
?
Dance with Papa!!
BABIIIN (BOING)
NO WAY.
SU (PUSH)
GOOD IDEA! IT'S IMPORTANT FOR A FATHER AND DAUGHTER TO HAVE PHYSICAL CONTACT!
S-STOP ...
GO ON, DANCE!
SOUL-KUN IS EXACTLY RIGHT!!
COME, MAKA! ♪
AAUGH! SOUL!! MAKE SURE NOBODY TAKES MY FOOD!
HNN !?
... ...
MAN, IS SHE GREEDY ...
HUH?
MAKA DOESN'T LIKE RAW FISH, SO THEN WHY DID SHE GET SALMON?
STRANGE GIRL...
...
OH ...
I GET IT ...

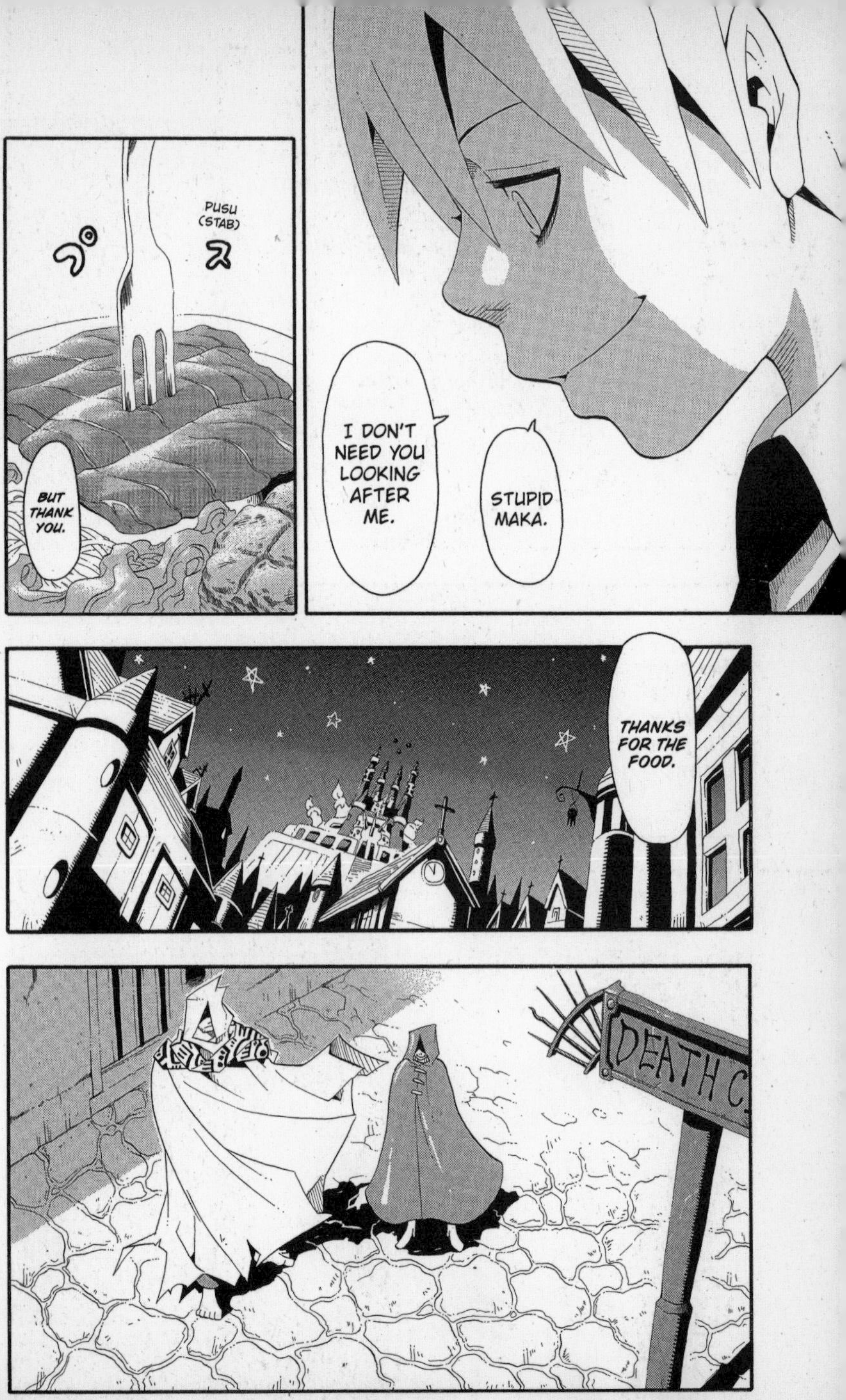
STUPID MAKA.
I DON'T NEED YOU LOOKING AFTER ME.
PUSU (STAB)
プス
BUT THANK YOU.
THANKS FOR THE FOOD.
DEATH C

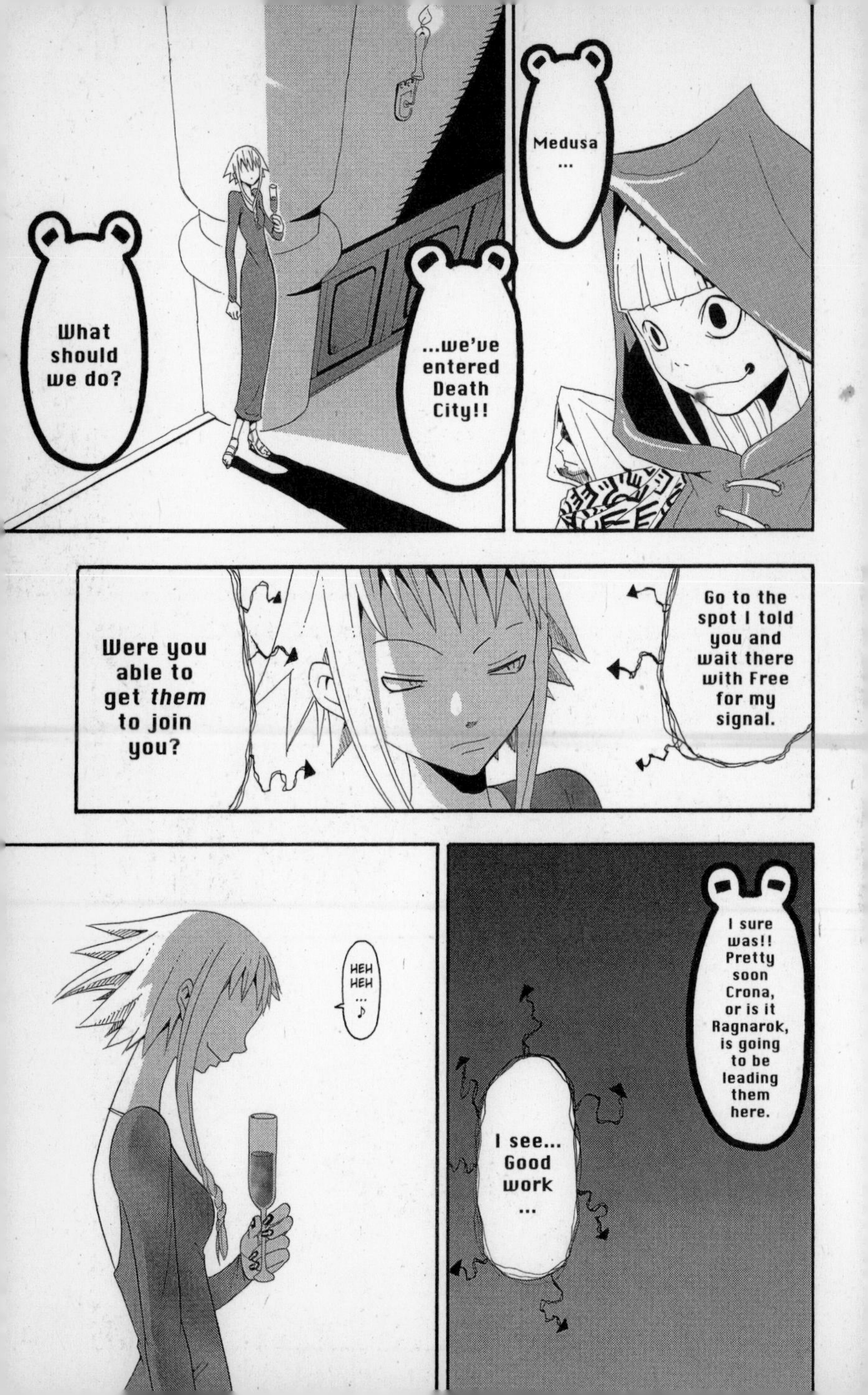
Medusa ...
...we've entered Death City!!
What should we do?
Go to the spot I told you and wait there with Free for my signal.
Were you able to get *them* to join you?
I sure was!! Pretty soon Crona, or is it Ragnarok, is going to be leading them here.
I see... Good work ...
HEH HEH ... ♪

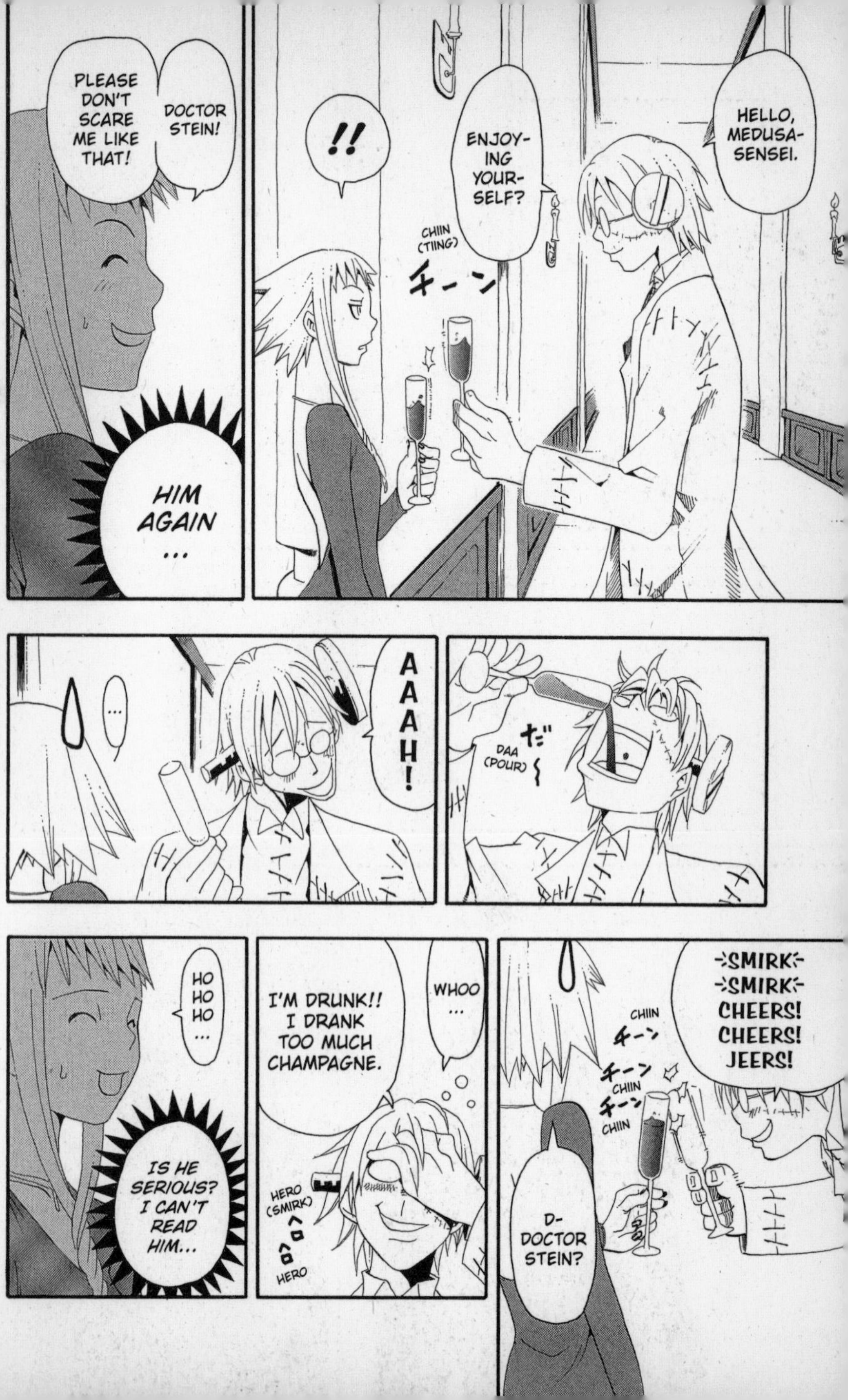
HELLO, MEDUSA-SENSEI.
ENJOYING YOURSELF?
!!
CHIIN (TIING)
チーン
DOCTOR STEIN!
PLEASE DON'T SCARE ME LIKE THAT!
HIM AGAIN...
だ
DAA (POUR)
AAAAH!
...
-SMIRK- -SMIRK- CHEERS! CHEERS! JEERS!
チーン
CHIIN
チーン
CHIIN
チーン
CHIIN
D- DOCTOR STEIN?
WHOO...
I'M DRUNK!! I DRANK TOO MUCH CHAMPAGNE.
HERO (SMIRK)
へロ
へロ
HERO
HO HO HO...
IS HE SERIOUS? I CAN'T READ HIM...

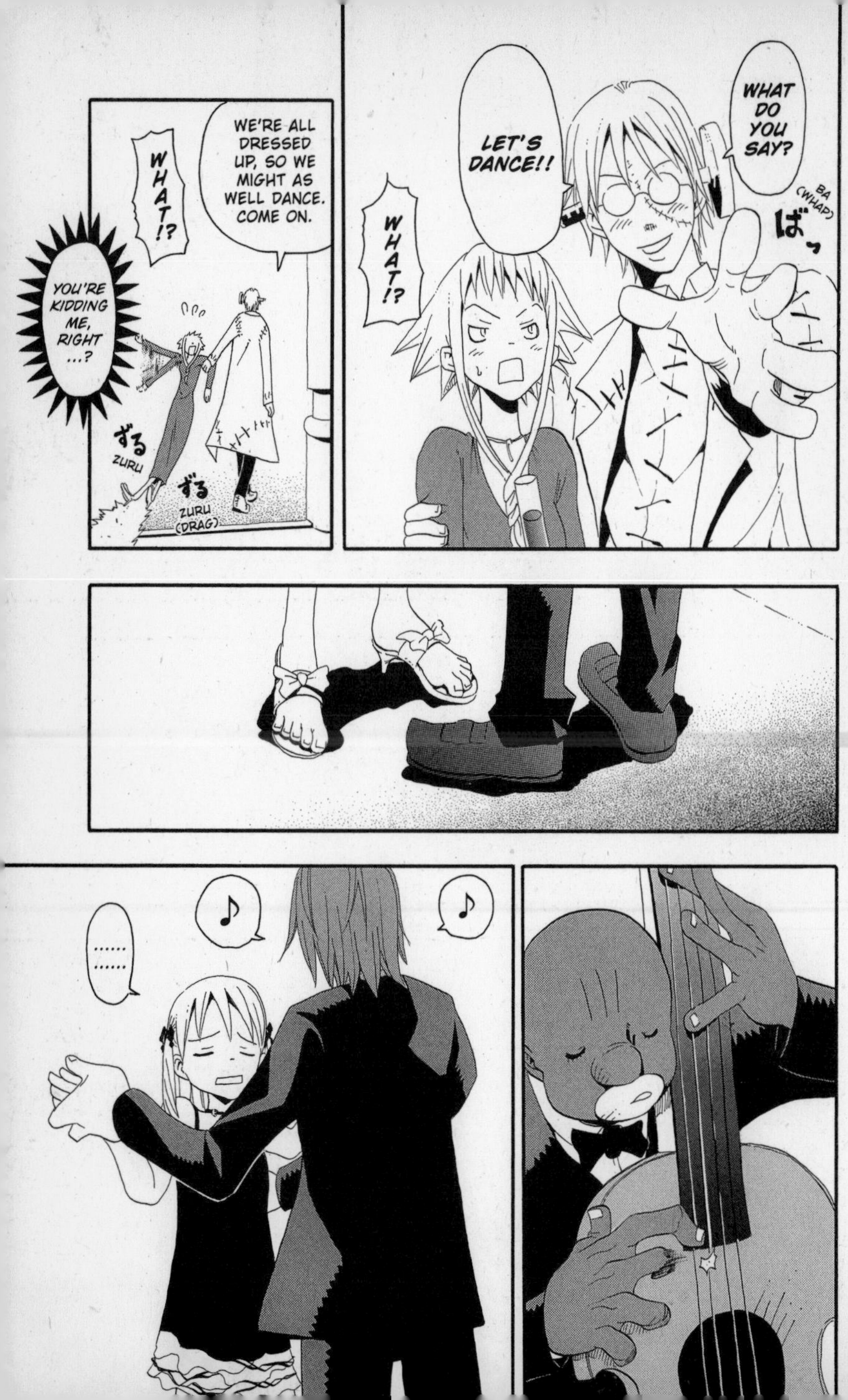
WHAT DO YOU SAY?
BA (WHAP)
ばっ
LET'S DANCE!!
WHAT!?
WE'RE ALL DRESSED UP, SO WE MIGHT AS WELL DANCE. COME ON.
WHAT!?
YOU'RE KIDDING ME, RIGHT ...?
ずる
ZURU
ずる
ZURU (DRAG)
♪
♪
......
......

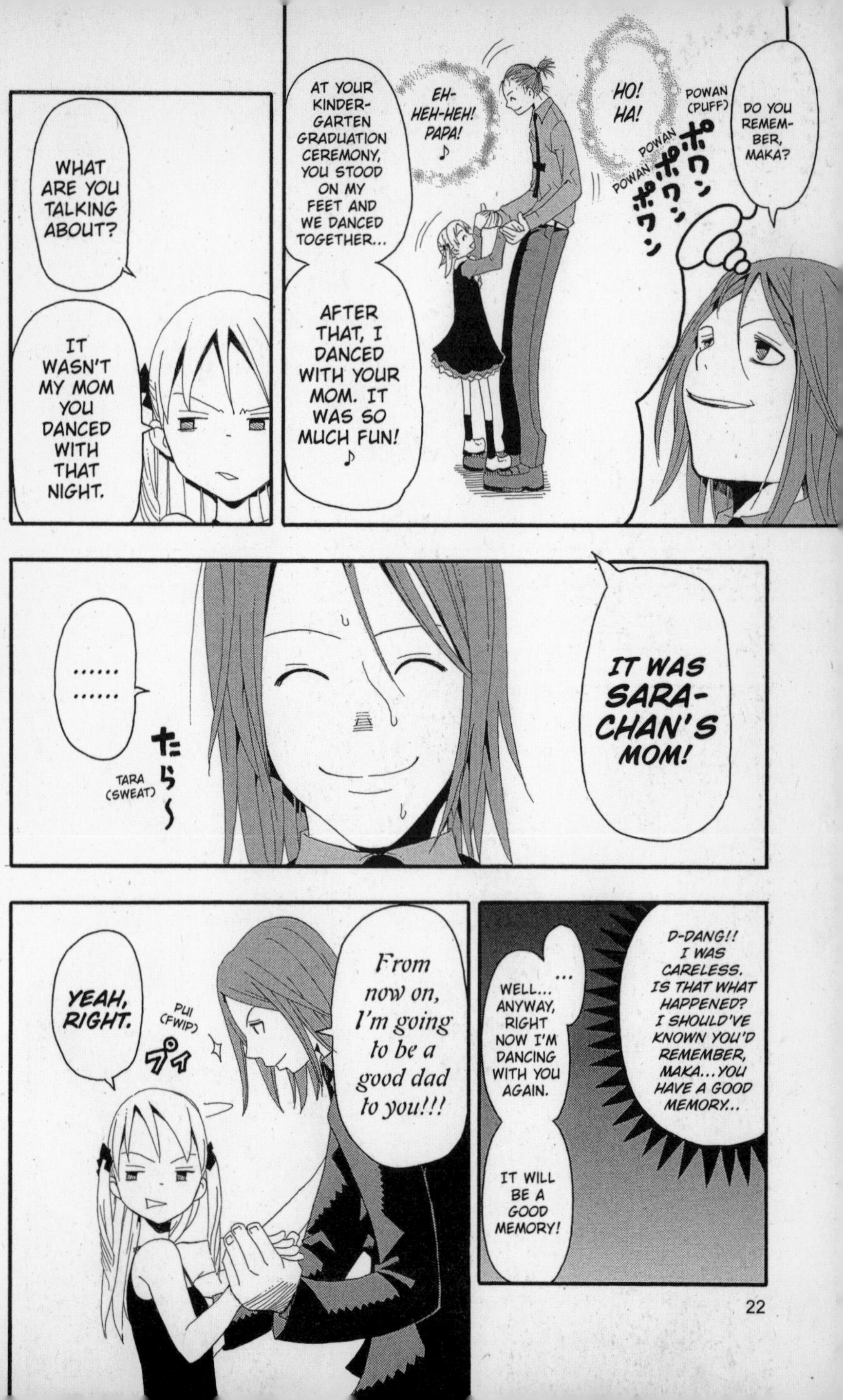
DO YOU REMEMBER, MAKA?
POWAN (PUFF)
ポワン
POWAN
ポワン
POWAN
ポワン
HO! HA!
EH-HEH-HEH! PAPA! ♪
AT YOUR KINDER-GARTEN GRADUATION CEREMONY, YOU STOOD ON MY FEET AND WE DANCED TOGETHER...
AFTER THAT, I DANCED WITH YOUR MOM. IT WAS SO MUCH FUN! ♪
WHAT ARE YOU TALKING ABOUT?
IT WASN'T MY MOM YOU DANCED WITH THAT NIGHT.
IT WAS SARA-CHAN'S MOM!
たら～
TARA (SWEAT)
......
......
D-DANG!! I WAS CARELESS. IS THAT WHAT HAPPENED? I SHOULD'VE KNOWN YOU'D REMEMBER, MAKA...YOU HAVE A GOOD MEMORY...
...
WELL... ANYWAY, RIGHT NOW I'M DANCING WITH YOU AGAIN.
IT WILL BE A GOOD MEMORY!
From now on, I'm going to be a good dad to you!!!
PUI (FWIP)
プイ
YEAH, RIGHT.

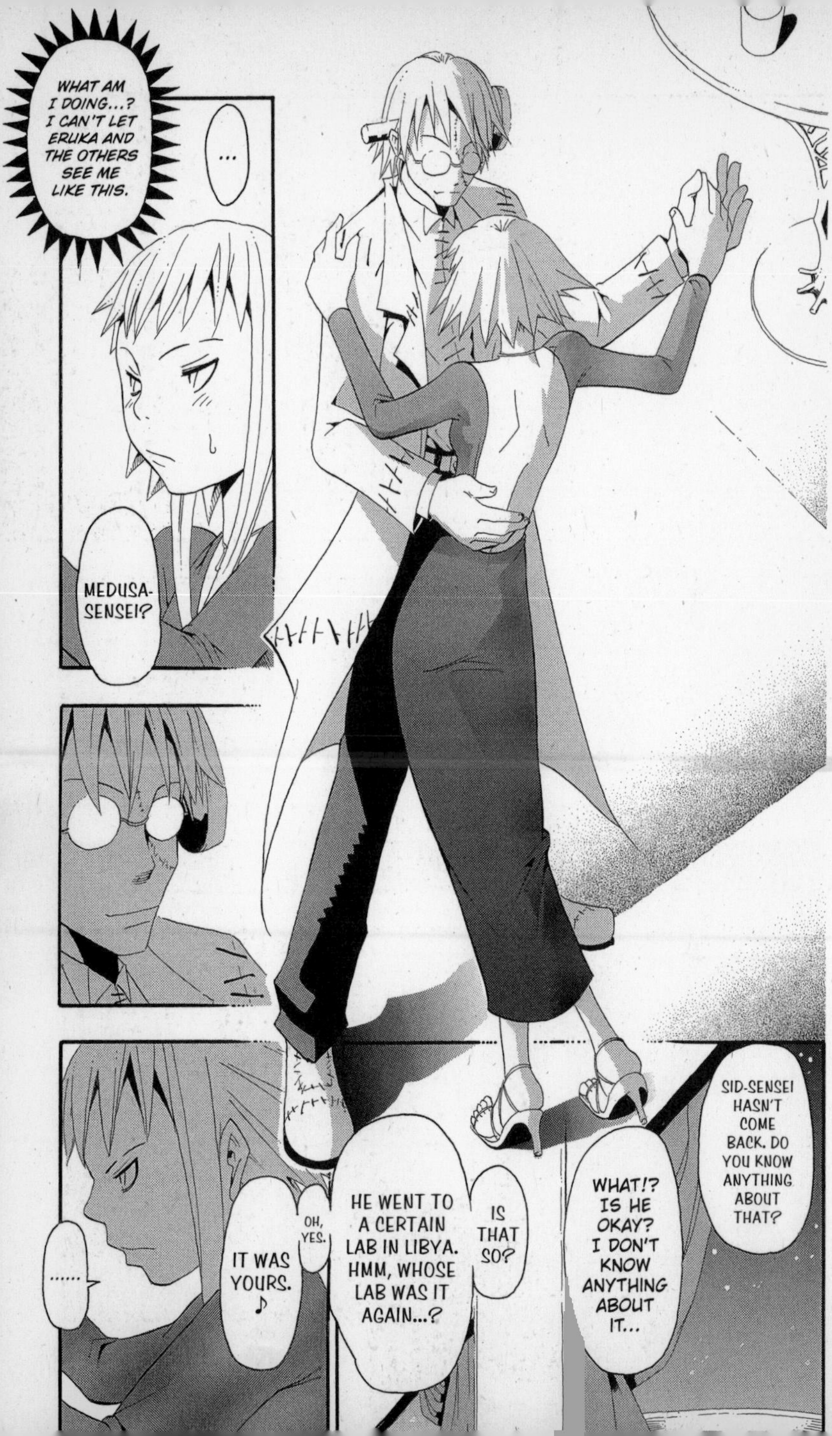
WHAT AM I DOING...? I CAN'T LET ERUKA AND THE OTHERS SEE ME LIKE THIS.
...
MEDUSA-SENSEI?
SID-SENSEI HASN'T COME BACK. DO YOU KNOW ANYTHING ABOUT THAT?
WHAT!? IS HE OKAY? I DON'T KNOW ANYTHING ABOUT IT...
IS THAT SO?
HE WENT TO A CERTAIN LAB IN LIBYA. HMM, WHOSE LAB WAS IT AGAIN...?
OH, YES.
IT WAS YOURS. ♪
......

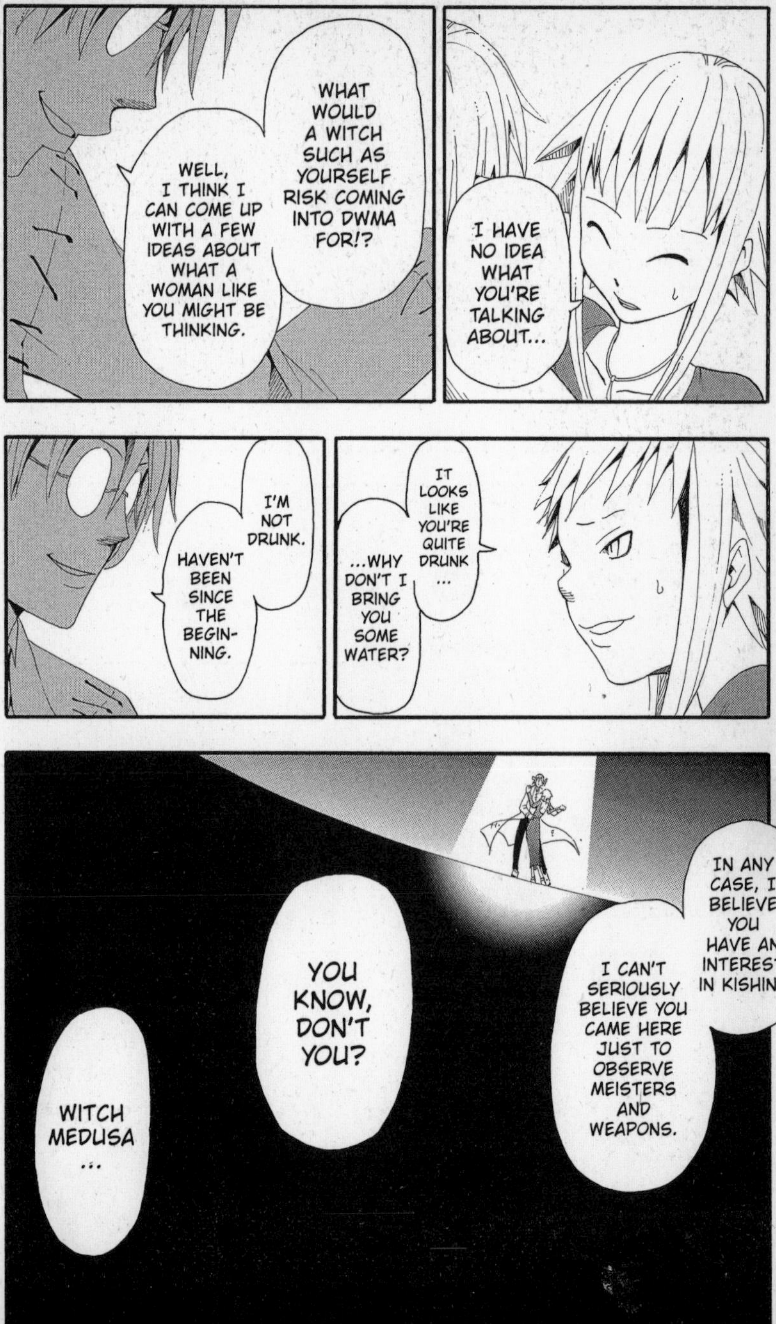
I HAVE NO IDEA WHAT YOU'RE TALKING ABOUT...
WHAT WOULD A WITCH SUCH AS YOURSELF RISK COMING INTO DWMA FOR!?
WELL, I THINK I CAN COME UP WITH A FEW IDEAS ABOUT WHAT A WOMAN LIKE YOU MIGHT BE THINKING.
IT LOOKS LIKE YOU'RE QUITE DRUNK...
...WHY DON'T I BRING YOU SOME WATER?
I'M NOT DRUNK.
HAVEN'T BEEN SINCE THE BEGIN-NING.
IN ANY CASE, I BELIEVE YOU HAVE AN INTEREST IN KISHIN?
I CAN'T SERIOUSLY BELIEVE YOU CAME HERE JUST TO OBSERVE MEISTERS AND WEAPONS.
YOU KNOW, DON'T YOU?
WITCH MEDUSA...

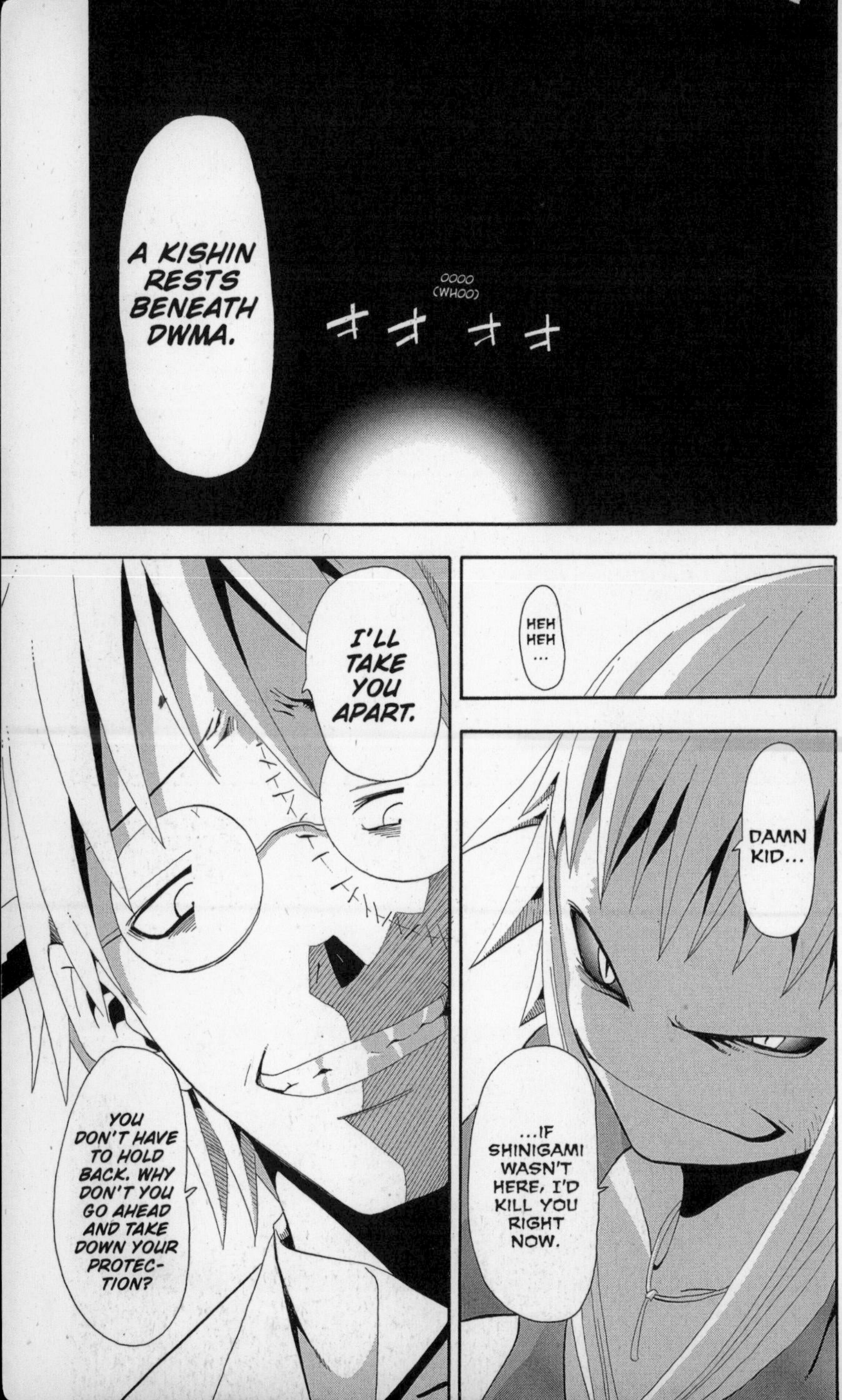
A KISHIN RESTS BENEATH DWMA.
オオオオ
OOOO (WHOO)
HEH HEH ...
DAMN KID...
...IF SHINIGAMI WASN'T HERE, I'D KILL YOU RIGHT NOW.
I'LL TAKE YOU APART.
YOU DON'T HAVE TO HOLD BACK. WHY DON'T YOU GO AHEAD AND TAKE DOWN YOUR PROTECTION?

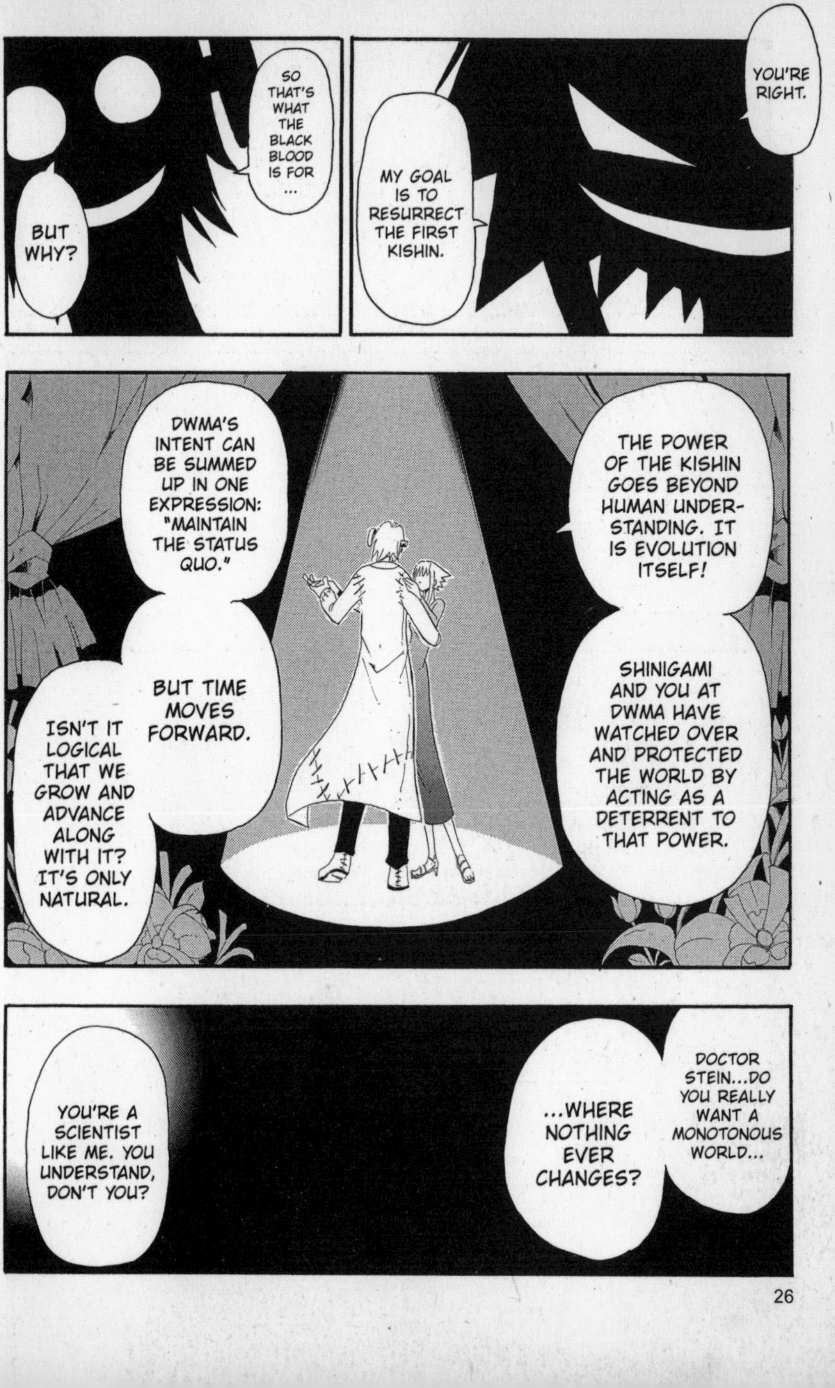
YOU'RE RIGHT.
MY GOAL IS TO RESURRECT THE FIRST KISHIN.
SO THAT'S WHAT THE BLACK BLOOD IS FOR...
BUT WHY?
THE POWER OF THE KISHIN GOES BEYOND HUMAN UNDER-STANDING. IT IS EVOLUTION ITSELF!
SHINIGAMI AND YOU AT DWMA HAVE WATCHED OVER AND PROTECTED THE WORLD BY ACTING AS A DETERRENT TO THAT POWER.
DWMA'S INTENT CAN BE SUMMED UP IN ONE EXPRESSION: "MAINTAIN THE STATUS QUO."
BUT TIME MOVES FORWARD.
ISN'T IT LOGICAL THAT WE GROW AND ADVANCE ALONG WITH IT? IT'S ONLY NATURAL.
DOCTOR STEIN...DO YOU REALLY WANT A MONOTONOUS WORLD...
...WHERE NOTHING EVER CHANGES?
YOU'RE A SCIENTIST LIKE ME. YOU UNDERSTAND, DON'T YOU?

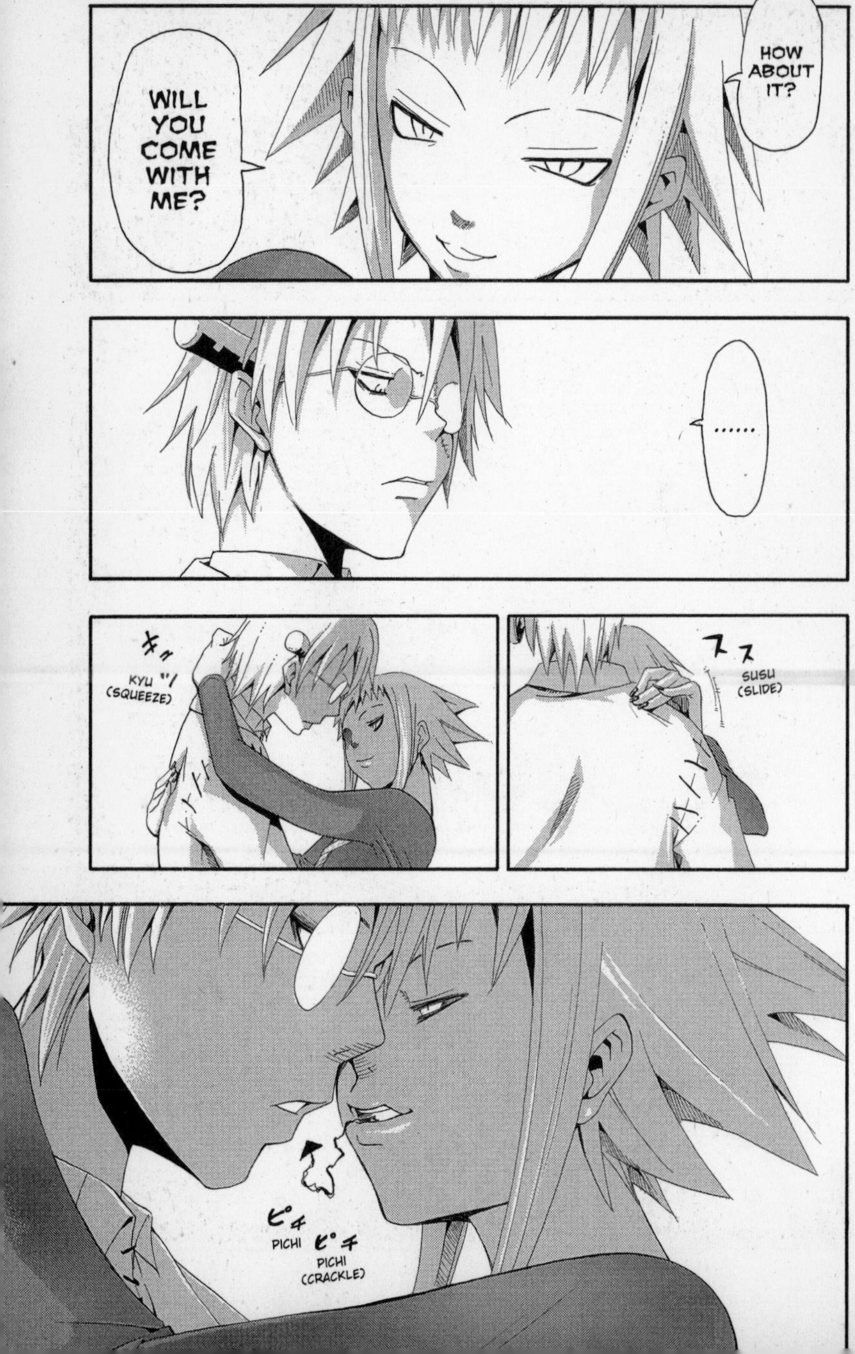
HOW ABOUT IT?
WILL YOU COME WITH ME?
......
スス
SUSU (SLIDE)
キュッ
KYU (SQUEEZE)
ピチ
PICHI
ピチ
PICHI (CRACKLE)

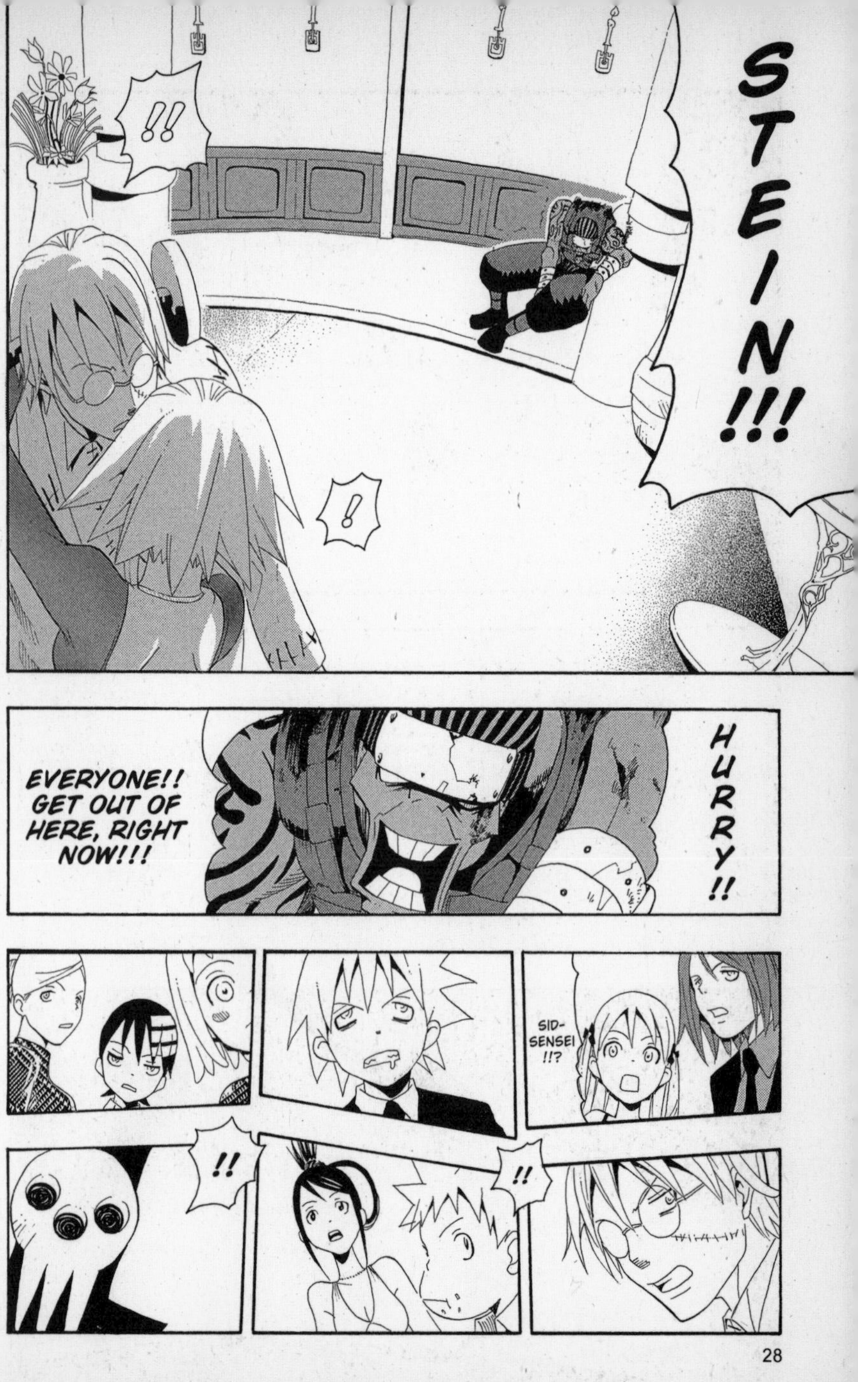
STEIN!!!
!!
!
HURRY!!
EVERYONE!! GET OUT OF HERE, RIGHT NOW!!!
SID-SENSEI!!?
!!
!!

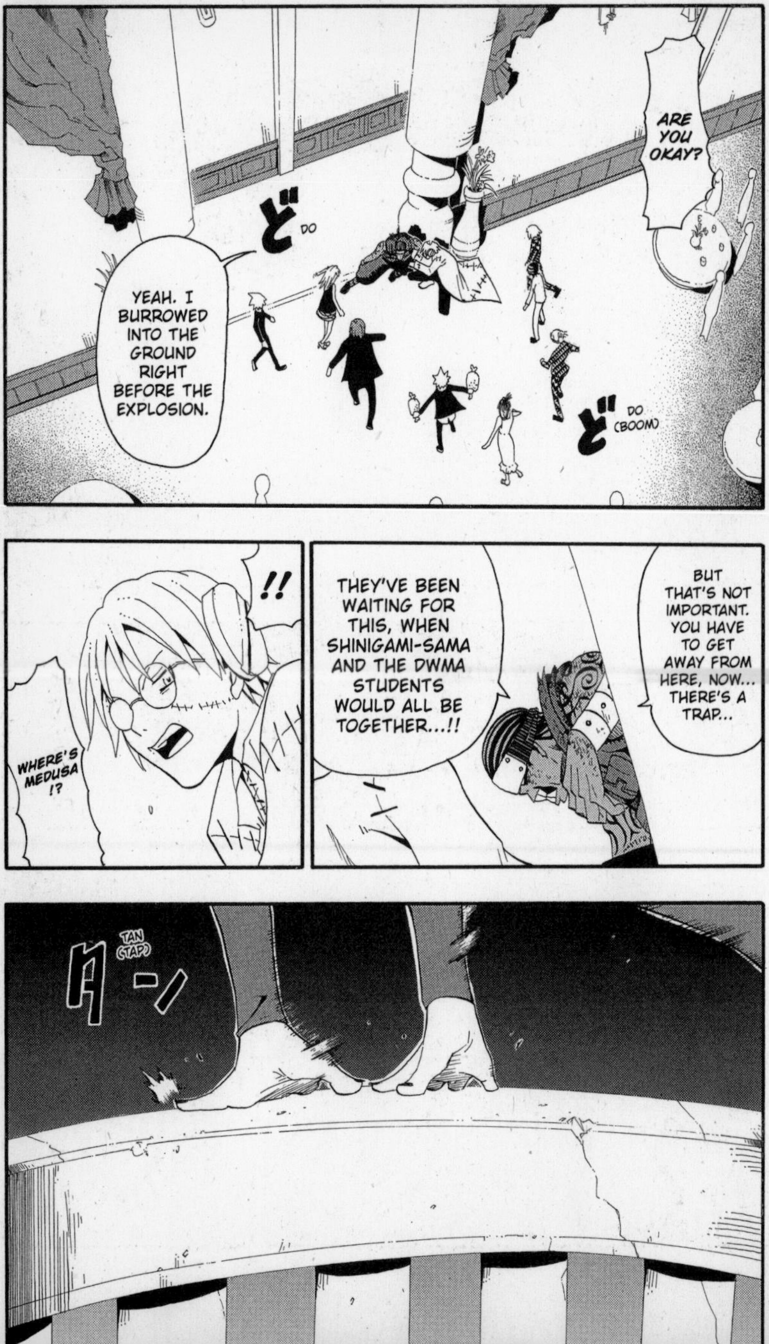
ARE YOU OKAY?
ど DO
YEAH. I BURROWED INTO THE GROUND RIGHT BEFORE THE EXPLOSION.
ど DO (BOOM)
BUT THAT'S NOT IMPORTANT. YOU HAVE TO GET AWAY FROM HERE, NOW... THERE'S A TRAP...
THEY'VE BEEN WAITING FOR THIS, WHEN SHINIGAMI-SAMA AND THE DWMA STUDENTS WOULD ALL BE TOGETHER...!!
!!
WHERE'S MEDUSA !?
TAN (TAP)
タ－ン

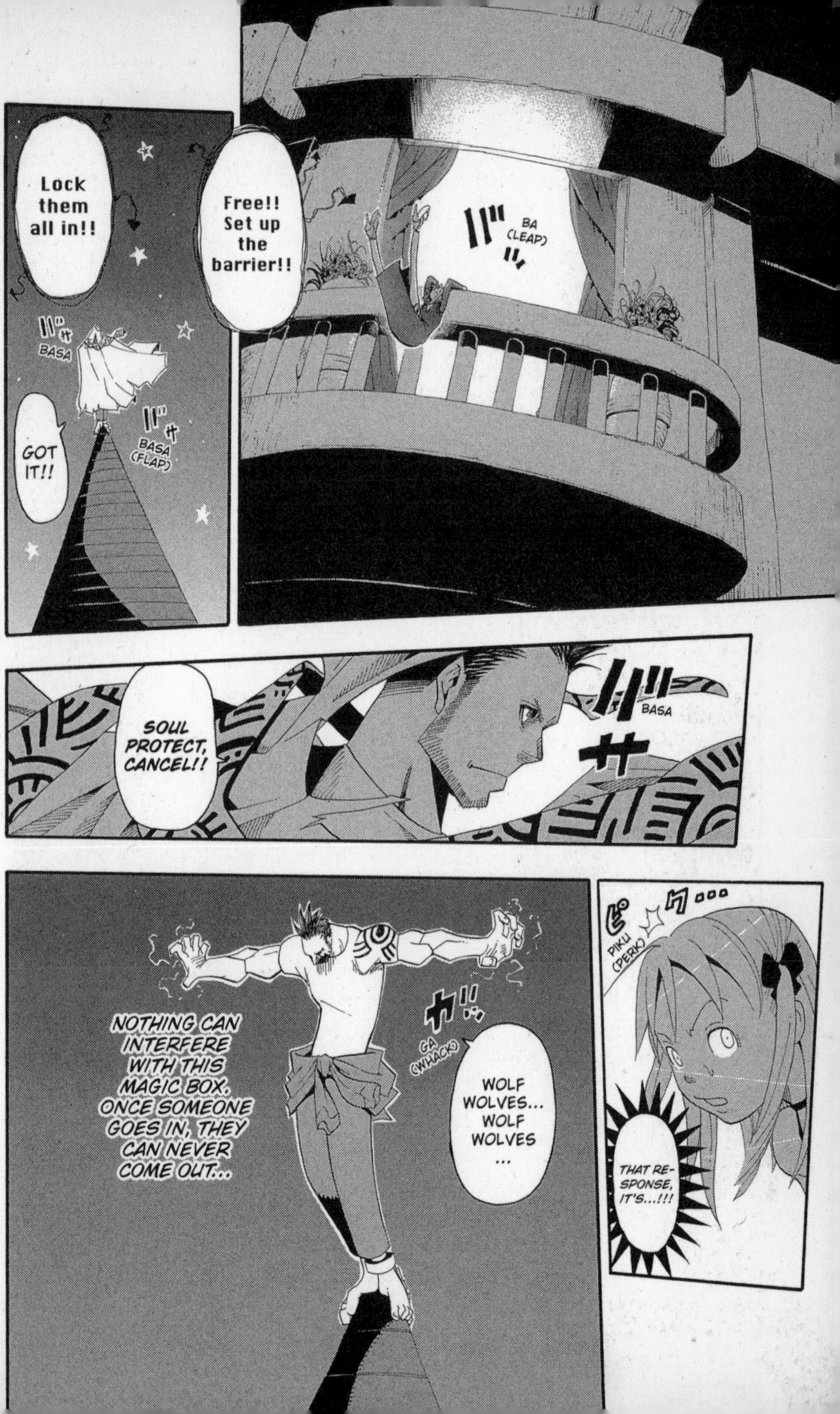
Free!! Set up the barrier!!
BA (LEAP)
Lock them all in!!
BASA
GOT IT!!
BASA (FLAP)
BASA
SOUL PROTECT, CANCEL!!
PIKU (PERK)
THAT RE-SPONSE, IT'S...!!!
GA (WHACK)
WOLF WOLVES... WOLF WOLVES ...
NOTHING CAN INTERFERE WITH THIS MAGIC BOX. ONCE SOMEONE GOES IN, THEY CAN NEVER COME OUT...

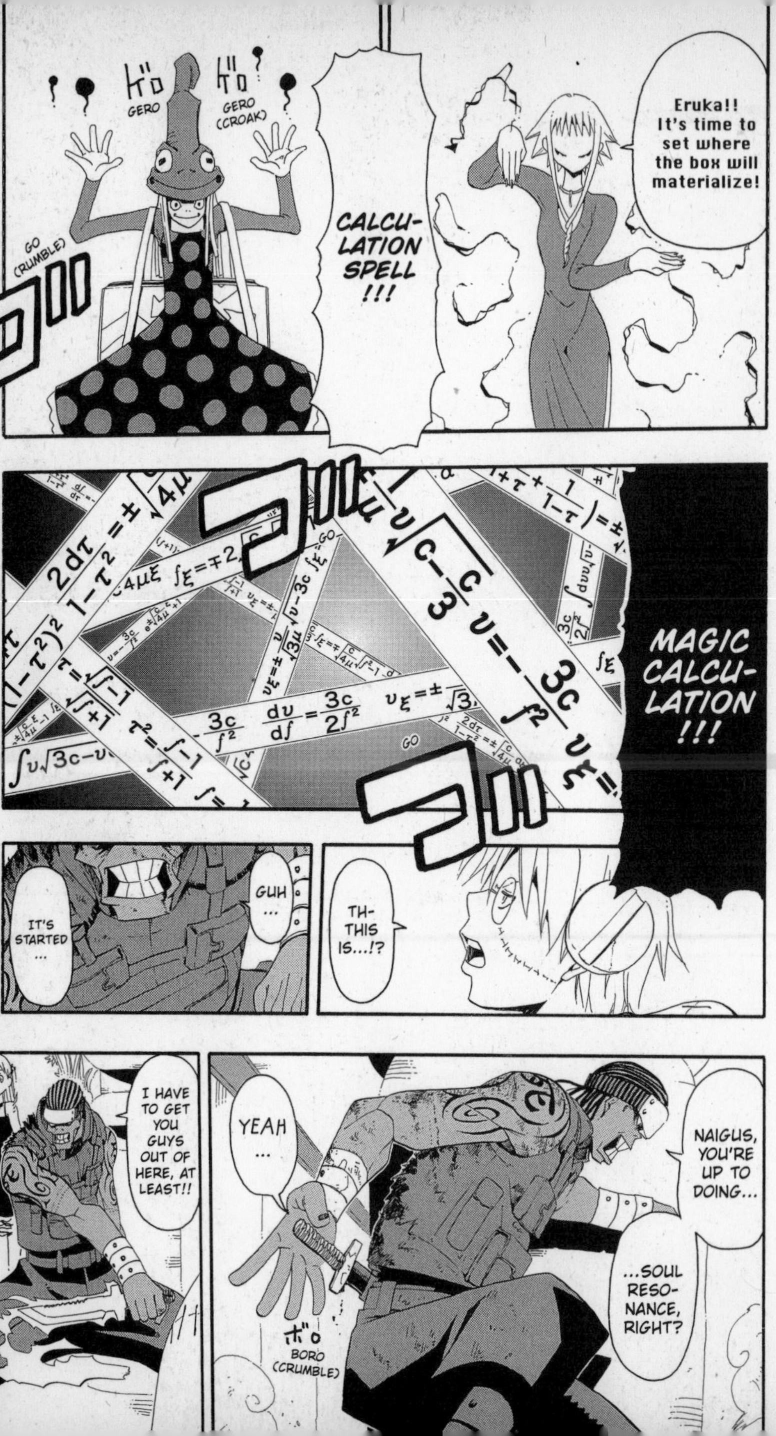
Eruka!! It's time to set where the box will materialize!
CALCULATION SPELL!!!
ゲロ GERO
ゲロ GERO (CROAK)
ゴ GO (RUMBLE)
MAGIC CALCULATION!!!
GO
GO
TH-THIS IS...!?
GUH ...
IT'S STARTED ...
NAIGUS, YOU'RE UP TO DOING...
...SOUL RESONANCE, RIGHT?
YEAH ...
ボロ BORO (CRUMBLE)
I HAVE TO GET YOU GUYS OUT OF HERE, AT LEAST!!
!?

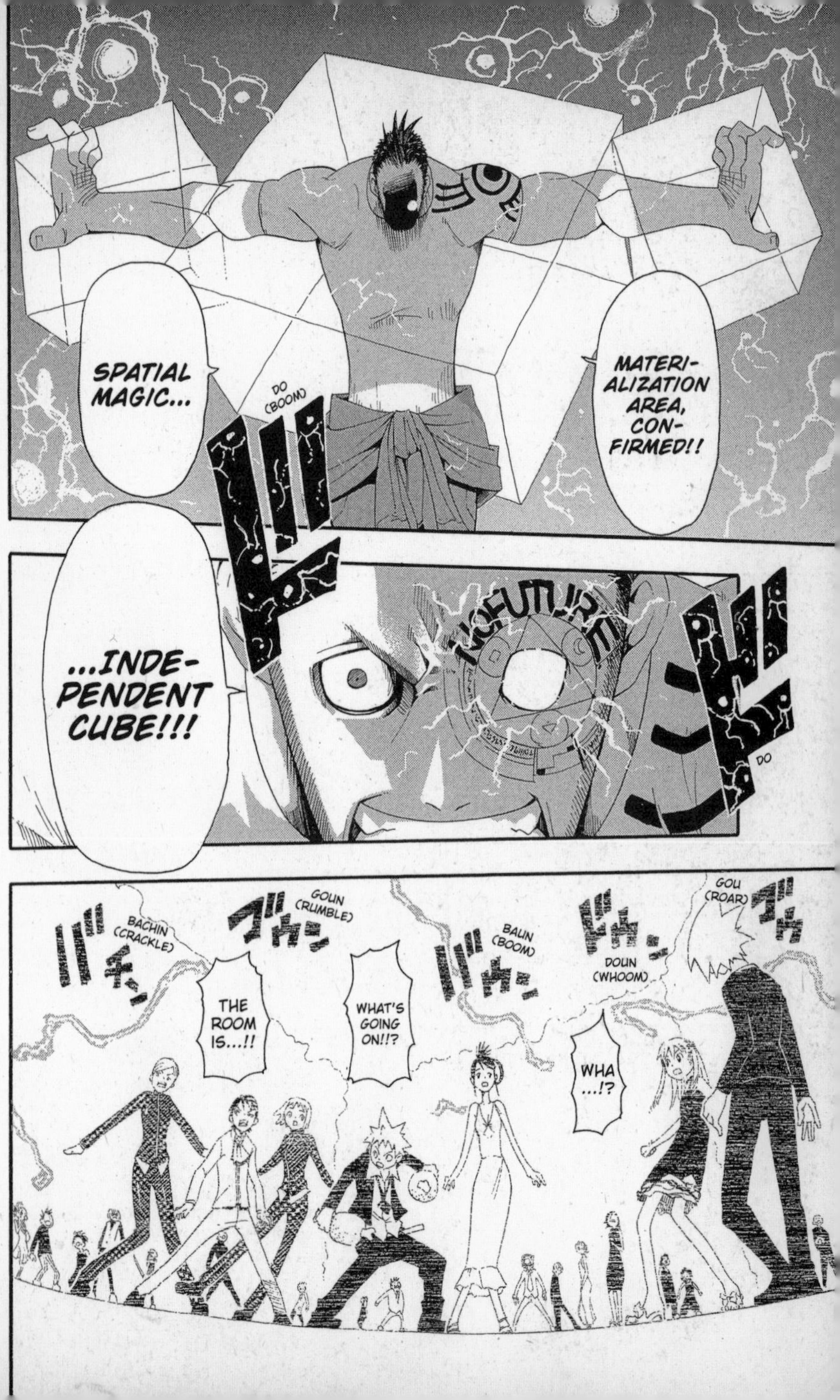
MATERI-
ALIZATION
AREA,
CON-
FIRMED!!
SPATIAL
MAGIC...
DO
(BOOM)
...INDE-
PENDENT
CUBE!!!
DO
GOU
(ROAR)
DOUN
(WHOOM)
WHA
...!?
BAUN
(BOOM)
WHAT'S
GOING
ON!!?
GOUN
(RUMBLE)
THE
ROOM
IS...!!
BACHIN
(CRACKLE)

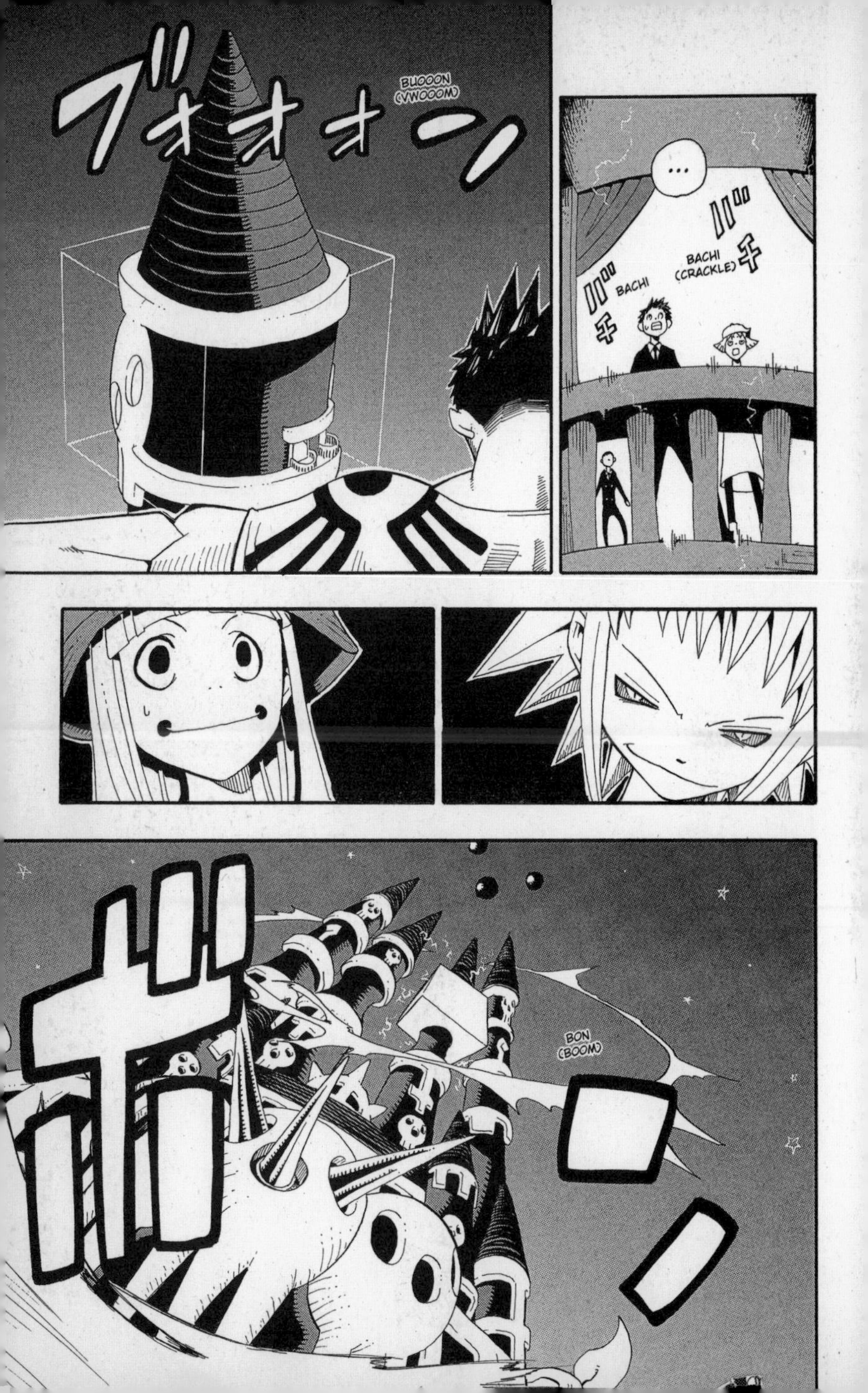
...
バチ
BACHI (CRACKLE)
バチ
BACHI
ブオオオーン
BUOOON (VWOOOM)
ボン
BON (BOOM)

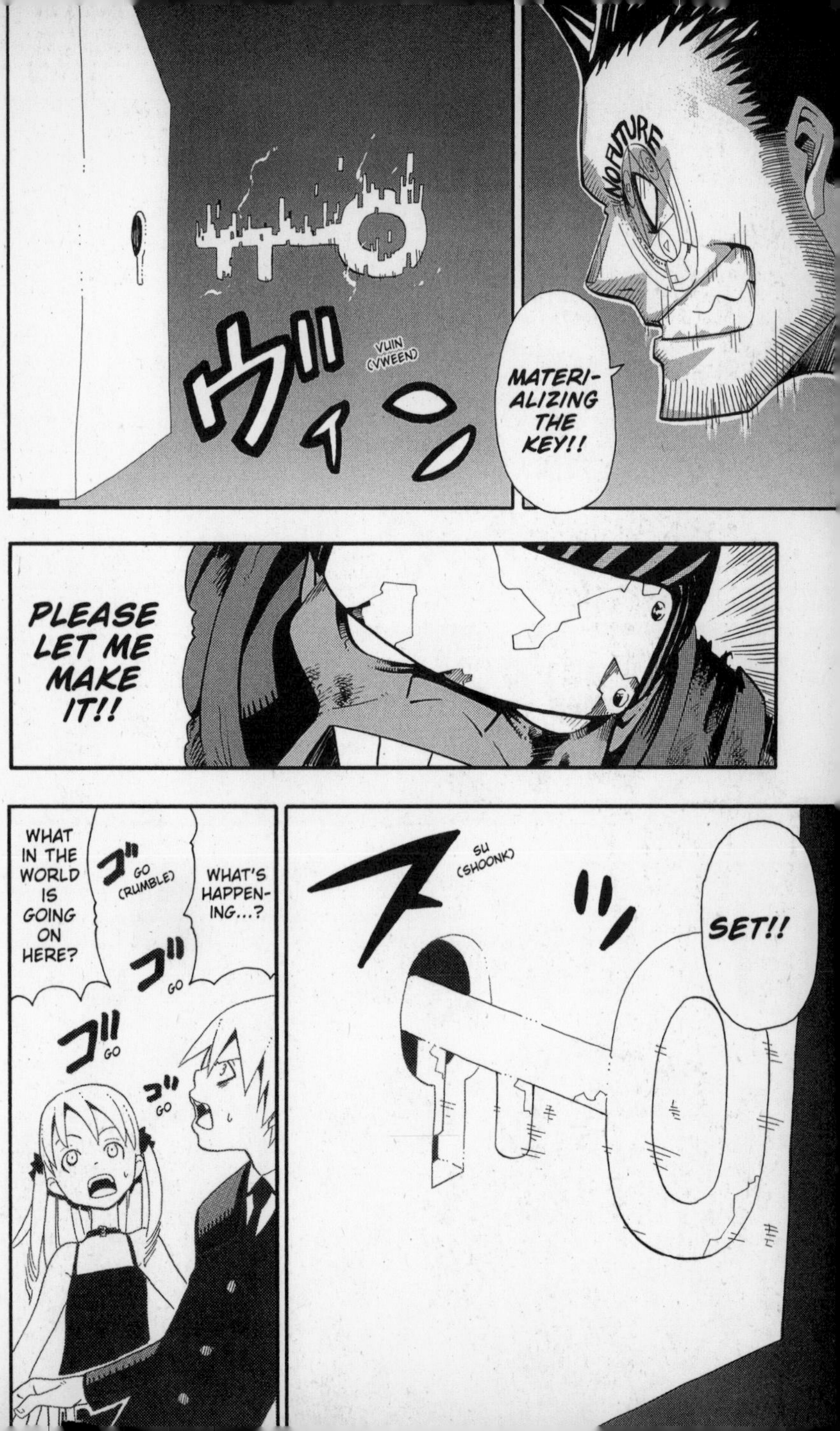
NO FUTURE
MATERI-ALIZING THE KEY!!
ヴィン
VUIN (VWEEN)
PLEASE LET ME MAKE IT!!
SET!!
スッ
SU (SHOONK)
WHAT'S HAPPEN-ING...?
WHAT IN THE WORLD IS GOING ON HERE?
ゴ GO (RUMBLE)
ゴ GO
ゴ GO
ゴ GO

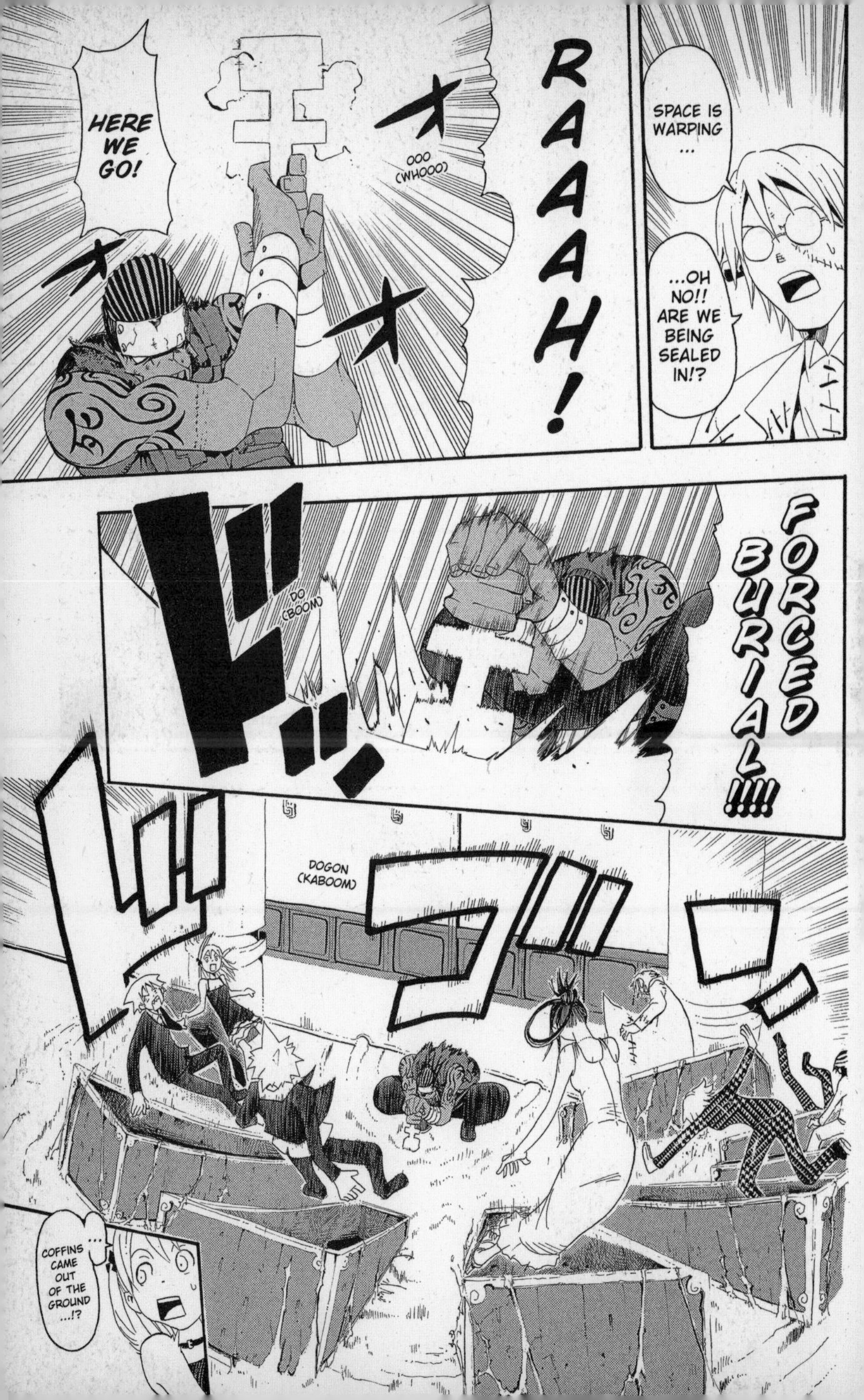
SPACE IS WARPING ...
...OH NO!! ARE WE BEING SEALED IN!?
HERE WE GO!
RAAAH!
OOO (WHOOO)
DO (BOOM)
FORCED BURIAL!!!!
DOGON (KABOOM)
... COFFINS CAME OUT OF THE GROUND ...!?

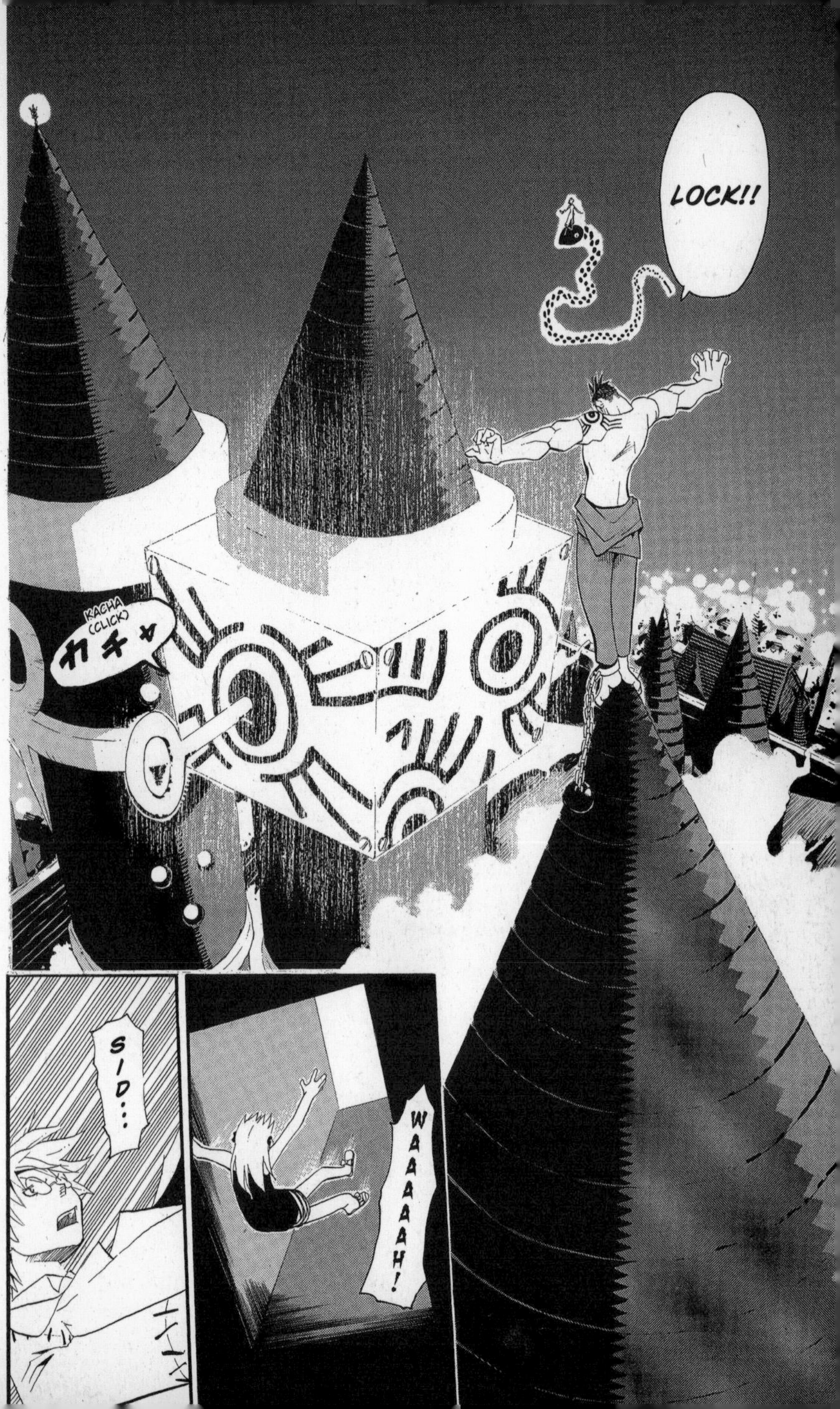
LOCK!!
KACHA (CLICK)
カチャ
WAAAAAH!
SID...

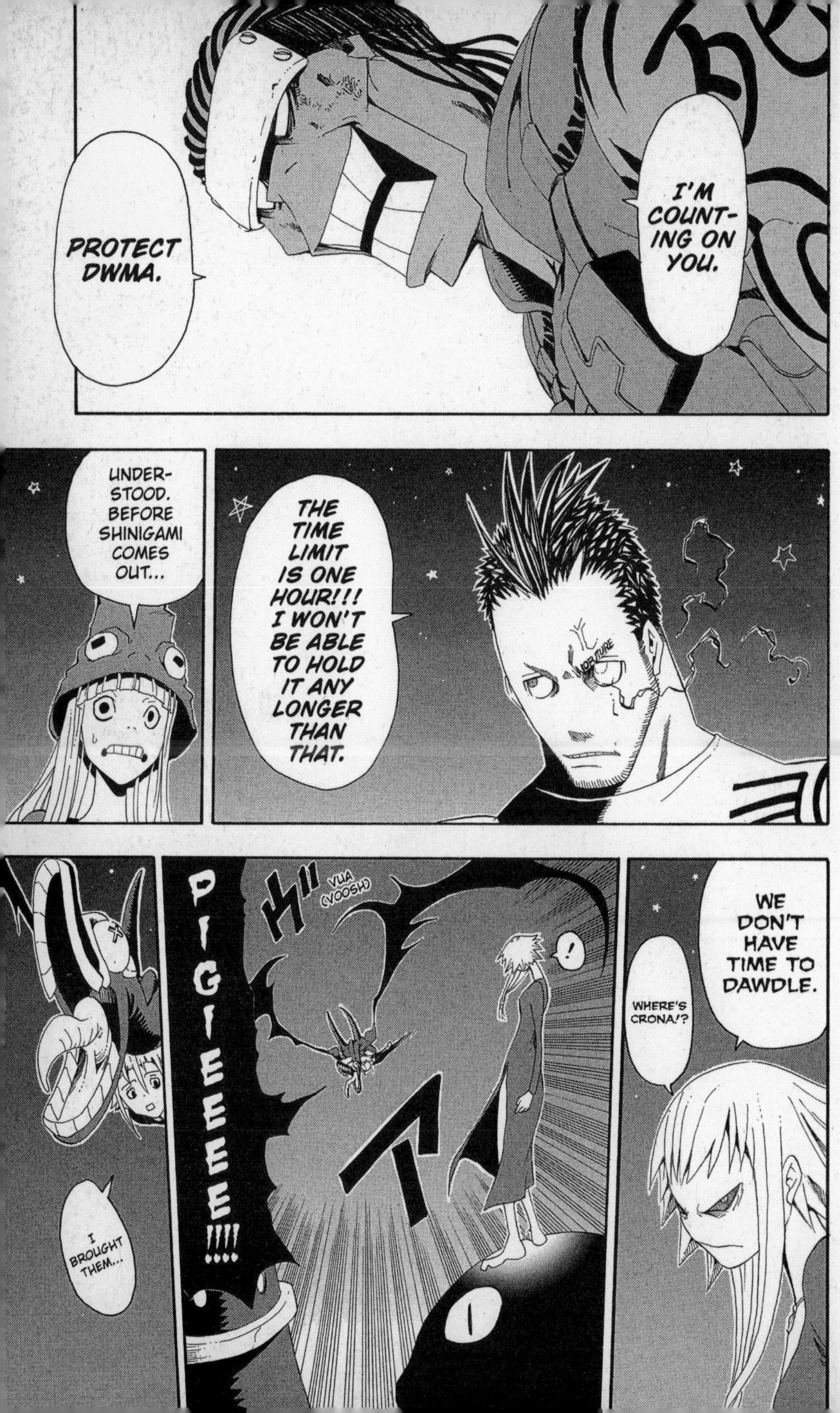
I'M COUNTING ON YOU.
PROTECT DWMA.
THE TIME LIMIT IS ONE HOUR!!! I WON'T BE ABLE TO HOLD IT ANY LONGER THAN THAT.
UNDERSTOOD. BEFORE SHINIGAMI COMES OUT...
WE DON'T HAVE TIME TO DAWDLE.
WHERE'S CRONA!?
VUA (VOOSH)
!
PIGIEEEE!!!!
I BROUGHT THEM...

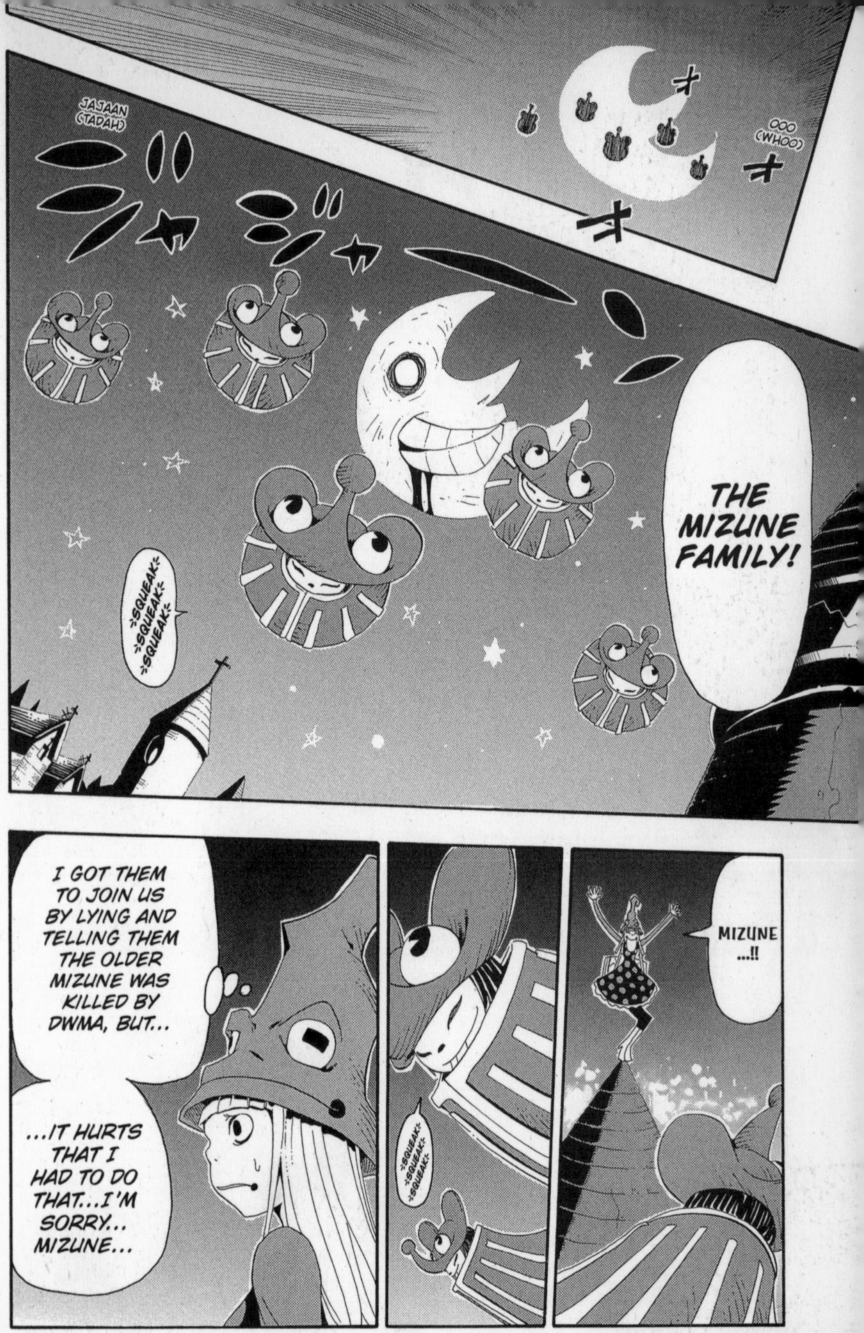
OOO (WHOO)
JAJAAN (TADAH)
THE MIZUNE FAMILY!
SQUEAK SQUEAK SQUEAK
MIZUNE ...!!
SQUEAK SQUEAK SQUEAK
I GOT THEM TO JOIN US BY LYING AND TELLING THEM THE OLDER MIZUNE WAS KILLED BY DWMA, BUT...
...IT HURTS THAT I HAD TO DO THAT...I'M SORRY... MIZUNE...

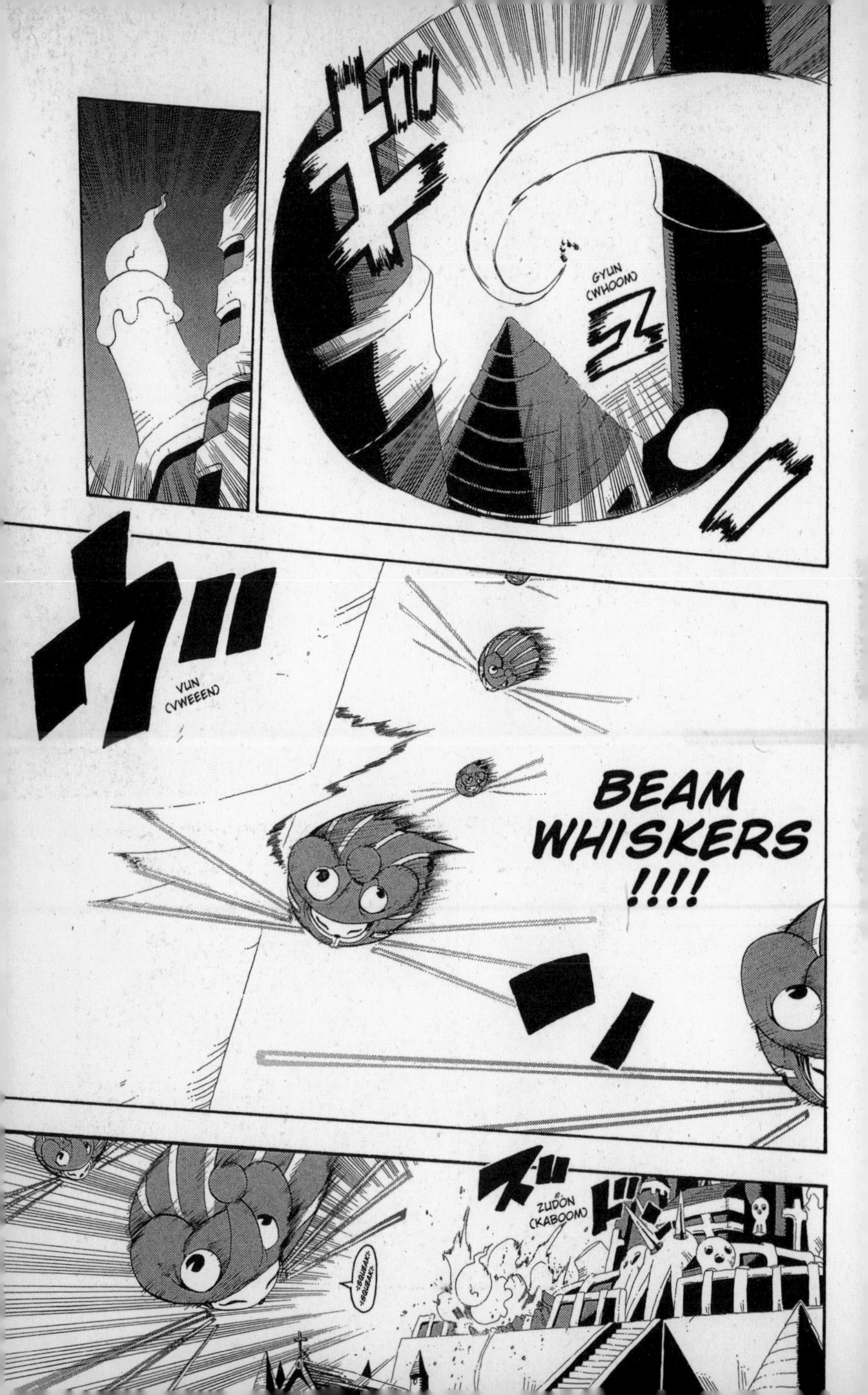
GYUN (WHOOM)
BEAM WHISKERS!!!!
VUN (VWEEEN)
ZUDON (KABOOM)
SQUEAK *SQUEAK*

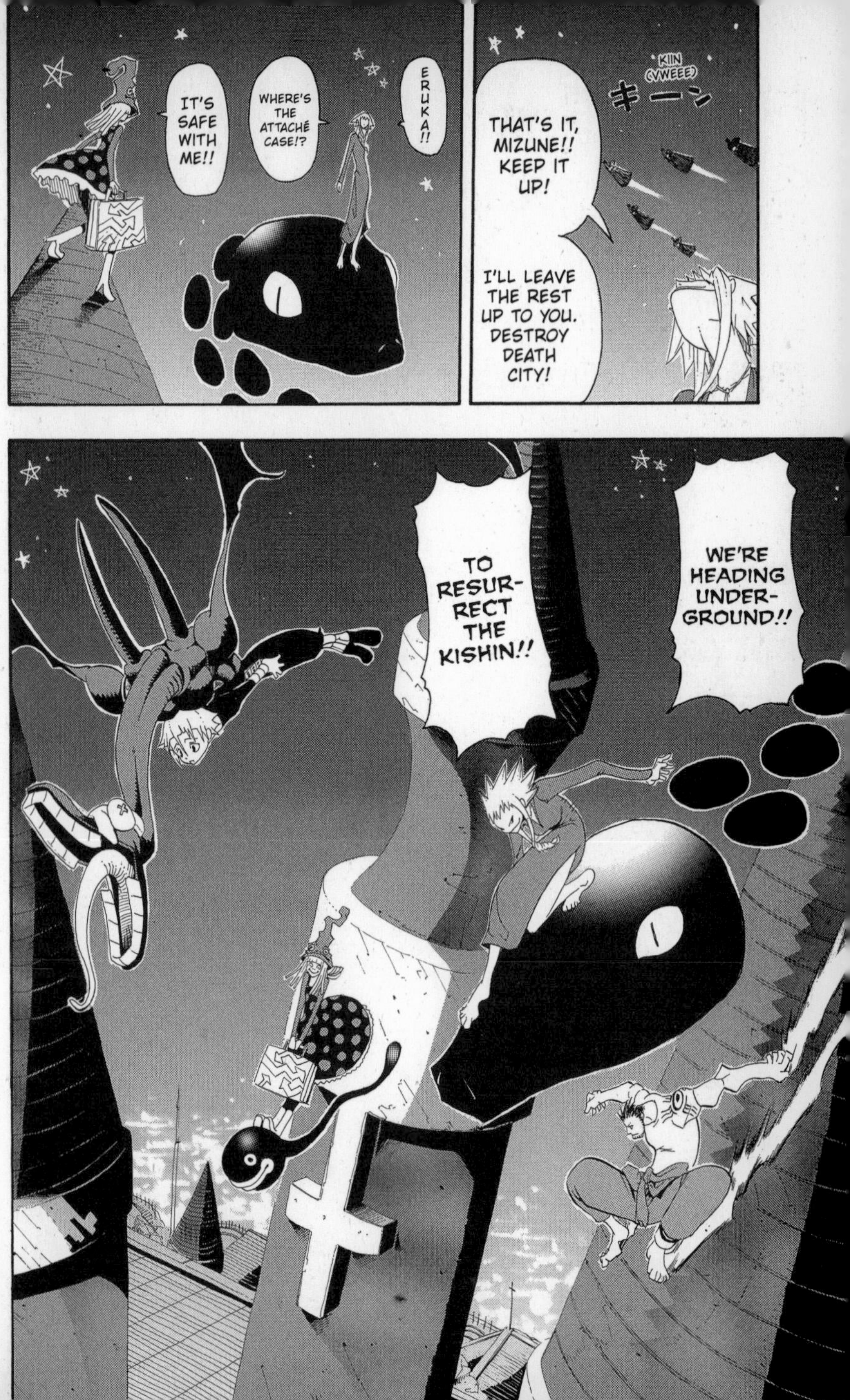
KIIN (VWEEE)
キーン
THAT'S IT, MIZUNE!! KEEP IT UP!
I'LL LEAVE THE REST UP TO YOU. DESTROY DEATH CITY!
ERUKA!!
WHERE'S THE ATTACHÉ CASE!?
IT'S SAFE WITH ME!!
WE'RE HEADING UNDER-GROUND!!
TO RESUR-RECT THE KISHIN!!

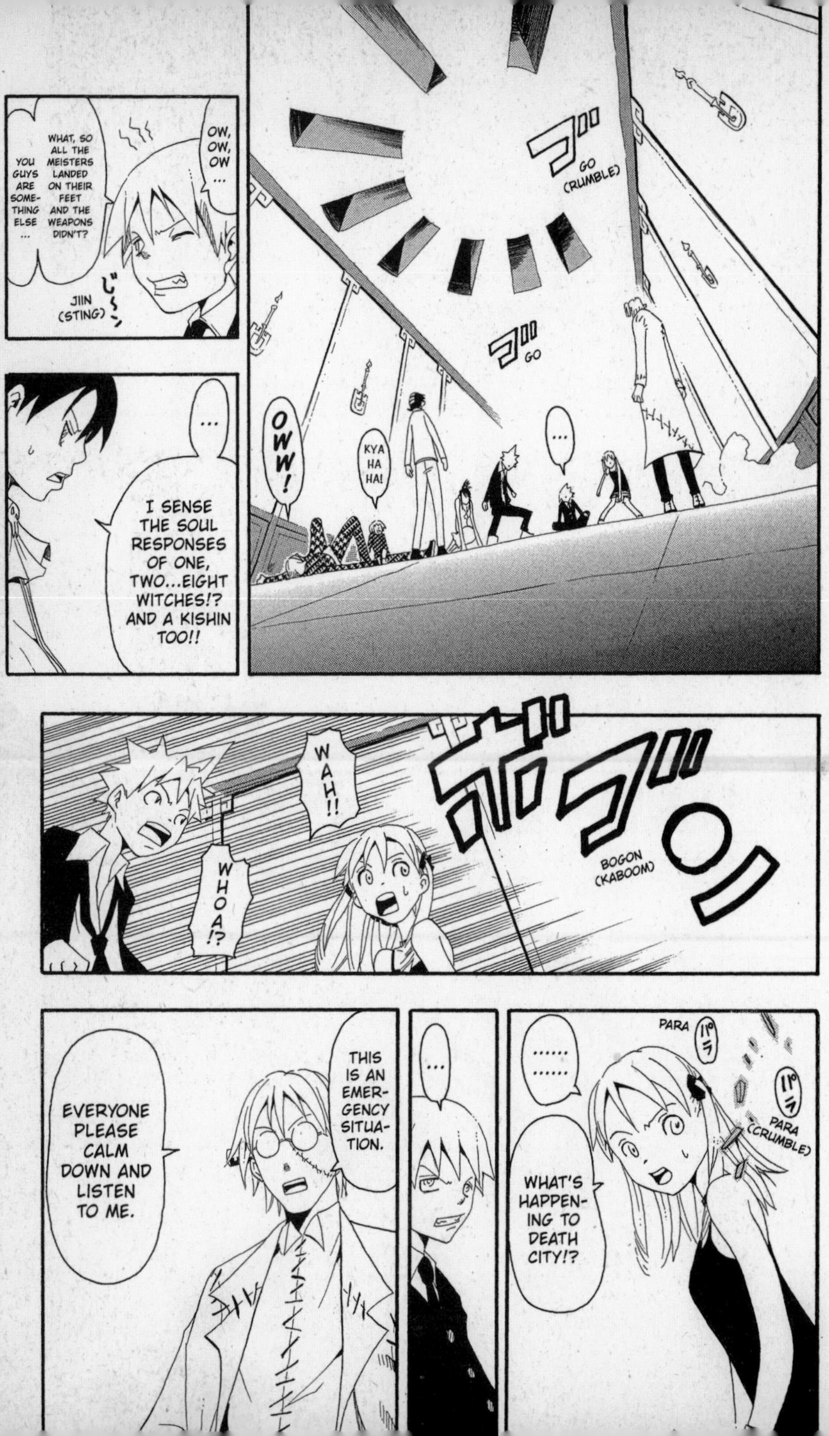
GO (RUMBLE)
GO
...
KYA HA HA!
OWW!
OW, OW, OW ...
WHAT, SO ALL THE MEISTERS LANDED ON THEIR FEET AND THE WEAPONS DIDN'T?
YOU GUYS ARE SOMETHING ELSE ...
JIIN (STING)
...
I SENSE THE SOUL RESPONSES OF ONE, TWO...EIGHT WITCHES!? AND A KISHIN TOO!!
BOGON (KABOOM)
WAH!!
WHOA!?
PARA
PARA (CRUMBLE)
......
......
WHAT'S HAPPENING TO DEATH CITY!?
...
THIS IS AN EMERGENCY SITUATION.
EVERYONE PLEASE CALM DOWN AND LISTEN TO ME.

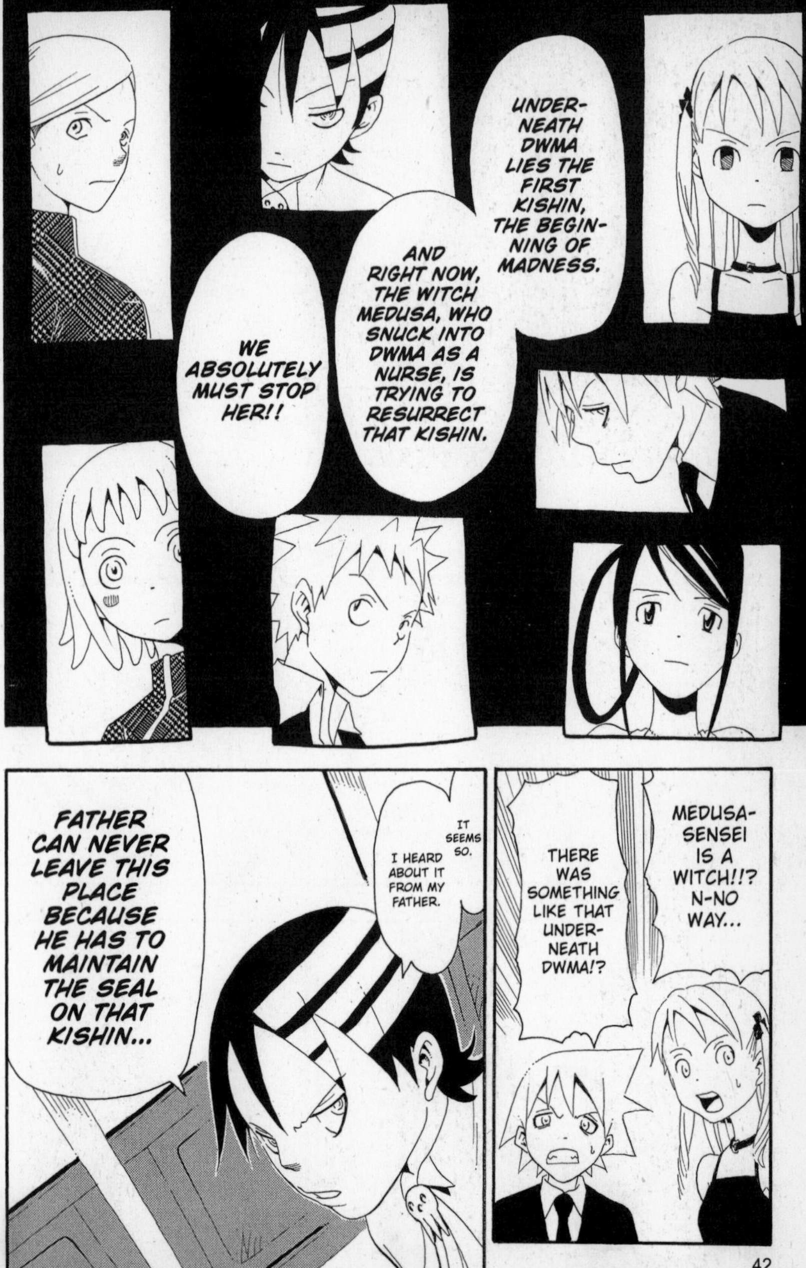
UNDER-NEATH DWMA LIES THE FIRST KISHIN, THE BEGIN-NING OF MADNESS.
AND RIGHT NOW, THE WITCH MEDUSA, WHO SNUCK INTO DWMA AS A NURSE, IS TRYING TO RESURRECT THAT KISHIN.
WE ABSOLUTELY MUST STOP HER!!
MEDUSA-SENSEI IS A WITCH!!? N-NO WAY...
THERE WAS SOMETHING LIKE THAT UNDER-NEATH DWMA!?
IT SEEMS SO.
I HEARD ABOUT IT FROM MY FATHER.
FATHER CAN NEVER LEAVE THIS PLACE BECAUSE HE HAS TO MAINTAIN THE SEAL ON THAT KISHIN...

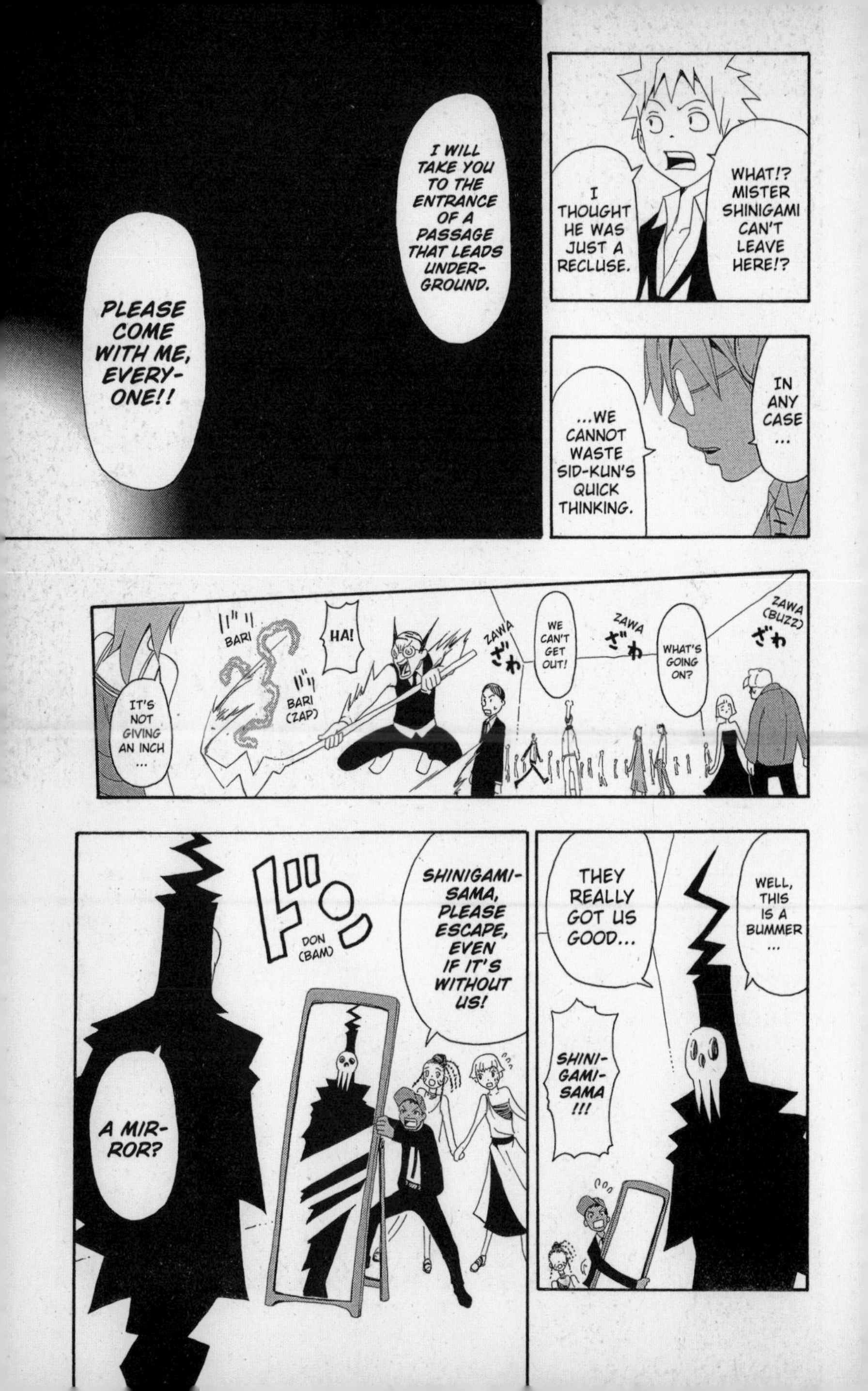
WHAT!? MISTER SHINIGAMI CAN'T LEAVE HERE!?
I THOUGHT HE WAS JUST A RECLUSE.
IN ANY CASE...
...WE CANNOT WASTE SID-KUN'S QUICK THINKING.
I WILL TAKE YOU TO THE ENTRANCE OF A PASSAGE THAT LEADS UNDER-GROUND.
PLEASE COME WITH ME, EVERY-ONE!!
ZAWA (BUZZ)
ざわ
WHAT'S GOING ON?
ZAWA
ざわ
WE CAN'T GET OUT!
ZAWA
ざわ
HA!
バリ
BARI
バリ
BARI (ZAP)
IT'S NOT GIVING AN INCH...
WELL, THIS IS A BUMMER...
THEY REALLY GOT US GOOD...
SHINI-GAMI-SAMA!!!
SHINIGAMI-SAMA, PLEASE ESCAPE, EVEN IF IT'S WITHOUT US!
ドン
DON (BAM)
A MIR-ROR?

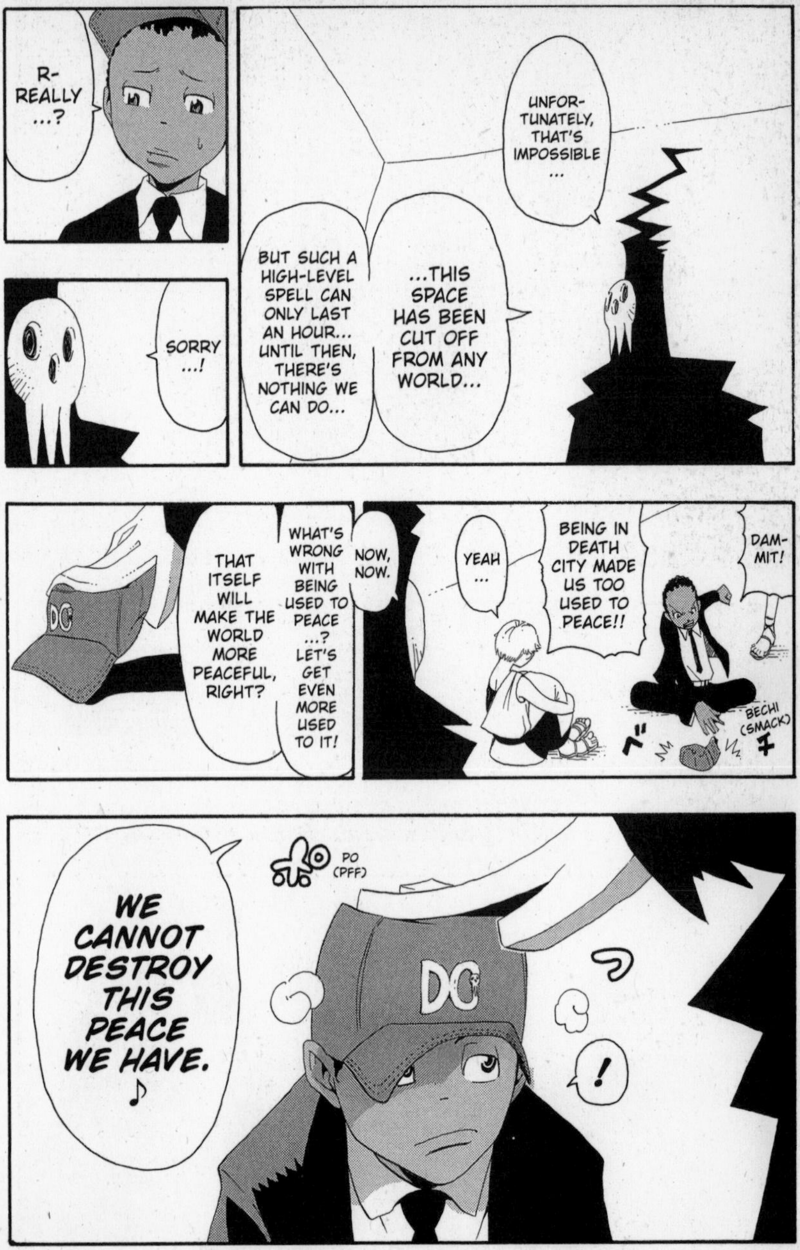
UNFORTUNATELY, THAT'S IMPOSSIBLE...
...THIS SPACE HAS BEEN CUT OFF FROM ANY WORLD...
BUT SUCH A HIGH-LEVEL SPELL CAN ONLY LAST AN HOUR... UNTIL THEN, THERE'S NOTHING WE CAN DO...
R-REALLY...?
SORRY...!
DAM-MIT!
BEING IN DEATH CITY MADE US TOO USED TO PEACE!!
YEAH...
BECHI (SMACK)
NOW, NOW.
WHAT'S WRONG WITH BEING USED TO PEACE...? LET'S GET EVEN MORE USED TO IT!
THAT ITSELF WILL MAKE THE WORLD MORE PEACEFUL, RIGHT?
PO (PFF)
WE CANNOT DESTROY THIS PEACE WE HAVE. ♪
!

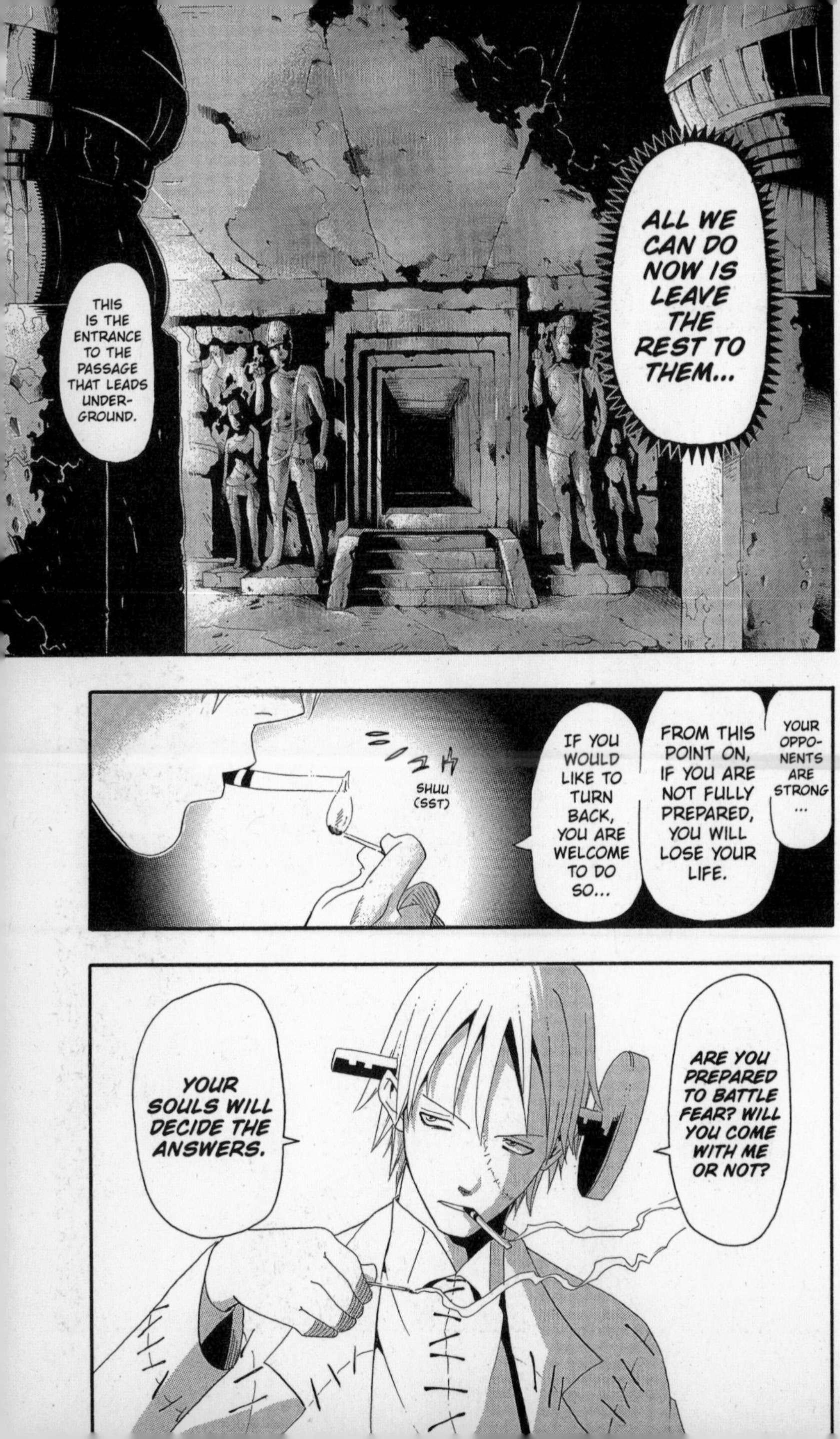
ALL WE CAN DO NOW IS LEAVE THE REST TO THEM...
THIS IS THE ENTRANCE TO THE PASSAGE THAT LEADS UNDERGROUND.
YOUR OPPONENTS ARE STRONG...
FROM THIS POINT ON, IF YOU ARE NOT FULLY PREPARED, YOU WILL LOSE YOUR LIFE.
IF YOU WOULD LIKE TO TURN BACK, YOU ARE WELCOME TO DO SO...
SHUU (SST)
ARE YOU PREPARED TO BATTLE FEAR? WILL YOU COME WITH ME OR NOT?
YOUR SOULS WILL DECIDE THE ANSWERS.

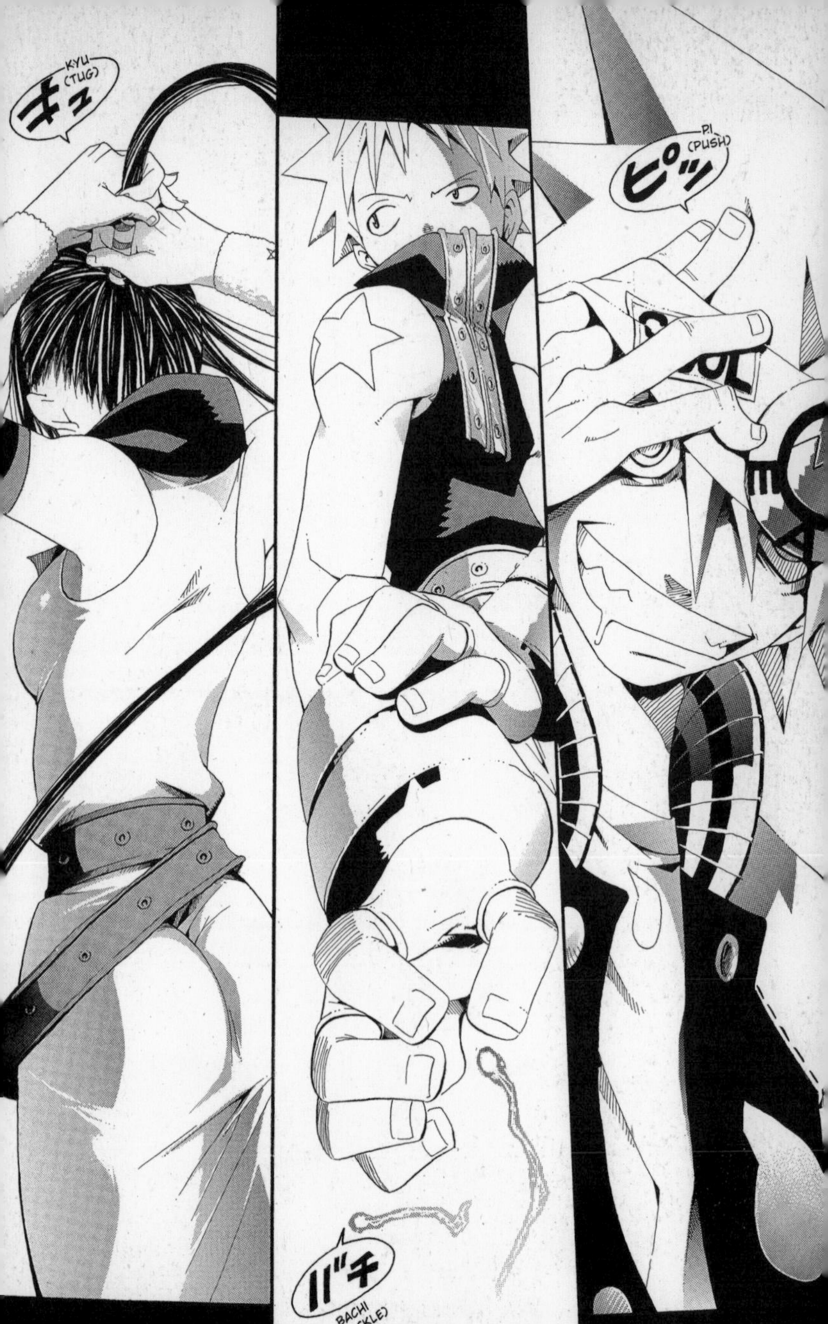
ピッ
PI (PUSH)
バチ
BACHI (CRACKLE)
キュ
KYU (TUG)

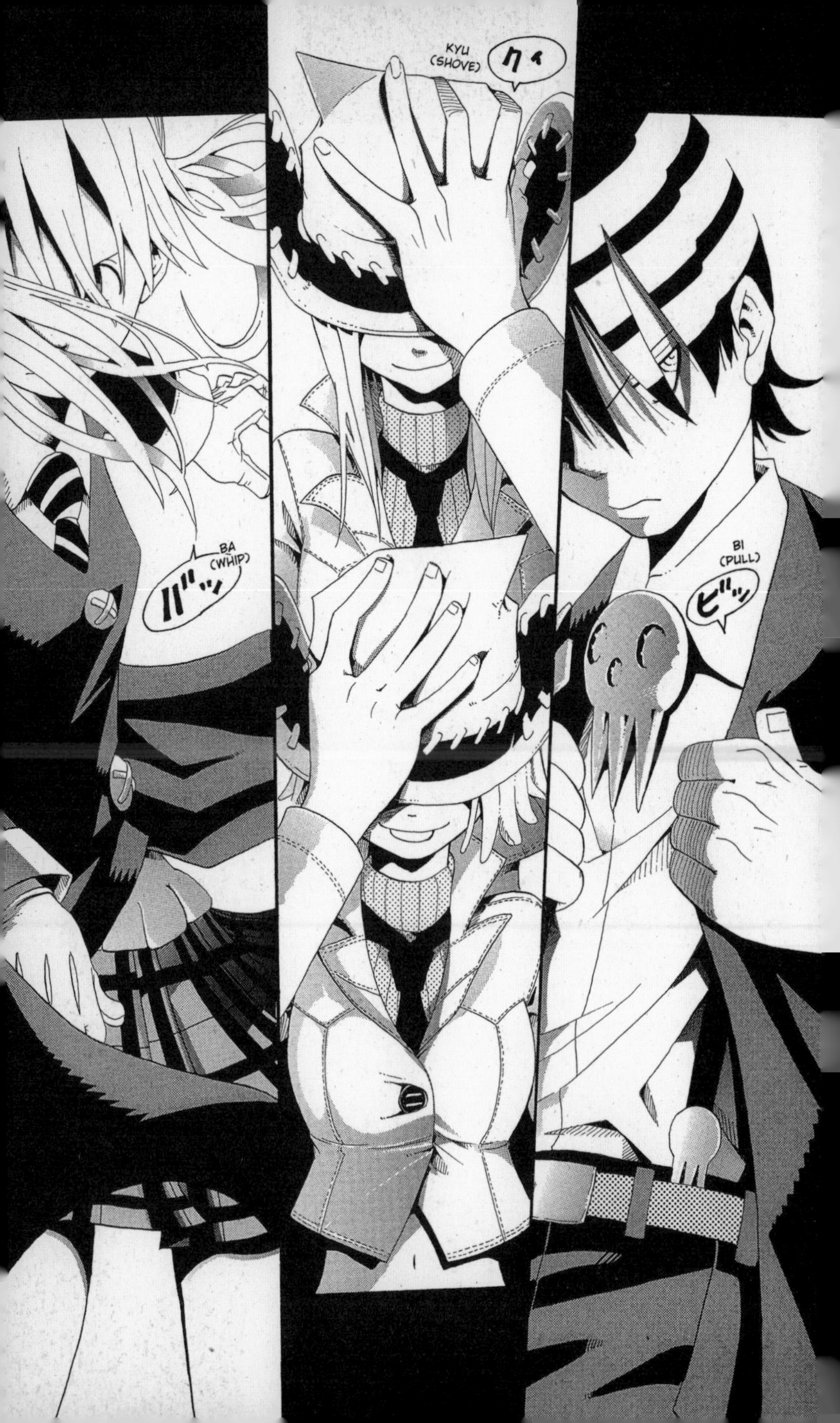
BI (PULL)
ビッ
KYU (SHOVE)
キュ
BA (WHIP)
バッ

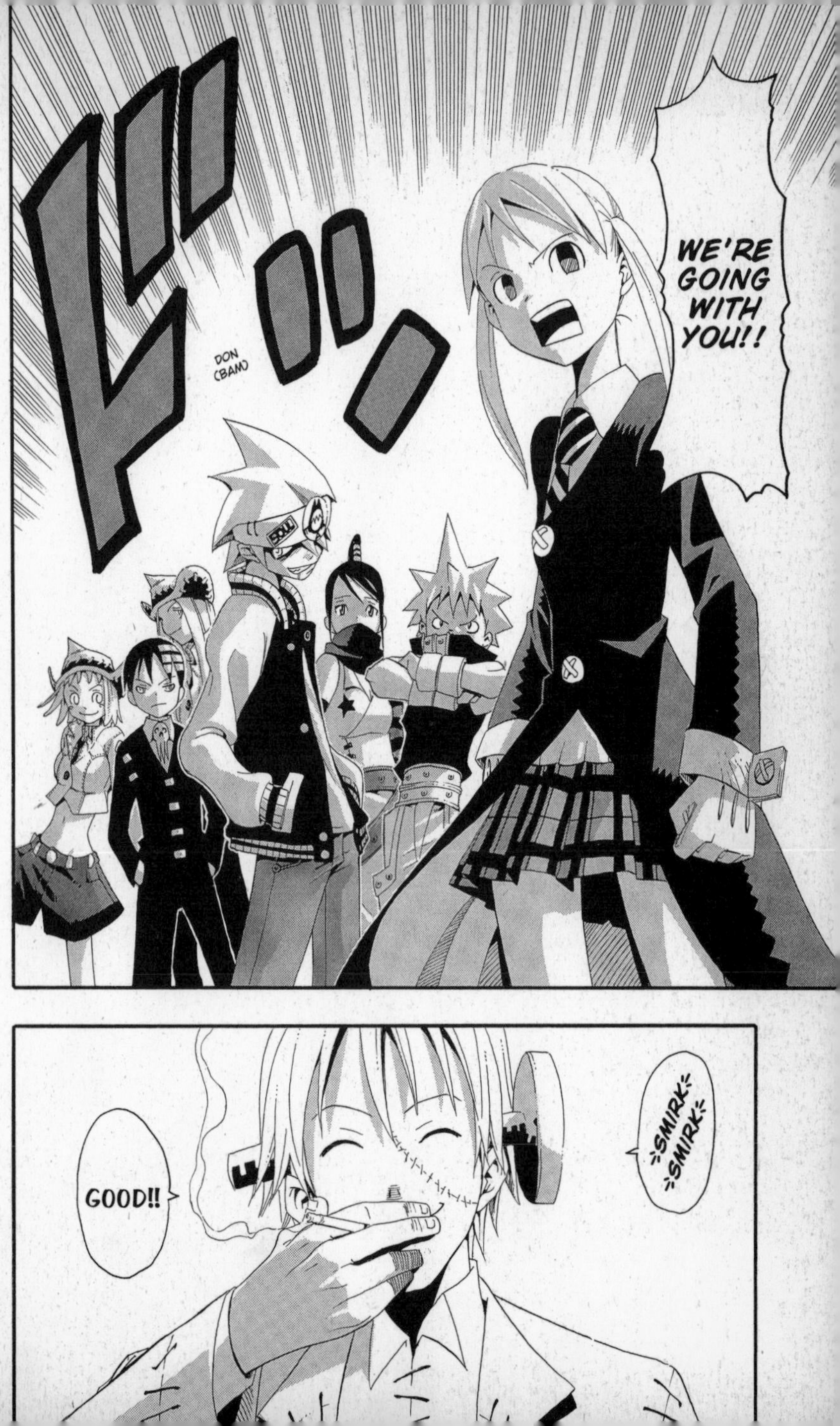
WE'RE GOING WITH YOU!!
DON (BAM)
SMIRK SMIRK
GOOD!!

SOUL EATER

CHAPTER 16: A FIGHT TO THE DEATH AT THE ANNIVERSARY CELEBRATION (PART 1)

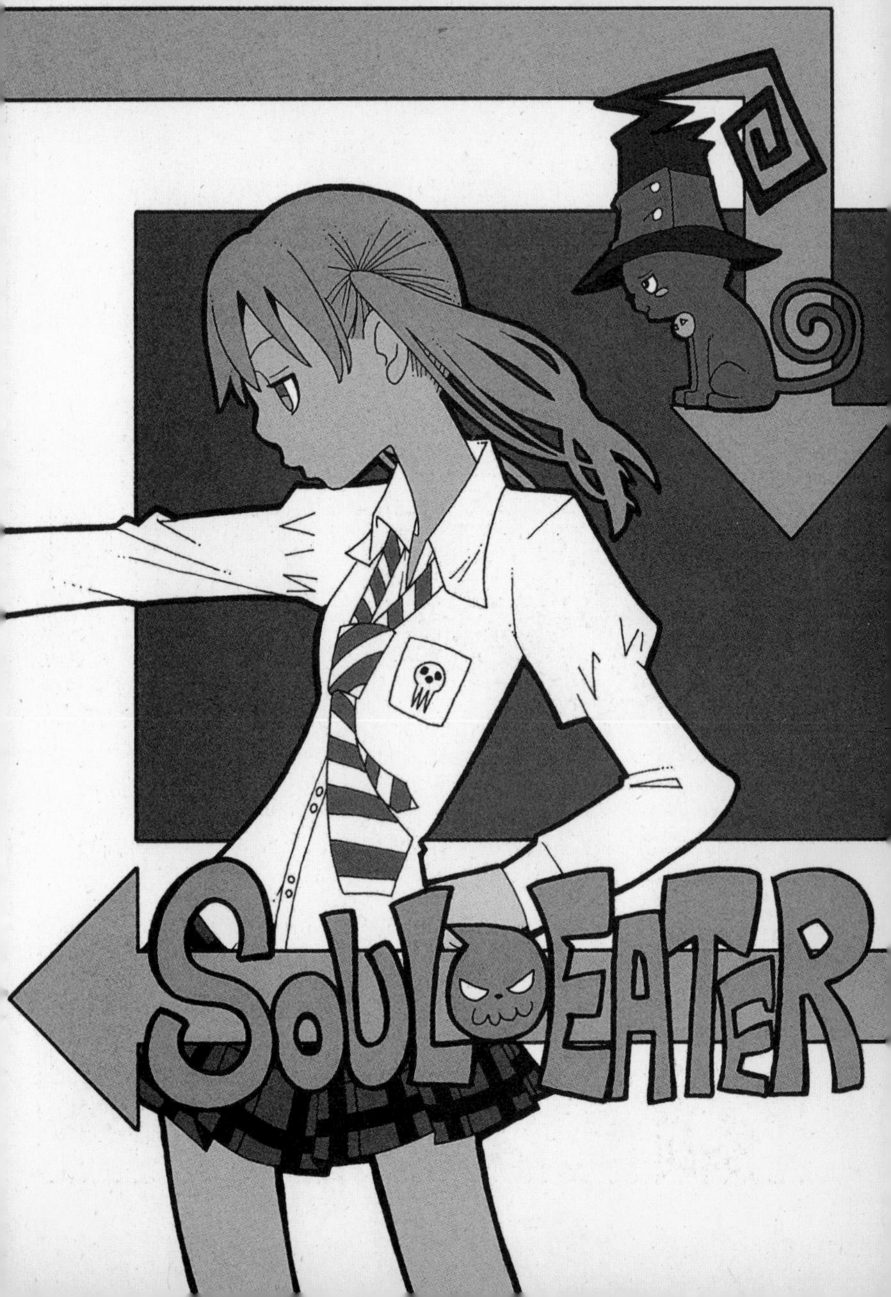
SOUL EATER

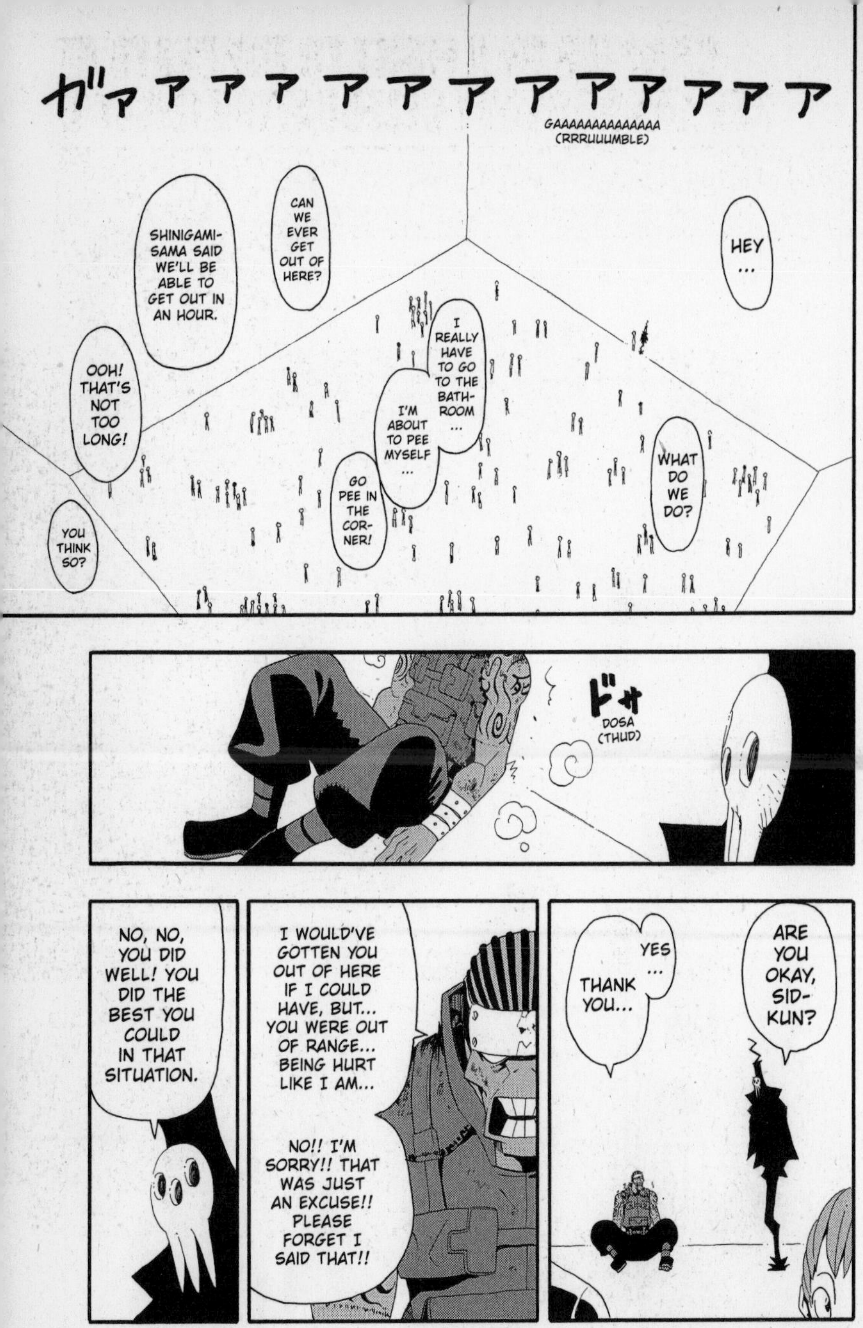
ガァァァァァァァァァァァァ
GAAAAAAAAAAAAAA
(RRRUUUMBLE)
HEY...
WHAT DO WE DO?
CAN WE EVER GET OUT OF HERE?
SHINIGAMI-SAMA SAID WE'LL BE ABLE TO GET OUT IN AN HOUR.
OOH! THAT'S NOT TOO LONG!
YOU THINK SO?
I REALLY HAVE TO GO TO THE BATHROOM...
I'M ABOUT TO PEE MYSELF...
GO PEE IN THE CORNER!
ドォ
DOSA
(THUD)
ARE YOU OKAY, SID-KUN?
YES...
THANK YOU...
I WOULD'VE GOTTEN YOU OUT OF HERE IF I COULD HAVE, BUT... YOU WERE OUT OF RANGE... BEING HURT LIKE I AM...
NO!! I'M SORRY!! THAT WAS JUST AN EXCUSE!! PLEASE FORGET I SAID THAT!!
NO, NO, YOU DID WELL! YOU DID THE BEST YOU COULD IN THAT SITUATION.

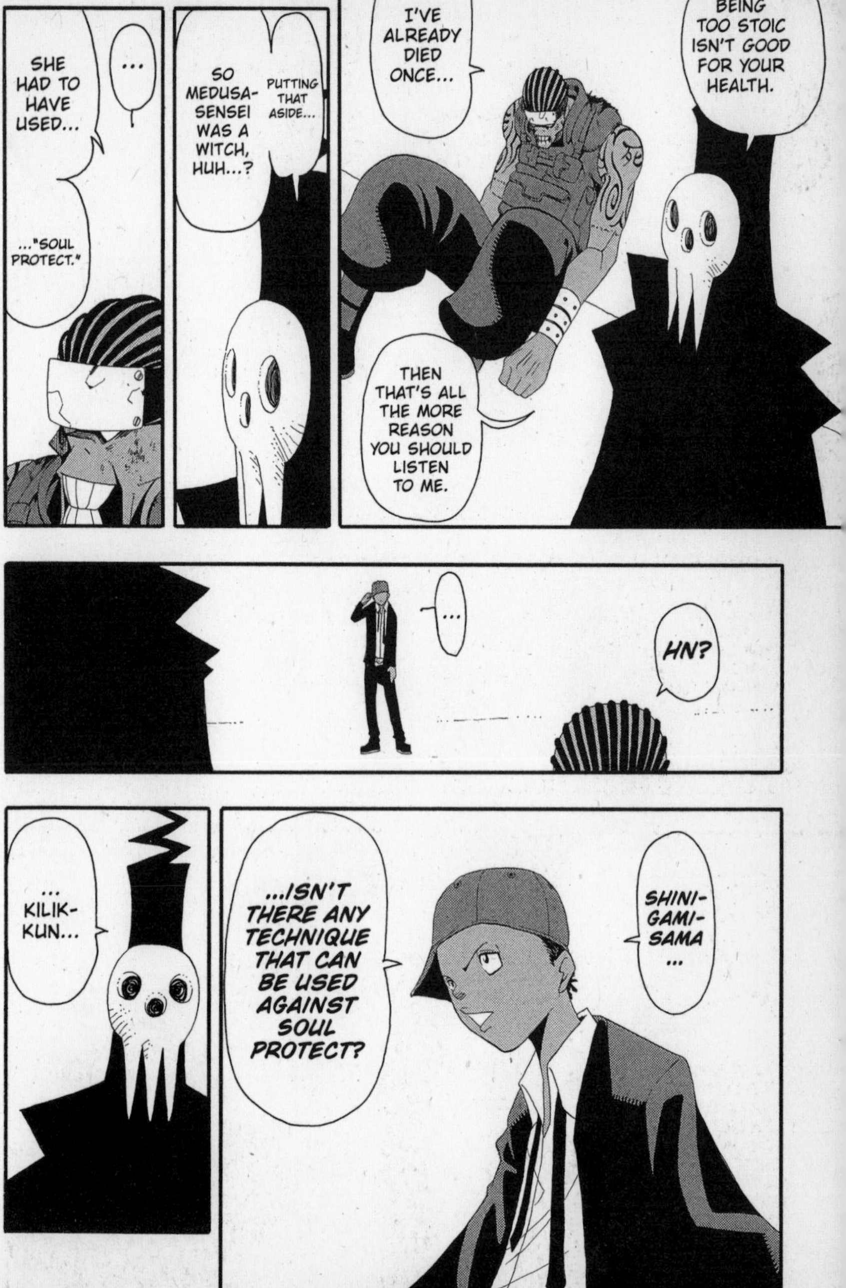
BEING TOO STOIC ISN'T GOOD FOR YOUR HEALTH.
I'VE ALREADY DIED ONCE...
THEN THAT'S ALL THE MORE REASON YOU SHOULD LISTEN TO ME.
PUTTING THAT ASIDE...
SO MEDUSA-SENSEI WAS A WITCH, HUH...?
...
SHE HAD TO HAVE USED...
..."SOUL PROTECT."
HN?
...
SHINI-GAMI-SAMA...
...ISN'T THERE ANY TECHNIQUE THAT CAN BE USED AGAINST SOUL PROTECT?
...KILIK-KUN...

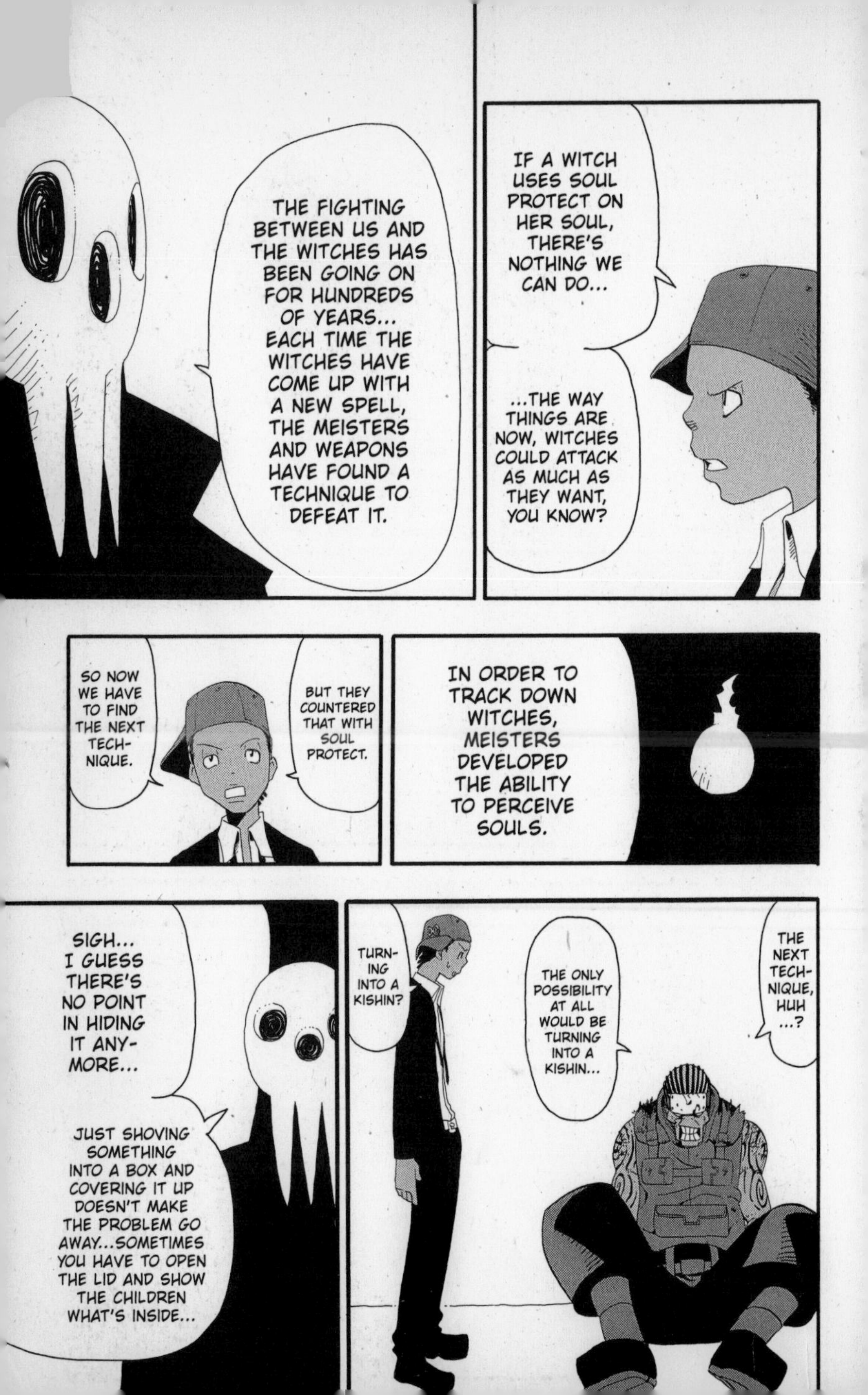
IF A WITCH USES SOUL PROTECT ON HER SOUL, THERE'S NOTHING WE CAN DO...
...THE WAY THINGS ARE NOW, WITCHES COULD ATTACK AS MUCH AS THEY WANT, YOU KNOW?
THE FIGHTING BETWEEN US AND THE WITCHES HAS BEEN GOING ON FOR HUNDREDS OF YEARS... EACH TIME THE WITCHES HAVE COME UP WITH A NEW SPELL, THE MEISTERS AND WEAPONS HAVE FOUND A TECHNIQUE TO DEFEAT IT.
IN ORDER TO TRACK DOWN WITCHES, MEISTERS DEVELOPED THE ABILITY TO PERCEIVE SOULS.
BUT THEY COUNTERED THAT WITH SOUL PROTECT.
SO NOW WE HAVE TO FIND THE NEXT TECHNIQUE.
THE NEXT TECHNIQUE, HUH ...?
THE ONLY POSSIBILITY AT ALL WOULD BE TURNING INTO A KISHIN...
TURNING INTO A KISHIN?
SIGH... I GUESS THERE'S NO POINT IN HIDING IT ANYMORE...
JUST SHOVING SOMETHING INTO A BOX AND COVERING IT UP DOESN'T MAKE THE PROBLEM GO AWAY...SOMETIMES YOU HAVE TO OPEN THE LID AND SHOW THE CHILDREN WHAT'S INSIDE...

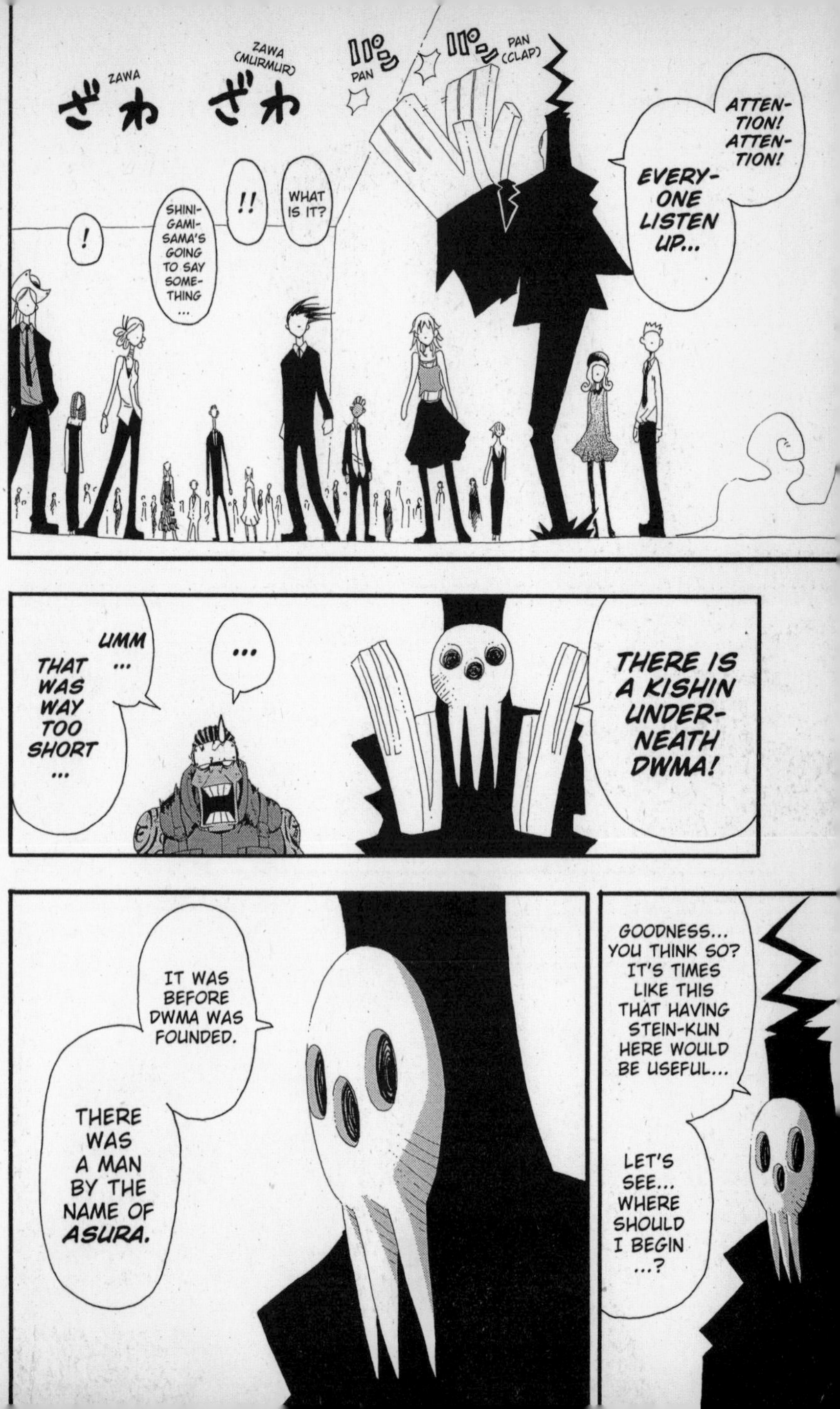
PAN (CLAP)
PAN
ATTENTION! ATTENTION!
EVERYONE LISTEN UP...
WHAT IS IT?
!!
SHINIGAMI-SAMA'S GOING TO SAY SOMETHING...
!
ZAWA (MURMUR)
ざわ
ZAWA
ざわ
THERE IS A KISHIN UNDERNEATH DWMA!
...
UMM... THAT WAS WAY TOO SHORT...
GOODNESS... YOU THINK SO? IT'S TIMES LIKE THIS THAT HAVING STEIN-KUN HERE WOULD BE USEFUL...
LET'S SEE... WHERE SHOULD I BEGIN...?
IT WAS BEFORE DWMA WAS FOUNDED.
THERE WAS A MAN BY THE NAME OF ASURA.

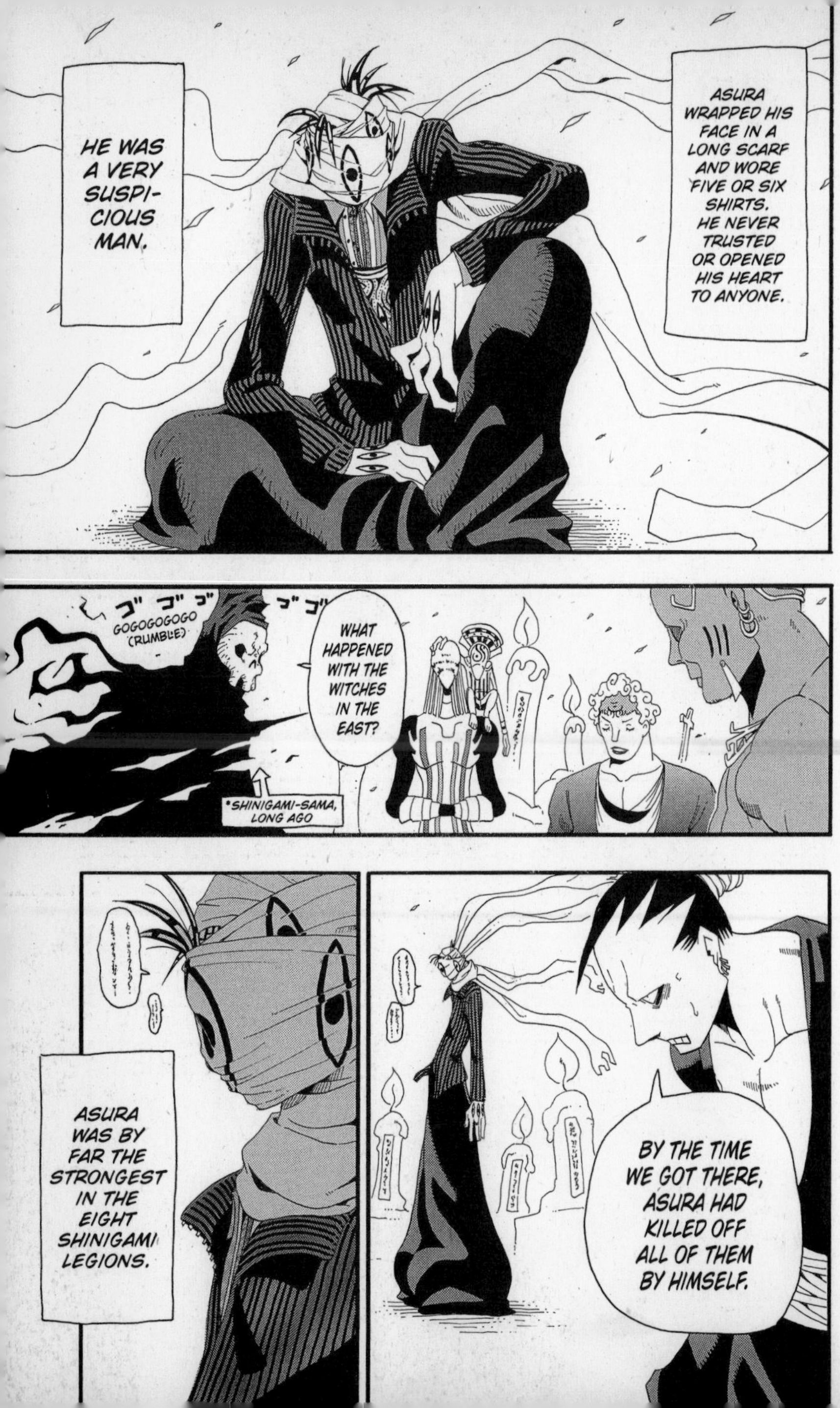
ASURA WRAPPED HIS FACE IN A LONG SCARF AND WORE FIVE OR SIX SHIRTS. HE NEVER TRUSTED OR OPENED HIS HEART TO ANYONE.
HE WAS A VERY SUSPI-CIOUS MAN.
WHAT HAPPENED WITH THE WITCHES IN THE EAST?
ゴゴゴ ゴゴ
GOGOGOGOGO (RUMBLE)
*SHINIGAMI-SAMA, LONG AGO
BY THE TIME WE GOT THERE, ASURA HAD KILLED OFF ALL OF THEM BY HIMSELF.
ASURA WAS BY FAR THE STRONGEST IN THE EIGHT SHINIGAMI LEGIONS.

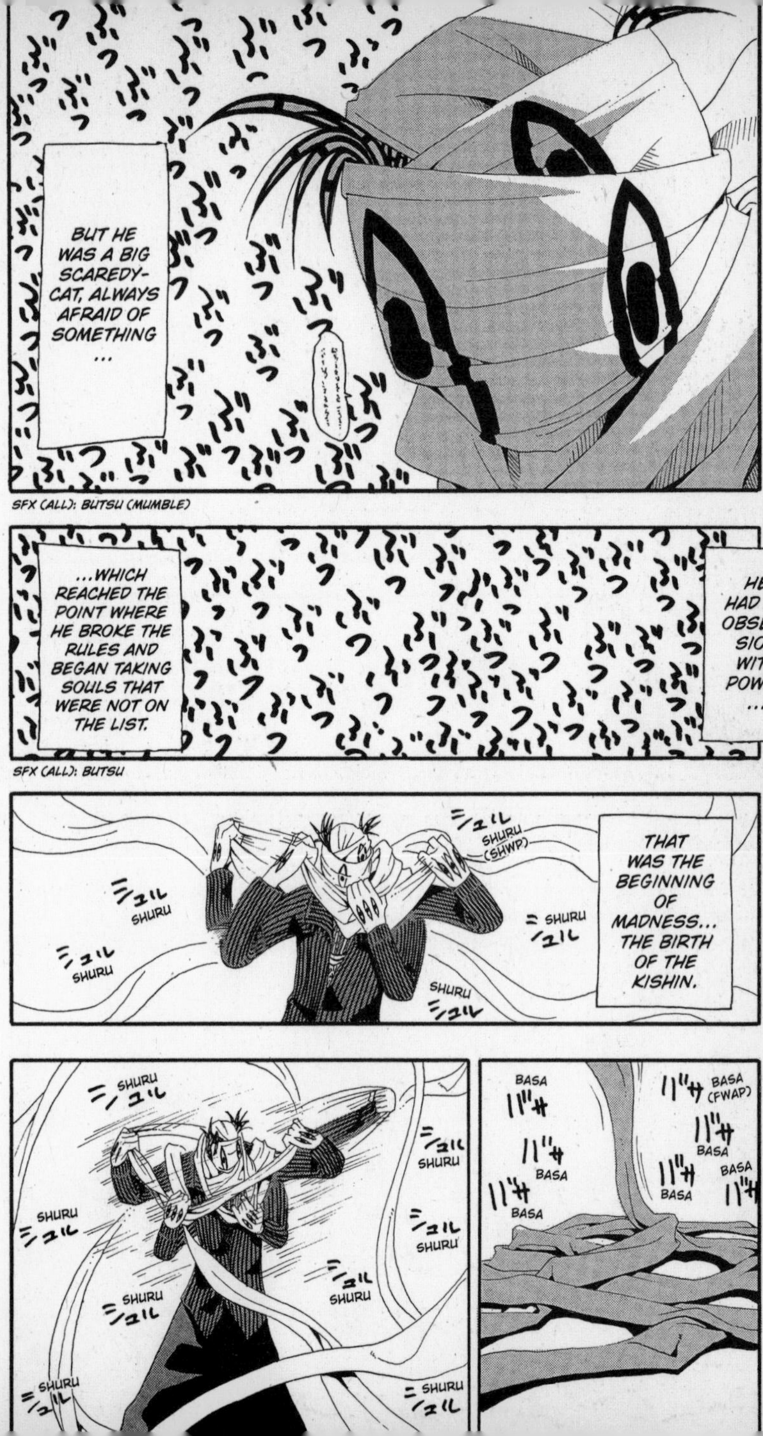

BUT HE WAS A BIG SCAREDY-CAT, ALWAYS AFRAID OF SOMETHING ...
SFX (ALL): BUTSU (MUMBLE)
HE HAD AN OBSESSION WITH POWER ...
...WHICH REACHED THE POINT WHERE HE BROKE THE RULES AND BEGAN TAKING SOULS THAT WERE NOT ON THE LIST.
SFX (ALL): BUTSU
SHURU (SHWP)
THAT WAS THE BEGINNING OF MADNESS... THE BIRTH OF THE KISHIN.
SHURU
SHURU
SHURU
SHURU
BASA (FWAP)
BASA
BASA
BASA
BASA
BASA
SHURU
SHURU
SHURU
SHURU
SHURU
SHURU
SHURU
SHURU

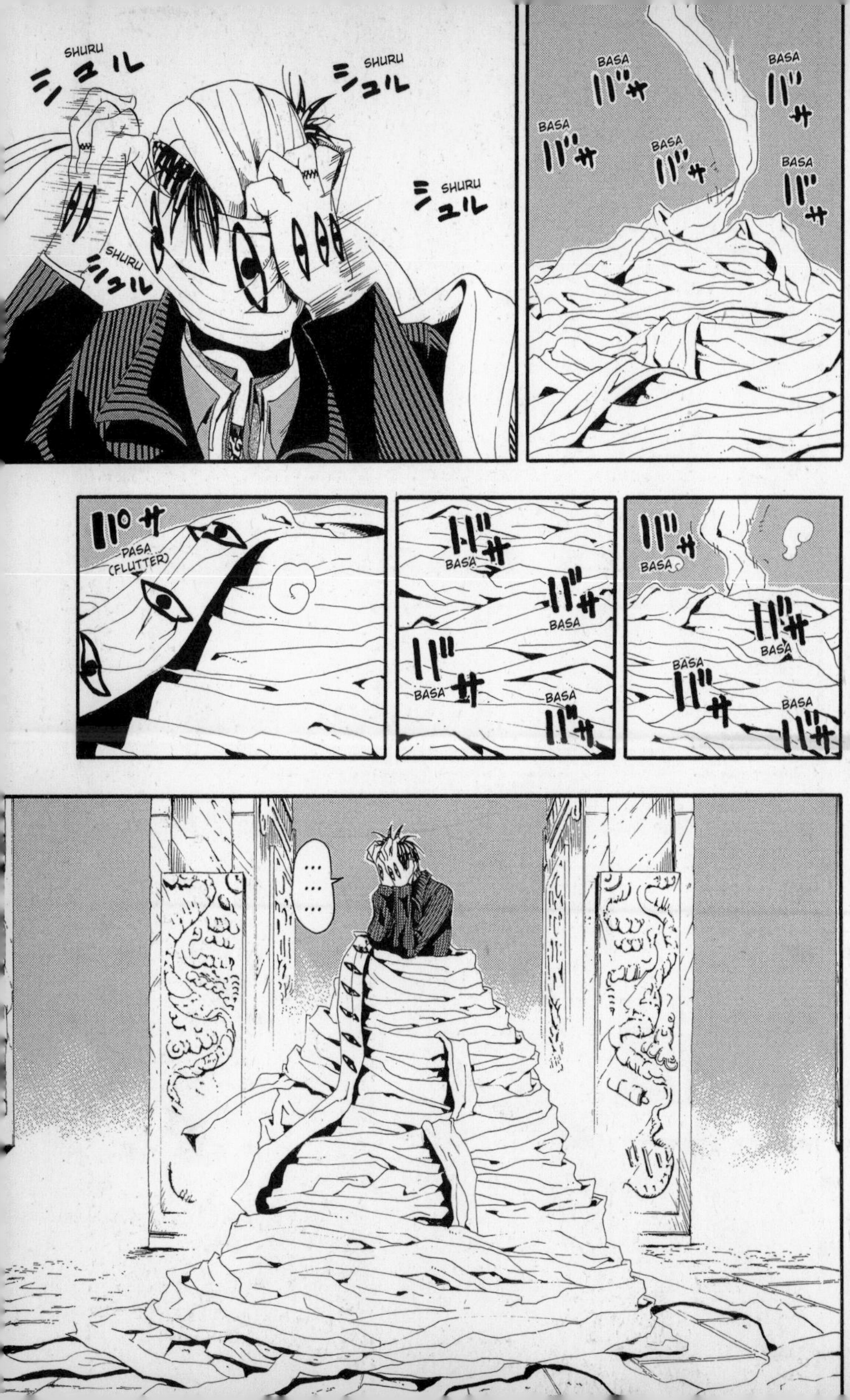

バサ
BASA
バサ
BASA
バサ
BASA
バサ
BASA
バサ
BASA
シュル
SHURU
シュル
SHURU
シュル
SHURU
シュル
SHURU
バサ
BASA
バサ
BASA
バサ
BASA
バサ
BASA
バサ
BASA
バサ
BASA
バサ
BASA
バサ
BASA
パサ
PASA (FLUTTER)
....

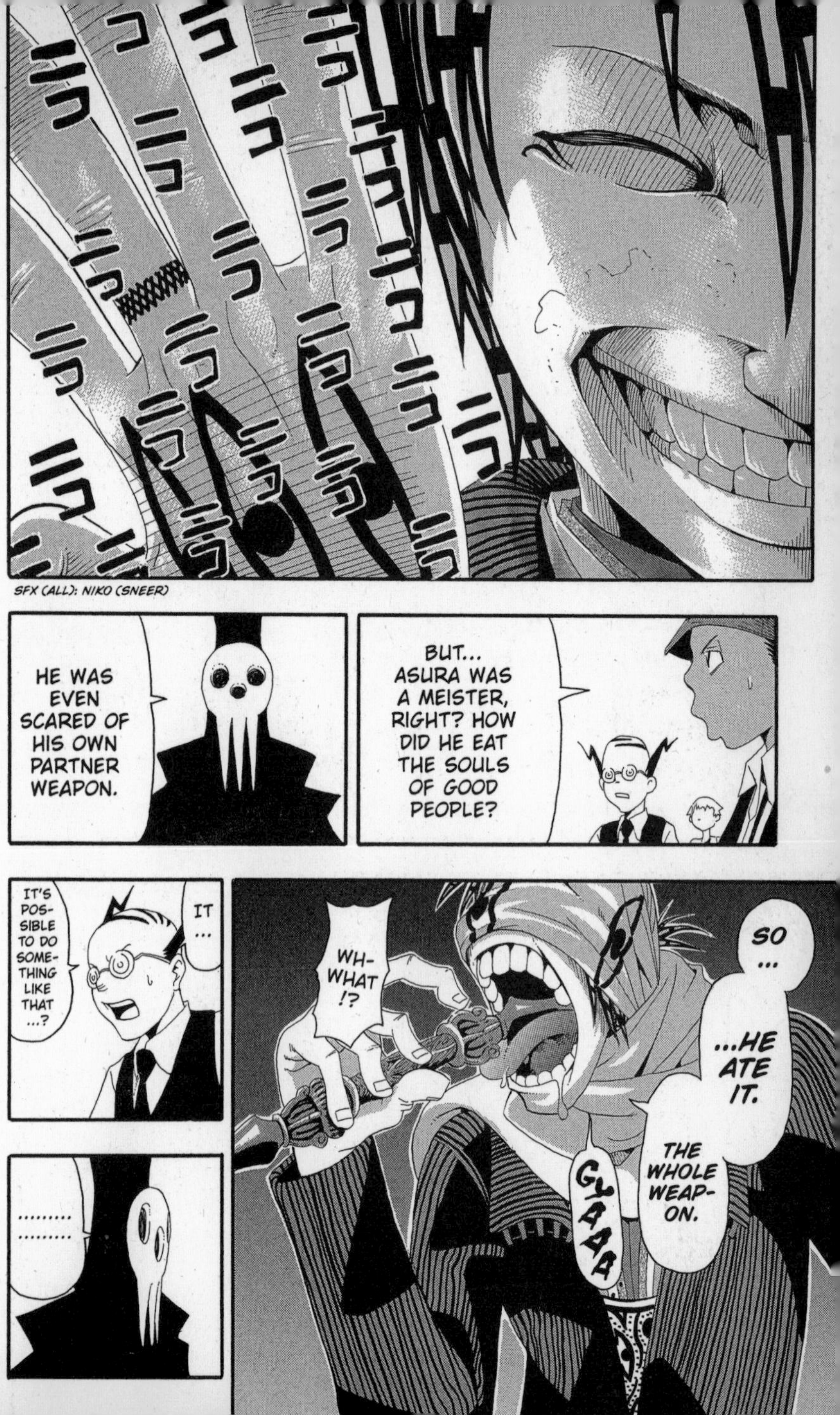
SFX (ALL): NIKO (SNEER)
BUT... ASURA WAS A MEISTER, RIGHT? HOW DID HE EAT THE SOULS OF GOOD PEOPLE?
HE WAS EVEN SCARED OF HIS OWN PARTNER WEAPON.
SO ...
...HE ATE IT.
WH-WHAT!?
THE WHOLE WEAP-ON.
GYAAA
IT ...
IT'S POS-SIBLE TO DO SOME-THING LIKE THAT ...?
....
....

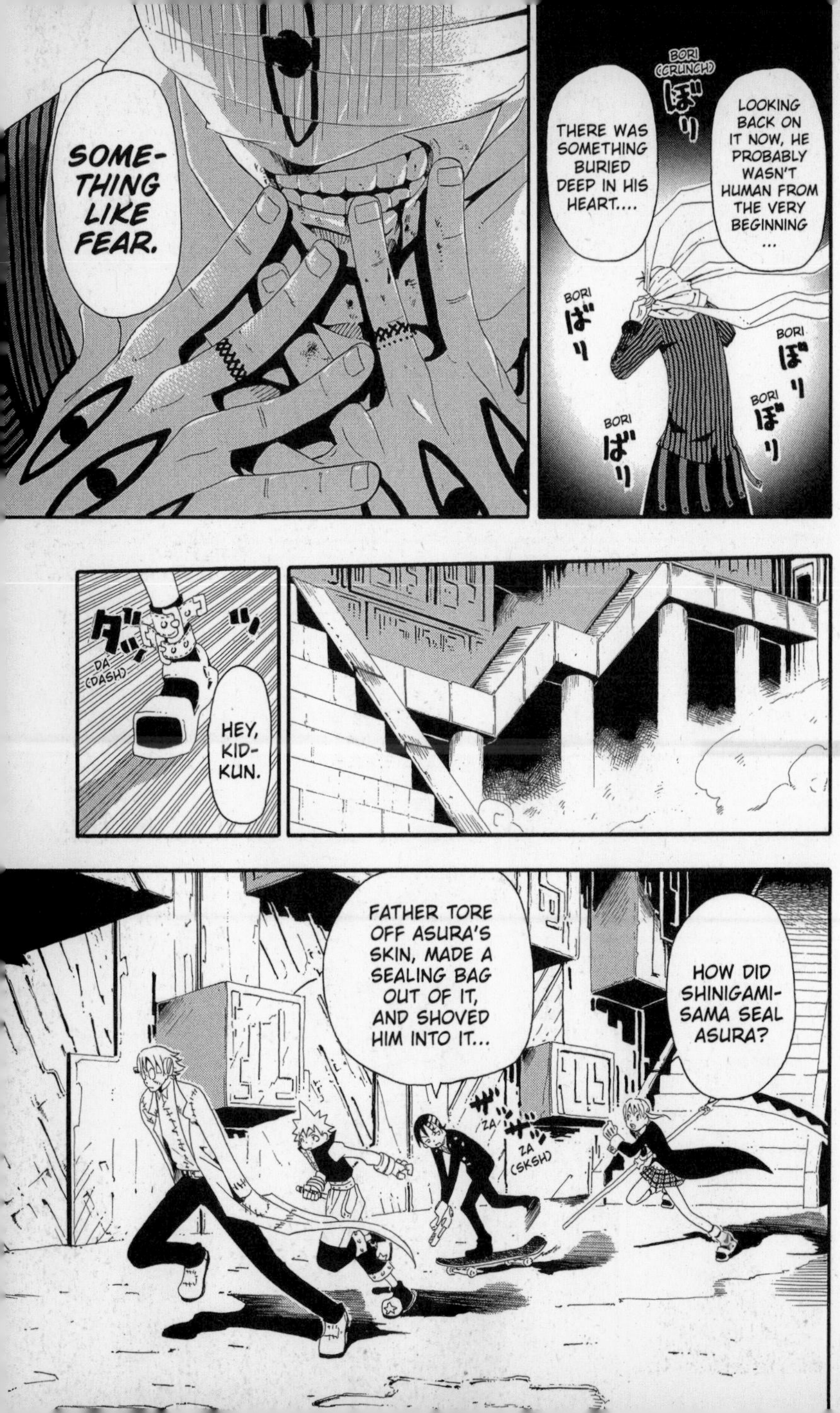

BORI (CRUNCH)
ぼり
LOOKING BACK ON IT NOW, HE PROBABLY WASN'T HUMAN FROM THE VERY BEGINNING ...
THERE WAS SOMETHING BURIED DEEP IN HIS HEART....
BORI
ぼり
BORI
ぼり
BORI
ばり
BORI
ばり
SOME-THING LIKE FEAR.
ダッ
DA (DASH)
HEY, KID-KUN.
HOW DID SHINIGAMI-SAMA SEAL ASURA?
ザッ
ZA
ザッ
ZA (SKSH)
FATHER TORE OFF ASURA'S SKIN, MADE A SEALING BAG OUT OF IT, AND SHOVED HIM INTO IT...

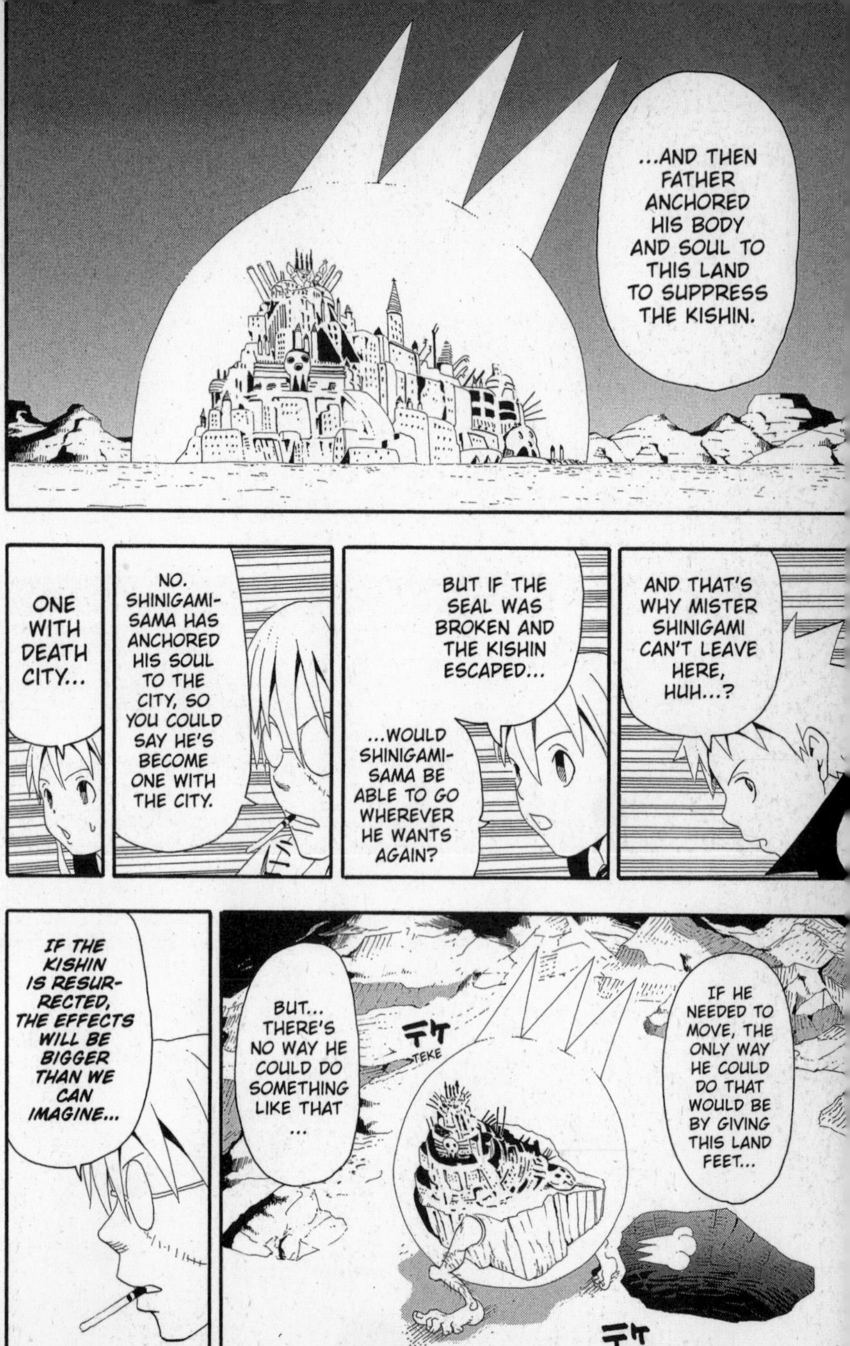
...AND THEN FATHER ANCHORED HIS BODY AND SOUL TO THIS LAND TO SUPPRESS THE KISHIN.
AND THAT'S WHY MISTER SHINIGAMI CAN'T LEAVE HERE, HUH...?
BUT IF THE SEAL WAS BROKEN AND THE KISHIN ESCAPED...
...WOULD SHINIGAMI-SAMA BE ABLE TO GO WHEREVER HE WANTS AGAIN?
NO. SHINIGAMI-SAMA HAS ANCHORED HIS SOUL TO THE CITY, SO YOU COULD SAY HE'S BECOME ONE WITH THE CITY.
ONE WITH DEATH CITY...
IF HE NEEDED TO MOVE, THE ONLY WAY HE COULD DO THAT WOULD BE BY GIVING THIS LAND FEET...
テケ
TEKE
テケ
TEKE (PLOD)
BUT... THERE'S NO WAY HE COULD DO SOMETHING LIKE THAT ...
IF THE KISHIN IS RESURRECTED, THE EFFECTS WILL BE BIGGER THAN WE CAN IMAGINE...

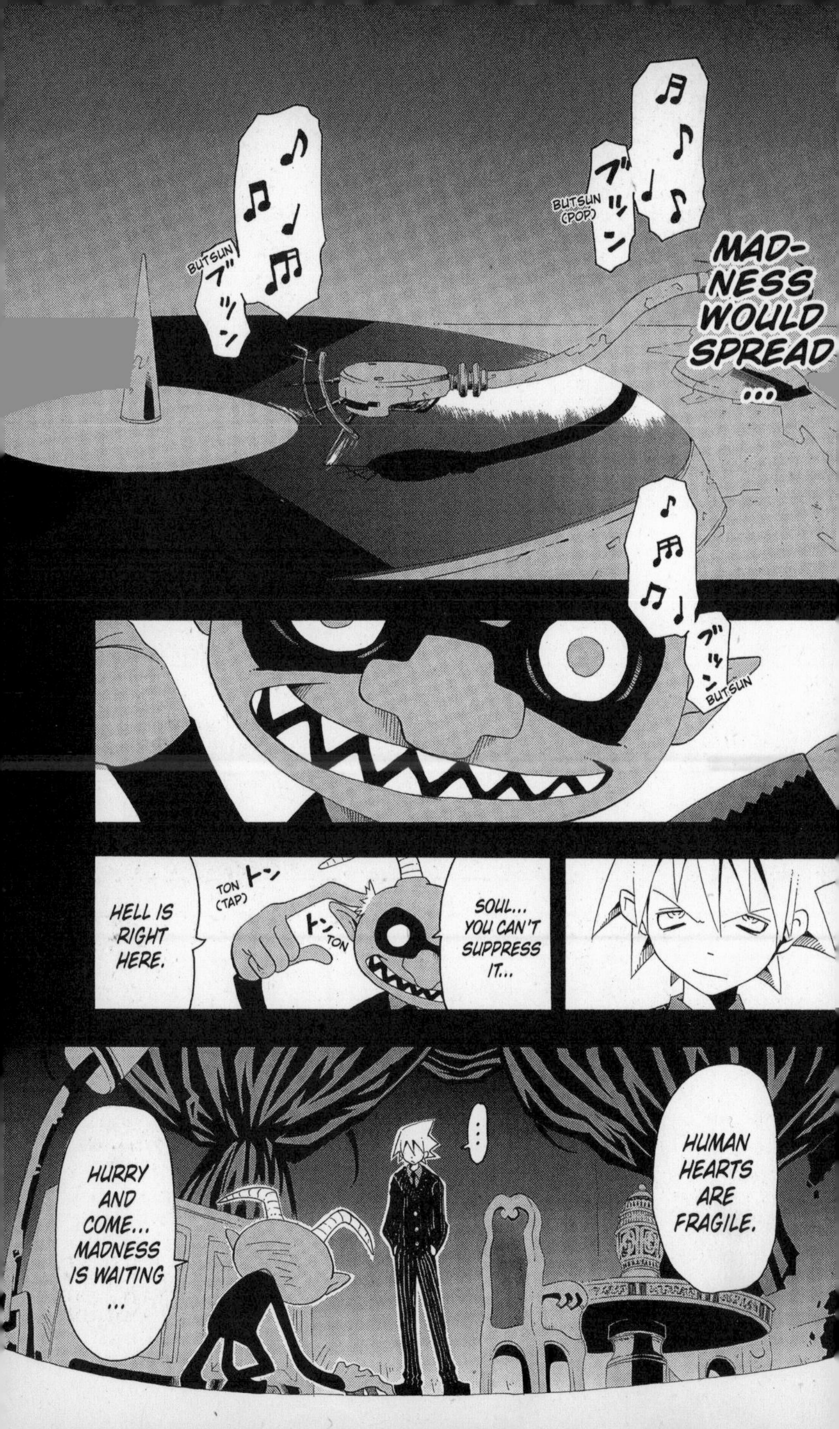
MADNESS WOULD SPREAD...
BUTSUN (POP) ブツン
BUTSUN ブツン
ブツン BUTSUN
SOUL... YOU CAN'T SUPPRESS IT...
TON トン (TAP)
トン TON
HELL IS RIGHT HERE.
HUMAN HEARTS ARE FRAGILE.
...
HURRY AND COME... MADNESS IS WAITING...

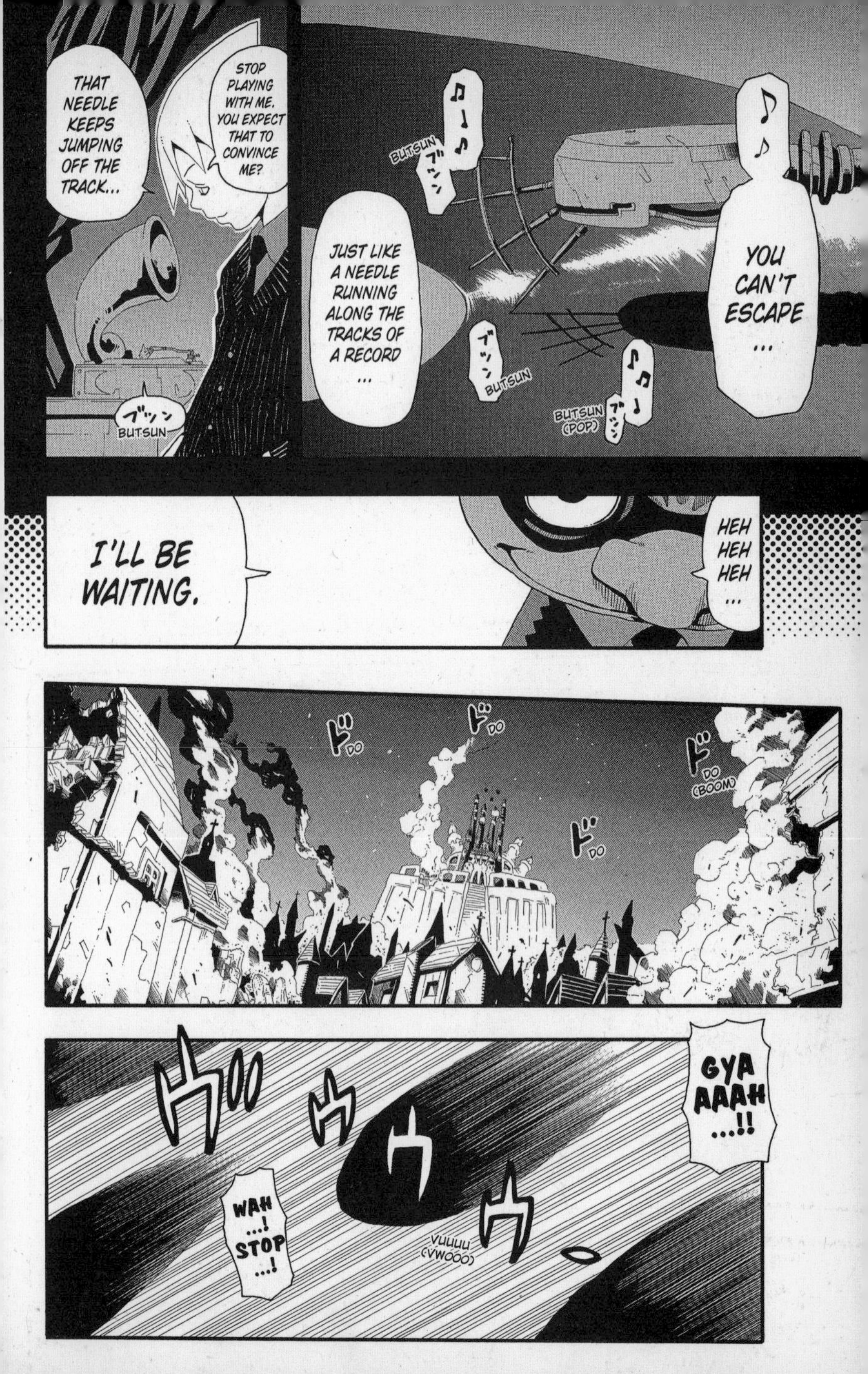
YOU CAN'T ESCAPE ...
ブツン BUTSUN
JUST LIKE A NEEDLE RUNNING ALONG THE TRACKS OF A RECORD ...
ブツン BUTSUN
ブツン BUTSUN (POP)
STOP PLAYING WITH ME. YOU EXPECT THAT TO CONVINCE ME?
THAT NEEDLE KEEPS JUMPING OFF THE TRACK...
ブツン BUTSUN
HEH HEH HEH ...
I'LL BE WAITING.
ド DO (BOOM)
ド DO
ド DO
ド DO
GYA AAAH ...!!
WAH ...! STOP ...!
VUUUN (VWOOO)

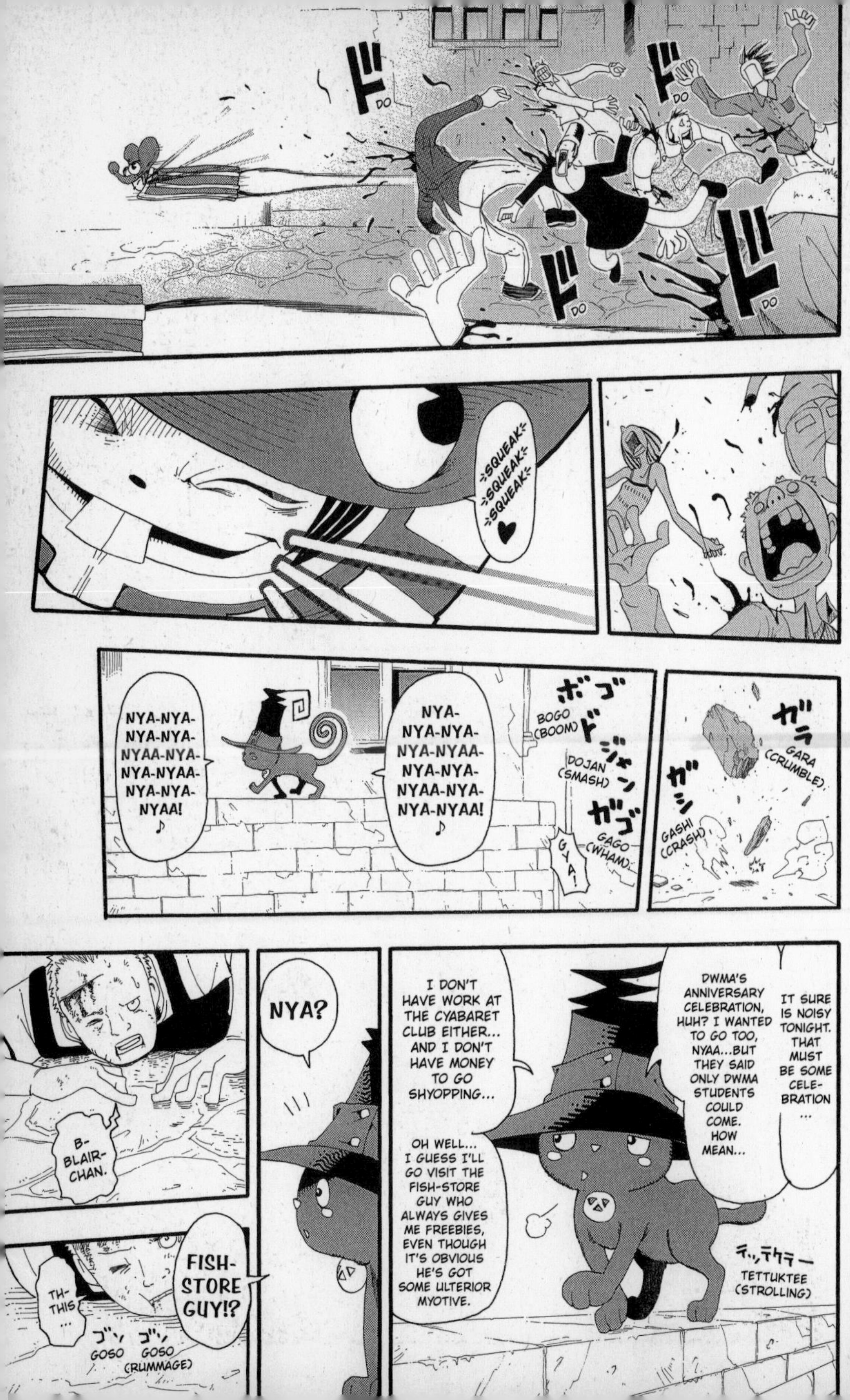
ド
DO
ド
DO
ド
DO
ド
DO
SQUEAK SQUEAK SQUEAK ♥
ガラ
GARA (CRUMBLE)
ガシ
GASHI (CRASH)
ボゴ
BOGO (BOOM)
ドジャーン
DOJAN (SMASH)
ガゴ
GAGO (WHAM)
GYA!
NYA-NYA-NYA-NYAA-NYA-NYA-NYAA-NYA-NYAA-NYA-NYA-NYAA! ♪
NYA-NYA-NYA-NYA-NYAA-NYA-NYA-NYAA-NYA-NYAA! ♪
IT SURE IS NOISY TONIGHT. THAT MUST BE SOME CELEBRATION...
DWMA'S ANNIVERSARY CELEBRATION, HUH? I WANTED TO GO TOO, NYAA...BUT THEY SAID ONLY DWMA STUDENTS COULD COME. HOW MEAN...
I DON'T HAVE WORK AT THE CYABARET CLUB EITHER... AND I DON'T HAVE MONEY TO GO SHYOPPING...
OH WELL... I GUESS I'LL GO VISIT THE FISH-STORE GUY WHO ALWAYS GIVES ME FREEBIES, EVEN THOUGH IT'S OBVIOUS HE'S GOT SOME ULTERIOR MYOTIVE.
テッテケテー
TETTUKTEE (STROLLING)
NYA?
B-BLAIR-CHAN.
FISH-STORE GUY!?
TH-THIS...
ゴソ ゴソ
GOSO GOSO (RUMMAGE)

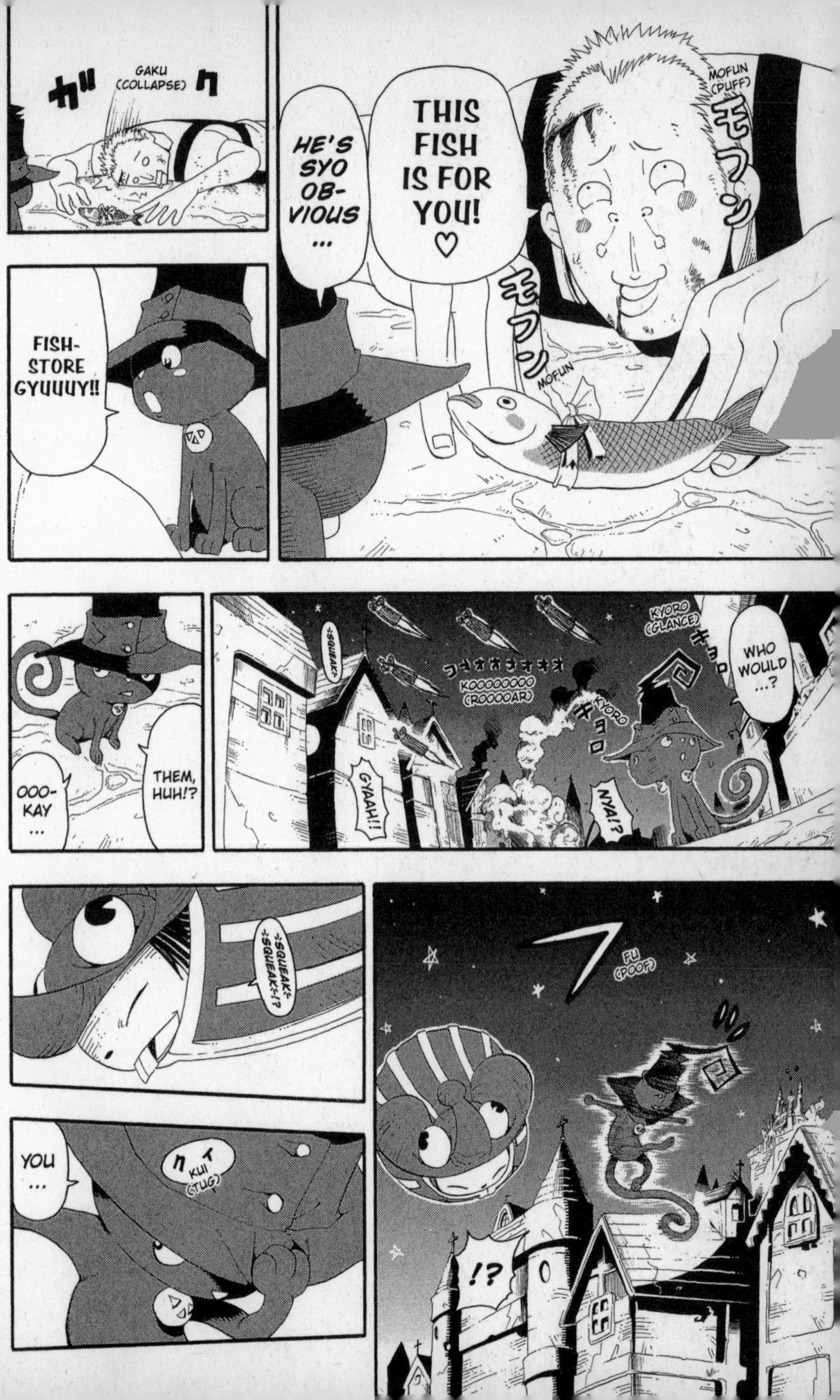
MOFUN (PUFF)
THIS FISH IS FOR YOU! ♡
HE'S SYO OB-VIOUS ...
MOFUN
GAKU (COLLAPSE)
FISH-STORE GYUUUY!!
WHO WOULD ...?
KYORO (GLANCE)
KYORO
KOOOOOOOO (ROOOOAR)
-SQUEAK-
NYA!?
GYAAH!!
THEM, HUH!?
OOO-KAY ...
FU (POOF)
!?
-SQUEAK- -SQUEAK-!?
YOU ...
KUI (TUG)

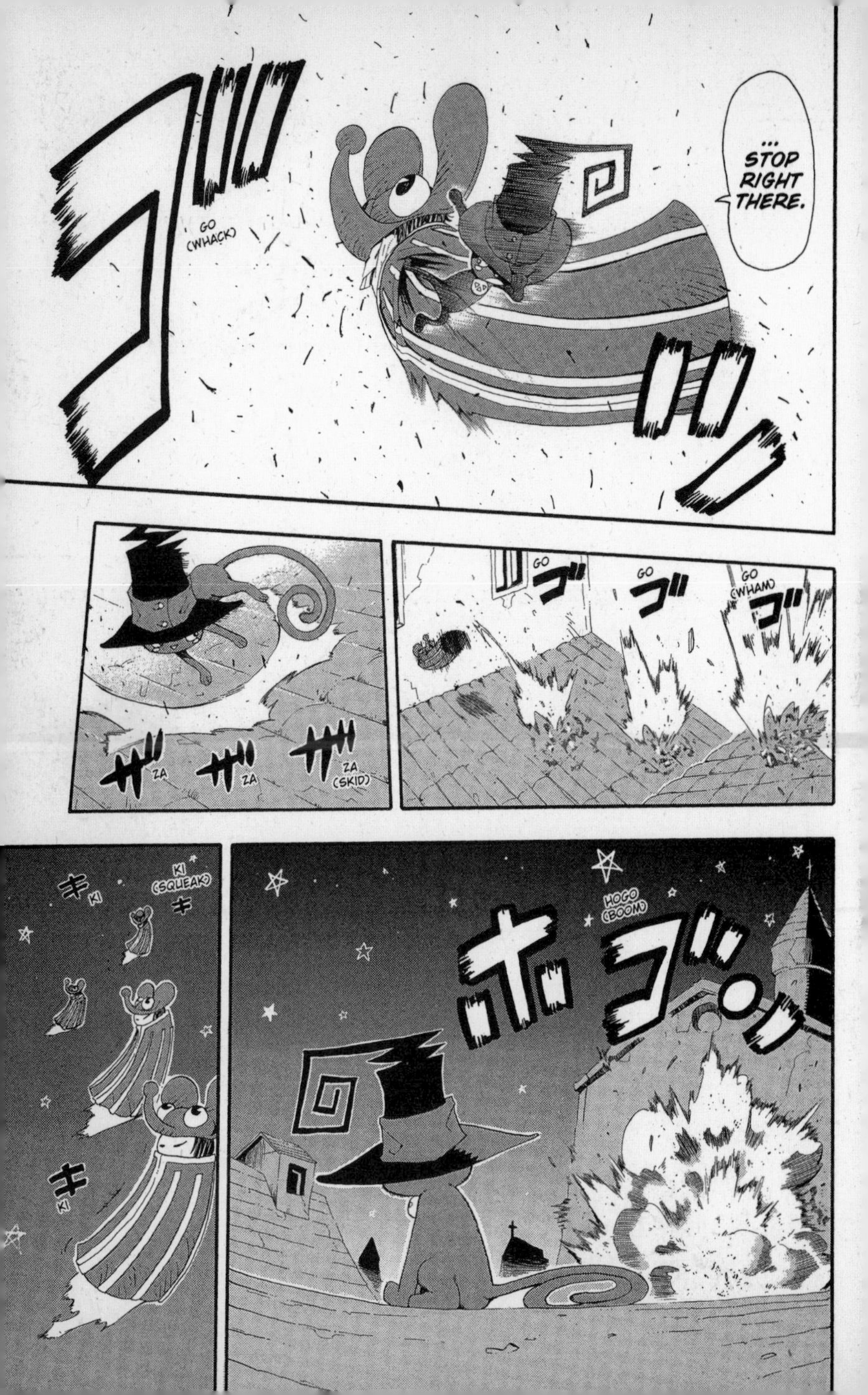
... STOP RIGHT THERE.
GO (WHACK)
GO
GO
GO (WHAM)
ZA
ZA
ZA (SKID)
HOGO (BOOM)
KI (SQUEAK)
KI
KI

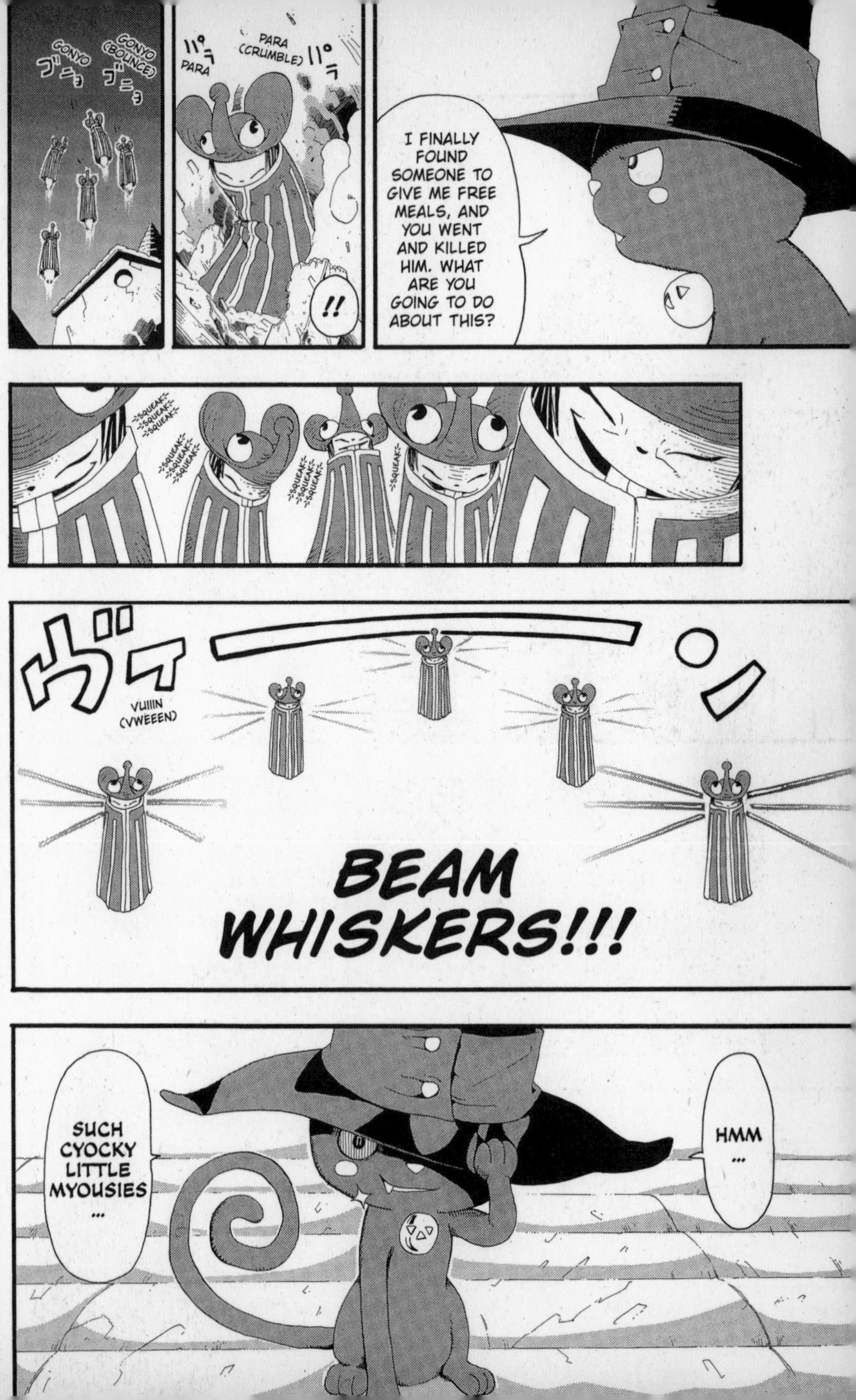
I FINALLY FOUND SOMEONE TO GIVE ME FREE MEALS, AND YOU WENT AND KILLED HIM. WHAT ARE YOU GOING TO DO ABOUT THIS?
PARA (CRUMBLE)
PARA
!!
GONYO (BOUNCE)
GONYO
SQUEAK SQUEAK SQUEAK
SQUEAK SQUEAK SQUEAK
SQUEAK SQUEAK SQUEAK
SQUEAK
VUIIIN (VWEEEN)
BEAM WHISKERS!!!
HMM ...
SUCH CYOCKY LITTLE MYOUSIES ...

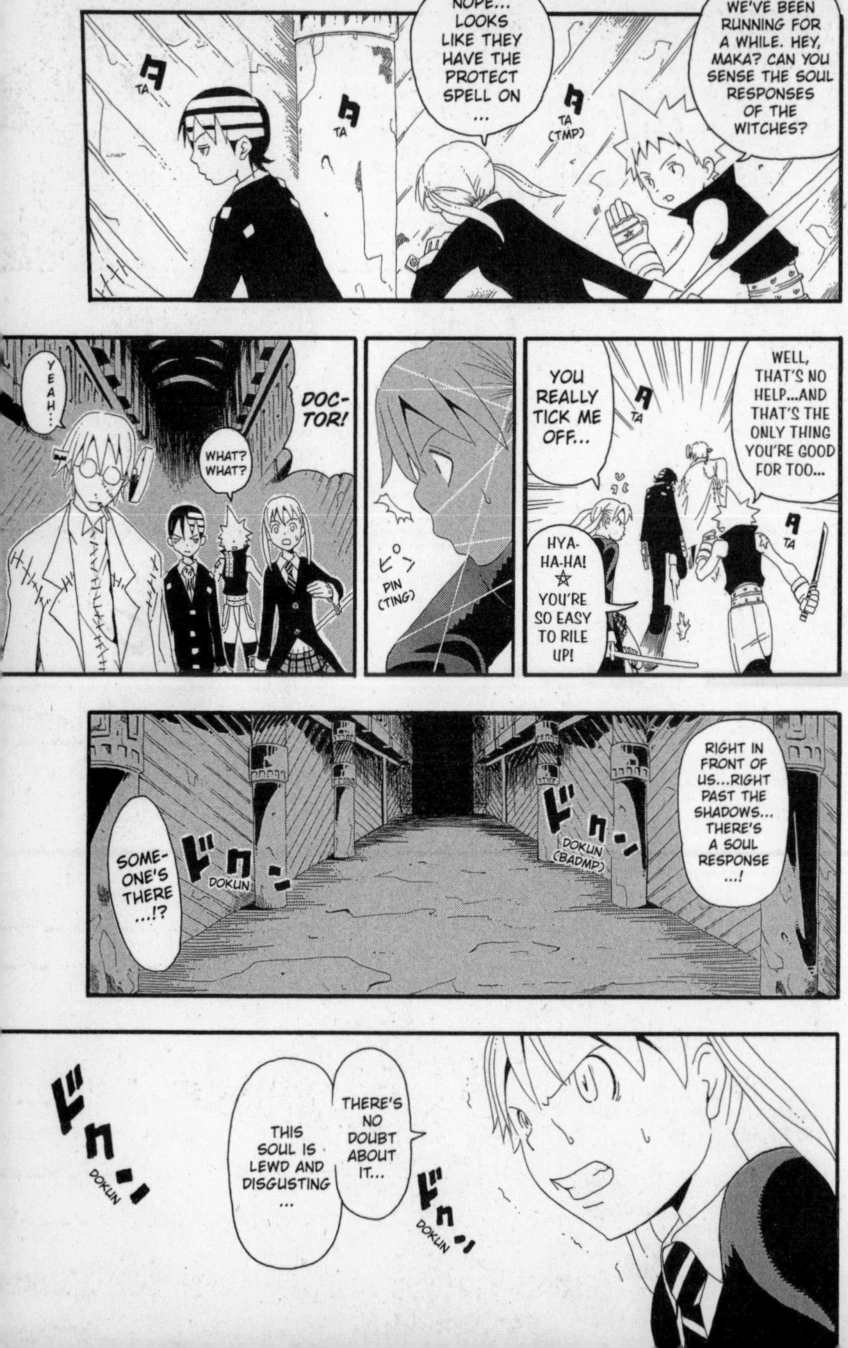

WE'VE BEEN RUNNING FOR A WHILE. HEY, MAKA? CAN YOU SENSE THE SOUL RESPONSES OF THE WITCHES?
TA (TMP)
NOPE... LOOKS LIKE THEY HAVE THE PROTECT SPELL ON ...
TA
TA
WELL, THAT'S NO HELP...AND THAT'S THE ONLY THING YOU'RE GOOD FOR TOO...
TA
TA
YOU REALLY TICK ME OFF...
HYA-HA-HA! ☆ YOU'RE SO EASY TO RILE UP!
PIN (TING)
DOC-TOR!
WHAT? WHAT?
YEAH...
RIGHT IN FRONT OF US...RIGHT PAST THE SHADOWS... THERE'S A SOUL RESPONSE ...!
DOKUN (BADMP)
DOKUN
SOME-ONE'S THERE ...!?
THERE'S NO DOUBT ABOUT IT...
DOKUN
THIS SOUL IS LEWD AND DISGUSTING ...
DOKUN

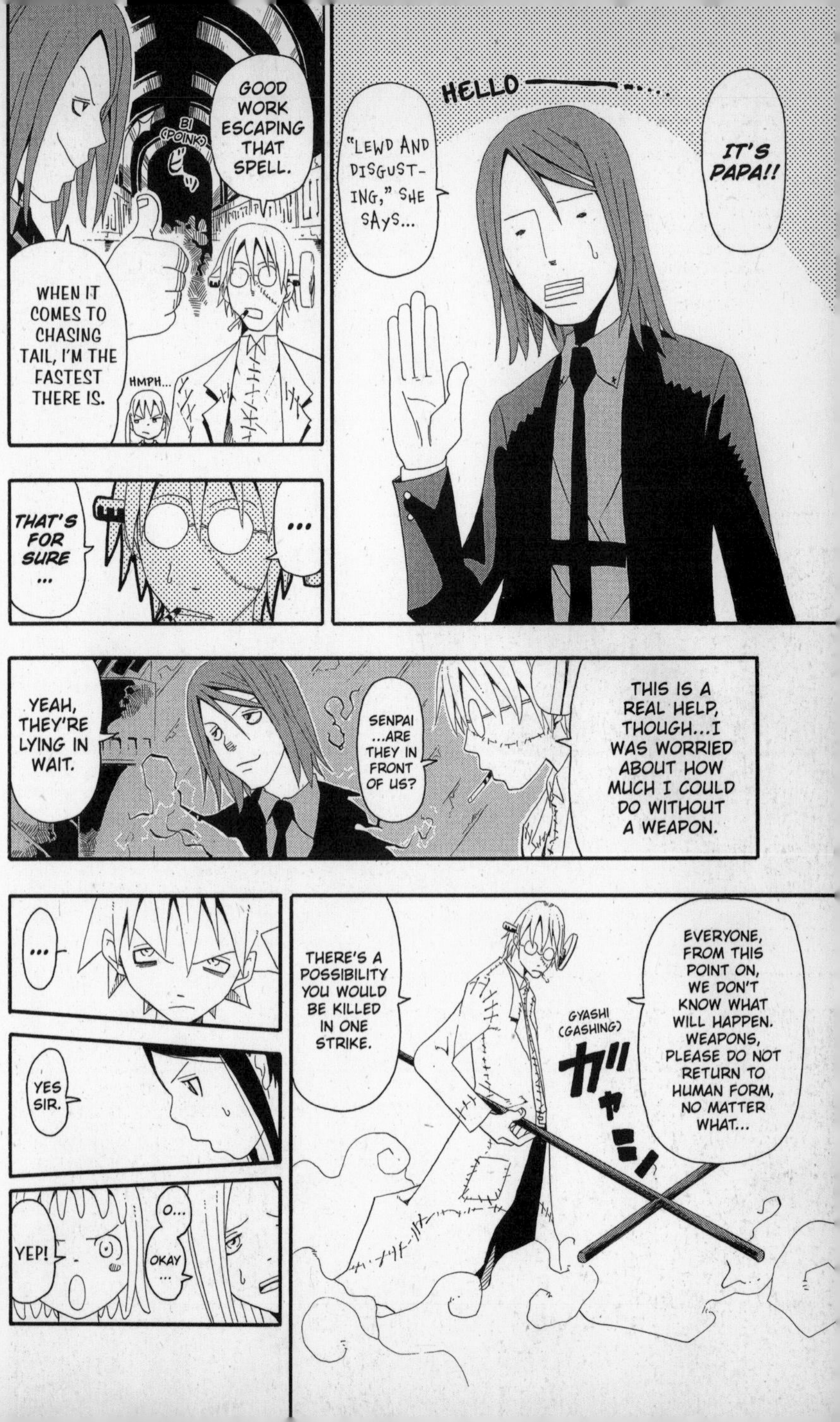
HELLO——....
IT'S PAPA!!
"LEWD AND DISGUST-ING," SHE SAYS...
GOOD WORK ESCAPING THAT SPELL.
BI (POINK)
WHEN IT COMES TO CHASING TAIL, I'M THE FASTEST THERE IS.
HMPH...
...
THAT'S FOR SURE ...
THIS IS A REAL HELP, THOUGH...I WAS WORRIED ABOUT HOW MUCH I COULD DO WITHOUT A WEAPON.
SENPAI ...ARE THEY IN FRONT OF US?
YEAH, THEY'RE LYING IN WAIT.
EVERYONE, FROM THIS POINT ON, WE DON'T KNOW WHAT WILL HAPPEN. WEAPONS, PLEASE DO NOT RETURN TO HUMAN FORM, NO MATTER WHAT...
GYASHI (GASHING)
THERE'S A POSSIBILITY YOU WOULD BE KILLED IN ONE STRIKE.
...
YES SIR.
O... OKAY ...
YEP!

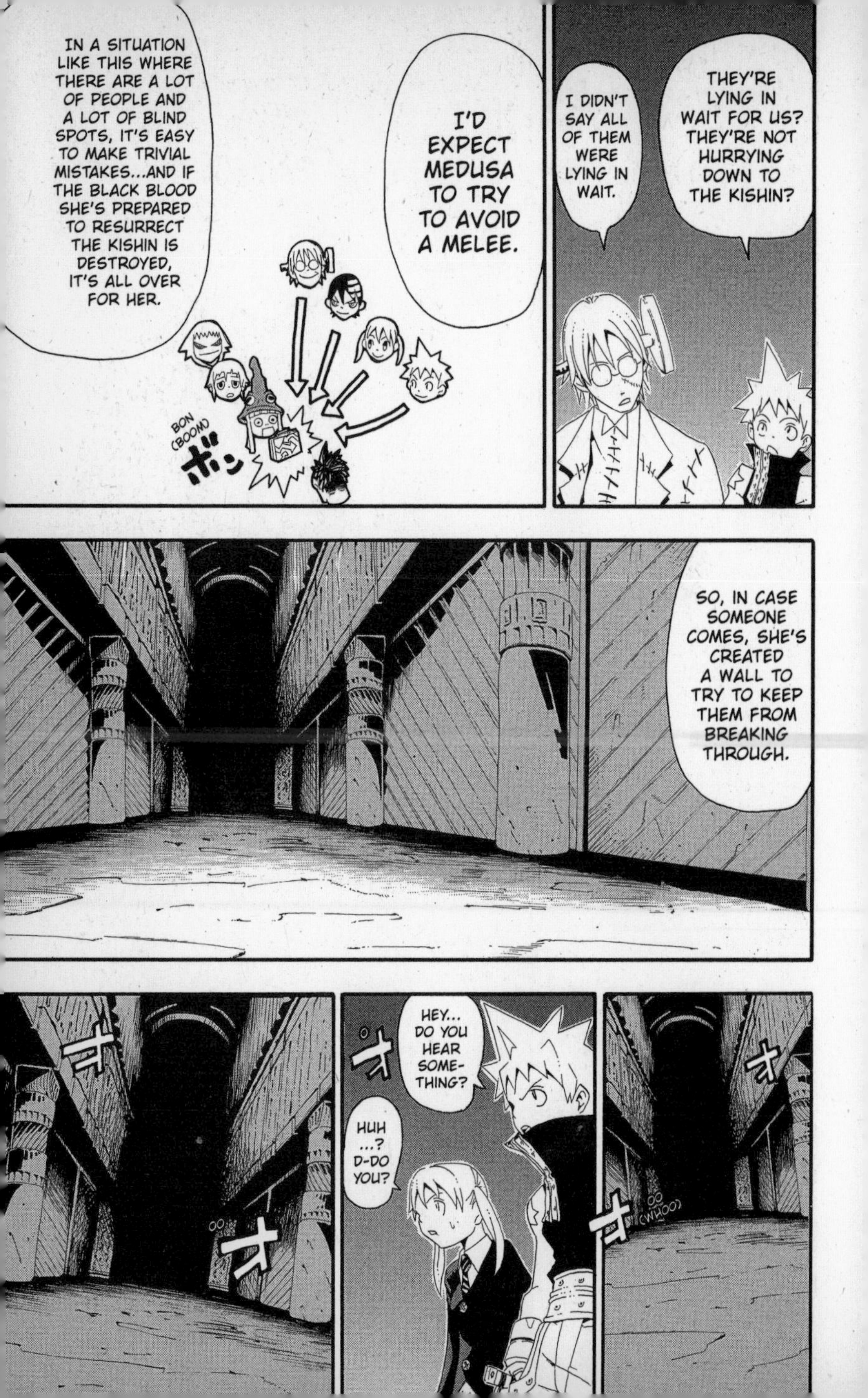
THEY'RE LYING IN WAIT FOR US? THEY'RE NOT HURRYING DOWN TO THE KISHIN?
I DIDN'T SAY ALL OF THEM WERE LYING IN WAIT.
I'D EXPECT MEDUSA TO TRY TO AVOID A MELEE.
IN A SITUATION LIKE THIS WHERE THERE ARE A LOT OF PEOPLE AND A LOT OF BLIND SPOTS, IT'S EASY TO MAKE TRIVIAL MISTAKES...AND IF THE BLACK BLOOD SHE'S PREPARED TO RESURRECT THE KISHIN IS DESTROYED, IT'S ALL OVER FOR HER.
BON (BOOM)
ボン
SO, IN CASE SOMEONE COMES, SHE'S CREATED A WALL TO TRY TO KEEP THEM FROM BREAKING THROUGH.
オ
OO (WHOO)
オ
オ
HEY... DO YOU HEAR SOMETHING?
HUH ...? D-DO YOU?
オ
オ
OO

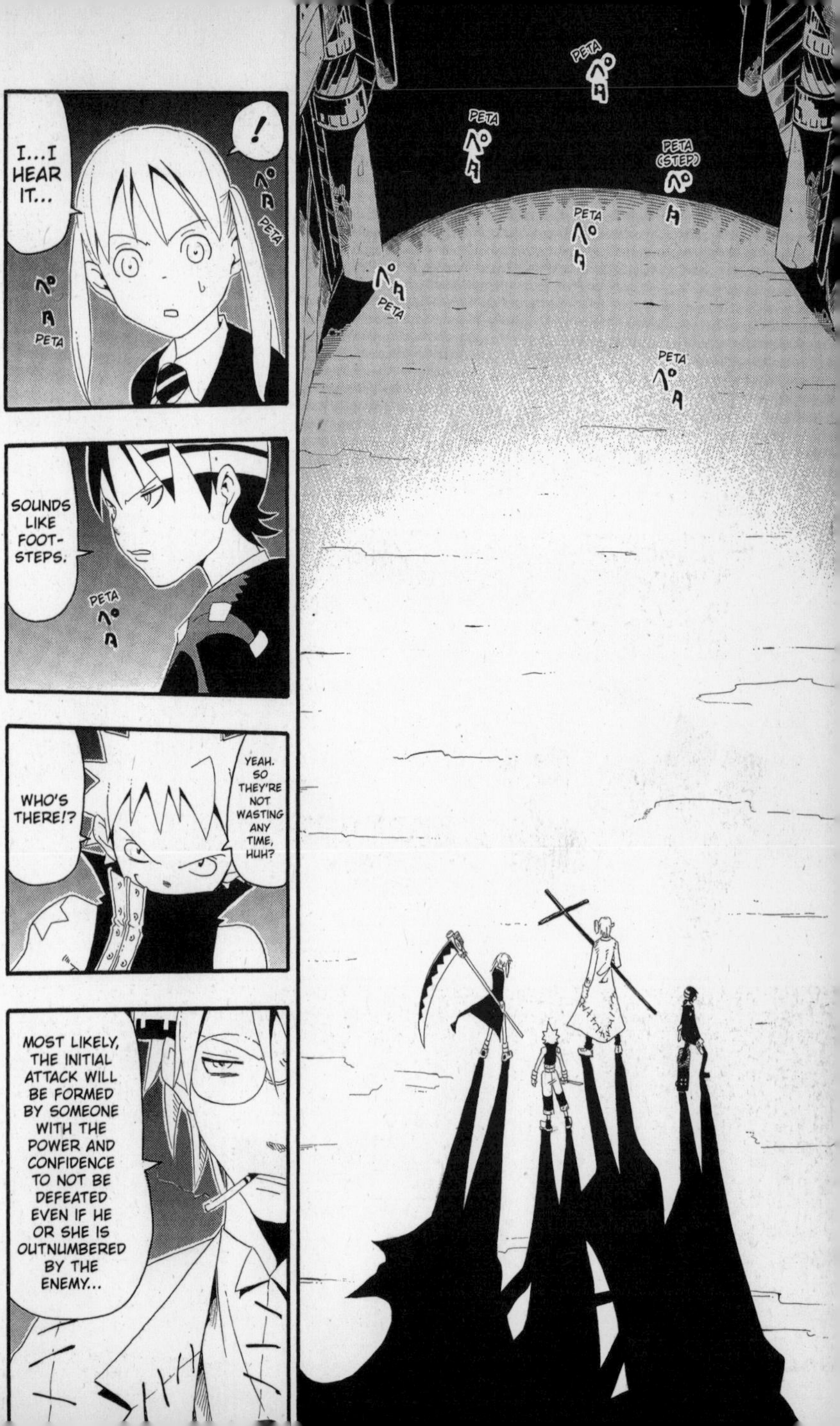

PETA ペタ
PETA (STEP) ペタ
PETA ペタ
PETA ペタ
ペタ PETA
PETA ペタ
!
ペタ PETA
I...I HEAR IT...
ペタ PETA
SOUNDS LIKE FOOT-STEPS.
PETA ペタ
YEAH. SO THEY'RE NOT WASTING ANY TIME, HUH?
WHO'S THERE!?
MOST LIKELY, THE INITIAL ATTACK WILL BE FORMED BY SOMEONE WITH THE POWER AND CONFIDENCE TO NOT BE DEFEATED EVEN IF HE OR SHE IS OUTNUMBERED BY THE ENEMY...

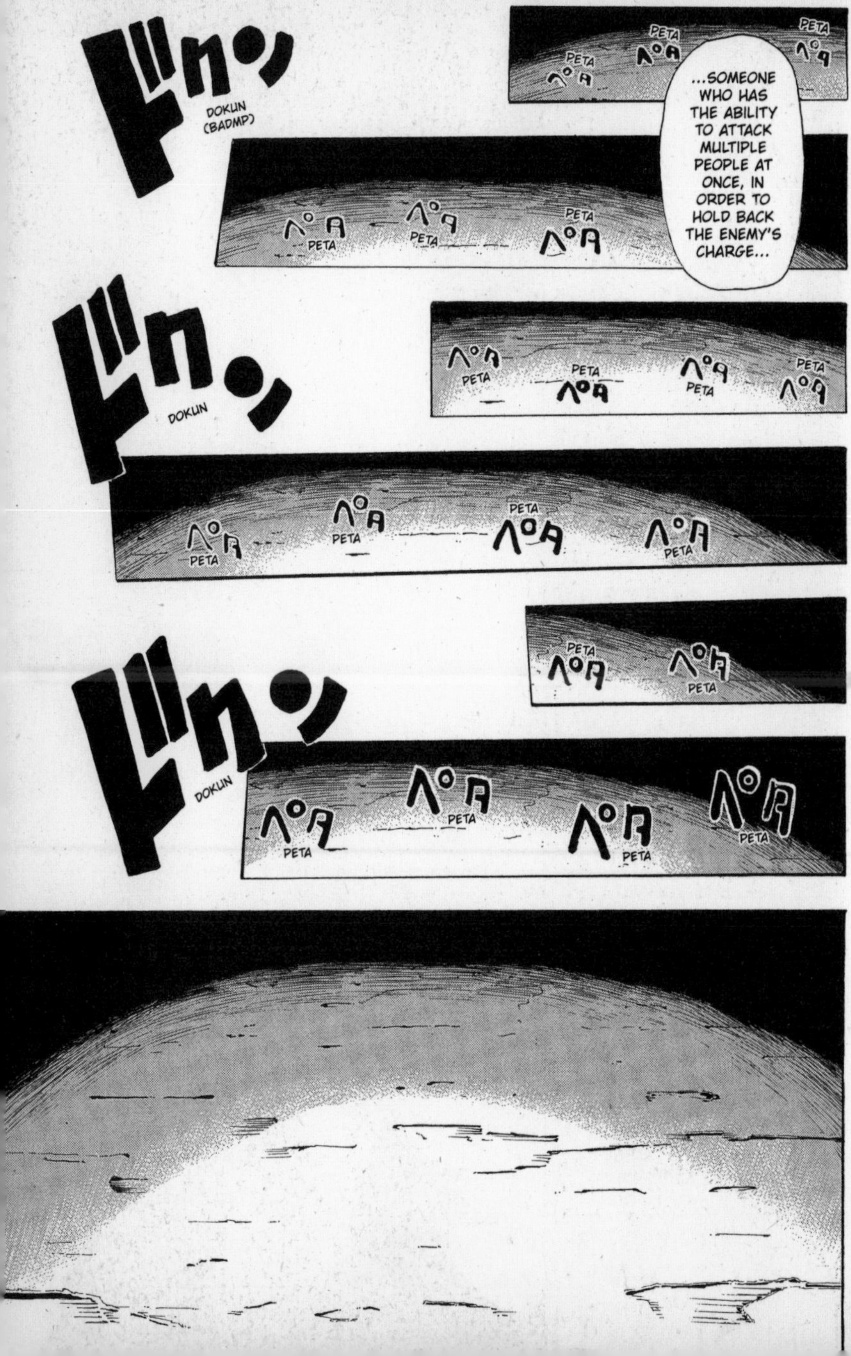
PETA
PETA
PETA
...SOMEONE WHO HAS THE ABILITY TO ATTACK MULTIPLE PEOPLE AT ONCE, IN ORDER TO HOLD BACK THE ENEMY'S CHARGE...
DOKUN (BADMP)
PETA
PETA
PETA
PETA
PETA
PETA
PETA
DOKUN
PETA
PETA
PETA
PETA
PETA
PETA
DOKUN
PETA
PETA
PETA
PETA

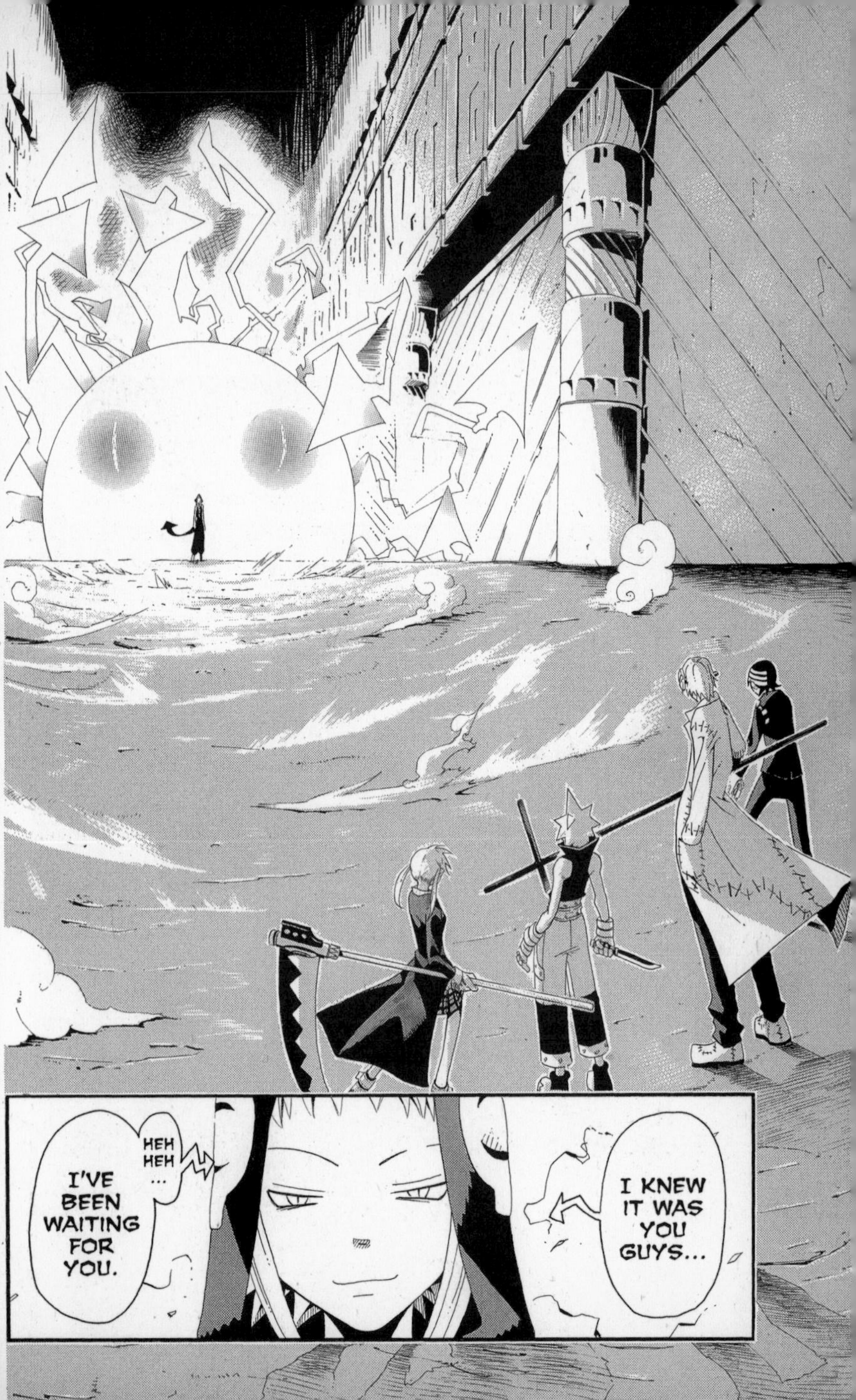
I KNEW IT WAS YOU GUYS...
HEH HEH ...
I'VE BEEN WAITING FOR YOU.

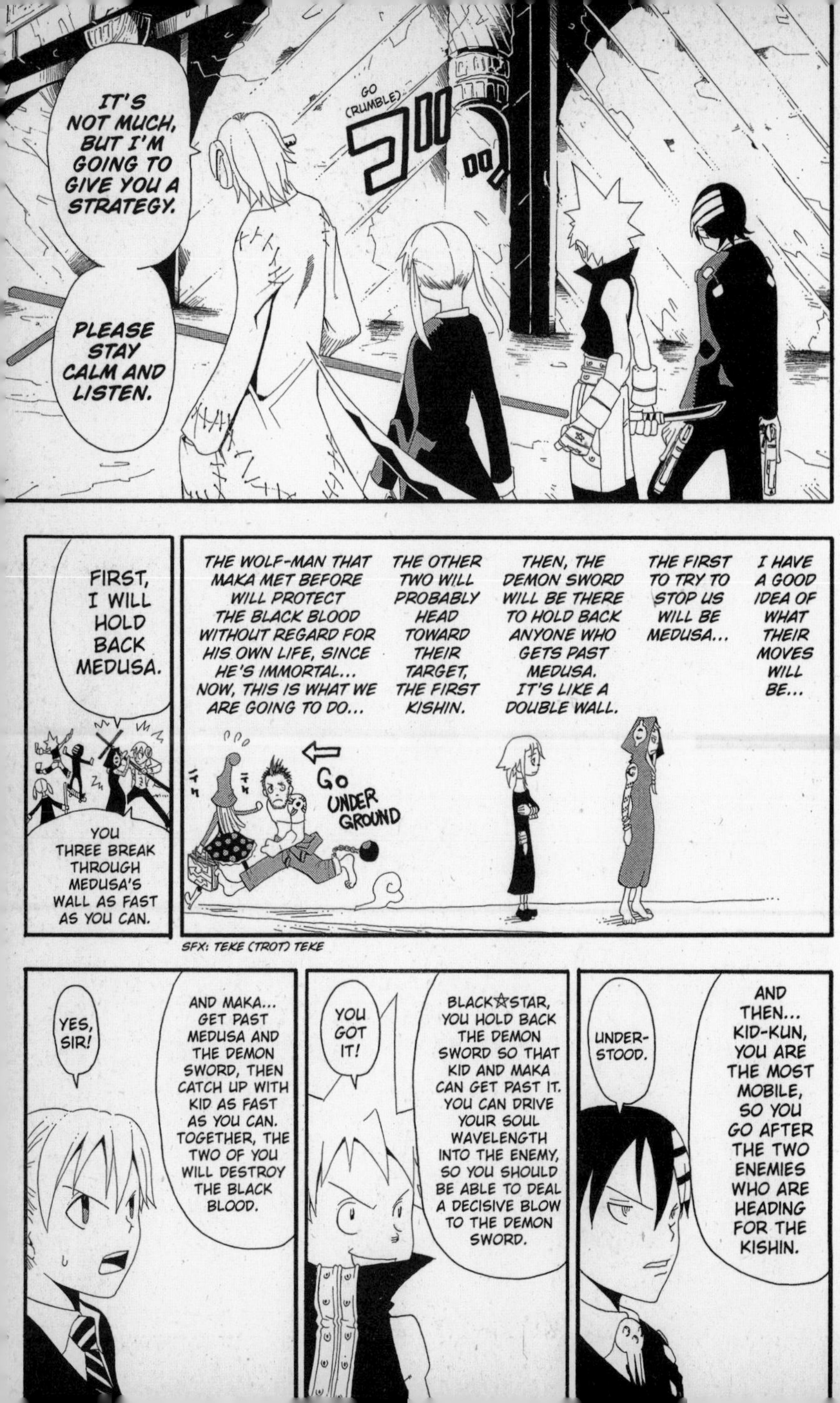
IT'S NOT MUCH, BUT I'M GOING TO GIVE YOU A STRATEGY.
GO (RUMBLE)
PLEASE STAY CALM AND LISTEN.
I HAVE A GOOD IDEA OF WHAT THEIR MOVES WILL BE...
THE FIRST TO TRY TO STOP US WILL BE MEDUSA...
THEN, THE DEMON SWORD WILL BE THERE TO HOLD BACK ANYONE WHO GETS PAST MEDUSA. IT'S LIKE A DOUBLE WALL.
THE OTHER TWO WILL PROBABLY HEAD TOWARD THEIR TARGET, THE FIRST KISHIN.
THE WOLF-MAN THAT MAKA MET BEFORE WILL PROTECT THE BLACK BLOOD WITHOUT REGARD FOR HIS OWN LIFE, SINCE HE'S IMMORTAL... NOW, THIS IS WHAT WE ARE GOING TO DO...
GO UNDER GROUND
SFX: TEKE (TROT) TEKE
FIRST, I WILL HOLD BACK MEDUSA.
YOU THREE BREAK THROUGH MEDUSA'S WALL AS FAST AS YOU CAN.
AND THEN... KID-KUN, YOU ARE THE MOST MOBILE, SO YOU GO AFTER THE TWO ENEMIES WHO ARE HEADING FOR THE KISHIN.
UNDER-STOOD.
BLACK☆STAR, YOU HOLD BACK THE DEMON SWORD SO THAT KID AND MAKA CAN GET PAST IT. YOU CAN DRIVE YOUR SOUL WAVELENGTH INTO THE ENEMY, SO YOU SHOULD BE ABLE TO DEAL A DECISIVE BLOW TO THE DEMON SWORD.
YOU GOT IT!
AND MAKA... GET PAST MEDUSA AND THE DEMON SWORD, THEN CATCH UP WITH KID AS FAST AS YOU CAN. TOGETHER, THE TWO OF YOU WILL DESTROY THE BLACK BLOOD.
YES, SIR!

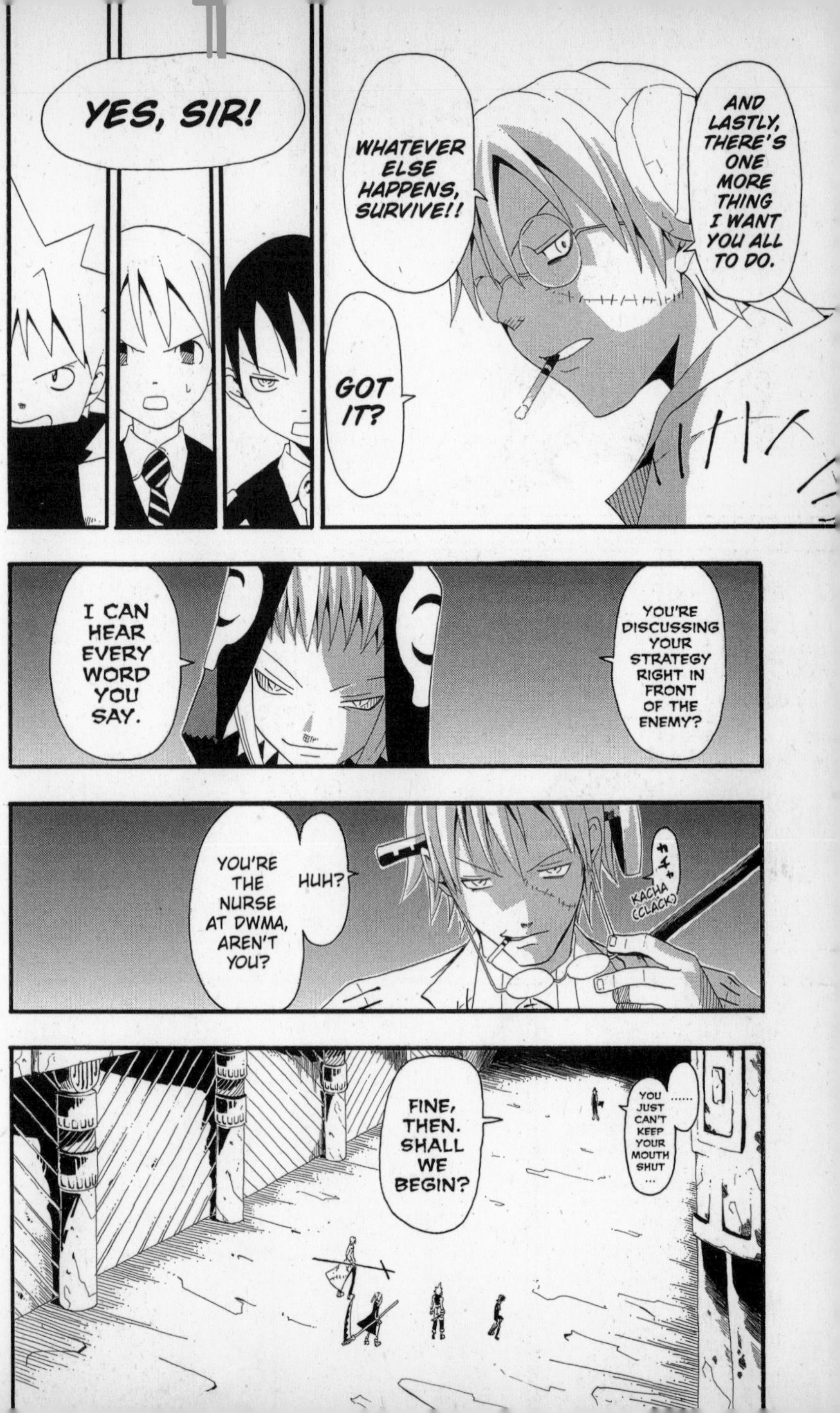
AND LASTLY, THERE'S ONE MORE THING I WANT YOU ALL TO DO.
WHATEVER ELSE HAPPENS, SURVIVE!!
GOT IT?
YES, SIR!
YOU'RE DISCUSSING YOUR STRATEGY RIGHT IN FRONT OF THE ENEMY?
I CAN HEAR EVERY WORD YOU SAY.
カチャ
KACHA (CLACK)
HUH?
YOU'RE THE NURSE AT DWMA, AREN'T YOU?
......
YOU JUST CAN'T KEEP YOUR MOUTH SHUT ...
FINE, THEN. SHALL WE BEGIN?

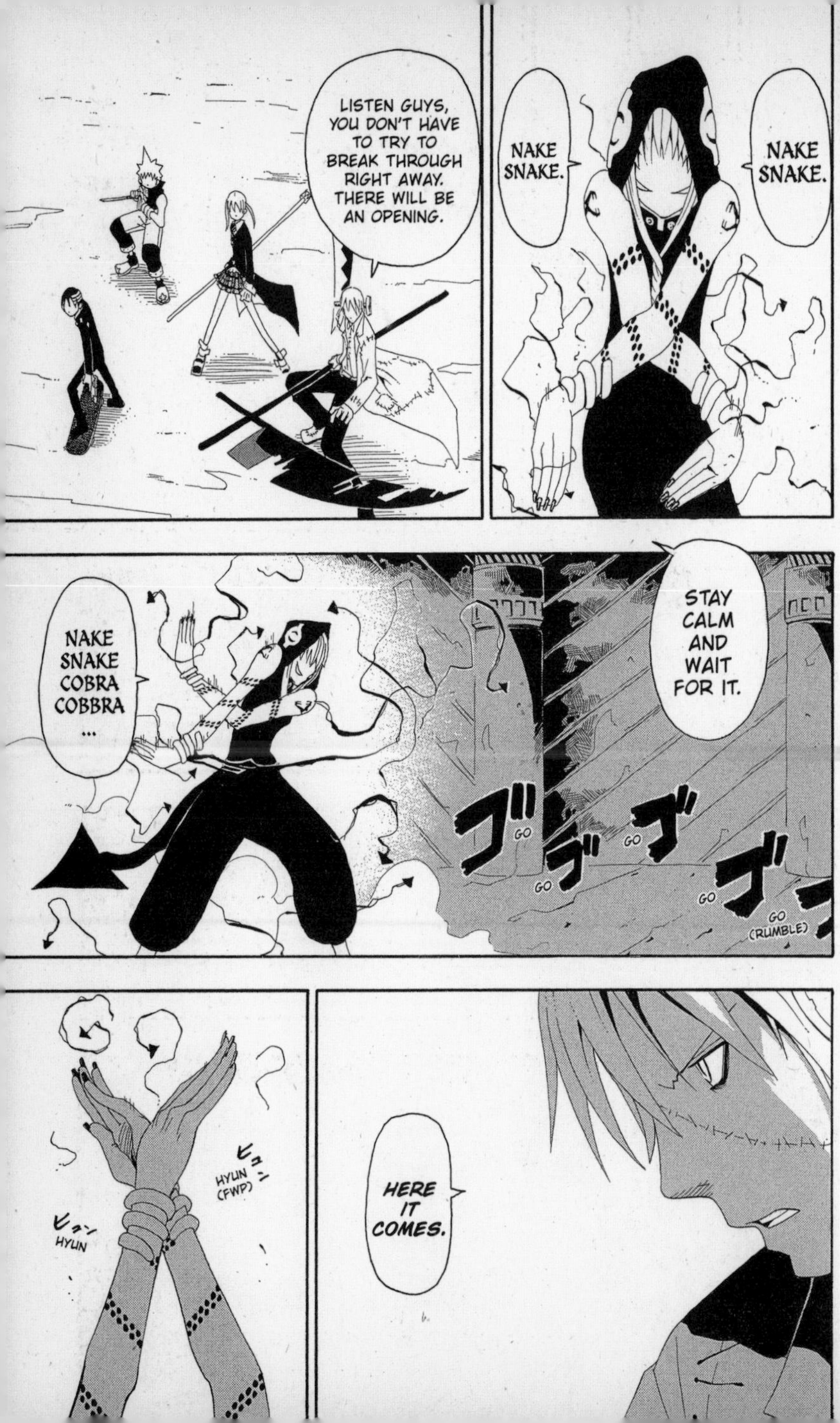
NAKE SNAKE.
NAKE SNAKE.
LISTEN GUYS, YOU DON'T HAVE TO TRY TO BREAK THROUGH RIGHT AWAY. THERE WILL BE AN OPENING.
STAY CALM AND WAIT FOR IT.
GO GO GO GO GO (RUMBLE)
NAKE SNAKE COBRA COBBRA ...
HERE IT COMES.
HYUN (FWP)
HYUN

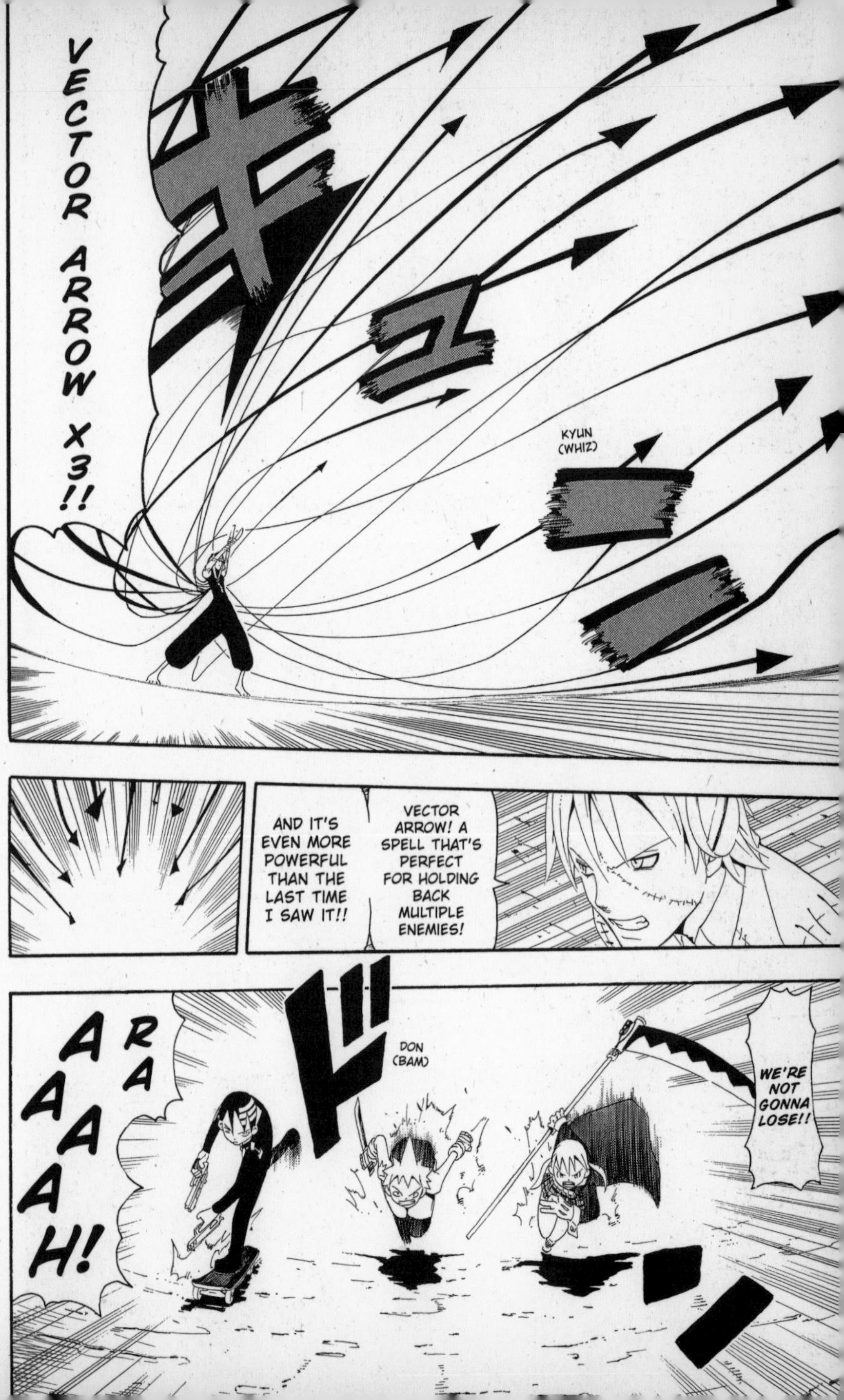
VECTOR ARROW X3!!
KYUN (WHIZ)
VECTOR ARROW! A SPELL THAT'S PERFECT FOR HOLDING BACK MULTIPLE ENEMIES!
AND IT'S EVEN MORE POWERFUL THAN THE LAST TIME I SAW IT!!
WE'RE NOT GONNA LOSE!!
DON (BAM)
RAAAAAH!

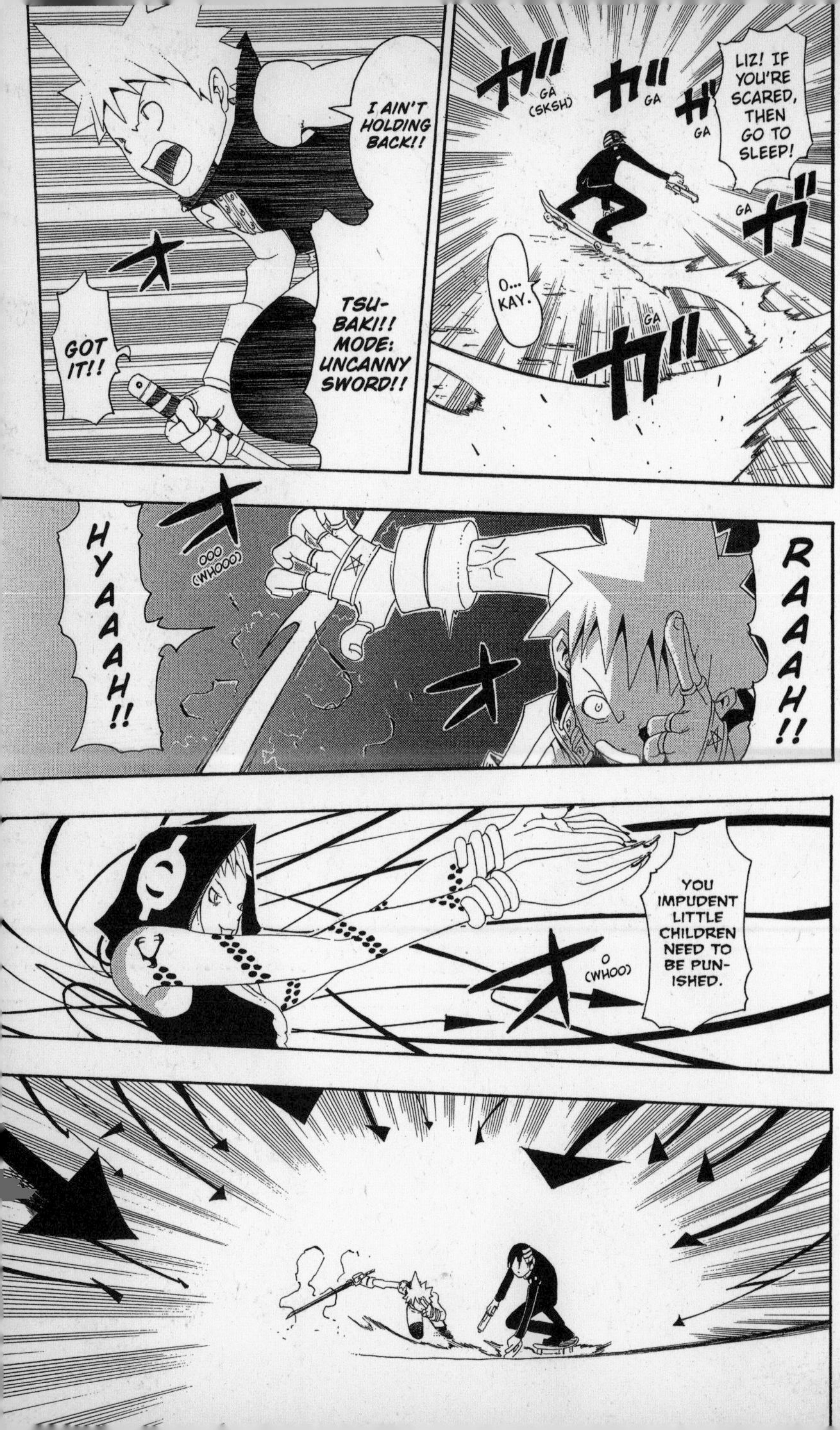
LIZ! IF YOU'RE SCARED, THEN GO TO SLEEP!
GA
GA
GA
GA (SKSH)
O... KAY.
GA
I AIN'T HOLDING BACK!!
TSU-BAKI!! MODE: UNCANNY SWORD!!
GOT IT!!
RAAAAH!!
OOO (WHOOOM)
HYAAAAH!!
YOU IMPUDENT LITTLE CHILDREN NEED TO BE PUN-ISHED.
O (WHOO)

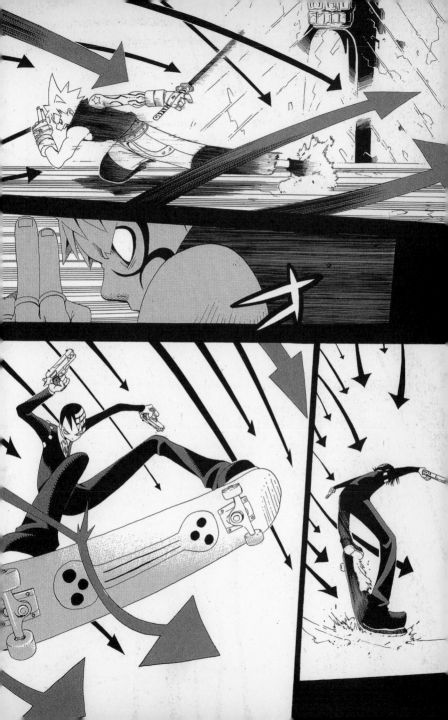

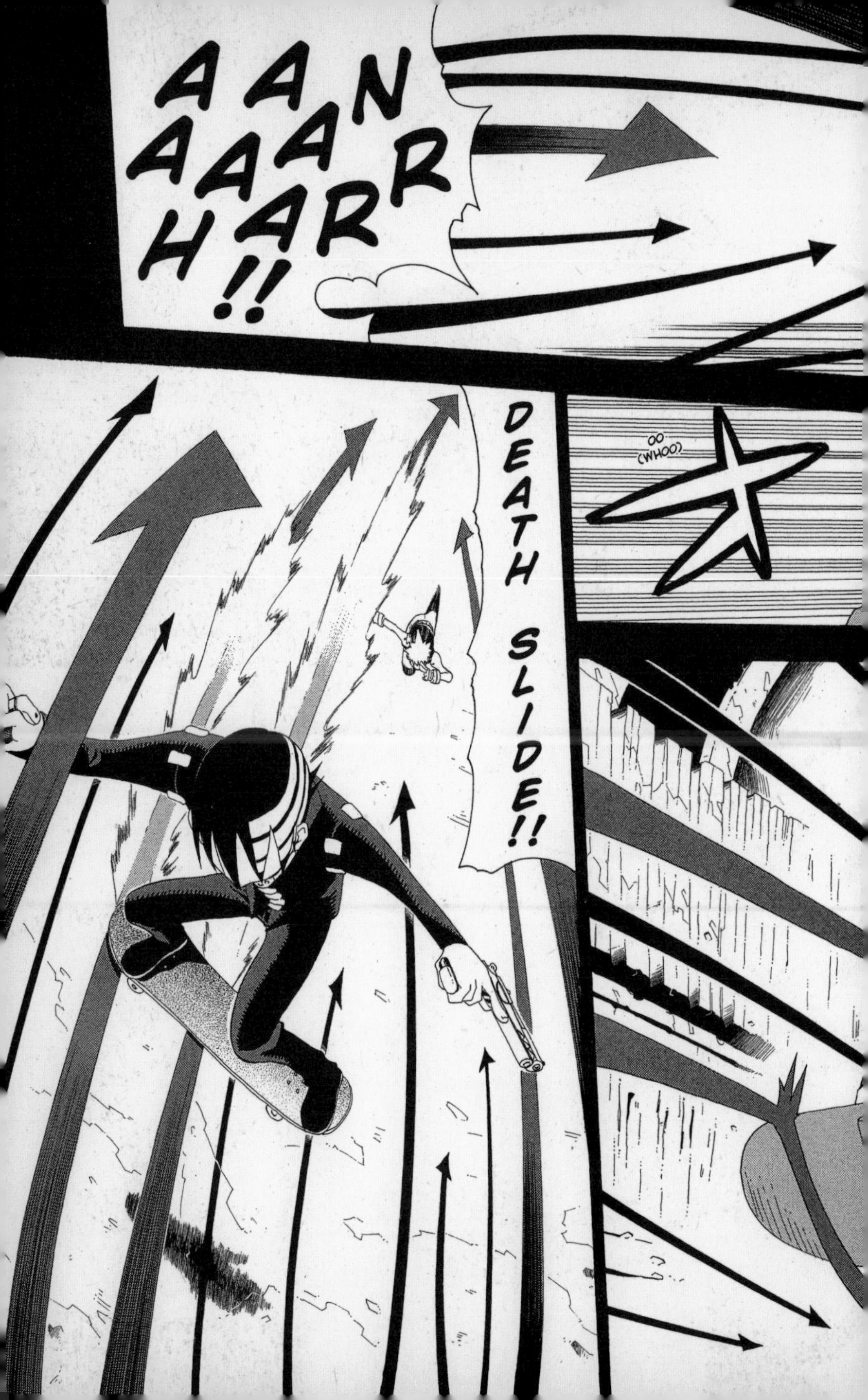
AAAAAAAAAHHARRN!!
DEATH SLIDE!!
OO-
(WHOO)

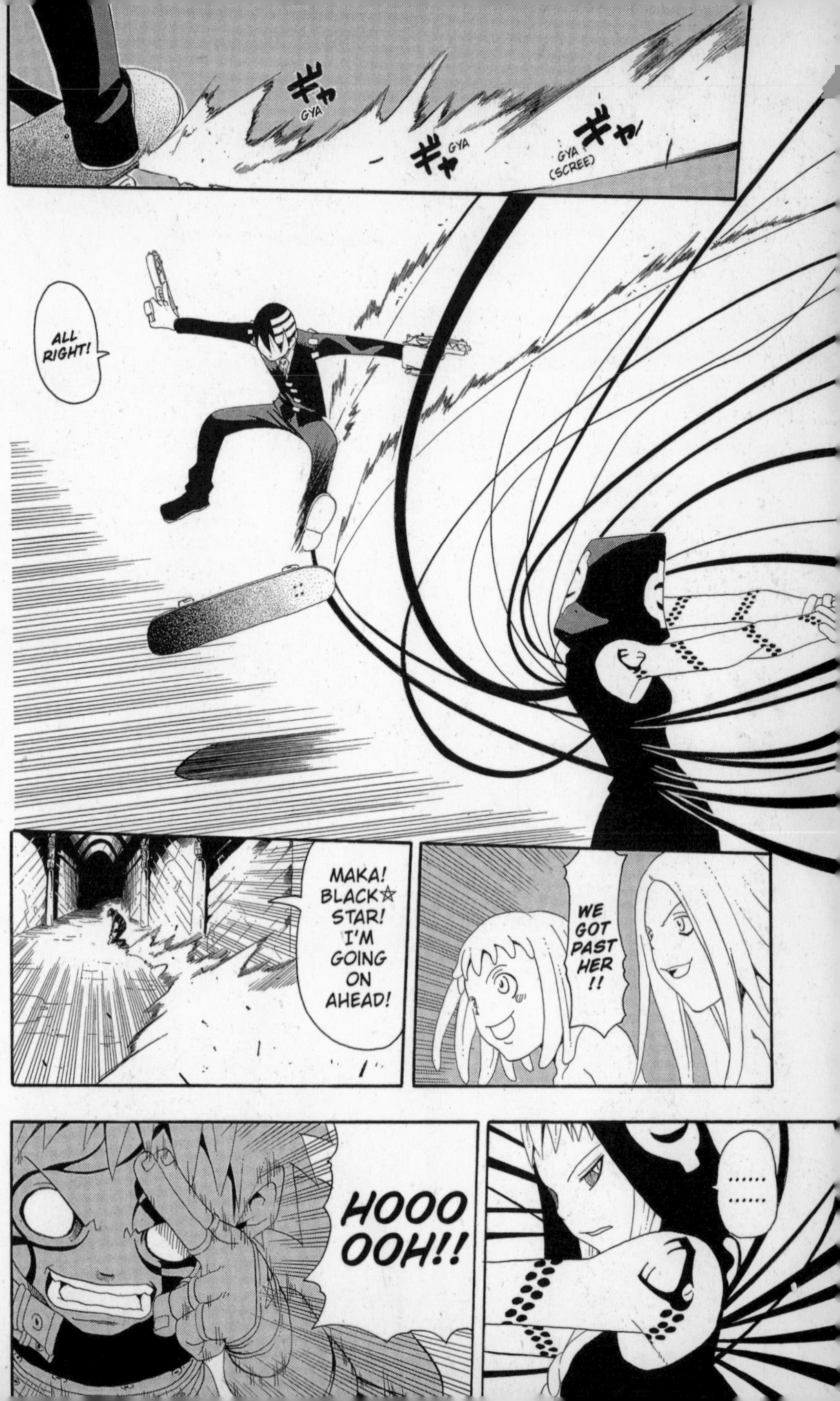
ギャ
GYA (SCREE)
ギャ
GYA
ギャ
GYA
ALL RIGHT!
WE GOT PAST HER!!
MAKA! BLACK☆STAR! I'M GOING ON AHEAD!
…… ……
HOOOOOH!!

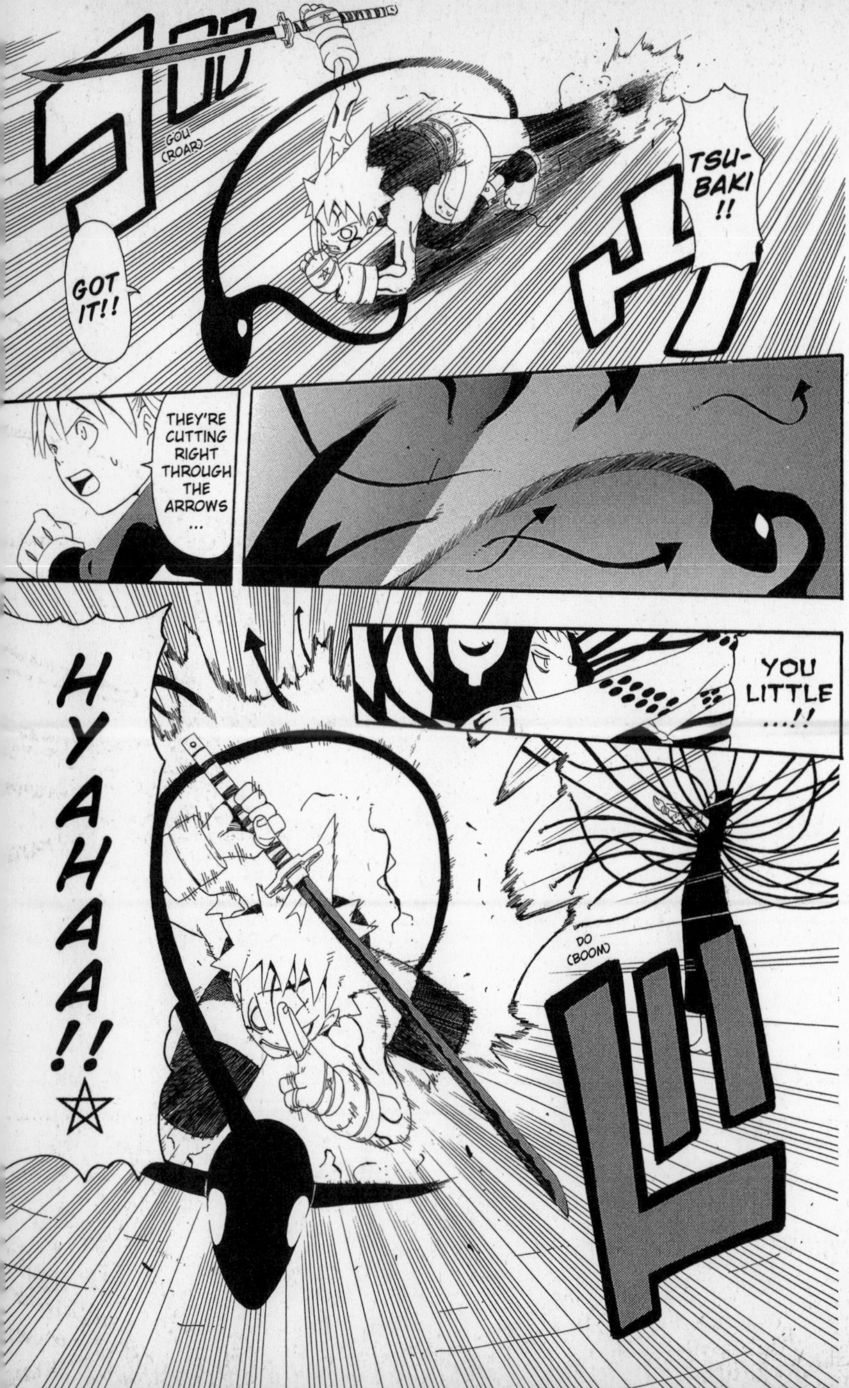
TSU-BAKI!!
GOU (ROAR)
GOT IT!!
THEY'RE CUTTING RIGHT THROUGH THE ARROWS ...
YOU LITTLE ...!!
DO (BOOM)
HYAHAAA!!☆

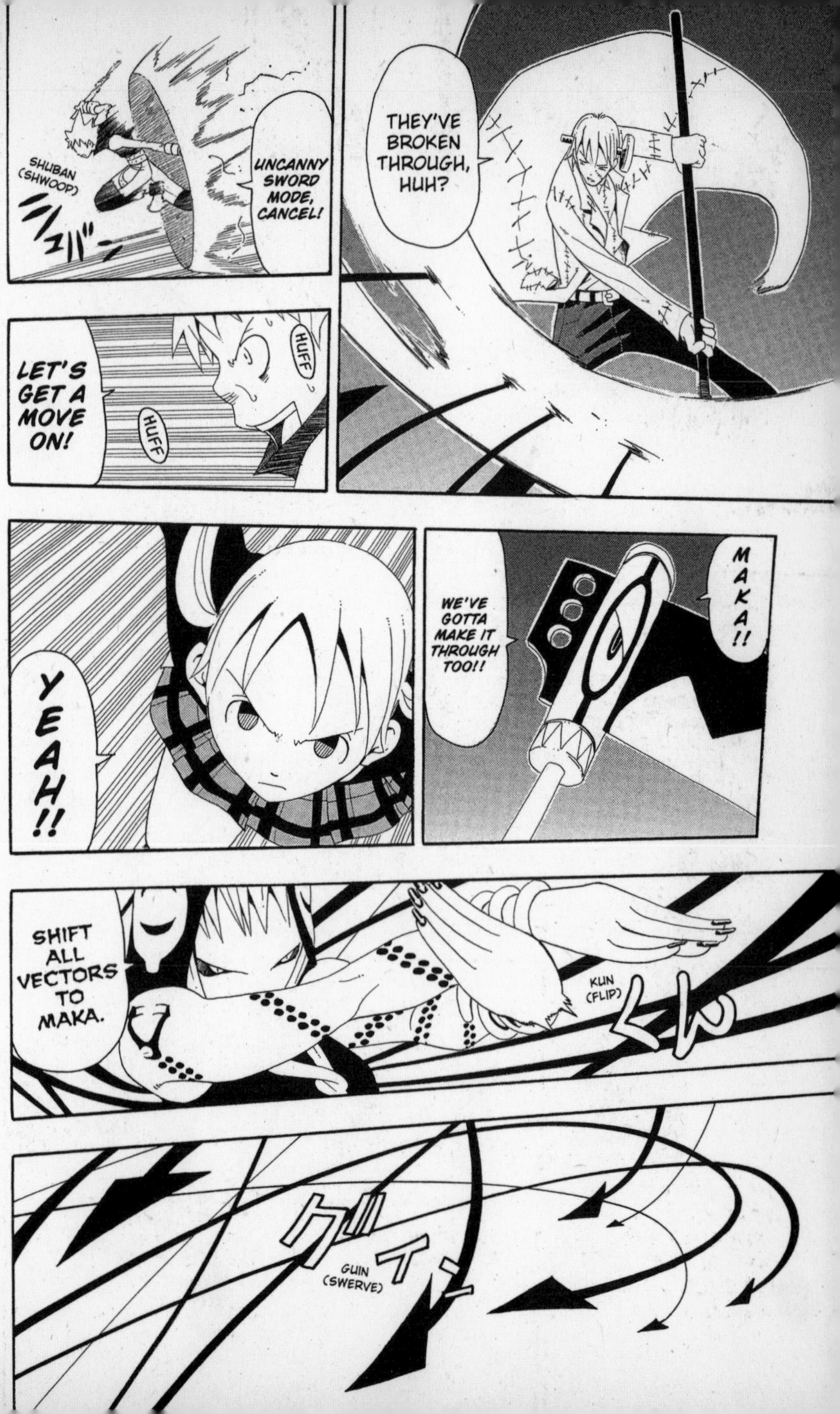
THEY'VE BROKEN THROUGH, HUH?
UNCANNY SWORD MODE, CANCEL!
SHUBAN (SHWOOP)
LET'S GET A MOVE ON!
HUFF
HUFF
MAKA!!
WE'VE GOTTA MAKE IT THROUGH TOO!!
YEAH!!
SHIFT ALL VECTORS TO MAKA.
KUN (FLIP)
GUIN (SWERVE)

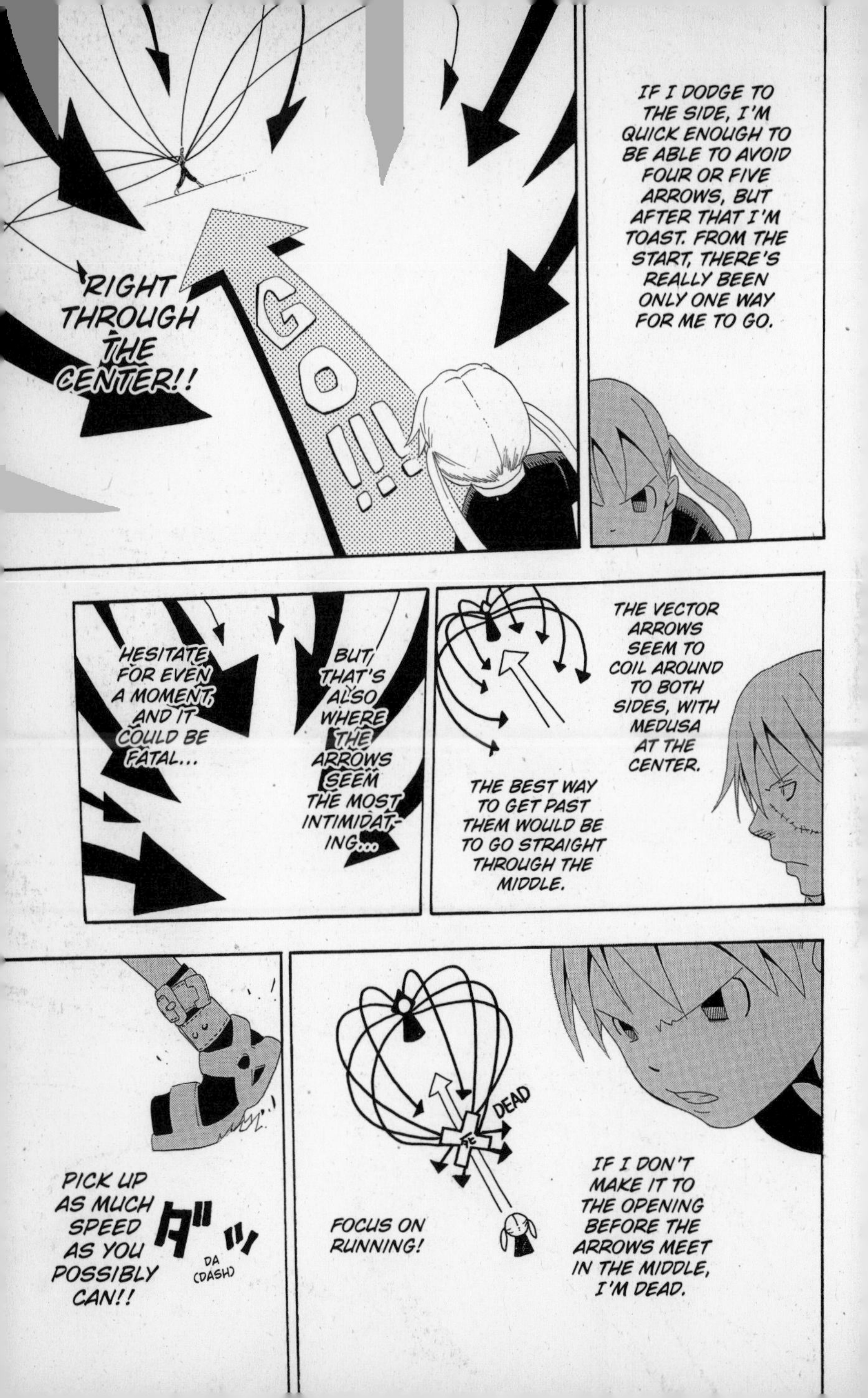
IF I DODGE TO THE SIDE, I'M QUICK ENOUGH TO BE ABLE TO AVOID FOUR OR FIVE ARROWS, BUT AFTER THAT I'M TOAST. FROM THE START, THERE'S REALLY BEEN ONLY ONE WAY FOR ME TO GO.
RIGHT THROUGH THE CENTER!!
GO!!
THE VECTOR ARROWS SEEM TO COIL AROUND TO BOTH SIDES, WITH MEDUSA AT THE CENTER.
THE BEST WAY TO GET PAST THEM WOULD BE TO GO STRAIGHT THROUGH THE MIDDLE.
BUT THAT'S ALSO WHERE THE ARROWS SEEM THE MOST INTIMIDATING...
HESITATE FOR EVEN A MOMENT, AND IT COULD BE FATAL...
IF I DON'T MAKE IT TO THE OPENING BEFORE THE ARROWS MEET IN THE MIDDLE, I'M DEAD.
DEAD
FOCUS ON RUNNING!
PICK UP AS MUCH SPEED AS YOU POSSIBLY CAN!!
ダッ
DA (DASH)

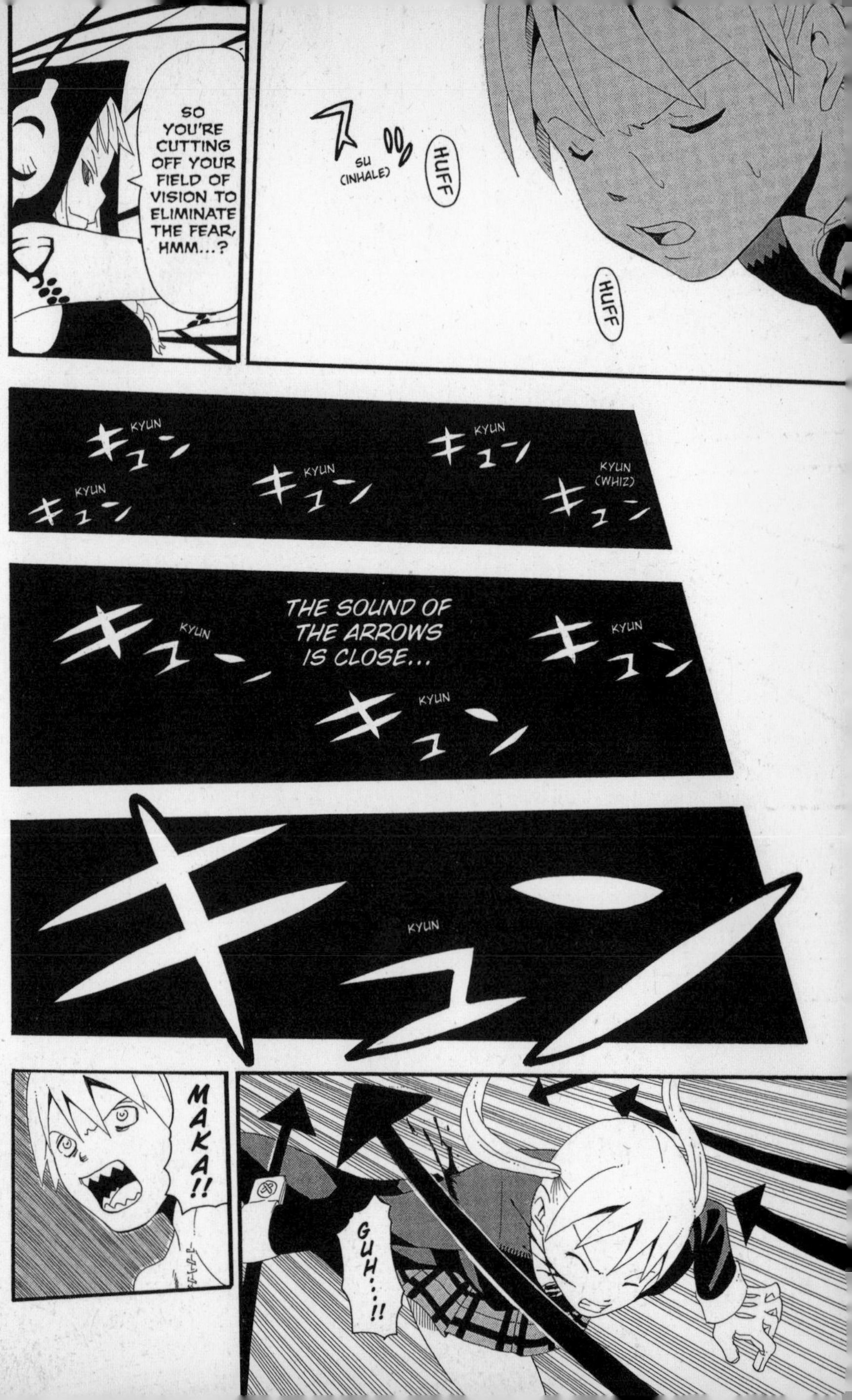
SU (INHALE)
HUFF
HUFF
SO YOU'RE CUTTING OFF YOUR FIELD OF VISION TO ELIMINATE THE FEAR, HMM...?
KYUN
KYUN (WHIZ)
KYUN
KYUN
KYUN
THE SOUND OF THE ARROWS IS CLOSE...
KYUN
KYUN
KYUN
KYUN
GUH...!!
MAKA!!

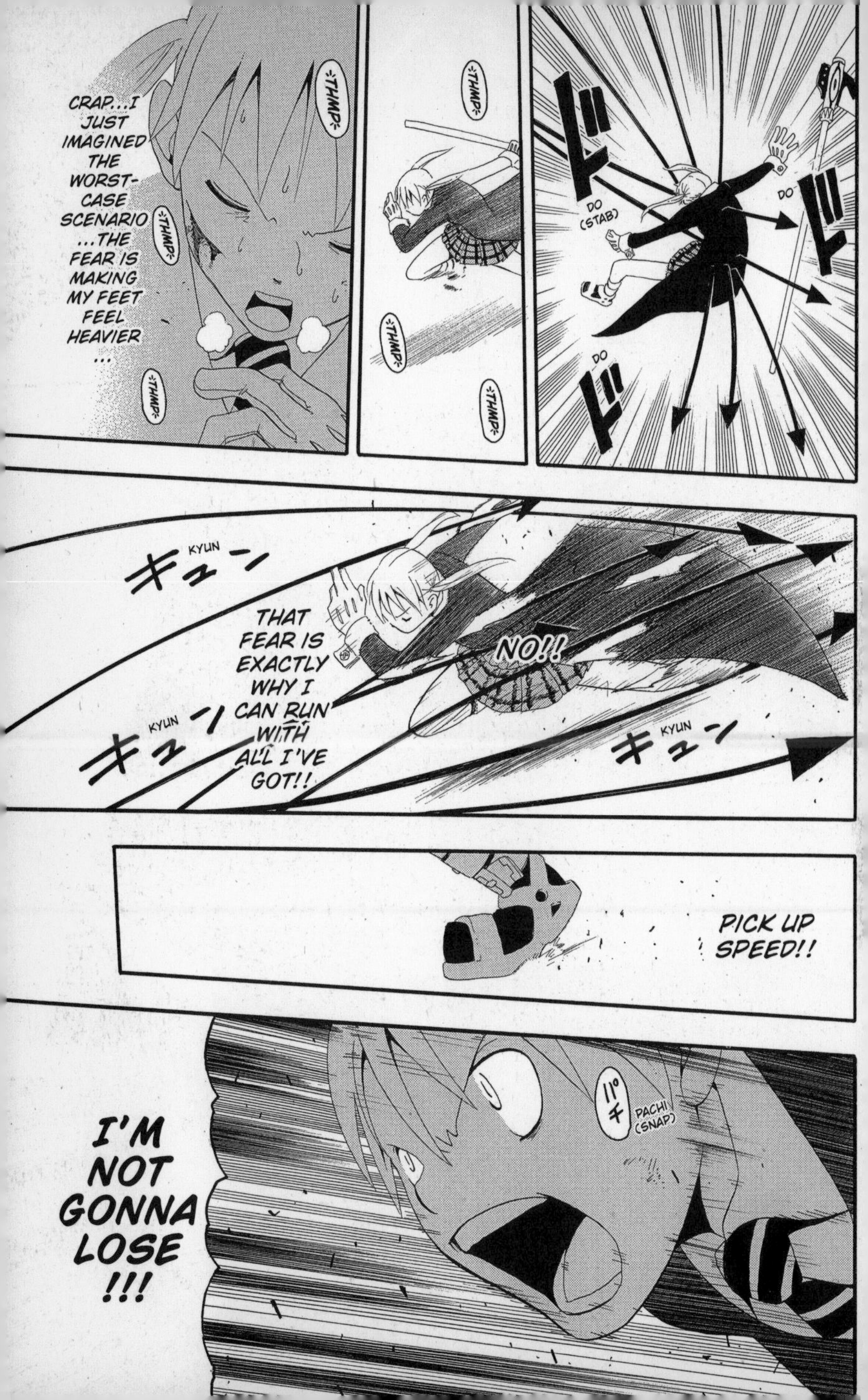
ド
DO (STAB)
ド
DO
ド
DO
THUMP
THUMP
THUMP
THUMP
CRAP...I JUST IMAGINED THE WORST-CASE SCENARIO ...THE FEAR IS MAKING MY FEET FEEL HEAVIER ...
THUMP
THUMP
キュン
KYUN
THAT FEAR IS EXACTLY WHY I CAN RUN WITH ALL I'VE GOT!!
NO!!
キュン
KYUN
キュン
KYUN
PICK UP SPEED!!
パチ
PACHI (SNAP)
I'M NOT GONNA LOSE!!!

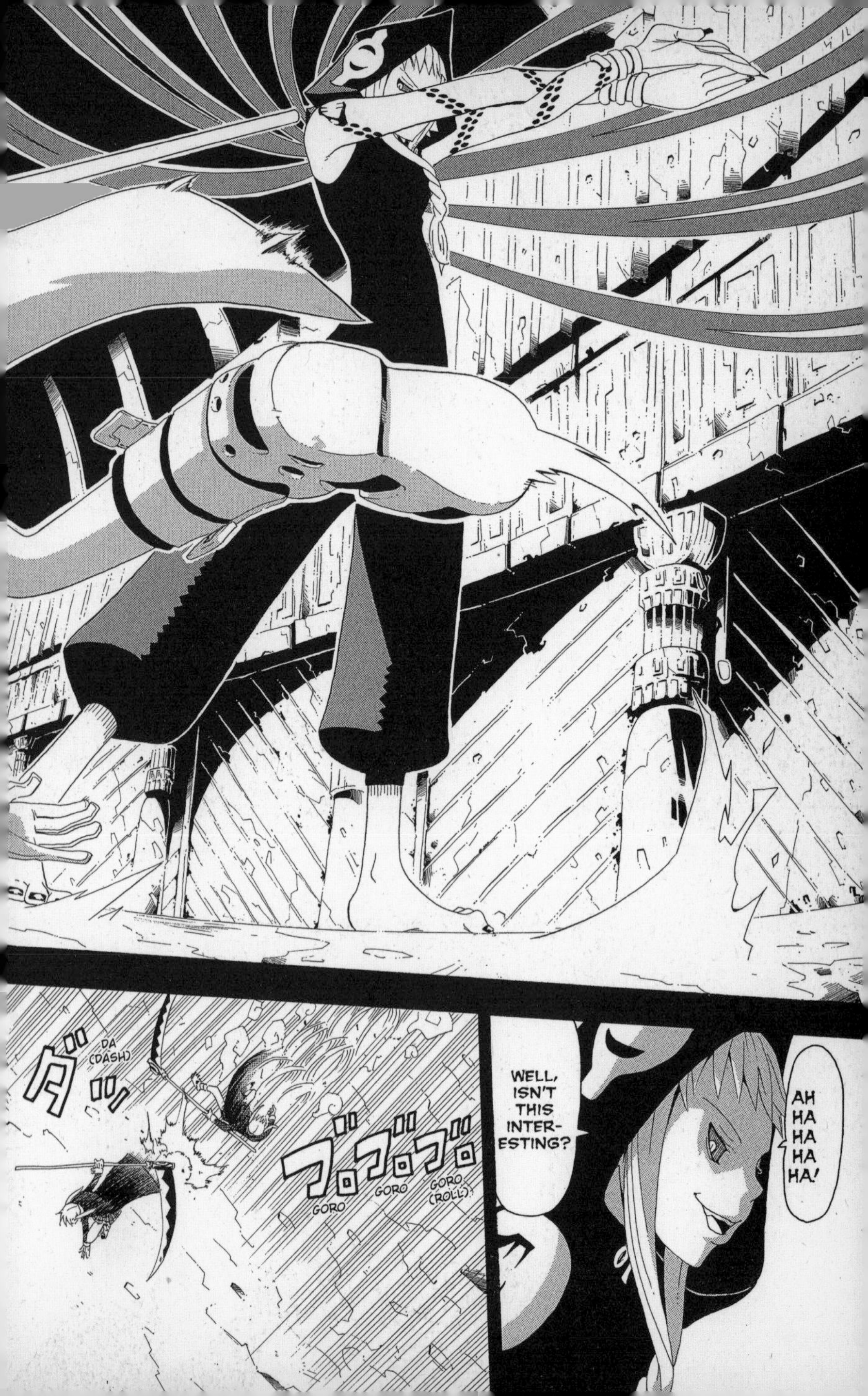
AH HA HA HA HA!
WELL, ISN'T THIS INTER-ESTING?
ダッ
DA (DASH)
ゴロゴロゴロ
GORO GORO GORO (ROLL)

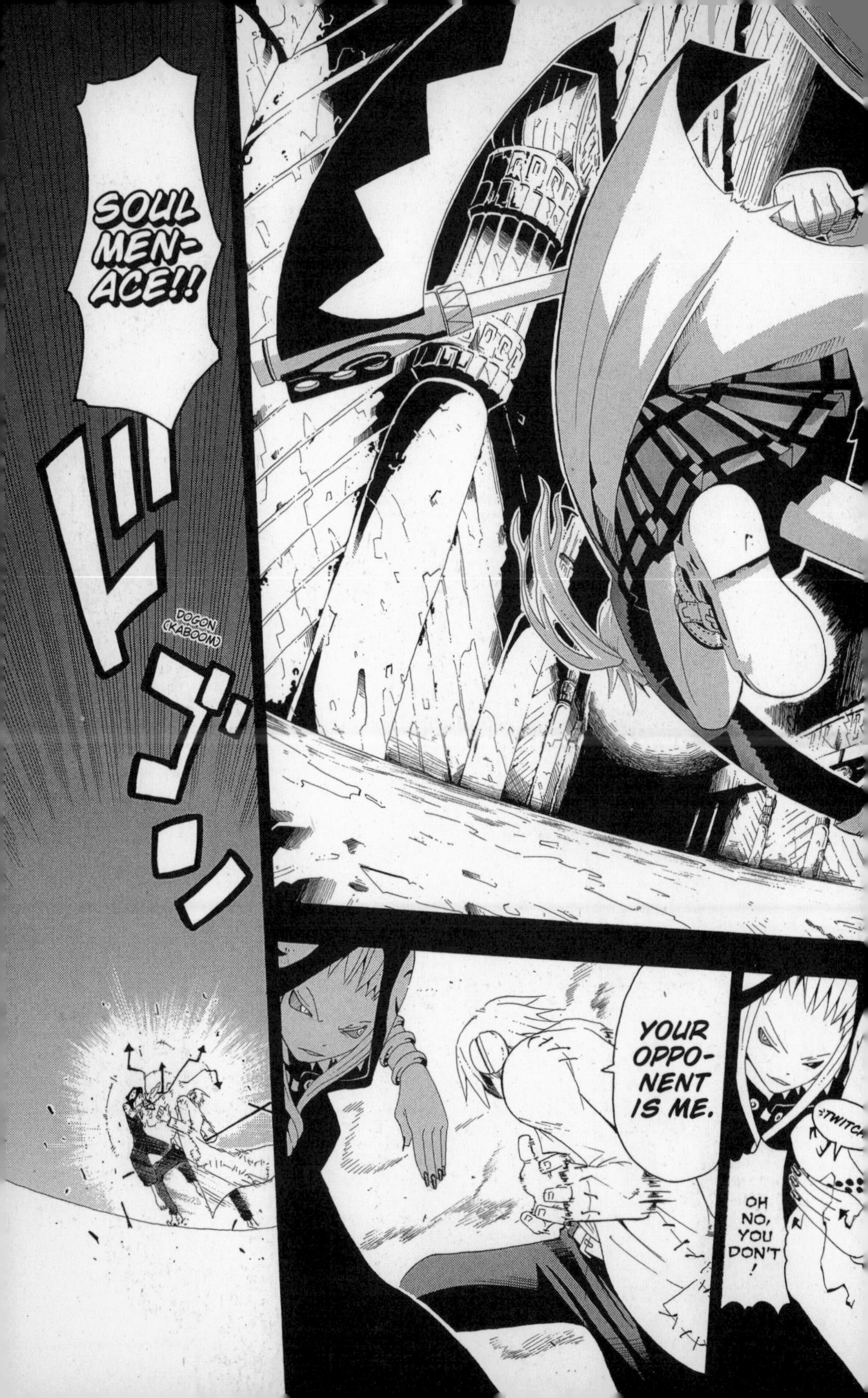
TWITCH
OH NO, YOU DON'T!
YOUR OPPONENT IS ME.
SOUL MENACE!!
DOGON (KABOOM)

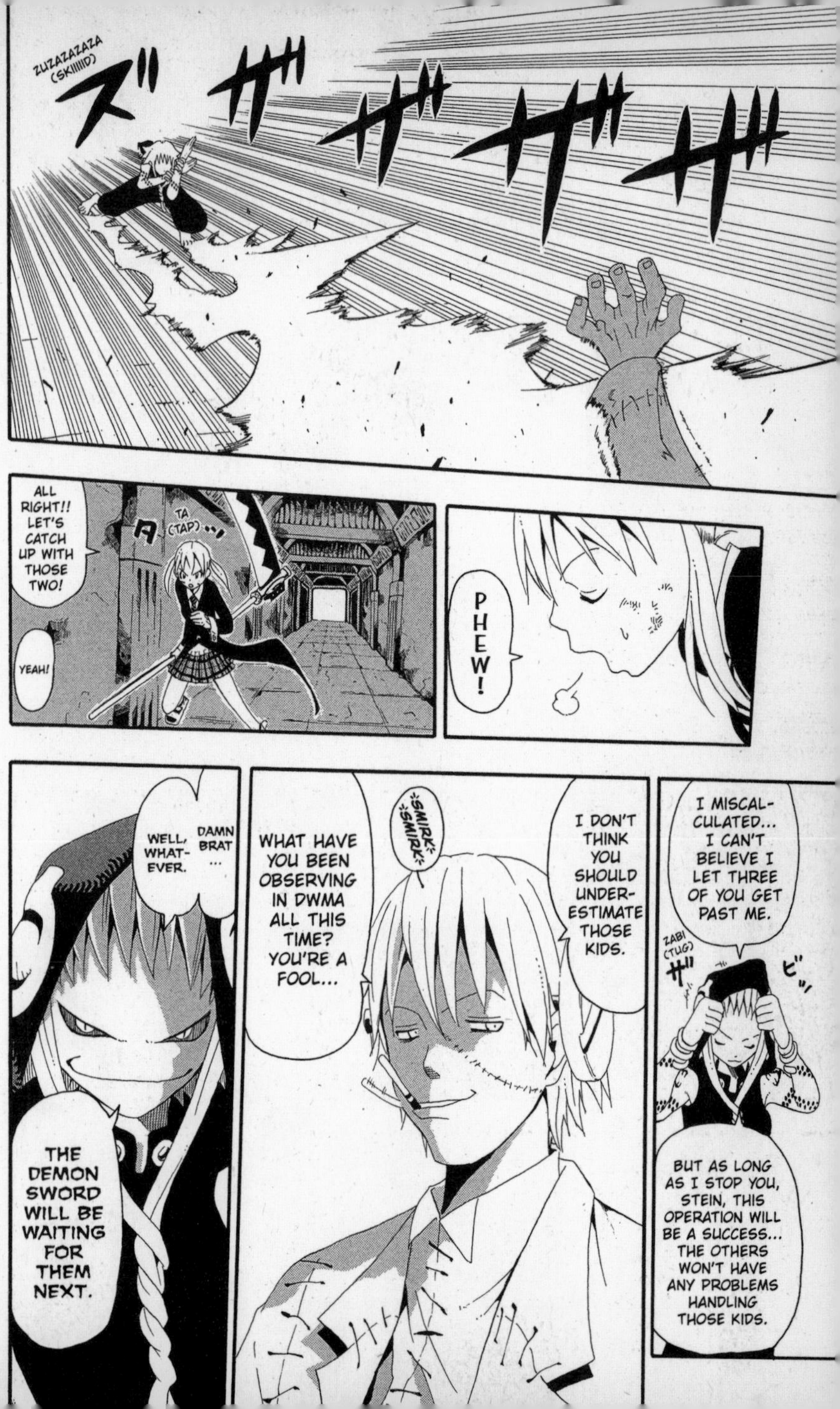

ZUZAZAZAZA (SKIIIIID)
ズザザザ
PHEW!
ALL RIGHT!! LET'S CATCH UP WITH THOSE TWO!
TA (TAP)
YEAH!
I MISCAL-CULATED... I CAN'T BELIEVE I LET THREE OF YOU GET PAST ME.
ZABI (TUG)
BUT AS LONG AS I STOP YOU, STEIN, THIS OPERATION WILL BE A SUCCESS... THE OTHERS WON'T HAVE ANY PROBLEMS HANDLING THOSE KIDS.
I DON'T THINK YOU SHOULD UNDER-ESTIMATE THOSE KIDS.
SMIRK SMIRK
WHAT HAVE YOU BEEN OBSERVING IN DWMA ALL THIS TIME? YOU'RE A FOOL...
DAMN BRAT ...
WELL, WHAT-EVER.
THE DEMON SWORD WILL BE WAITING FOR THEM NEXT.

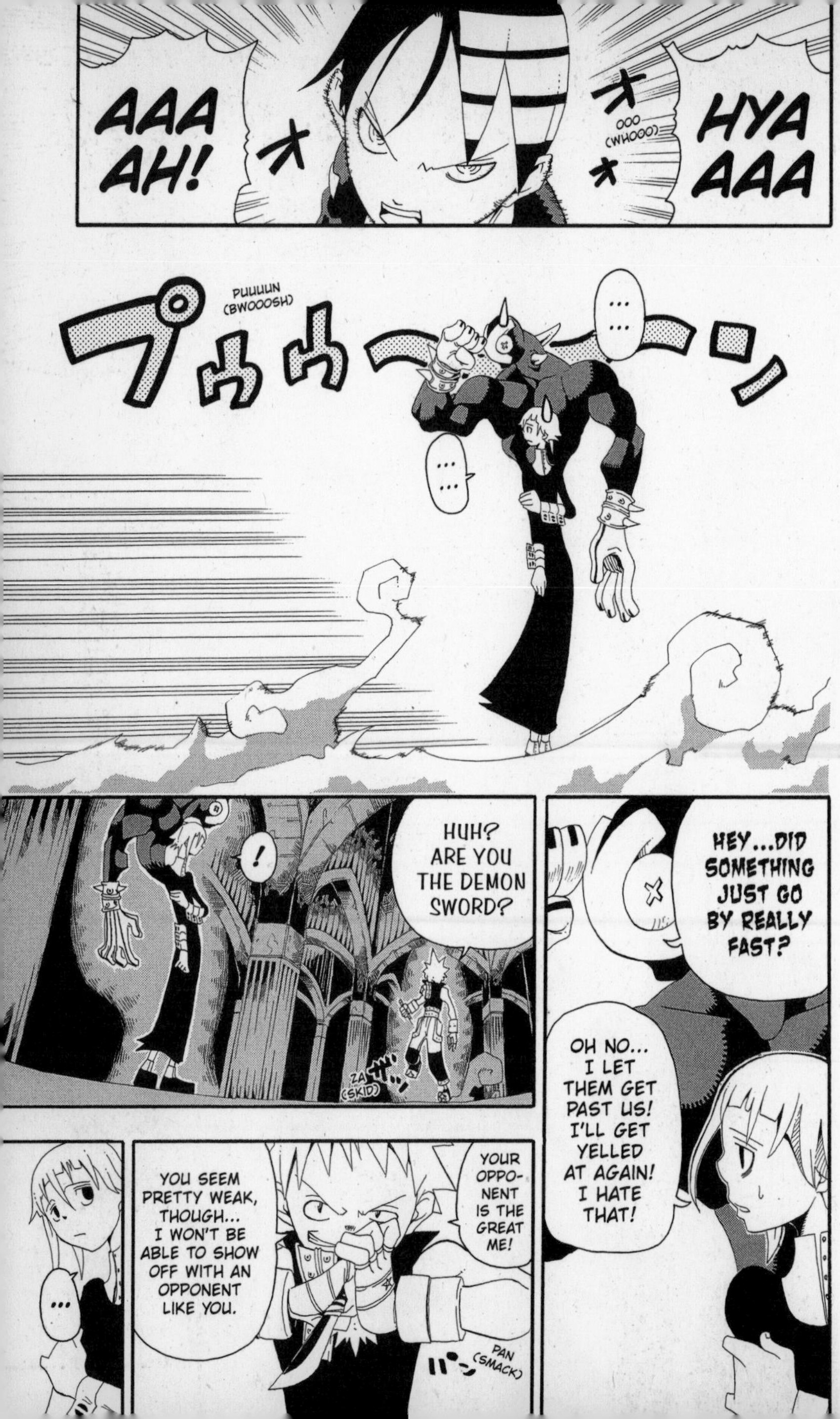
HYA AAA
OOO (WHOOO)
AAA AH!
……
PUUUUN (BWOOOSH)
……
HEY...DID SOMETHING JUST GO BY REALLY FAST?
OH NO... I LET THEM GET PAST US! I'LL GET YELLED AT AGAIN! I HATE THAT!
HUH? ARE YOU THE DEMON SWORD?
!
ZA (SKID)
YOUR OPPONENT IS THE GREAT ME!
YOU SEEM PRETTY WEAK, THOUGH... I WON'T BE ABLE TO SHOW OFF WITH AN OPPONENT LIKE YOU.
PAN (SMACK)
...

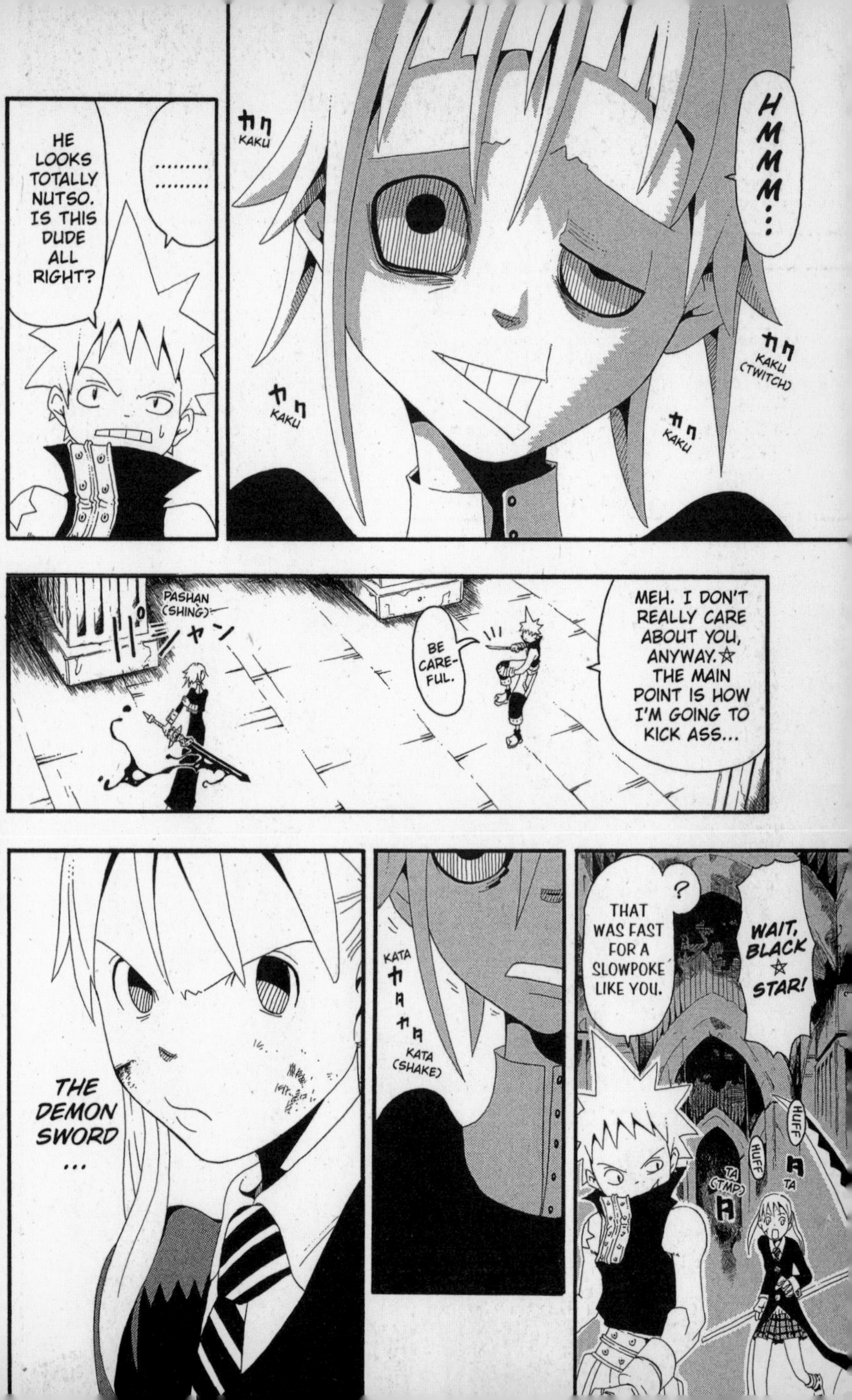
HMMM...
KAKU
KAKU (TWITCH)
KAKU
KAKU
....
....
HE LOOKS TOTALLY NUTSO. IS THIS DUDE ALL RIGHT?
MEH. I DON'T REALLY CARE ABOUT YOU, ANYWAY.☆ THE MAIN POINT IS HOW I'M GOING TO KICK ASS...
BE CARE-FUL.
PASHAN (SHING)
WAIT, BLACK☆STAR!
?
THAT WAS FAST FOR A SLOWPOKE LIKE YOU.
HUFF
HUFF
TA
TA (TMP)
KATA
KATA (SHAKE)
THE DEMON SWORD...

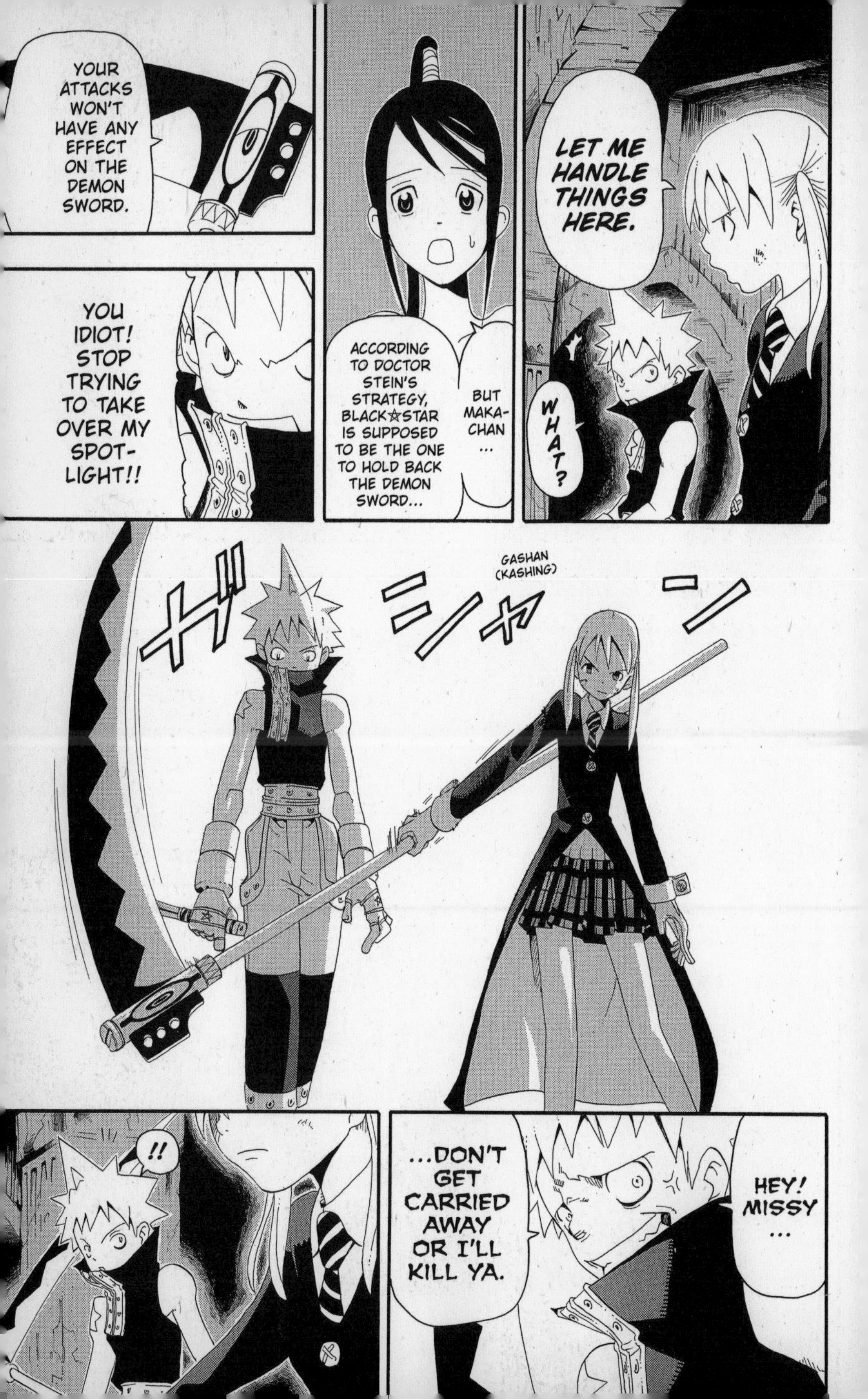
LET ME HANDLE THINGS HERE.
WHAT?
BUT MAKA-CHAN ...
ACCORDING TO DOCTOR STEIN'S STRATEGY, BLACK☆STAR IS SUPPOSED TO BE THE ONE TO HOLD BACK THE DEMON SWORD...
YOUR ATTACKS WON'T HAVE ANY EFFECT ON THE DEMON SWORD.
YOU IDIOT! STOP TRYING TO TAKE OVER MY SPOT-LIGHT!!
GASHAN (KASHING)
HEY! MISSY ...
...DON'T GET CARRIED AWAY OR I'LL KILL YA.
!!

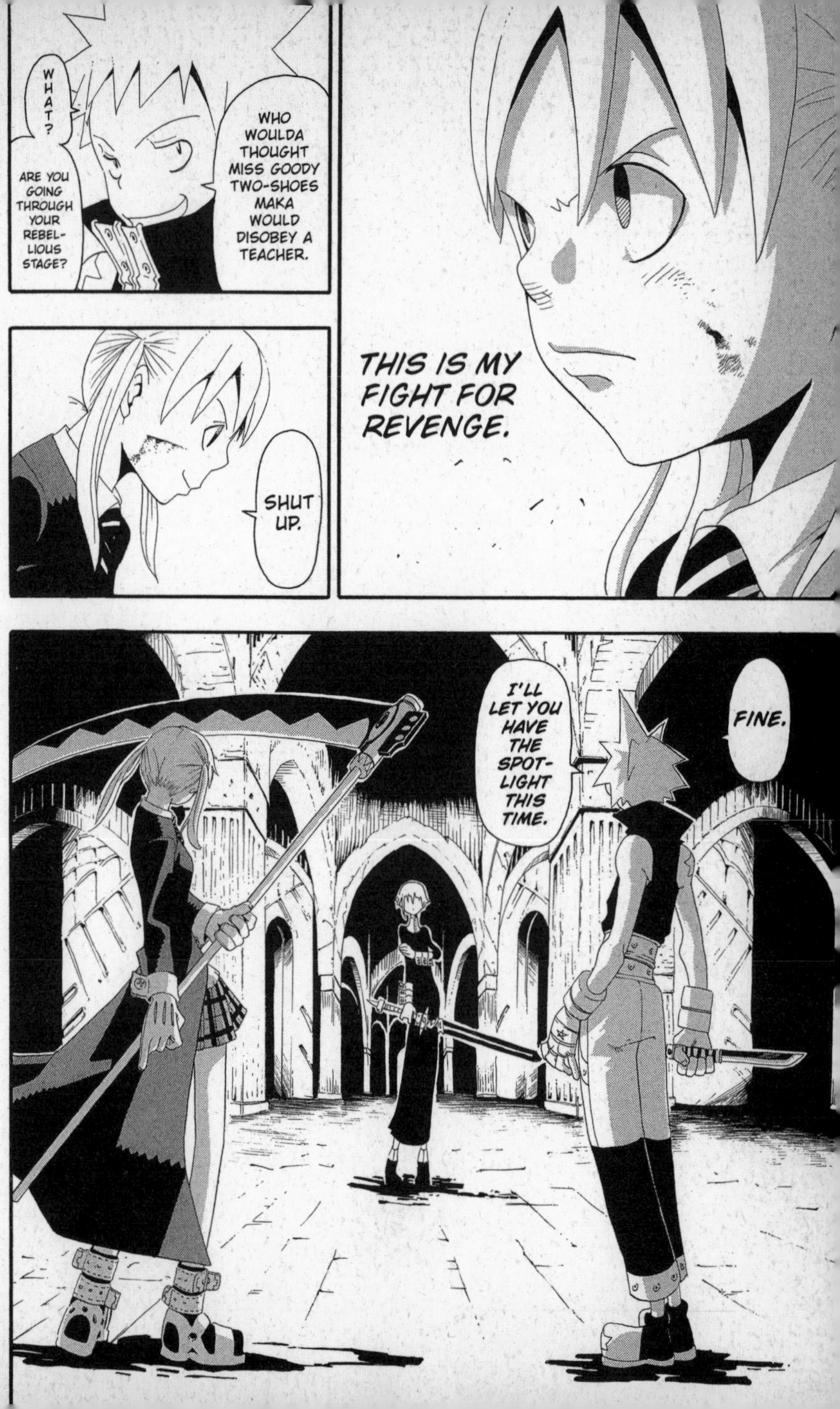
THIS IS MY FIGHT FOR REVENGE.
WHO WOULDA THOUGHT MISS GOODY TWO-SHOES MAKA WOULD DISOBEY A TEACHER.
WHAT?
ARE YOU GOING THROUGH YOUR REBEL-LIOUS STAGE?
SHUT UP.
FINE.
I'LL LET YOU HAVE THE SPOT-LIGHT THIS TIME.

SOUL EATER

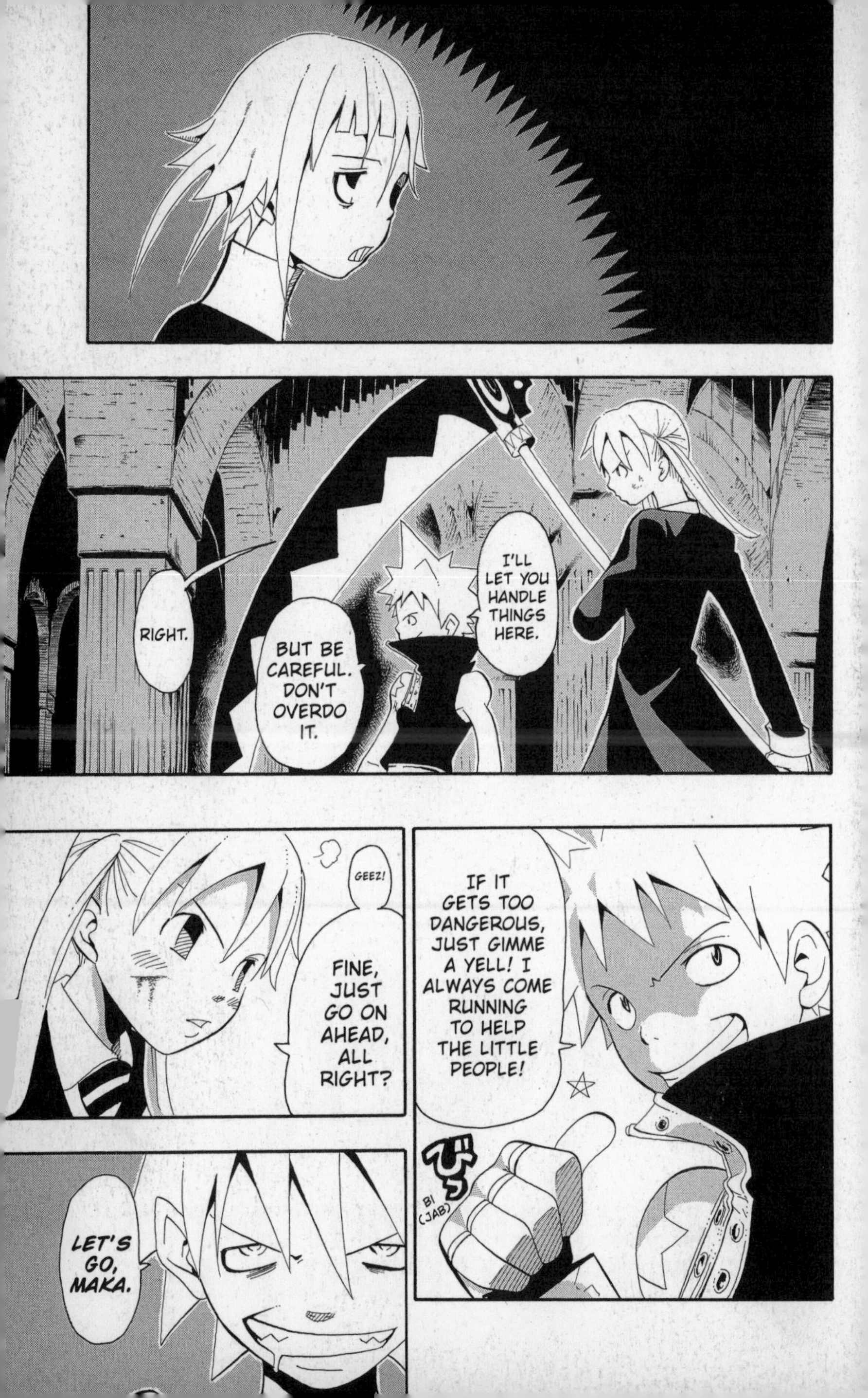
I'LL LET YOU HANDLE THINGS HERE.
BUT BE CAREFUL. DON'T OVERDO IT.
RIGHT.
IF IT GETS TOO DANGEROUS, JUST GIMME A YELL! I ALWAYS COME RUNNING TO HELP THE LITTLE PEOPLE!
びっ
BI (JAB)
GEEZ!
FINE, JUST GO ON AHEAD, ALL RIGHT?
LET'S GO, MAKA.

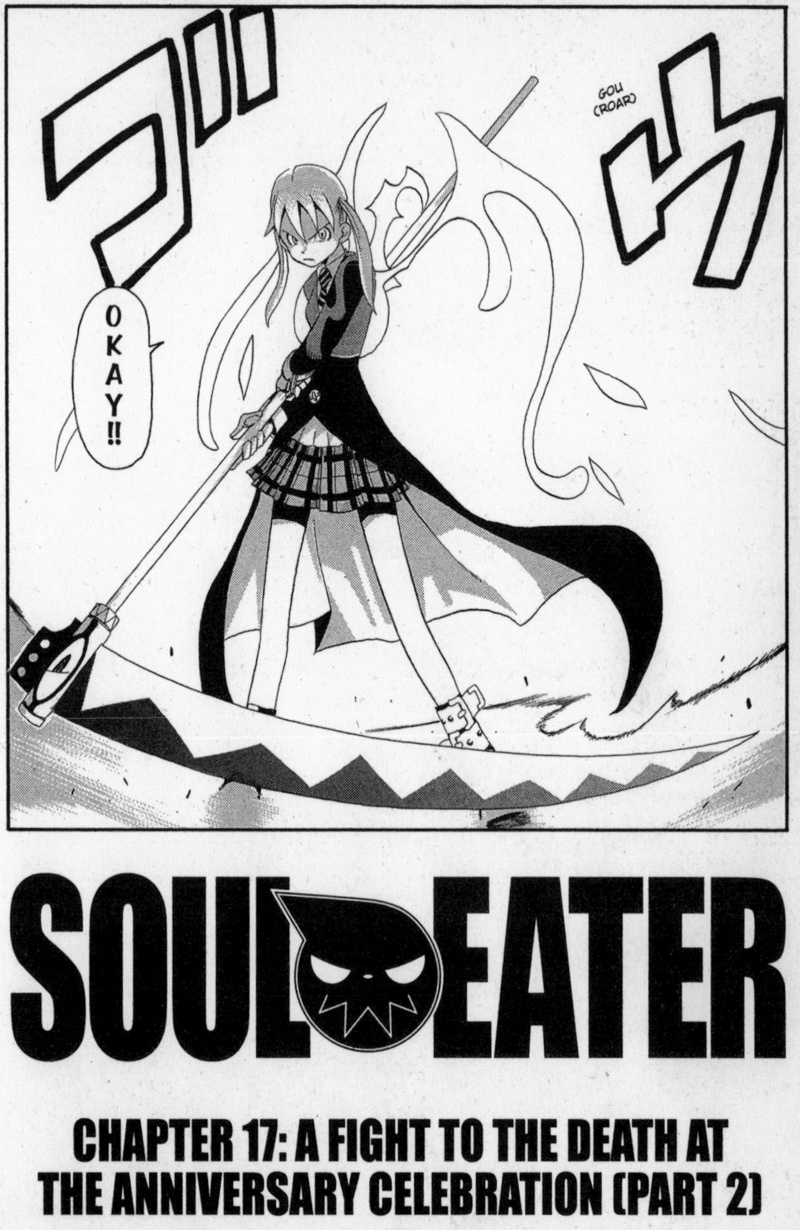
GOU (ROAR)
OKAY!!

SOUL EATER

CHAPTER 17: A FIGHT TO THE DEATH AT THE ANNIVERSARY CELEBRATION (PART 2)

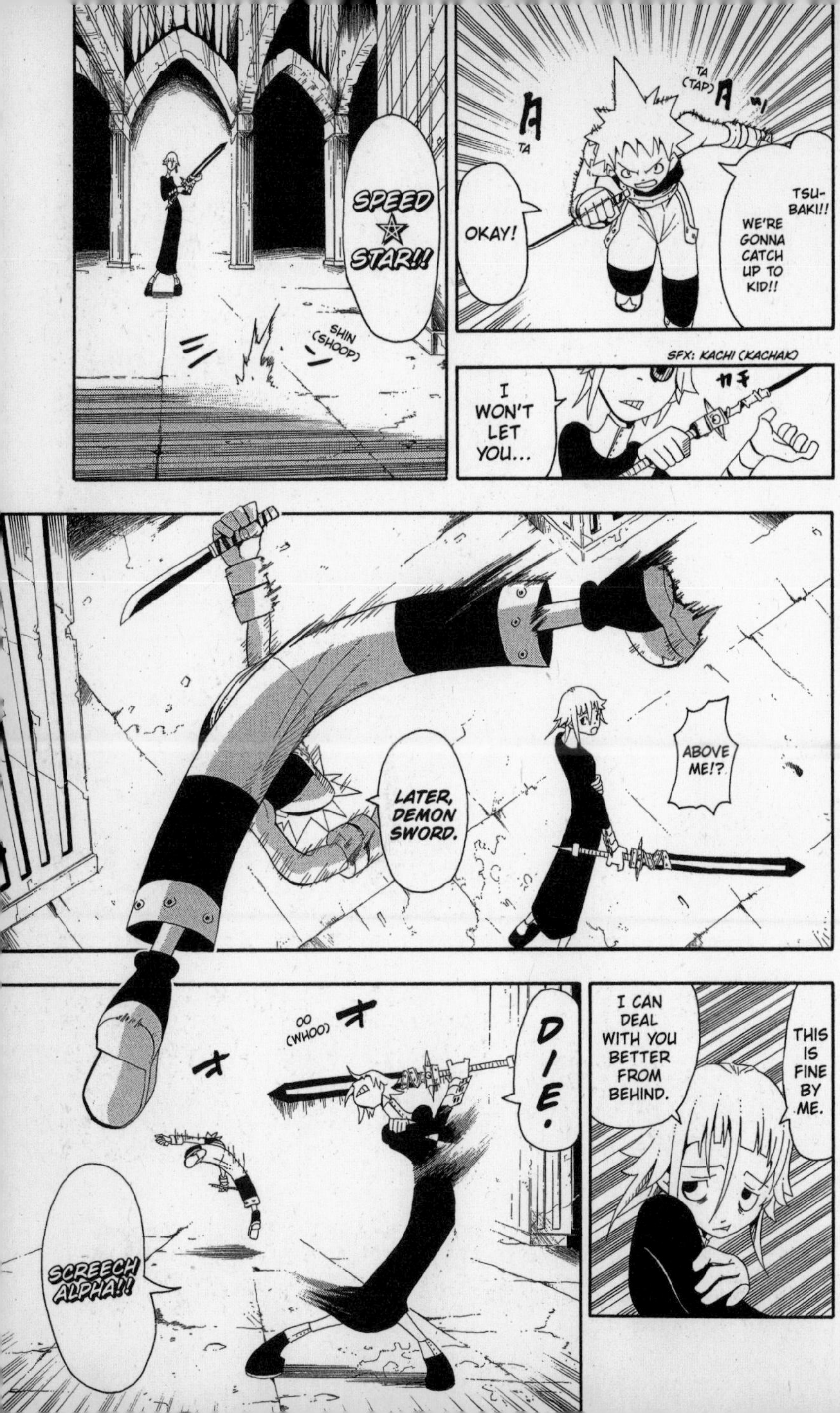
TSU-BAKI!! WE'RE GONNA CATCH UP TO KID!!
TA (TAP)
OKAY!
TA
SFX: KACHI (KACHAK)
I WON'T LET YOU...
SPEED ☆ STAR!!
SHIN (SHOOP)
ABOVE ME!?
LATER, DEMON SWORD.
THIS IS FINE BY ME.
I CAN DEAL WITH YOU BETTER FROM BEHIND.
DIE.
OO (WHOO)
SCREECH ALPHA!!

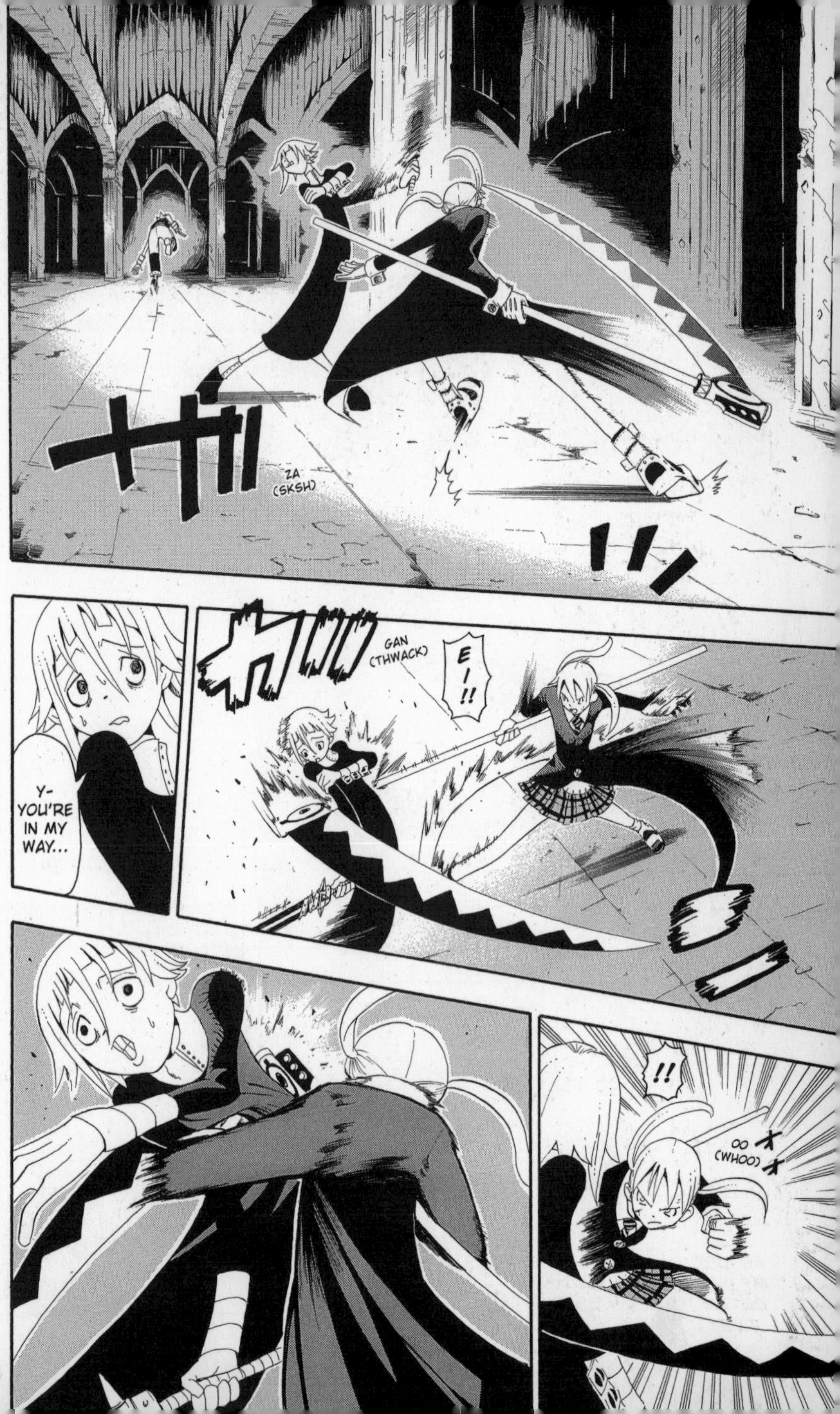
ZA
(SKSH)
GAN
(THWACK)
E-!!
Y-YOU'RE IN MY WAY...
!!
OO
(WHOO)

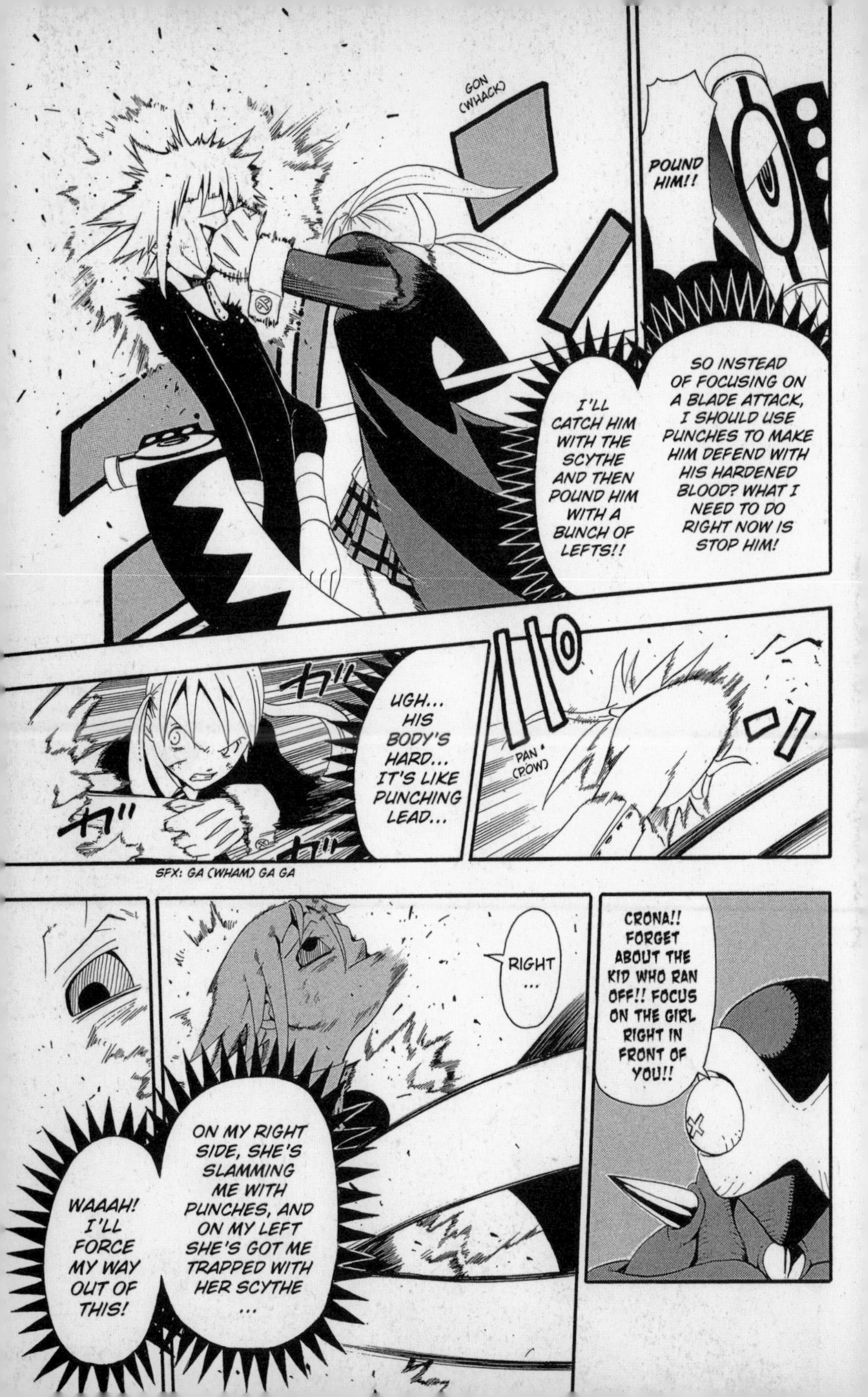
POUND HIM!!
GON (WHACK)
SO INSTEAD OF FOCUSING ON A BLADE ATTACK, I SHOULD USE PUNCHES TO MAKE HIM DEFEND WITH HIS HARDENED BLOOD? WHAT I NEED TO DO RIGHT NOW IS STOP HIM!
I'LL CATCH HIM WITH THE SCYTHE AND THEN POUND HIM WITH A BUNCH OF LEFTS!!
PAN (POW)
UGH... HIS BODY'S HARD... IT'S LIKE PUNCHING LEAD...
SFX: GA (WHAM) GA GA
CRONA!! FORGET ABOUT THE KID WHO RAN OFF!! FOCUS ON THE GIRL RIGHT IN FRONT OF YOU!!
RIGHT ...
ON MY RIGHT SIDE, SHE'S SLAMMING ME WITH PUNCHES, AND ON MY LEFT SHE'S GOT ME TRAPPED WITH HER SCYTHE ...
WAAAH! I'LL FORCE MY WAY OUT OF THIS!

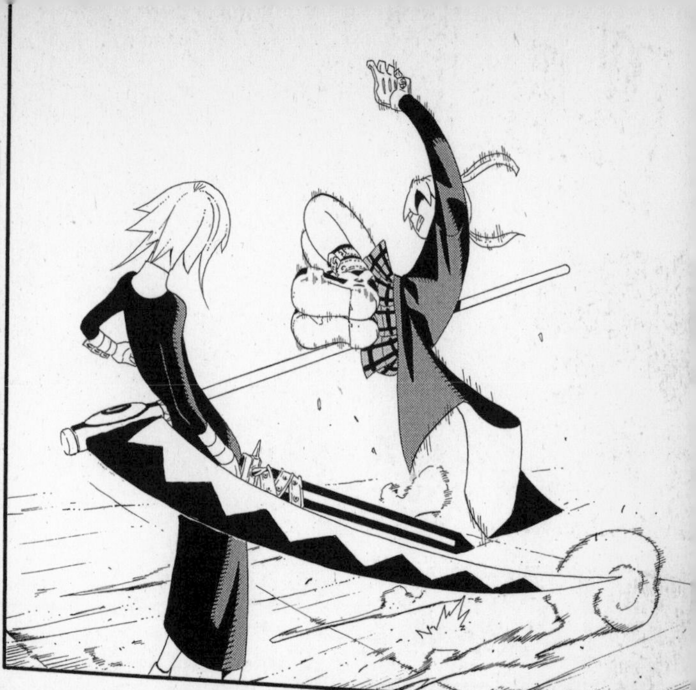

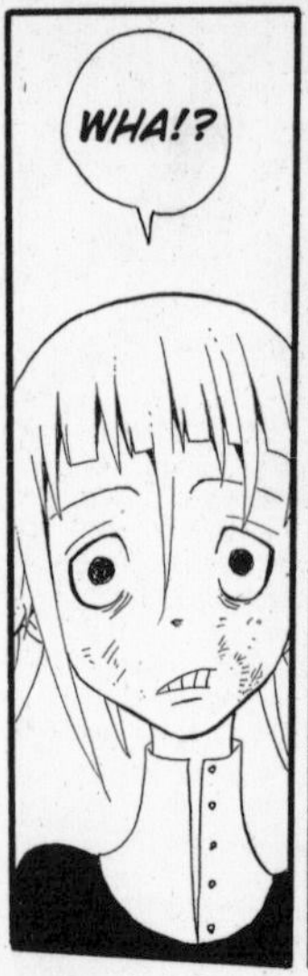
WHA!?

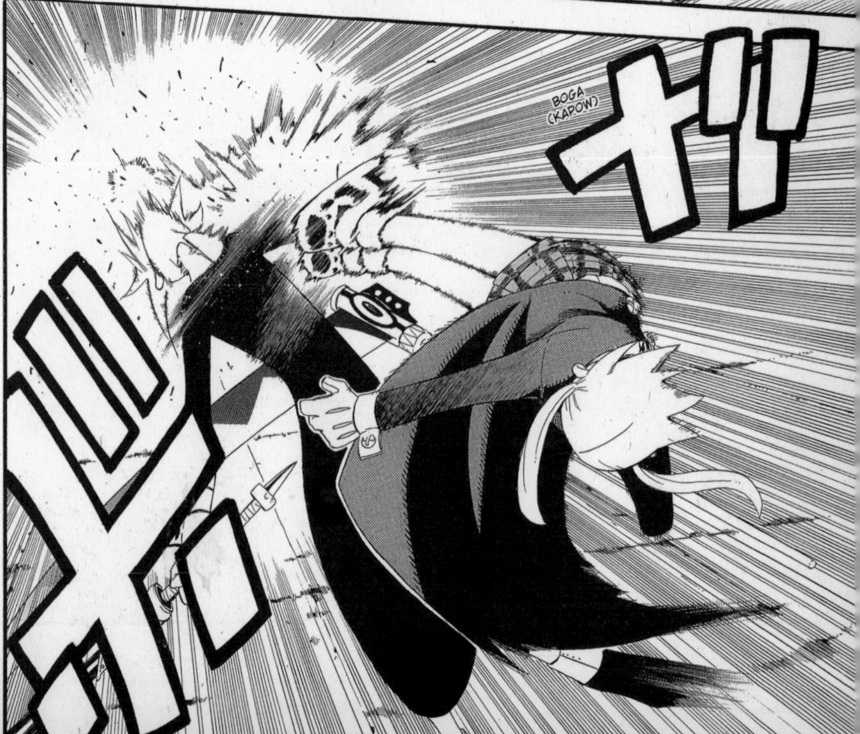
BOGA
(KAPOW)

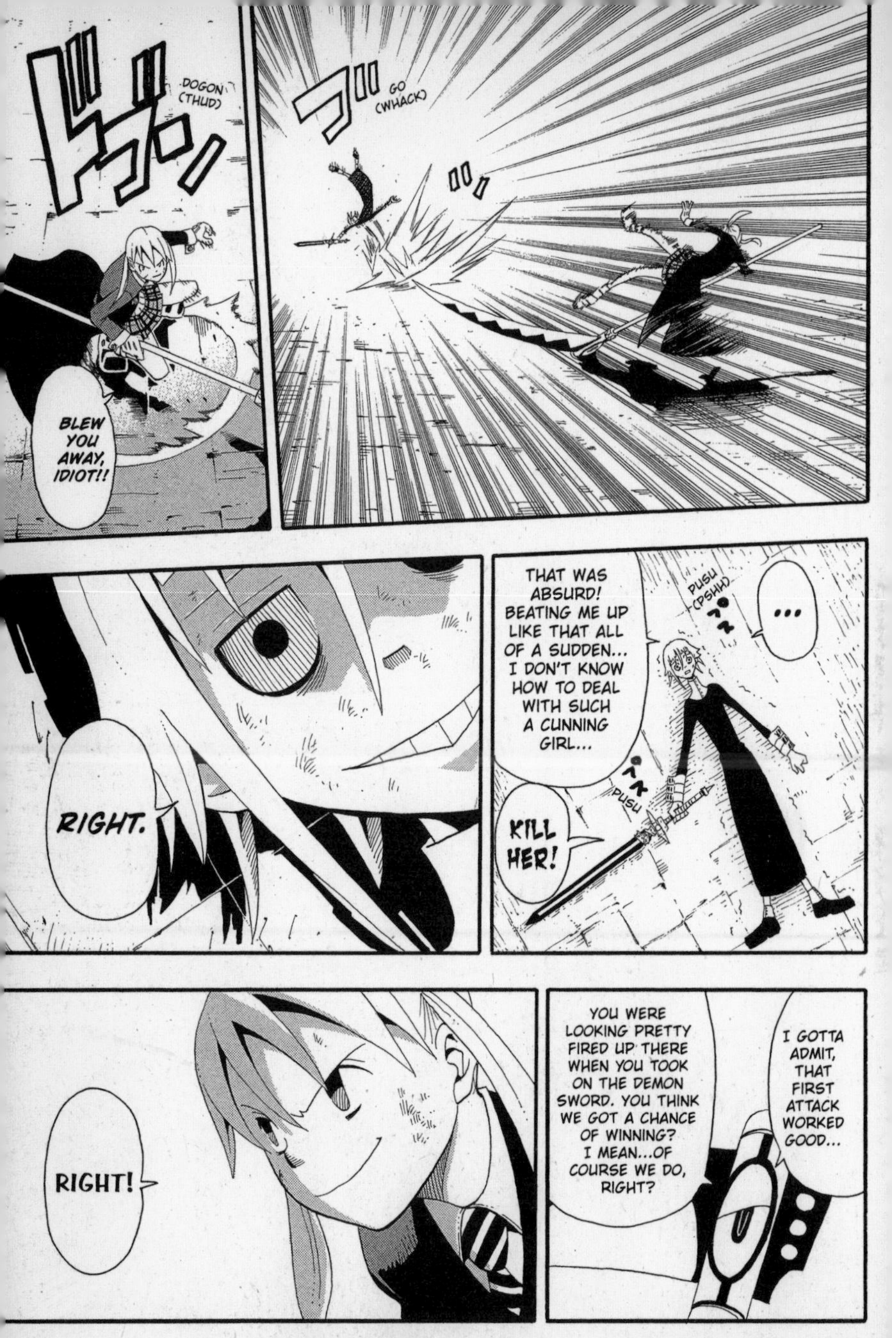
GO (WHACK)
DOGON (THUD)
BLEW YOU AWAY, IDIOT!!
...
PUSU (PSHH)
THAT WAS ABSURD! BEATING ME UP LIKE THAT ALL OF A SUDDEN... I DON'T KNOW HOW TO DEAL WITH SUCH A CUNNING GIRL...
PUSU
KILL HER!
RIGHT.
I GOTTA ADMIT, THAT FIRST ATTACK WORKED GOOD...
YOU WERE LOOKING PRETTY FIRED UP THERE WHEN YOU TOOK ON THE DEMON SWORD. YOU THINK WE GOT A CHANCE OF WINNING? I MEAN...OF COURSE WE DO, RIGHT?
RIGHT!

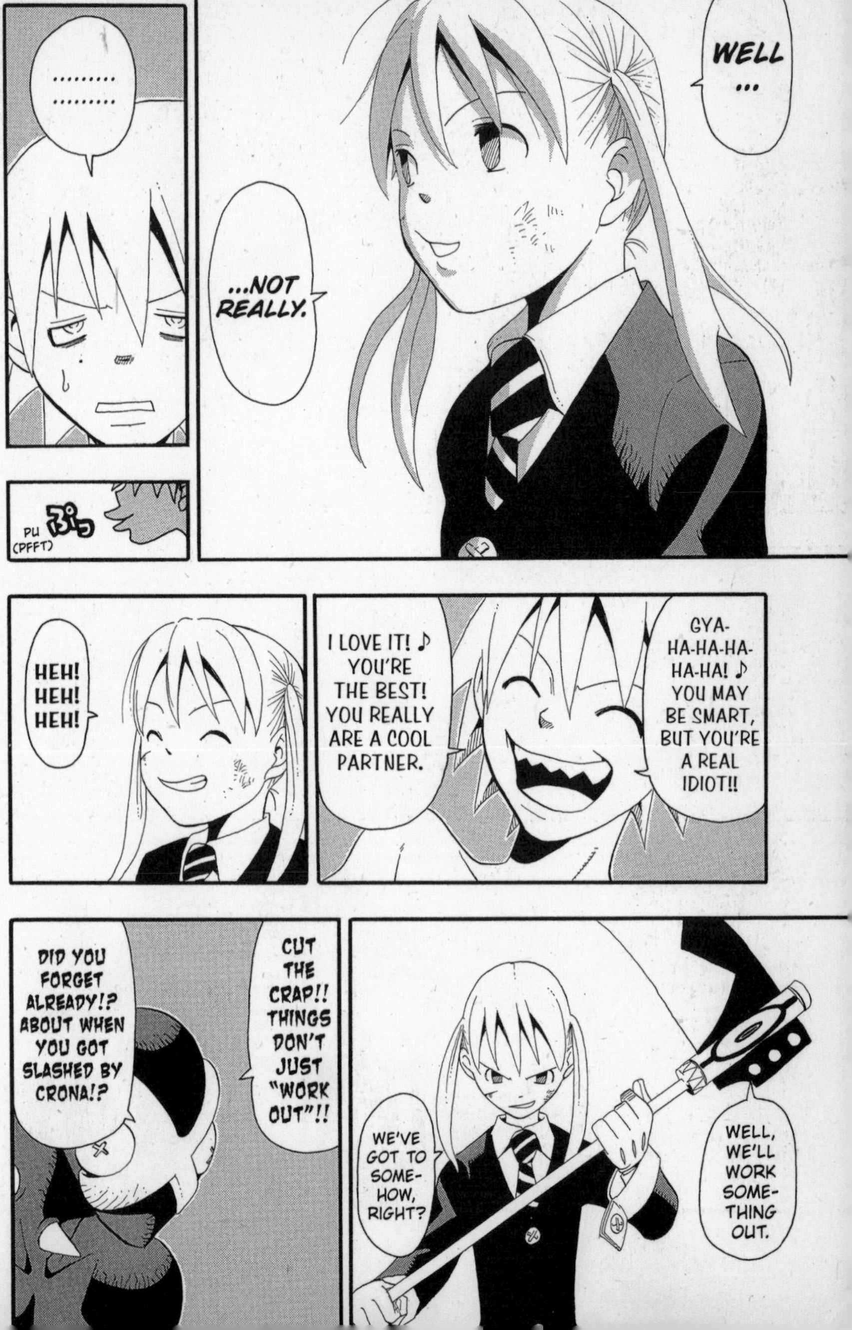
WELL ...
...NOT REALLY.
....
PU ぷっ (PFFT)
GYA-HA-HA-HA-HA-HA! ♪ YOU MAY BE SMART, BUT YOU'RE A REAL IDIOT!!
I LOVE IT! ♪ YOU'RE THE BEST! YOU REALLY ARE A COOL PARTNER.
HEH! HEH! HEH!
WELL, WE'LL WORK SOMETHING OUT.
WE'VE GOT TO SOMEHOW, RIGHT?
CUT THE CRAP!! THINGS DON'T JUST "WORK OUT"!!
DID YOU FORGET ALREADY!? ABOUT WHEN YOU GOT SLASHED BY CRONA!?

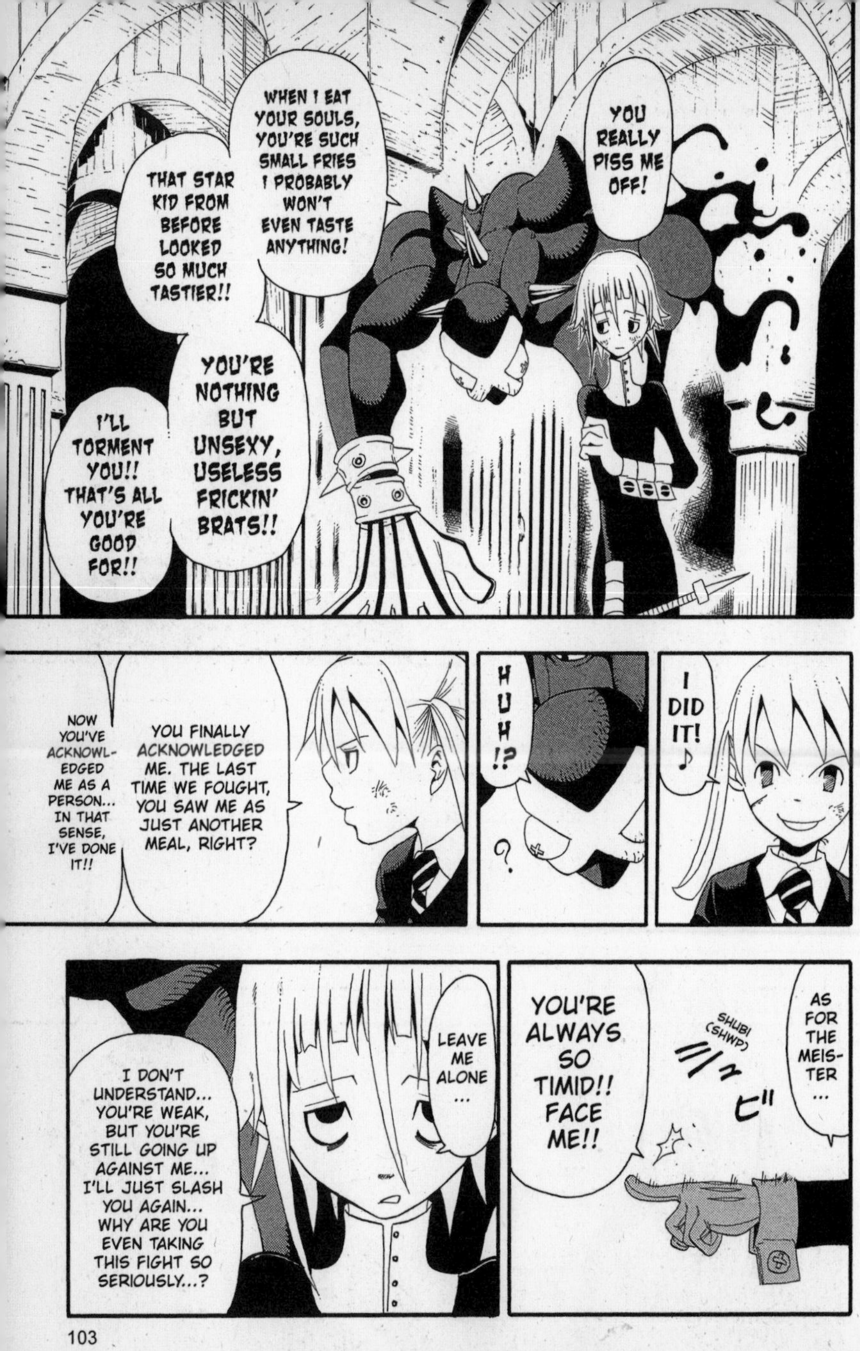
YOU REALLY PISS ME OFF!
WHEN I EAT YOUR SOULS, YOU'RE SUCH SMALL FRIES I PROBABLY WON'T EVEN TASTE ANYTHING!
THAT STAR KID FROM BEFORE LOOKED SO MUCH TASTIER!!
YOU'RE NOTHING BUT UNSEXY, USELESS FRICKIN' BRATS!!
I'LL TORMENT YOU!! THAT'S ALL YOU'RE GOOD FOR!!
I DID IT! ♪
HUH!?
?
YOU FINALLY ACKNOWLEDGED ME. THE LAST TIME WE FOUGHT, YOU SAW ME AS JUST ANOTHER MEAL, RIGHT?
NOW YOU'VE ACKNOWL-EDGED ME AS A PERSON... IN THAT SENSE, I'VE DONE IT!!
AS FOR THE MEISTER...
SHUBI (SHWP)
YOU'RE ALWAYS SO TIMID!! FACE ME!!
LEAVE ME ALONE...
I DON'T UNDERSTAND... YOU'RE WEAK, BUT YOU'RE STILL GOING UP AGAINST ME... I'LL JUST SLASH YOU AGAIN... WHY ARE YOU EVEN TAKING THIS FIGHT SO SERIOUSLY...?

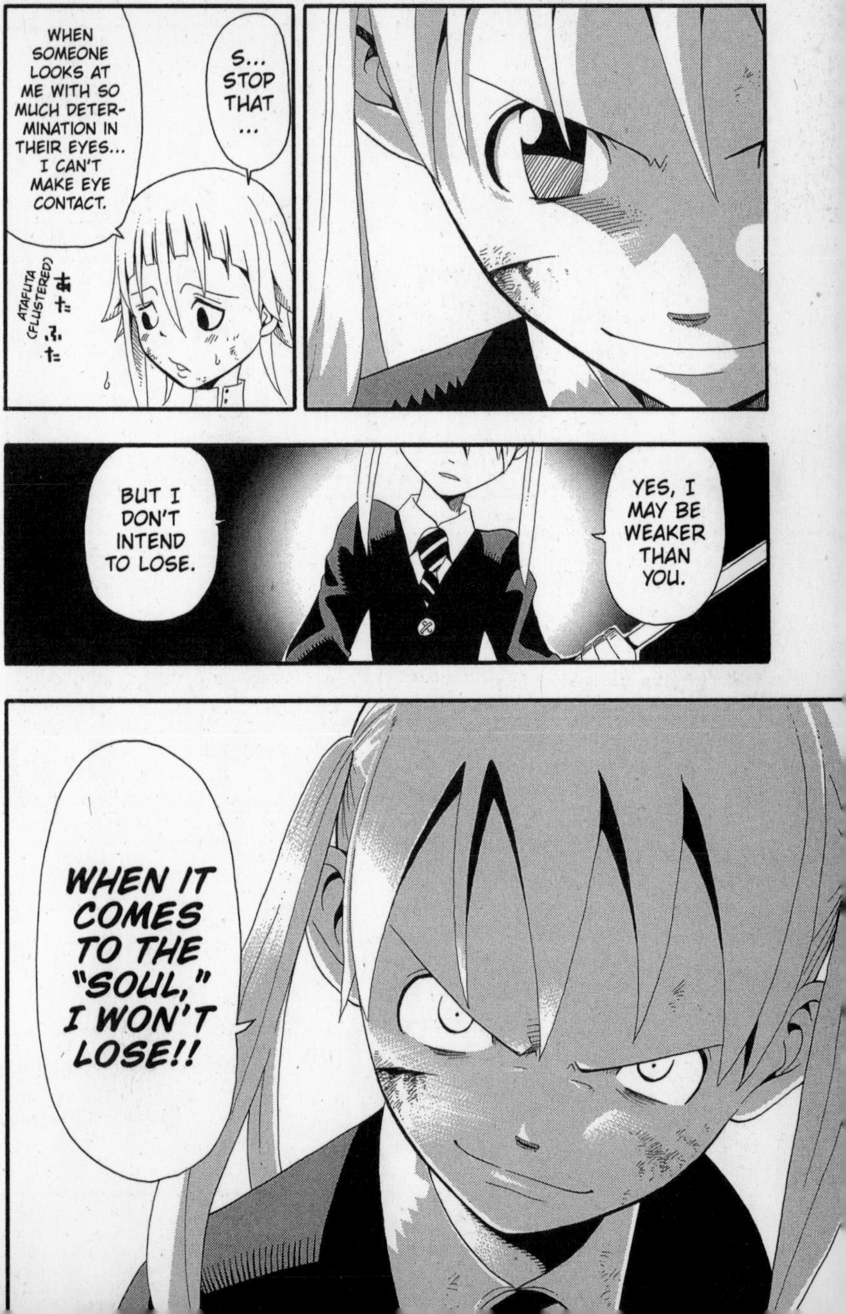
S... STOP THAT ...
WHEN SOMEONE LOOKS AT ME WITH SO MUCH DETERMINATION IN THEIR EYES... I CAN'T MAKE EYE CONTACT.
あたふたた
ATAFUTA (FLUSTERED)
YES, I MAY BE WEAKER THAN YOU.
BUT I DON'T INTEND TO LOSE.
WHEN IT COMES TO THE "SOUL," I WON'T LOSE!!

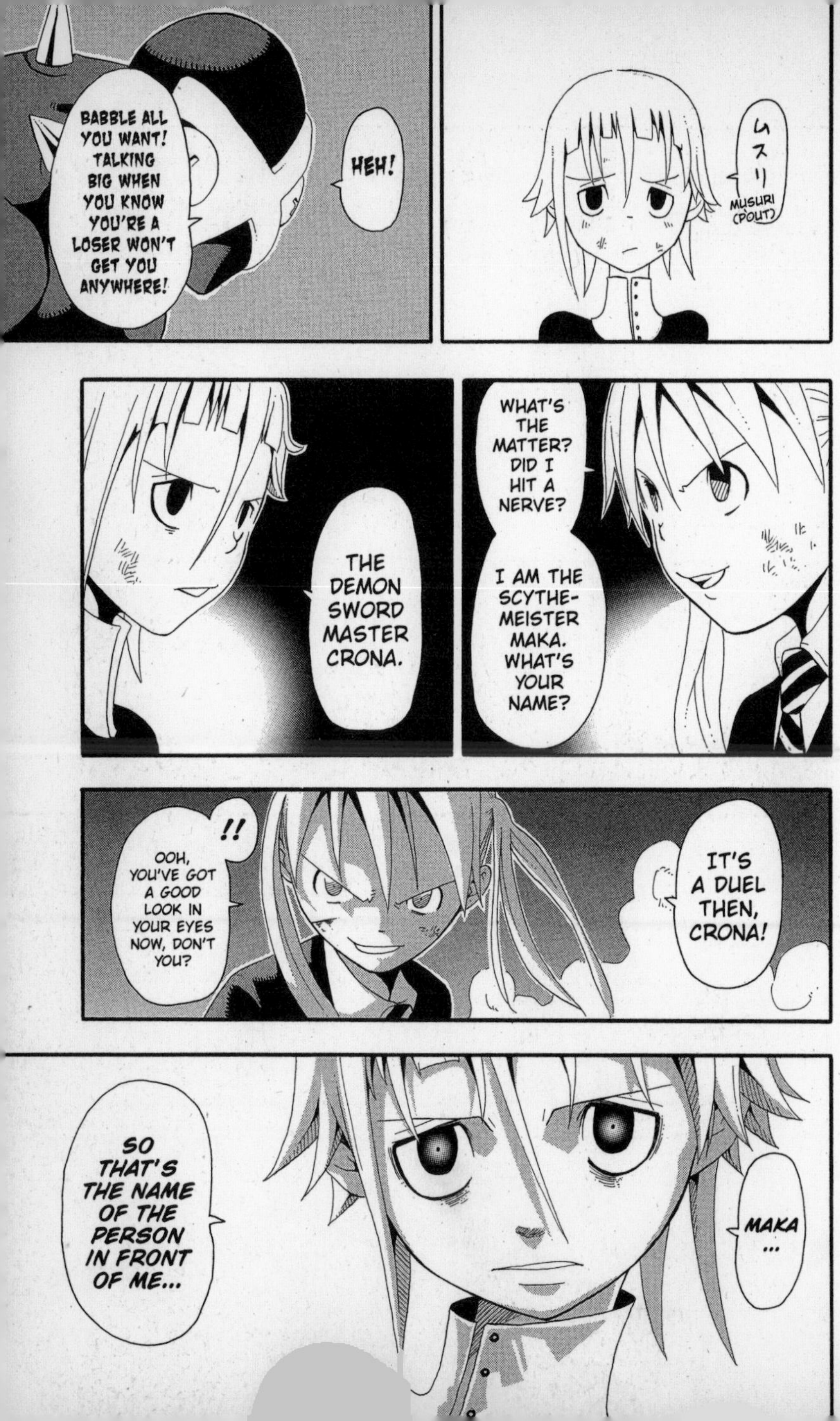
ムスリ
MUSURI (POUT)
HEH!
BABBLE ALL YOU WANT! TALKING BIG WHEN YOU KNOW YOU'RE A LOSER WON'T GET YOU ANYWHERE!
WHAT'S THE MATTER? DID I HIT A NERVE?
I AM THE SCYTHE-MEISTER MAKA. WHAT'S YOUR NAME?
THE DEMON SWORD MASTER CRONA.
IT'S A DUEL THEN, CRONA!
!!
OOH, YOU'VE GOT A GOOD LOOK IN YOUR EYES NOW, DON'T YOU?
MAKA...
SO THAT'S THE NAME OF THE PERSON IN FRONT OF ME...

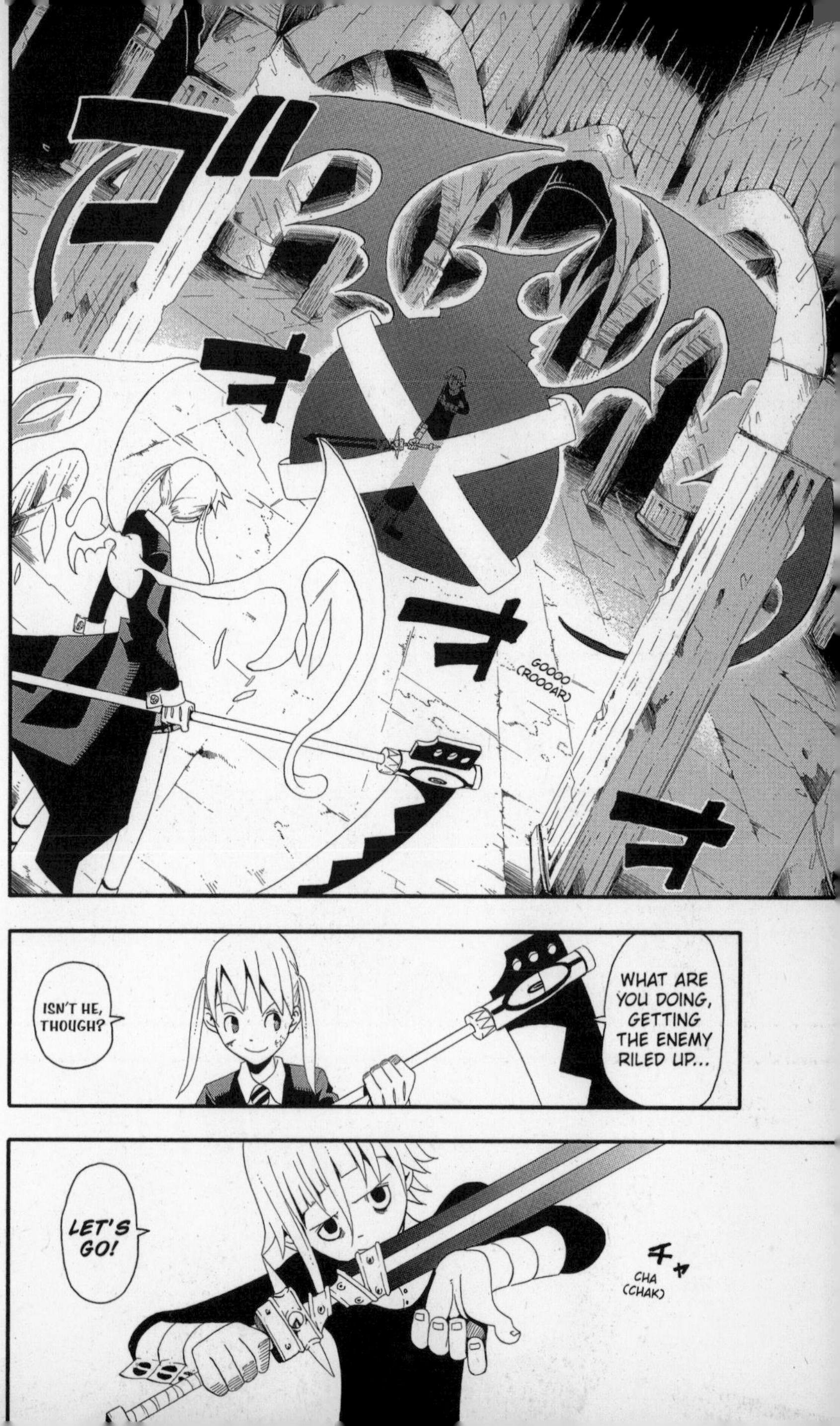
ゴォォォ
GOOOO (ROOOAR)
WHAT ARE YOU DOING, GETTING THE ENEMY RILED UP...
ISN'T HE, THOUGH?
チャ
CHA (CHAK)
LET'S GO!

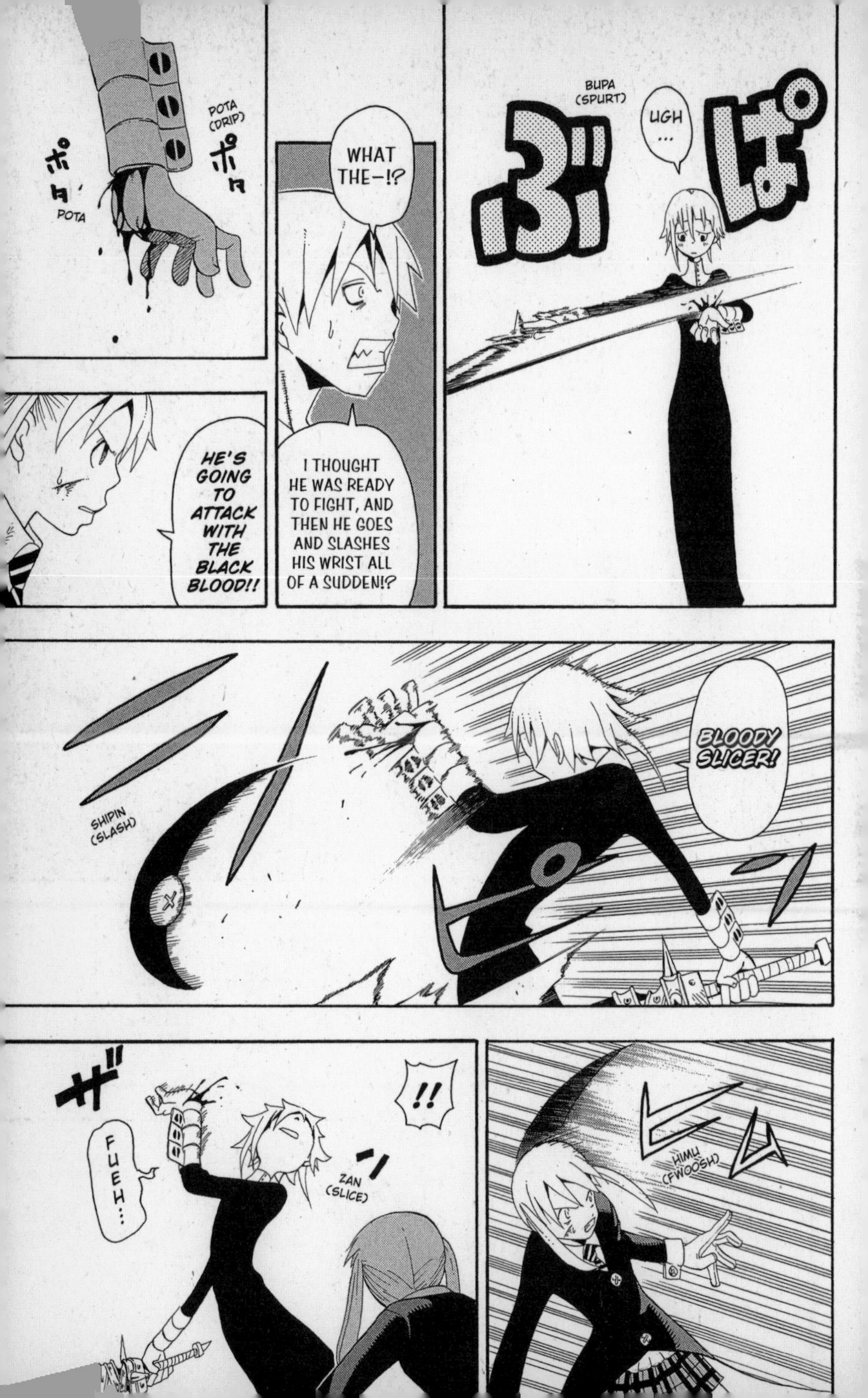

BUPA (SPURT)
ぶぱ
UGH...
WHAT THE-!?
I THOUGHT HE WAS READY TO FIGHT, AND THEN HE GOES AND SLASHES HIS WRIST ALL OF A SUDDEN!?
POTA (DRIP)
ポタ
ポタ
POTA
HE'S GOING TO ATTACK WITH THE BLACK BLOOD!!
BLOODY SLICER!
SHIPIN (SLASH)
HIMU (FWOOSH)
!!
ZAN (SLICE)
FUEH...

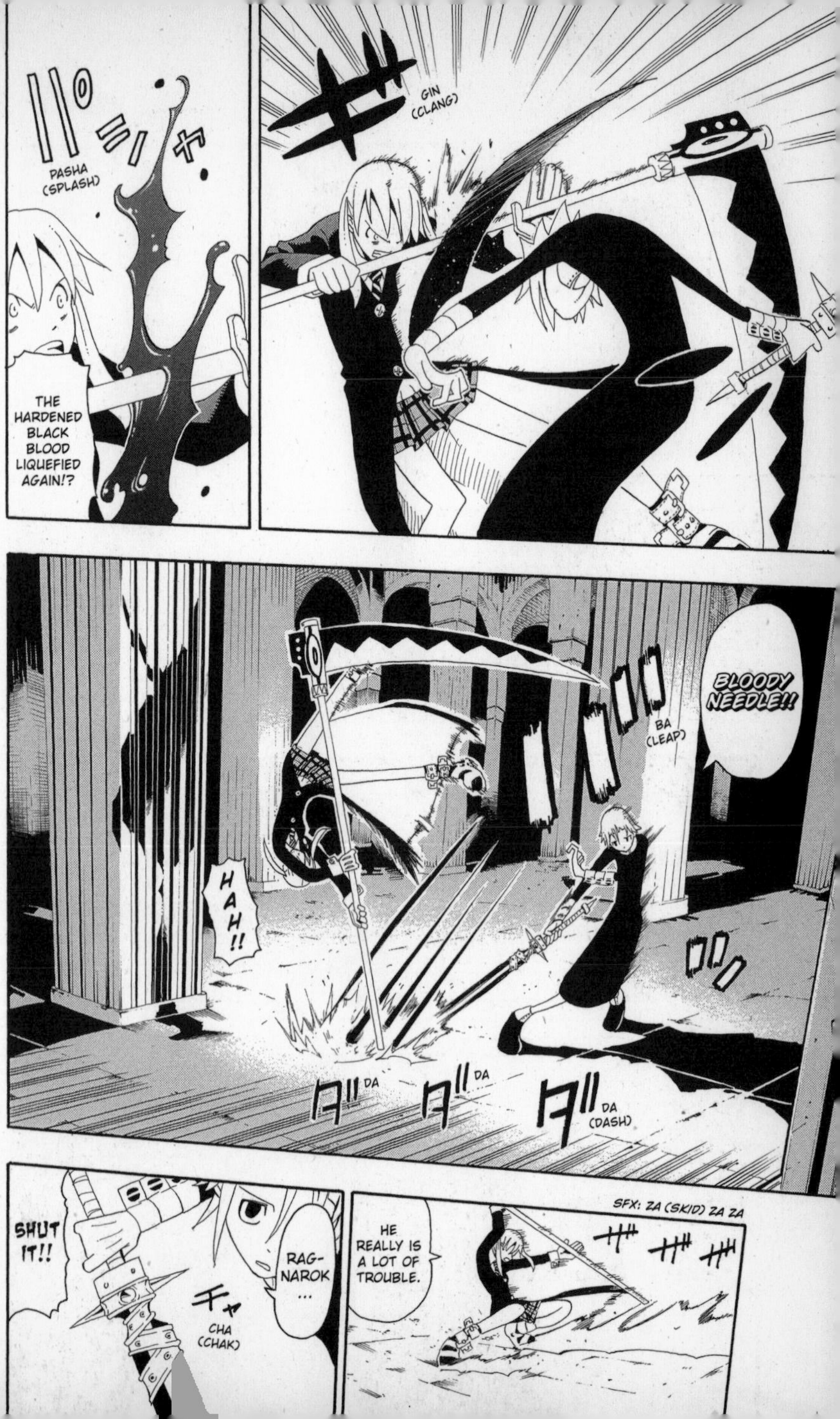
GIN
(CLANG)
PASHA
(SPLASH)
THE HARDENED BLACK BLOOD LIQUEFIED AGAIN!?
BLOODY NEEDLE!!
BA
(LEAP)
HAH!!
DA
DA
DA
(DASH)
SFX: ZA (SKID) ZA ZA
HE REALLY IS A LOT OF TROUBLE.
RAG-NAROK...
CHA
(CHAK)
SHUT IT!!

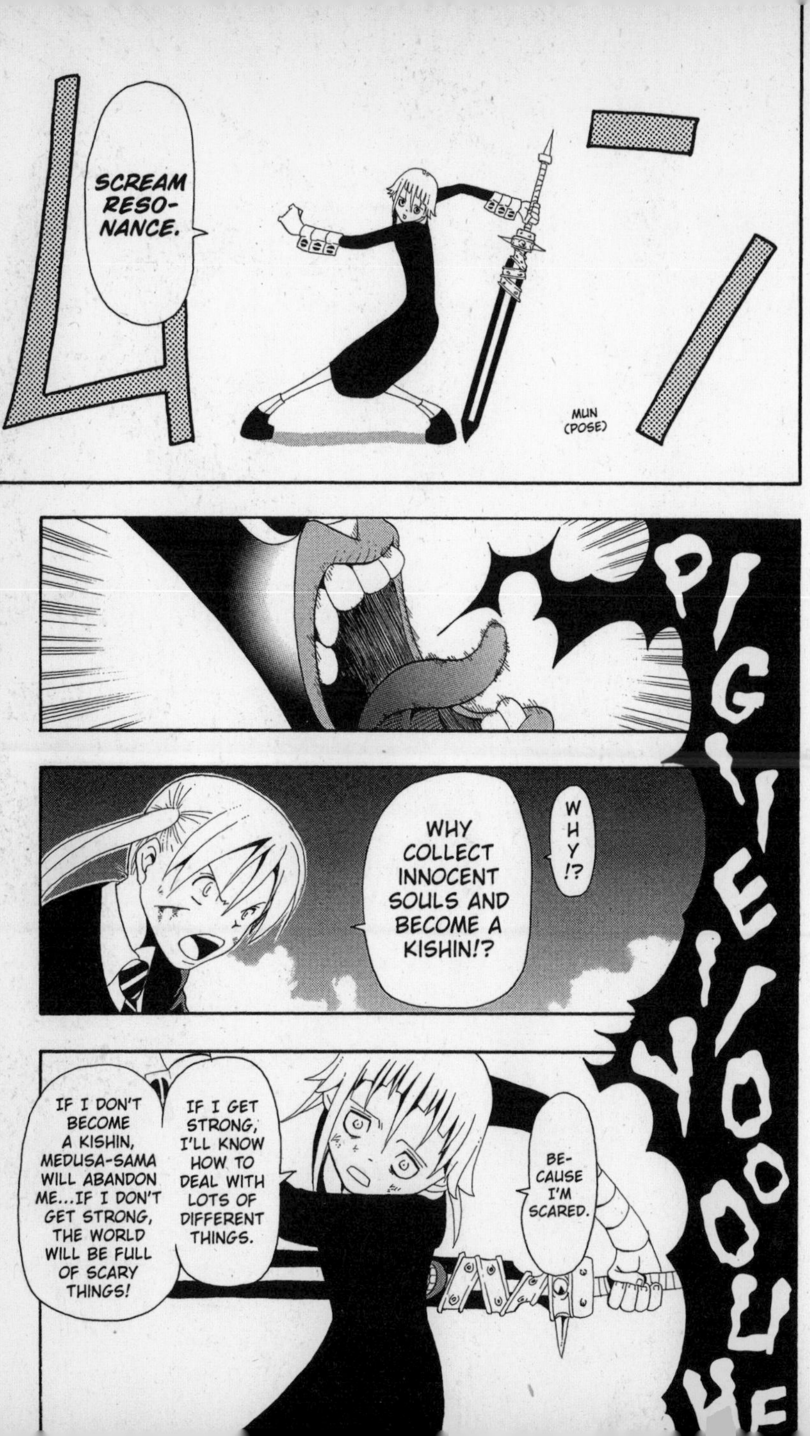

SCREAM RESO-NANCE.
MUN (POSE)
WHY!?
WHY COLLECT INNOCENT SOULS AND BECOME A KISHIN!?
BE-CAUSE I'M SCARED.
IF I GET STRONG, I'LL KNOW HOW TO DEAL WITH LOTS OF DIFFERENT THINGS.
IF I DON'T BECOME A KISHIN, MEDUSA-SAMA WILL ABANDON ME...IF I DON'T GET STRONG, THE WORLD WILL BE FULL OF SCARY THINGS!

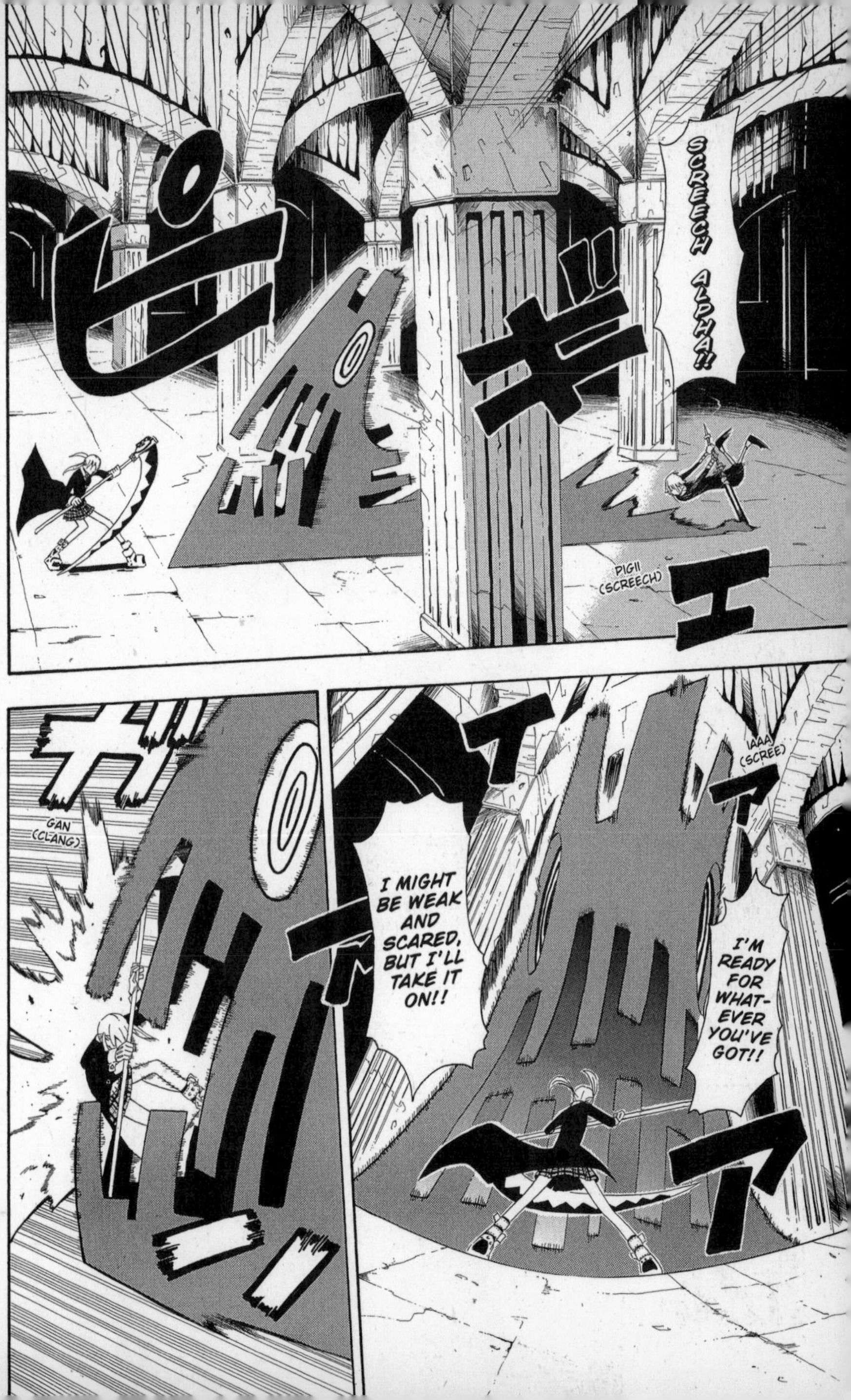
SCREECH ALPHA!!
PIGII (SCREECH)
IAAA (SCREE)
I'M READY FOR WHATEVER YOU'VE GOT!!
I MIGHT BE WEAK AND SCARED, BUT I'LL TAKE IT ON!!
GAN (CLANG)

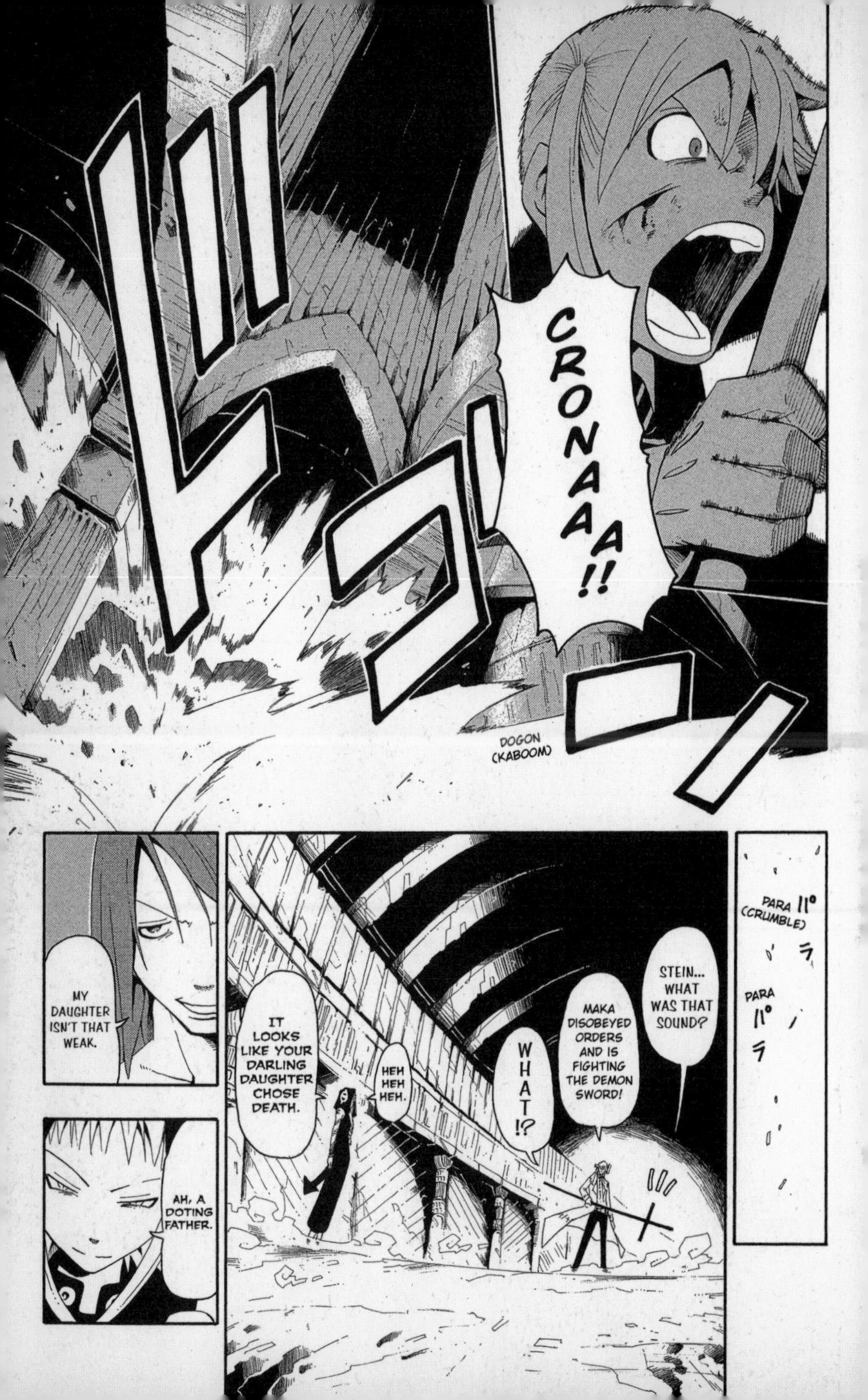
CRONAAA!!
DOGON (KABOOM)
PARA (CRUMBLE)
PARA
STEIN... WHAT WAS THAT SOUND?
MAKA DISOBEYED ORDERS AND IS FIGHTING THE DEMON SWORD!
WHAT!?
HEH HEH HEH.
IT LOOKS LIKE YOUR DARLING DAUGHTER CHOSE DEATH.
MY DAUGHTER ISN'T THAT WEAK.
AH, A DOTING FATHER.

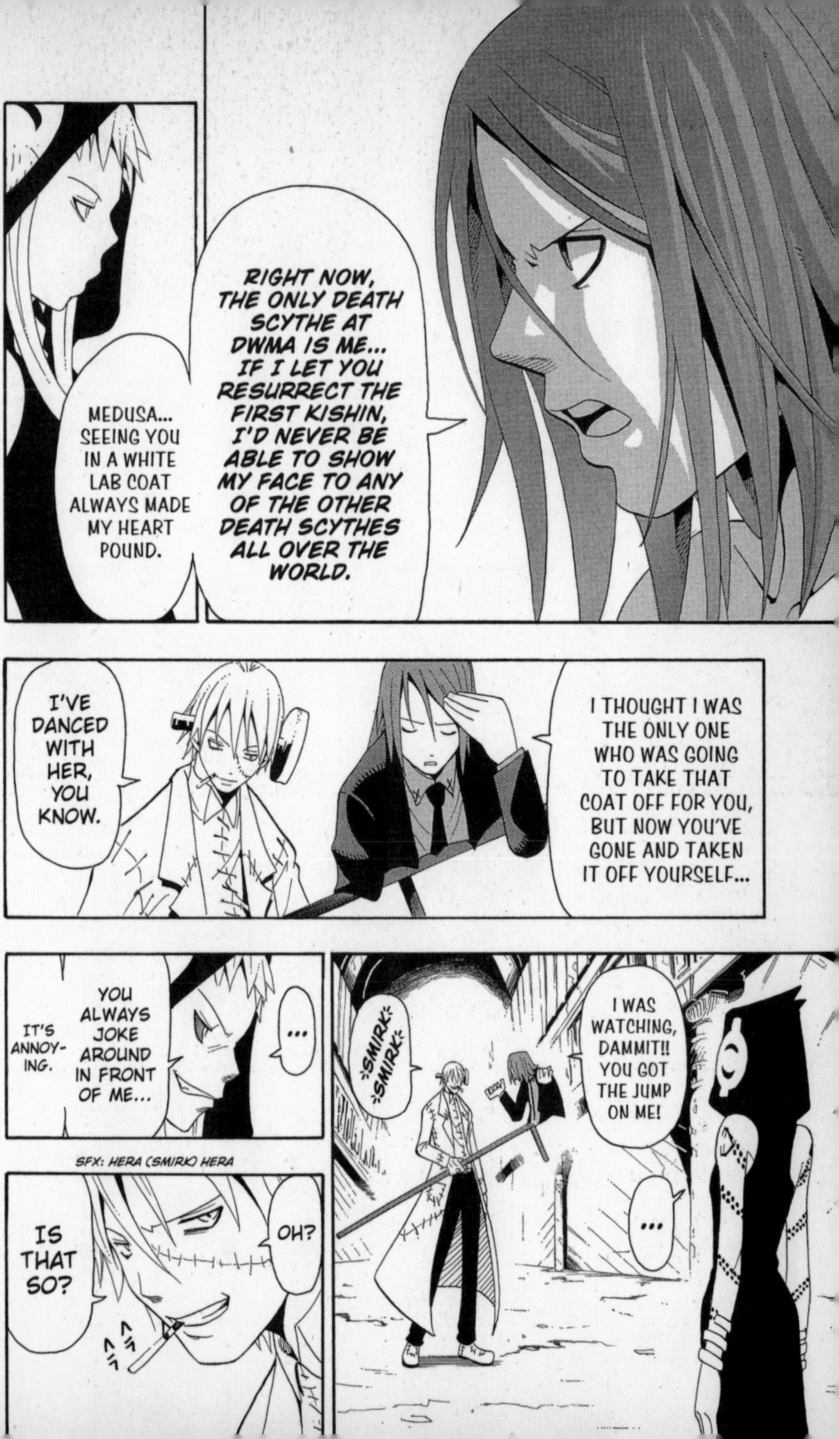
RIGHT NOW, THE ONLY DEATH SCYTHE AT DWMA IS ME... IF I LET YOU RESURRECT THE FIRST KISHIN, I'D NEVER BE ABLE TO SHOW MY FACE TO ANY OF THE OTHER DEATH SCYTHES ALL OVER THE WORLD.
MEDUSA... SEEING YOU IN A WHITE LAB COAT ALWAYS MADE MY HEART POUND.
I THOUGHT I WAS THE ONLY ONE WHO WAS GOING TO TAKE THAT COAT OFF FOR YOU, BUT NOW YOU'VE GONE AND TAKEN IT OFF YOURSELF...
I'VE DANCED WITH HER, YOU KNOW.
I WAS WATCHING, DAMMIT!! YOU GOT THE JUMP ON ME!
SMIRK SMIRK
...
...
YOU ALWAYS JOKE AROUND IN FRONT OF ME...
IT'S ANNOY-ING.
SFX: HERA (SMIRK) HERA
OH?
IS THAT SO?

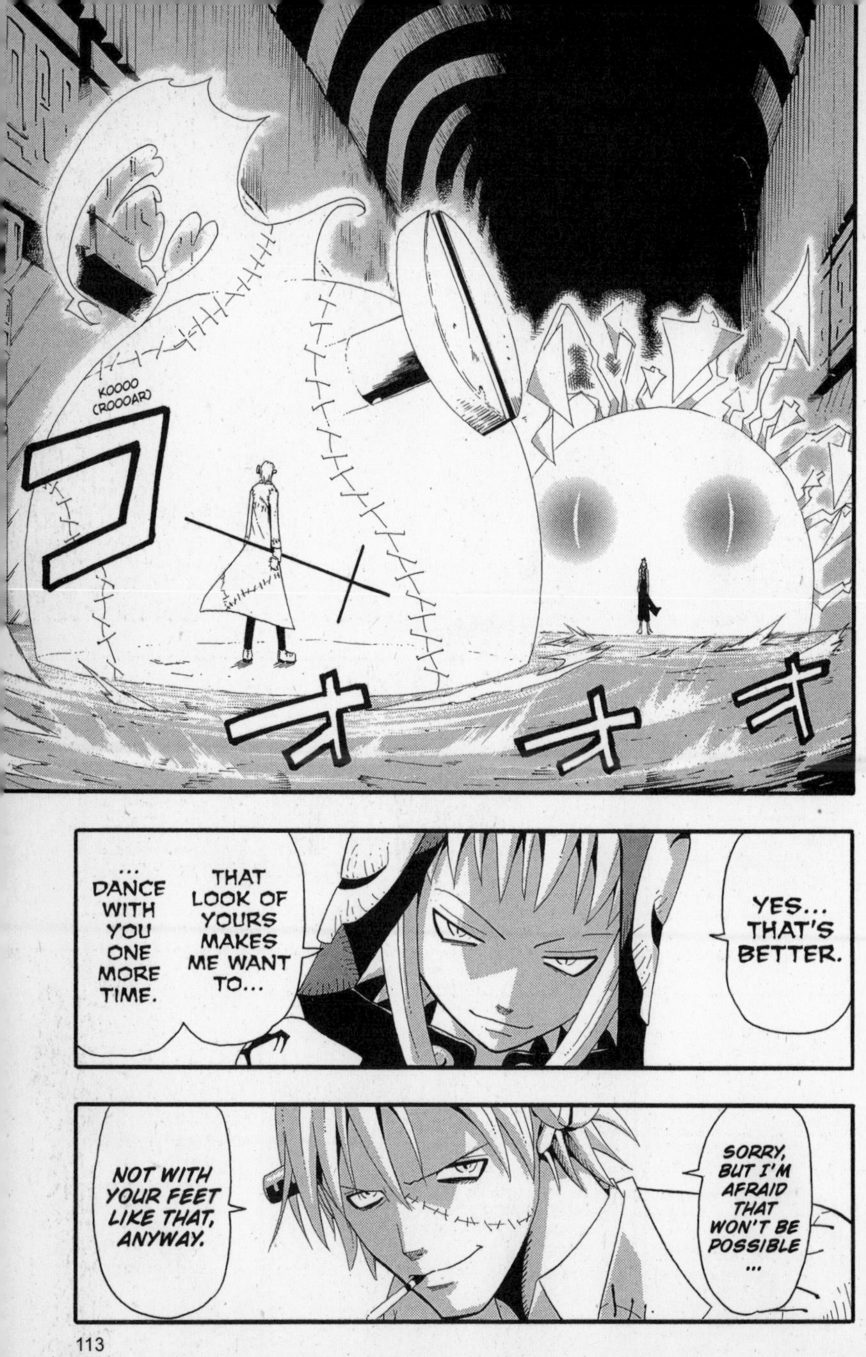
KOOOO (ROOOAR)
YES... THAT'S BETTER.
THAT LOOK OF YOURS MAKES ME WANT TO...
... DANCE WITH YOU ONE MORE TIME.
SORRY, BUT I'M AFRAID THAT WON'T BE POSSIBLE ...
NOT WITH YOUR FEET LIKE THAT, ANYWAY.

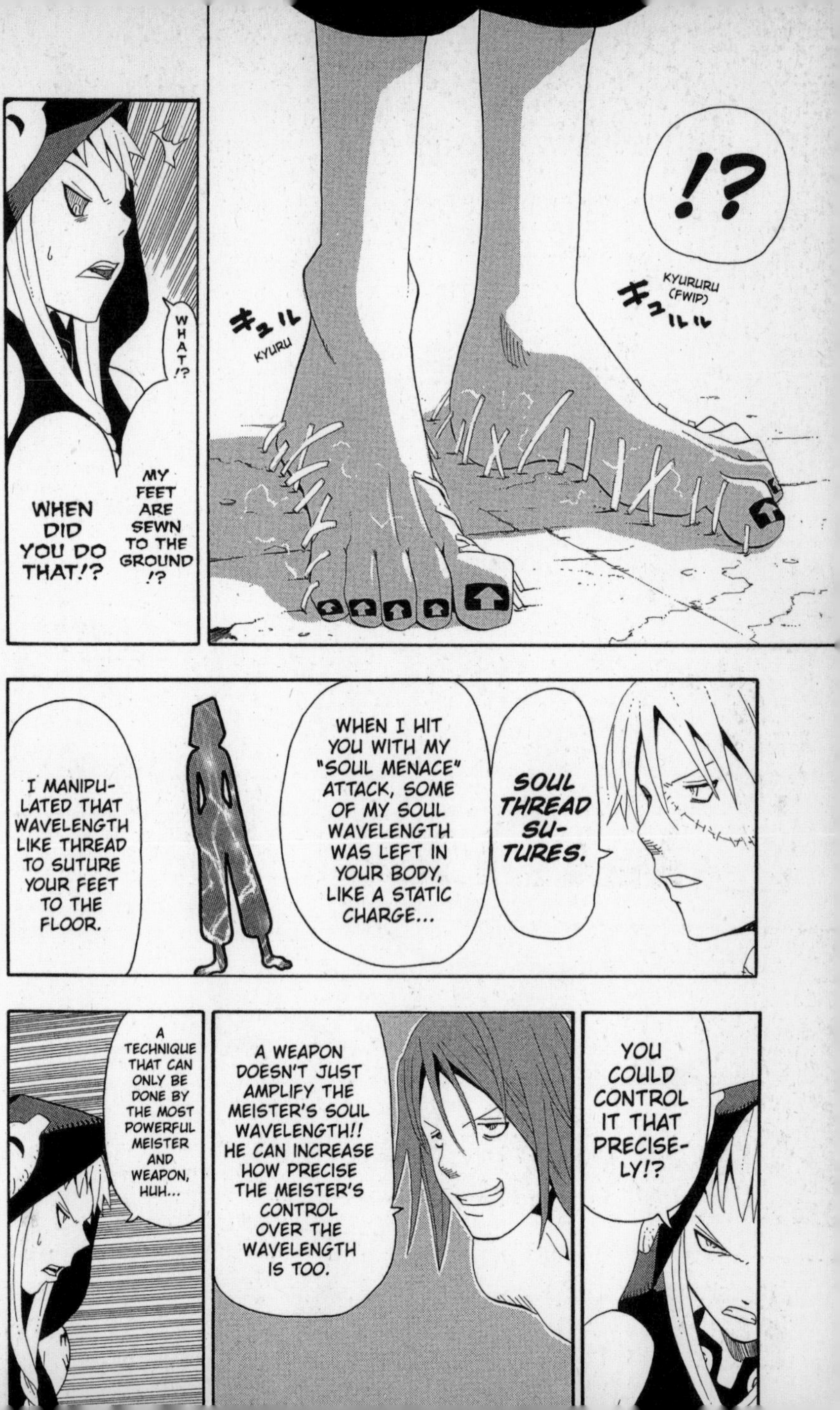
!?
KYURURU (FWIP)
キュルル
キュル
KYURU
WHAT!?
MY FEET ARE SEWN TO THE GROUND!?
WHEN DID YOU DO THAT!?
SOUL THREAD SUTURES.
WHEN I HIT YOU WITH MY "SOUL MENACE" ATTACK, SOME OF MY SOUL WAVELENGTH WAS LEFT IN YOUR BODY, LIKE A STATIC CHARGE...
I MANIPULATED THAT WAVELENGTH LIKE THREAD TO SUTURE YOUR FEET TO THE FLOOR.
YOU COULD CONTROL IT THAT PRECISELY!?
A WEAPON DOESN'T JUST AMPLIFY THE MEISTER'S SOUL WAVELENGTH!! HE CAN INCREASE HOW PRECISE THE MEISTER'S CONTROL OVER THE WAVELENGTH IS TOO.
A TECHNIQUE THAT CAN ONLY BE DONE BY THE MOST POWERFUL MEISTER AND WEAPON, HUH...

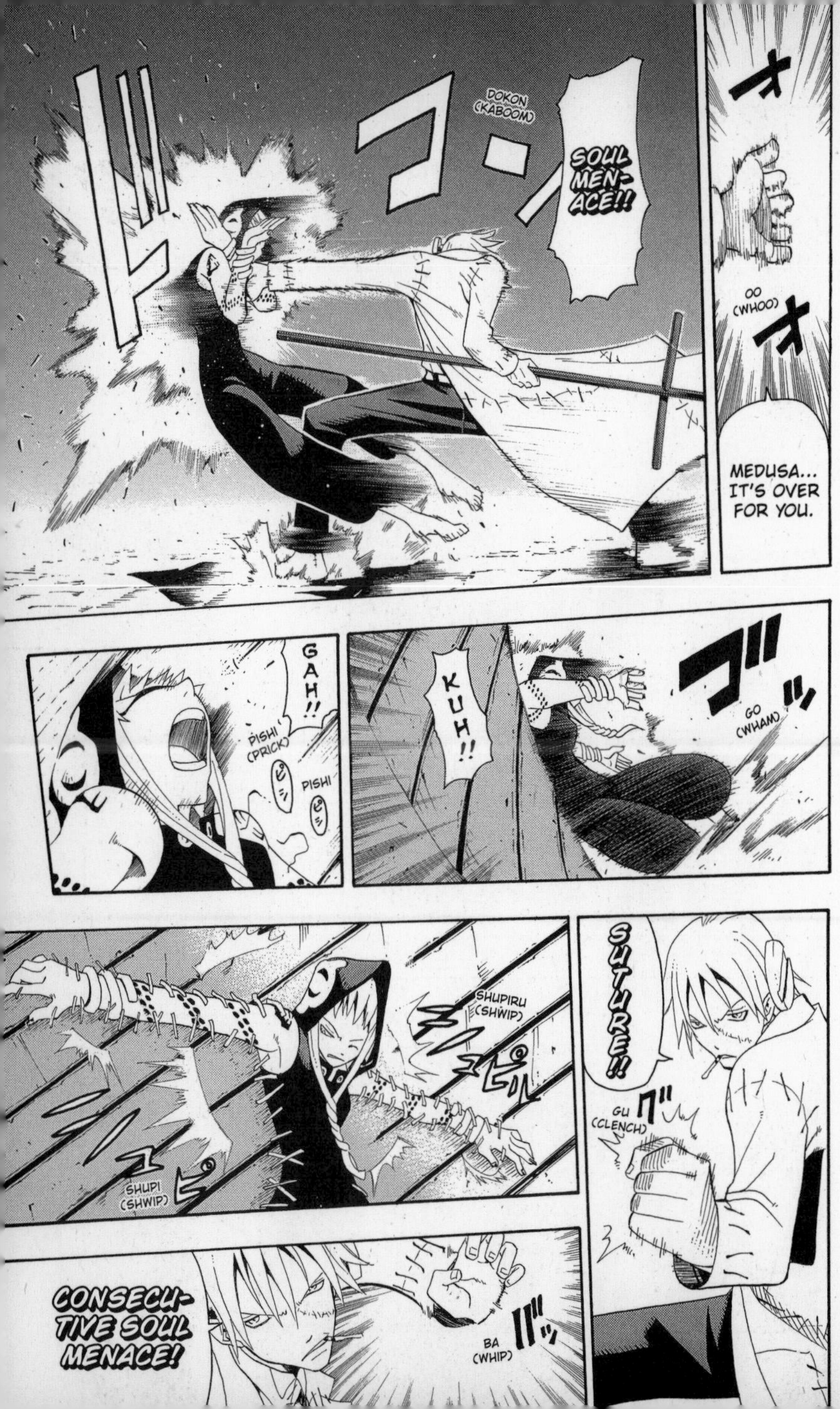
OO (WHOO)
MEDUSA... IT'S OVER FOR YOU.
DOKON (KABOOM)
SOUL MEN-ACE!!
GO (WHAM)
KUH!!
GAH!!
PISHI (PRICK)
PISHI
SUTURE!!
GU (CLENCH)
SHUPIRU (SHWIP)
SHUPI (SHWIP)
BA (WHIP)
CONSECU-TIVE SOUL MENACE!

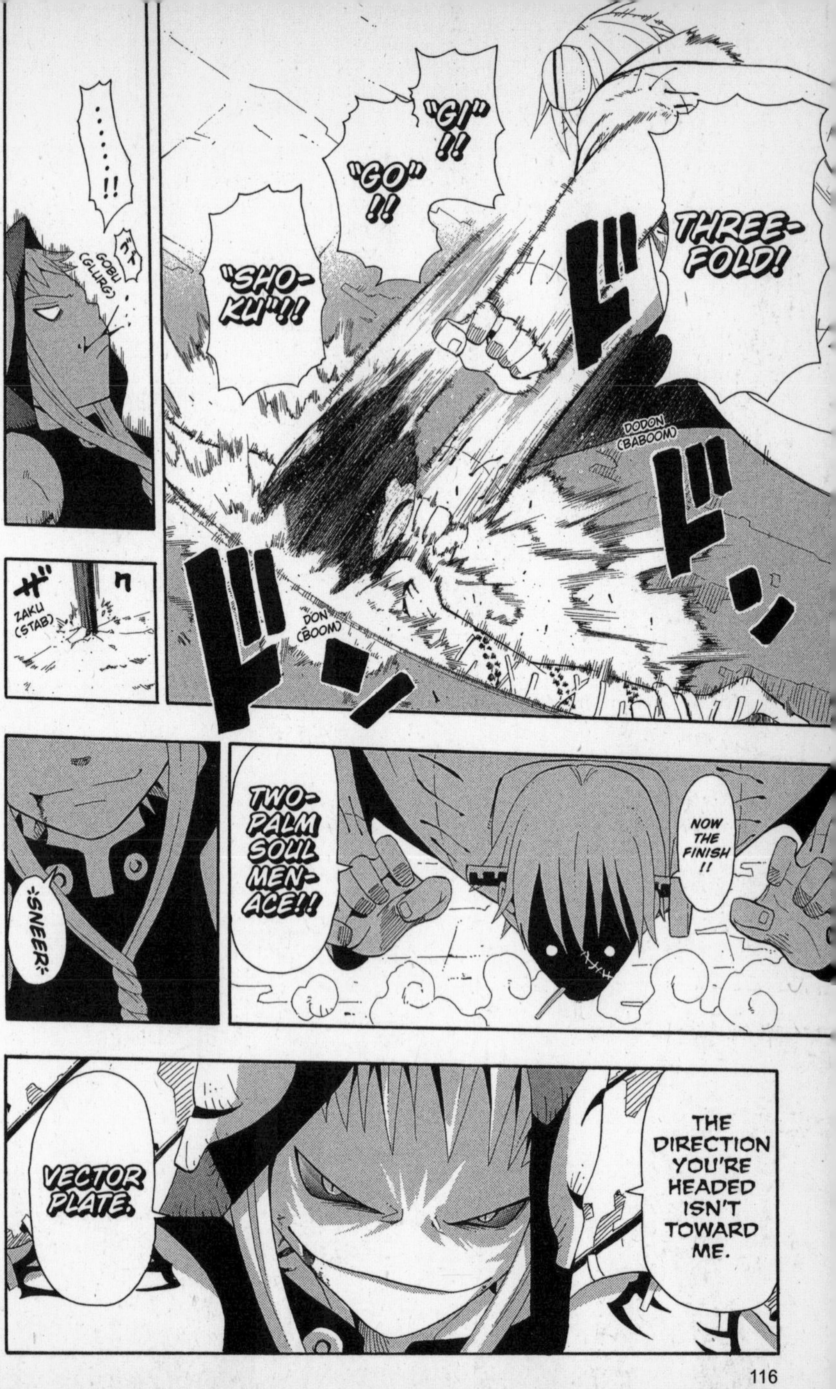
THREE-FOLD!
"GI"!!
"GO"!!
"SHO-KU"!!
DODON (BABOOM)
DON (BOOM)
......!!
GOBU (GLURG)
ZAKU (STAB)
NOW THE FINISH!!
TWO-PALM SOUL MEN-ACE!!
SNEER
THE DIRECTION YOU'RE HEADED ISN'T TOWARD ME.
VECTOR PLATE.

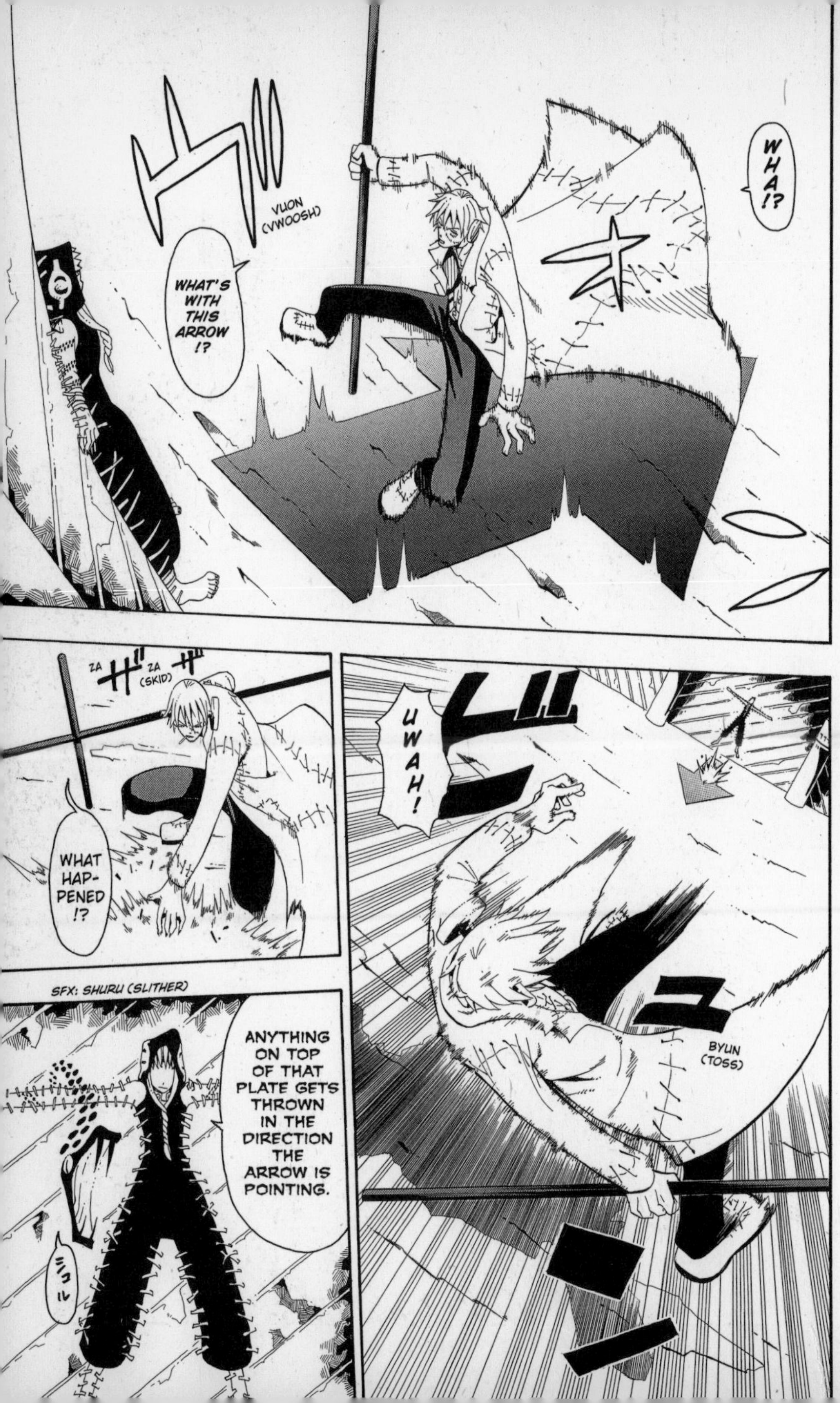
WHA!?
VUON (VWOOSH)
WHAT'S WITH THIS ARROW!?
UWAH!
BYUN (TOSS)
ZA ZA (SKID)
WHAT HAPPENED!?
SFX: SHURU (SLITHER)
ANYTHING ON TOP OF THAT PLATE GETS THROWN IN THE DIRECTION THE ARROW IS POINTING.

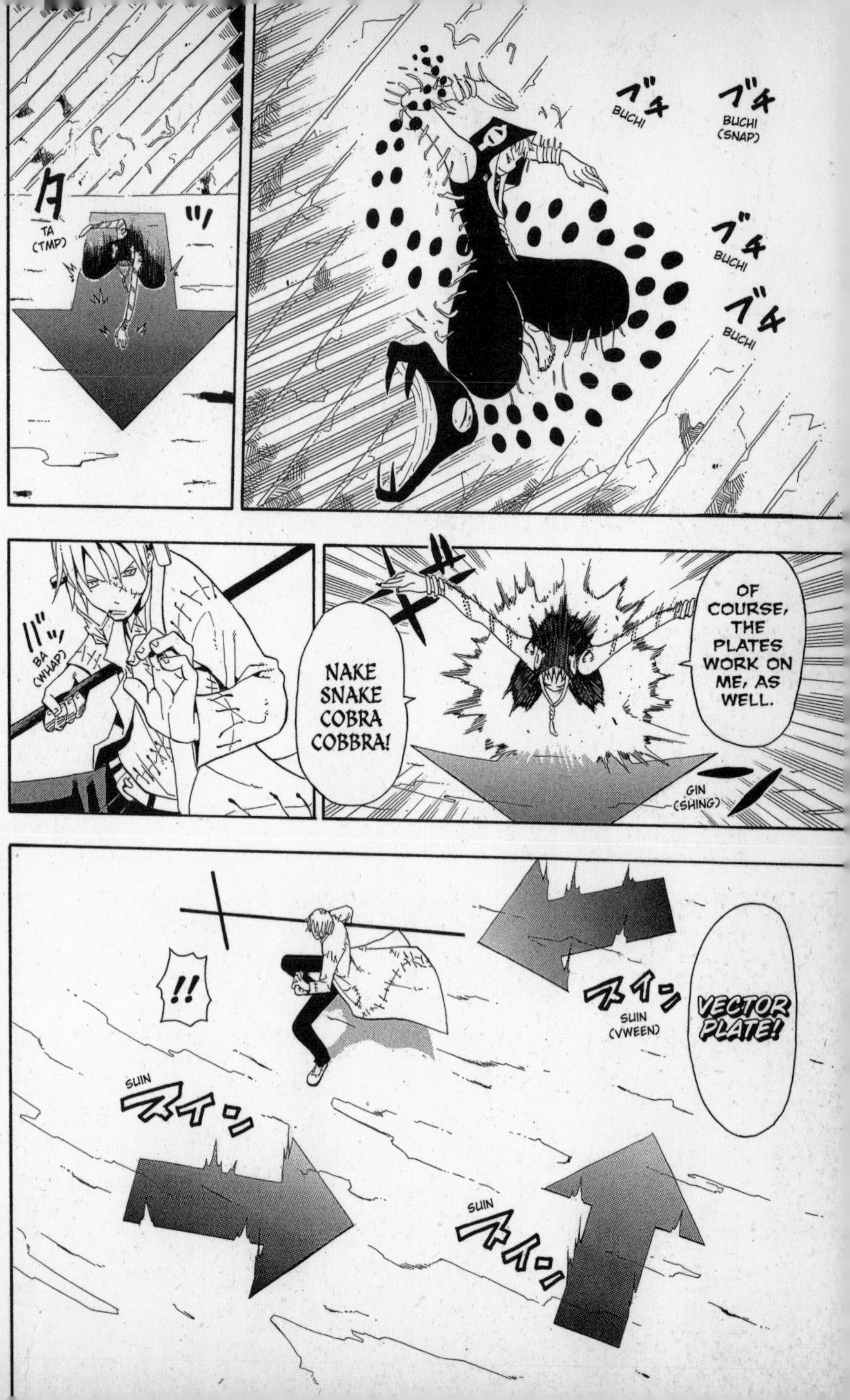
BUCHI (SNAP)
BUCHI
BUCHI
BUCHI
TA (TMP)
OF COURSE, THE PLATES WORK ON ME, AS WELL.
NAKE SNAKE COBRA COBBRA!
GIN (SHING)
BA (WHAP)
VECTOR PLATE!
SUIN (VWEEN)
!!
SUIN
SUIN

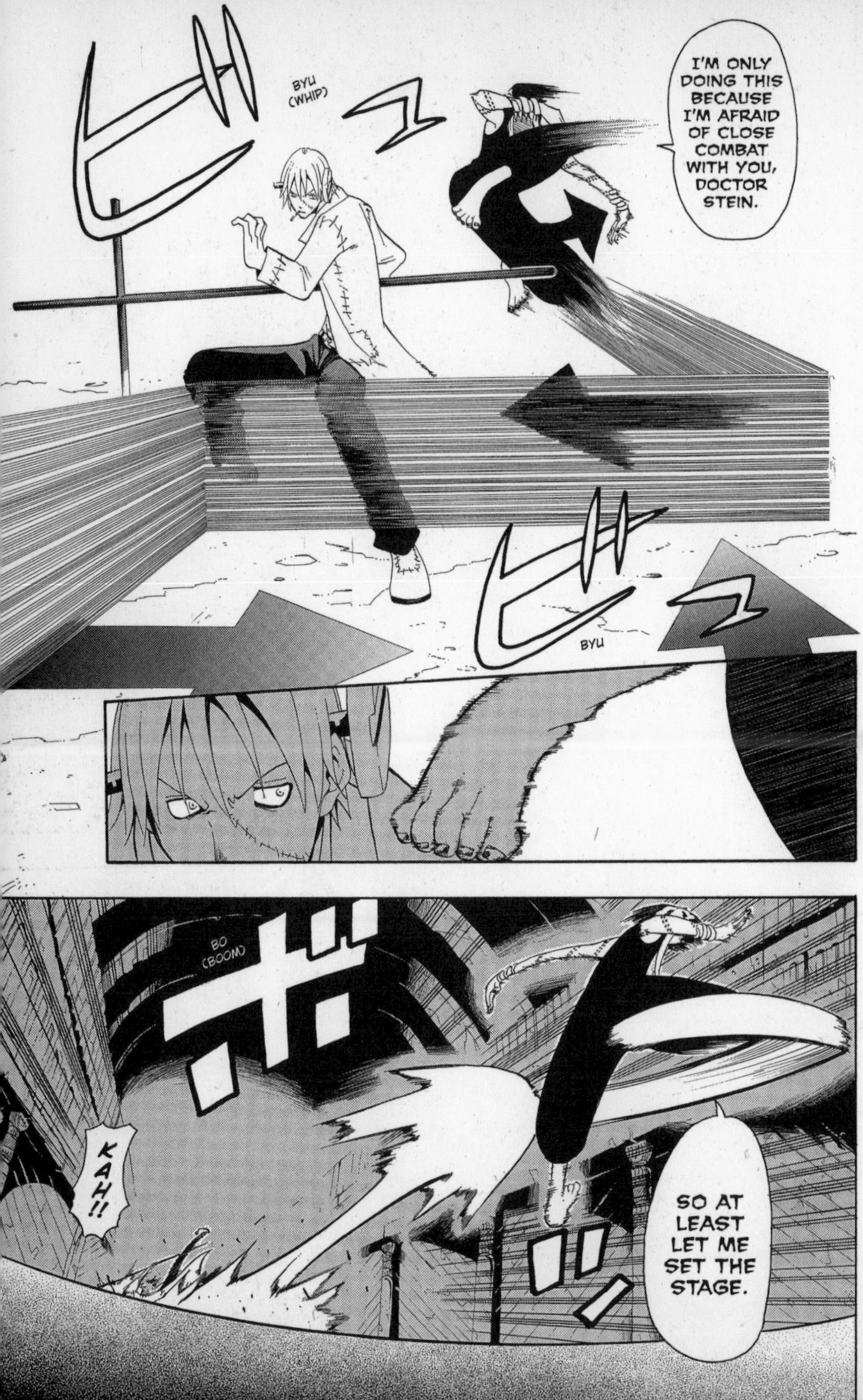
I'M ONLY DOING THIS BECAUSE I'M AFRAID OF CLOSE COMBAT WITH YOU, DOCTOR STEIN.
BYU (WHIP)
BYU
BO (BOOM)
SO AT LEAST LET ME SET THE STAGE.
KAH!!

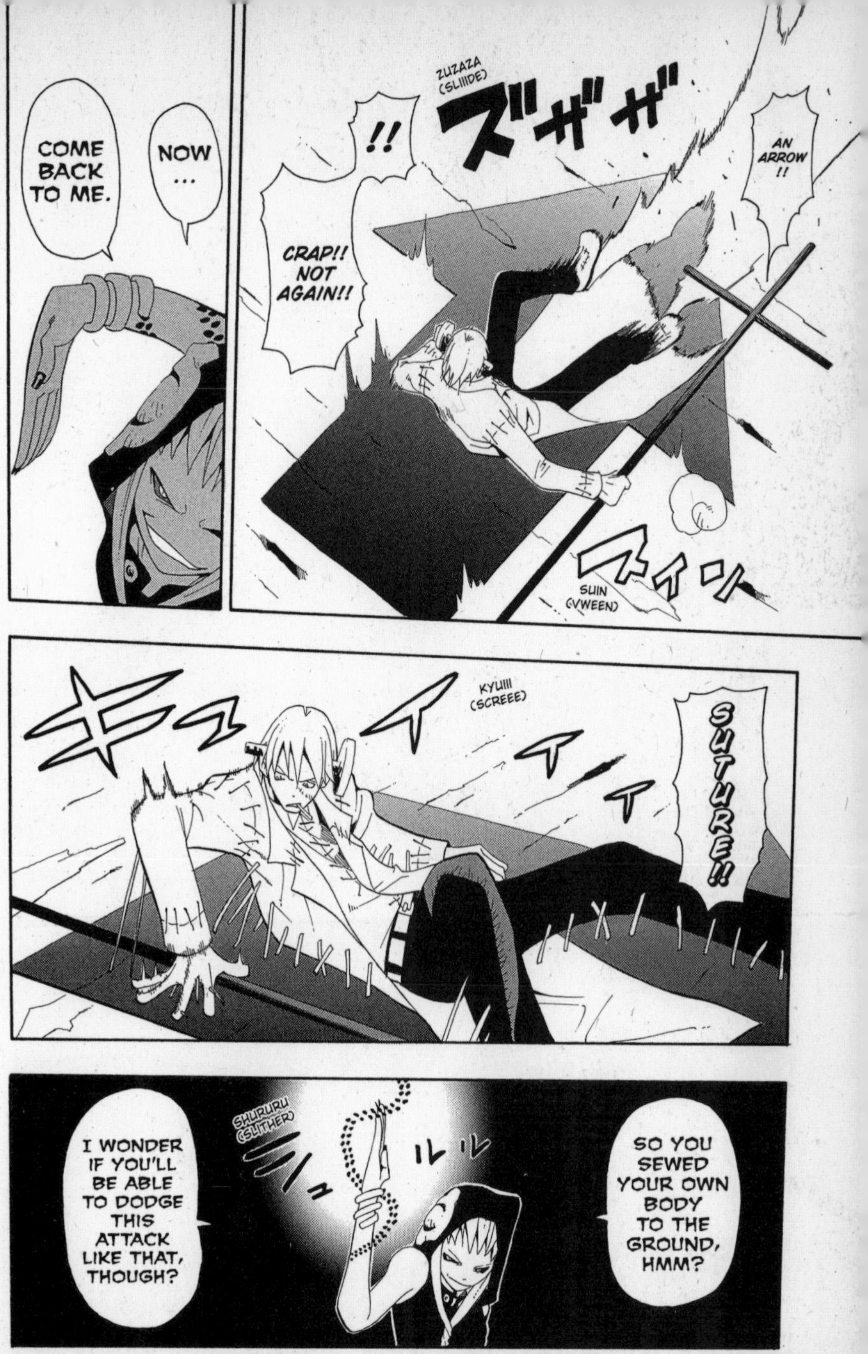
AN ARROW !!
ZUZAZA (SLIIIDE)
!!
CRAP!! NOT AGAIN!!
SUIN (VWEEN)
NOW ...
COME BACK TO ME.
SUTURE!!
KYUIII (SCREEE)
SO YOU SEWED YOUR OWN BODY TO THE GROUND, HMM?
SHURURU (SLITHER)
I WONDER IF YOU'LL BE ABLE TO DODGE THIS ATTACK LIKE THAT, THOUGH?

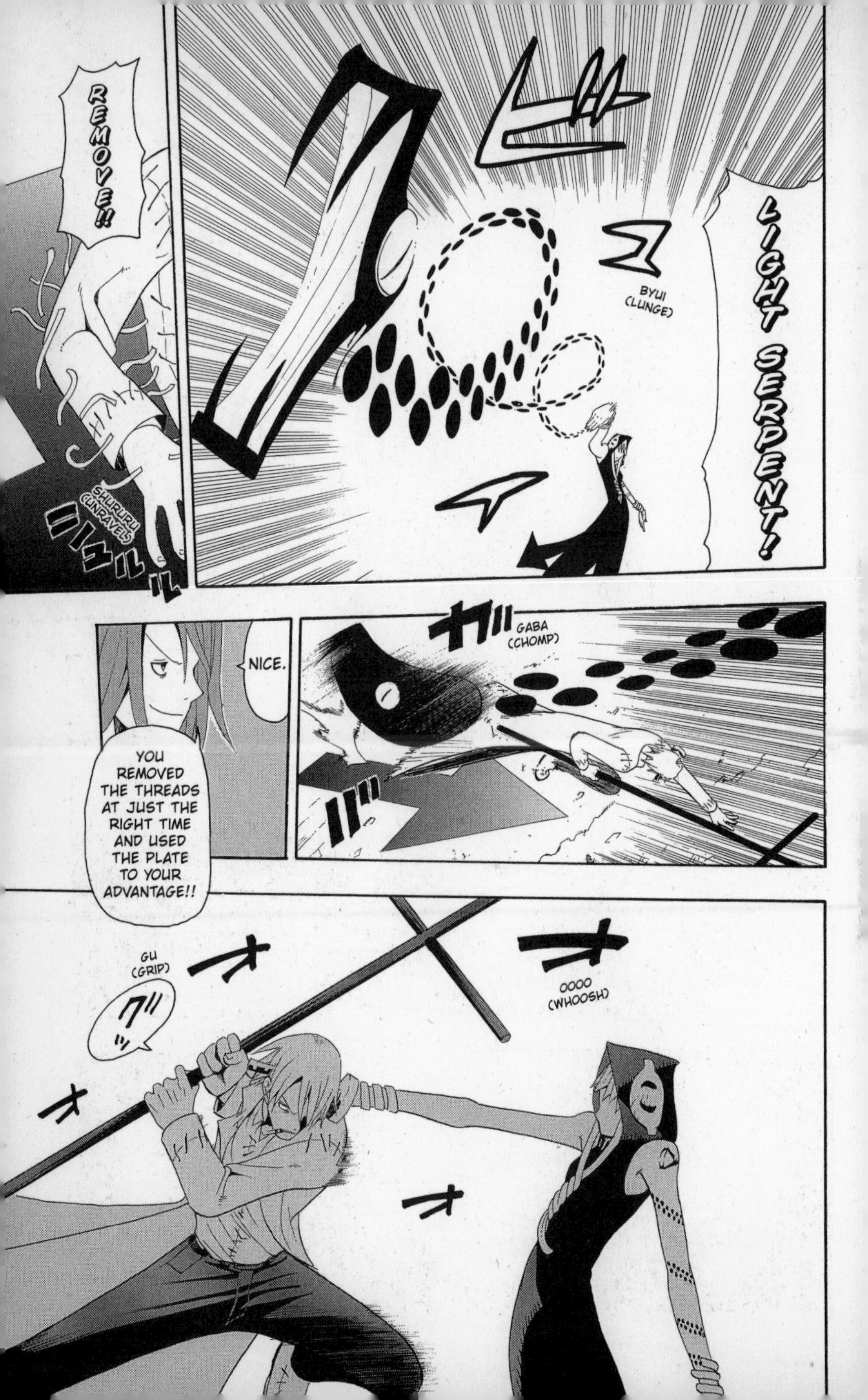
LIGHT SERPENT!
BYUI (LUNGE)
REMOVE!!
SHURURU (UNRAVELS)
GABA (CHOMP)
NICE.
YOU REMOVED THE THREADS AT JUST THE RIGHT TIME AND USED THE PLATE TO YOUR ADVANTAGE!!
OOOO (WHOOSH)
GU (GRIP)

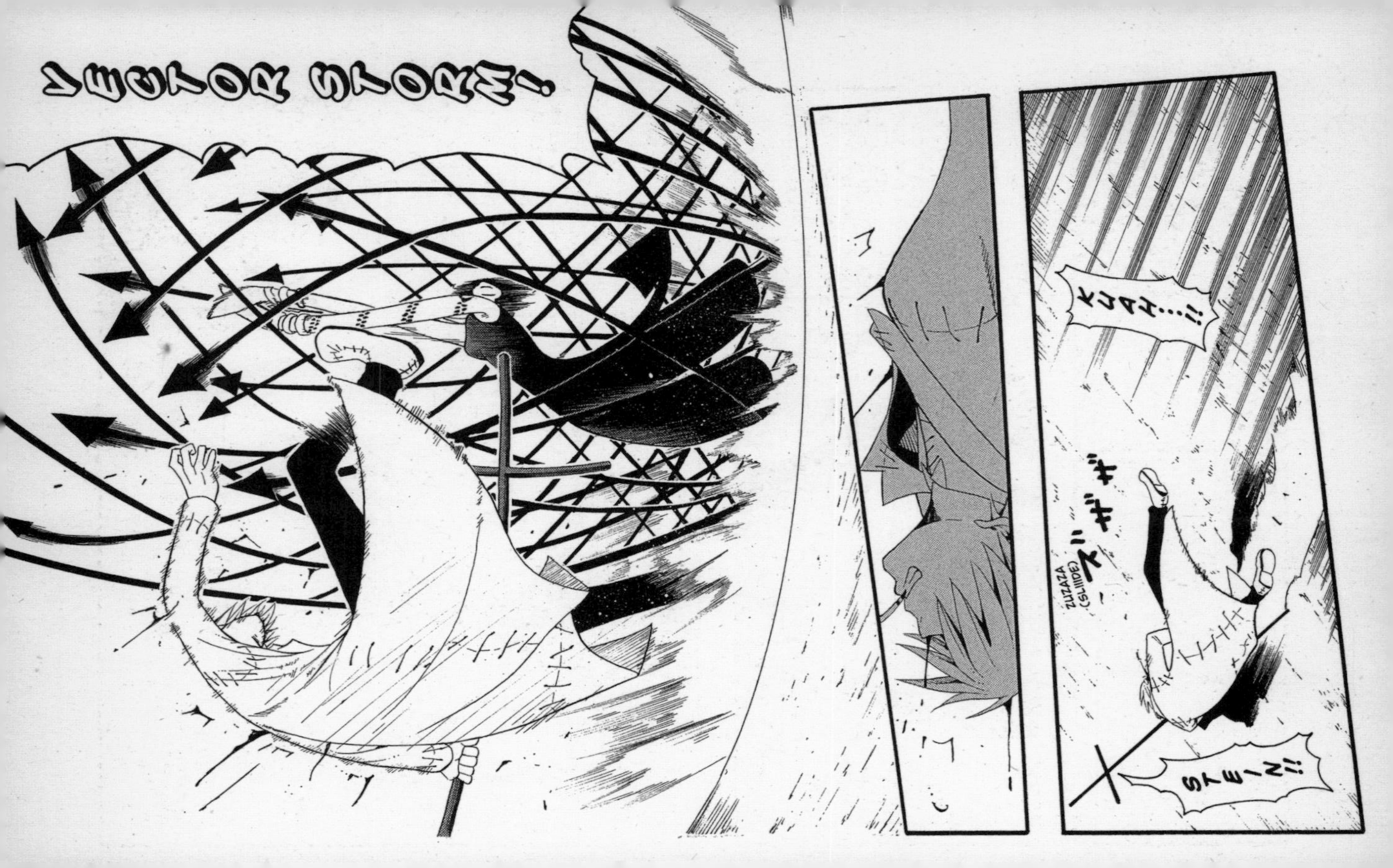
KUAH...!!
ZUZAZA (SLIIIDE)
STEIN!!
VECTOR STORM!

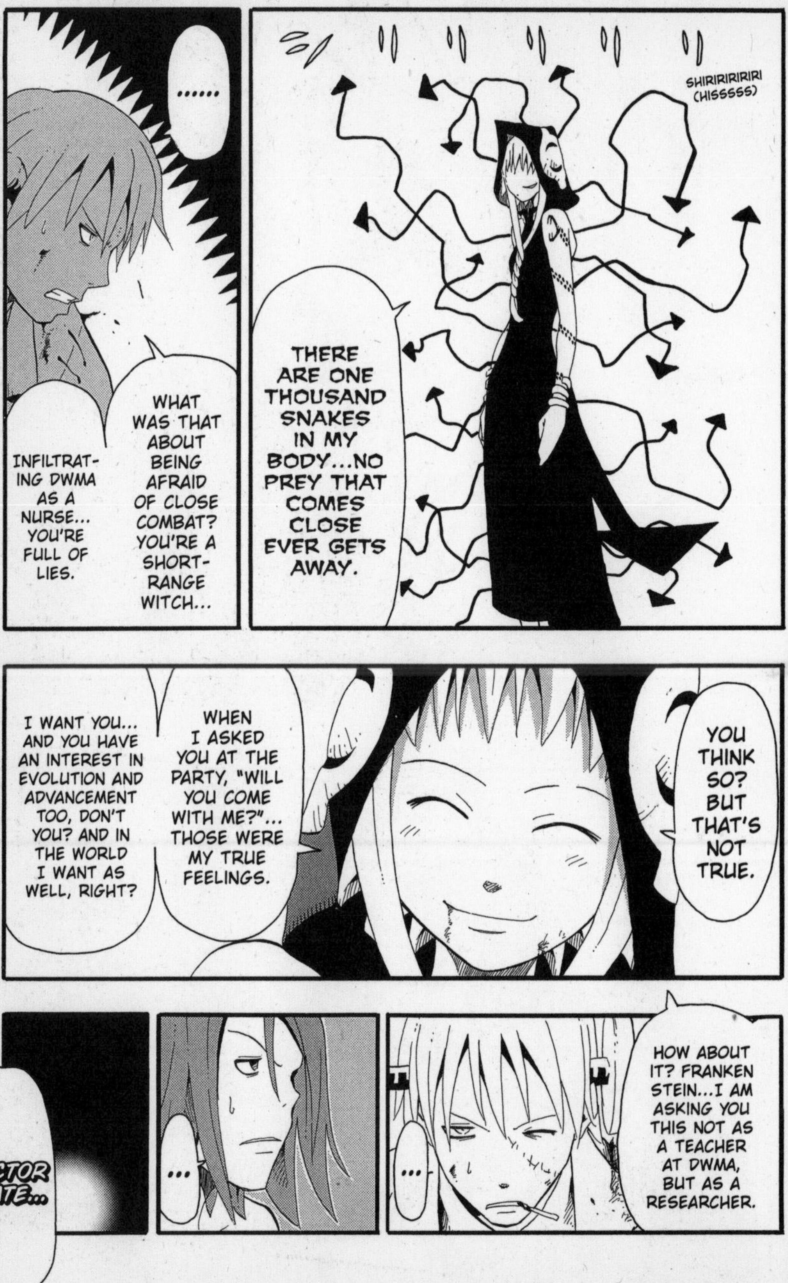
SHIRIRIRIRIRI (HISSSSS)
THERE ARE ONE THOUSAND SNAKES IN MY BODY...NO PREY THAT COMES CLOSE EVER GETS AWAY.
......
WHAT WAS THAT ABOUT BEING AFRAID OF CLOSE COMBAT? YOU'RE A SHORT-RANGE WITCH...
INFILTRAT-ING DWMA AS A NURSE... YOU'RE FULL OF LIES.
YOU THINK SO? BUT THAT'S NOT TRUE.
WHEN I ASKED YOU AT THE PARTY, "WILL YOU COME WITH ME?"... THOSE WERE MY TRUE FEELINGS.
I WANT YOU... AND YOU HAVE AN INTEREST IN EVOLUTION AND ADVANCEMENT TOO, DON'T YOU? AND IN THE WORLD I WANT AS WELL, RIGHT?
HOW ABOUT IT? FRANKEN STEIN...I AM ASKING YOU THIS NOT AS A TEACHER AT DWMA, BUT AS A RESEARCHER.
...
...
VECTOR PLATE...

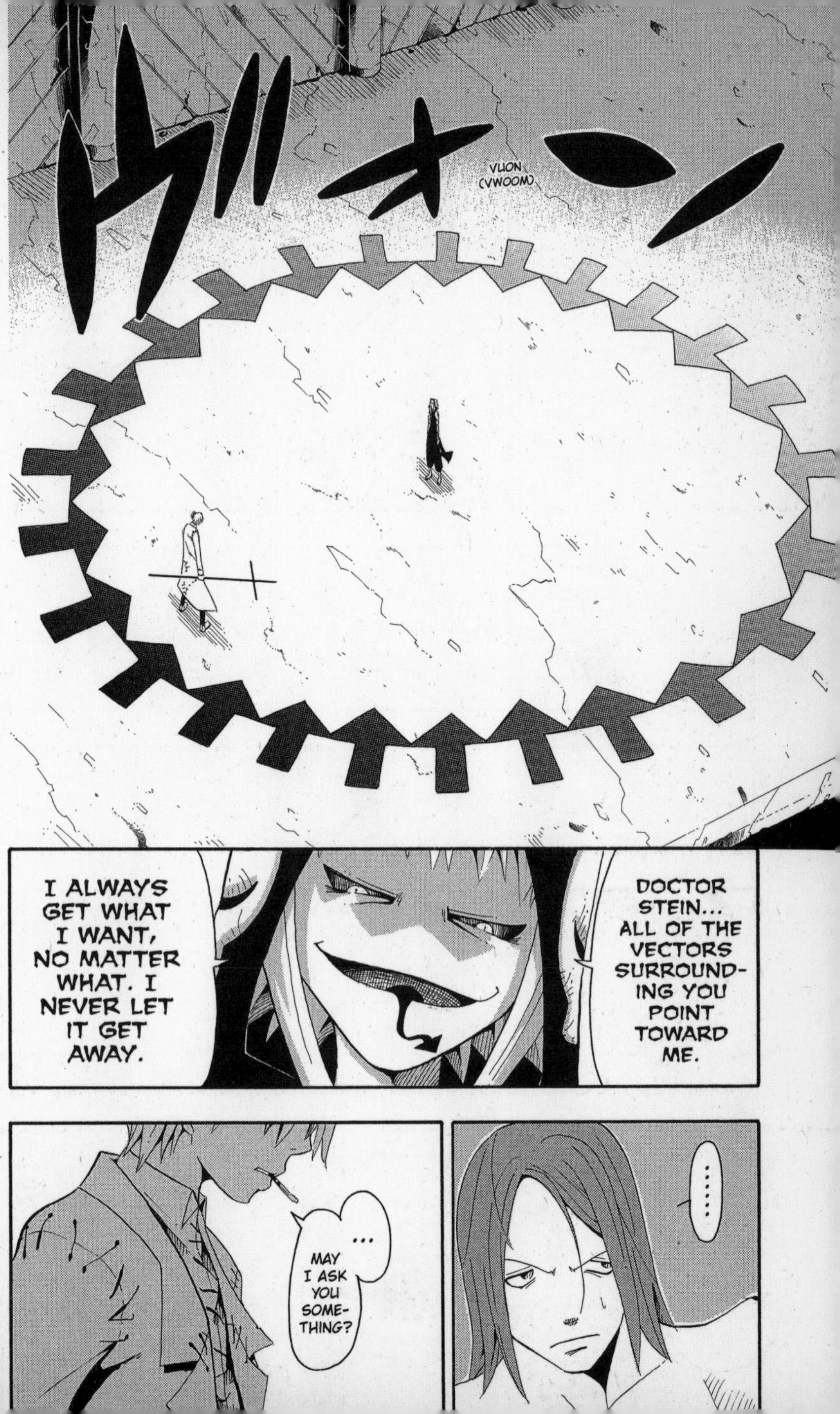
VUON (VWOOM)
DOCTOR STEIN... ALL OF THE VECTORS SURROUND-ING YOU POINT TOWARD ME.
I ALWAYS GET WHAT I WANT, NO MATTER WHAT. I NEVER LET IT GET AWAY.
......
... MAY I ASK YOU SOME-THING?

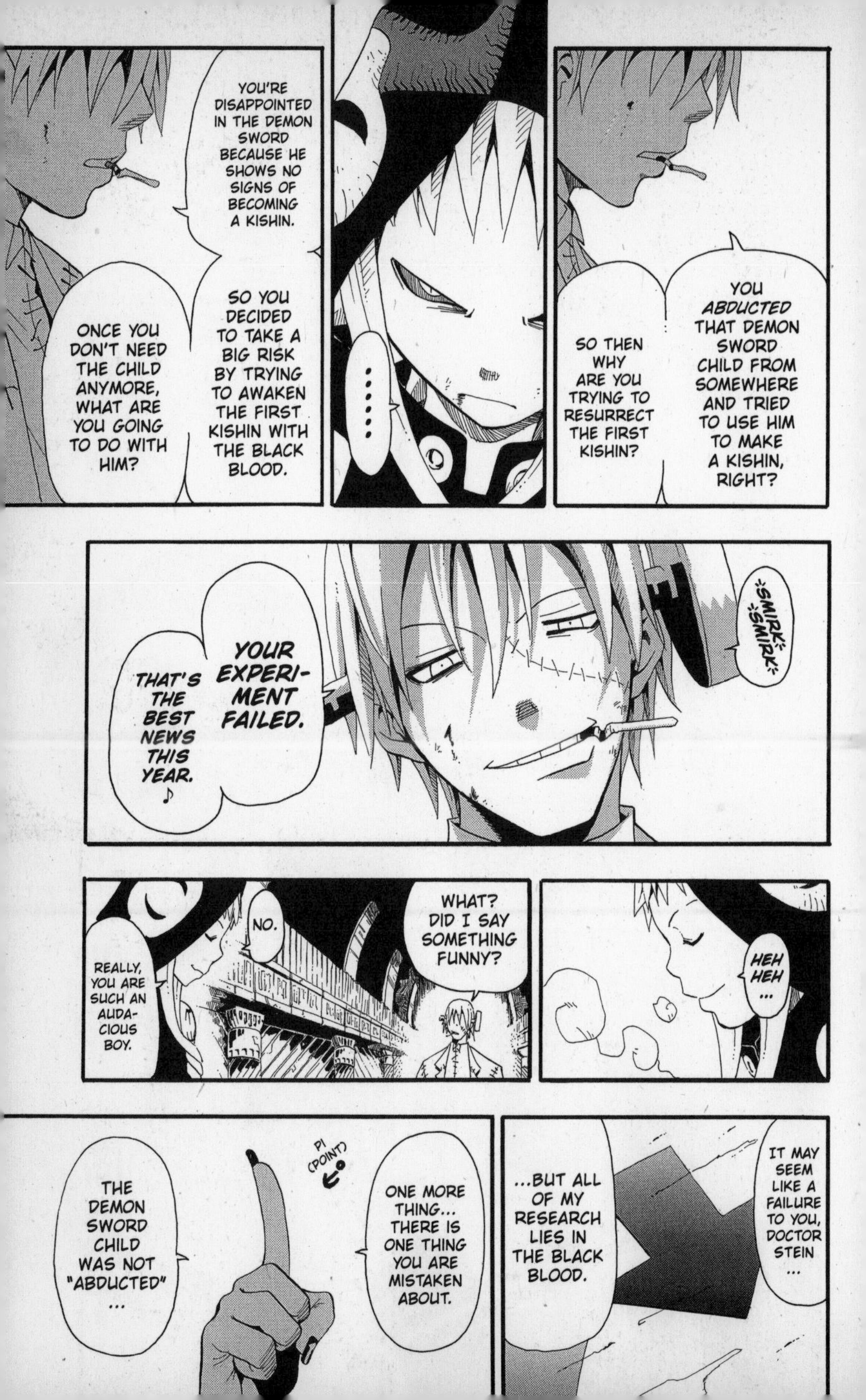
YOU ABDUCTED THAT DEMON SWORD CHILD FROM SOMEWHERE AND TRIED TO USE HIM TO MAKE A KISHIN, RIGHT?
SO THEN WHY ARE YOU TRYING TO RESURRECT THE FIRST KISHIN?
......
YOU'RE DISAPPOINTED IN THE DEMON SWORD BECAUSE HE SHOWS NO SIGNS OF BECOMING A KISHIN.
SO YOU DECIDED TO TAKE A BIG RISK BY TRYING TO AWAKEN THE FIRST KISHIN WITH THE BLACK BLOOD.
ONCE YOU DON'T NEED THE CHILD ANYMORE, WHAT ARE YOU GOING TO DO WITH HIM?
SMIRK *SMIRK*
YOUR EXPERIMENT FAILED.
THAT'S THE BEST NEWS THIS YEAR. ♪
HEH HEH ...
WHAT? DID I SAY SOMETHING FUNNY?
NO.
REALLY, YOU ARE SUCH AN AUDACIOUS BOY.
IT MAY SEEM LIKE A FAILURE TO YOU, DOCTOR STEIN ...
...BUT ALL OF MY RESEARCH LIES IN THE BLACK BLOOD.
PI (POINT)
ONE MORE THING... THERE IS ONE THING YOU ARE MISTAKEN ABOUT.
THE DEMON SWORD CHILD WAS NOT "ABDUCTED" ...

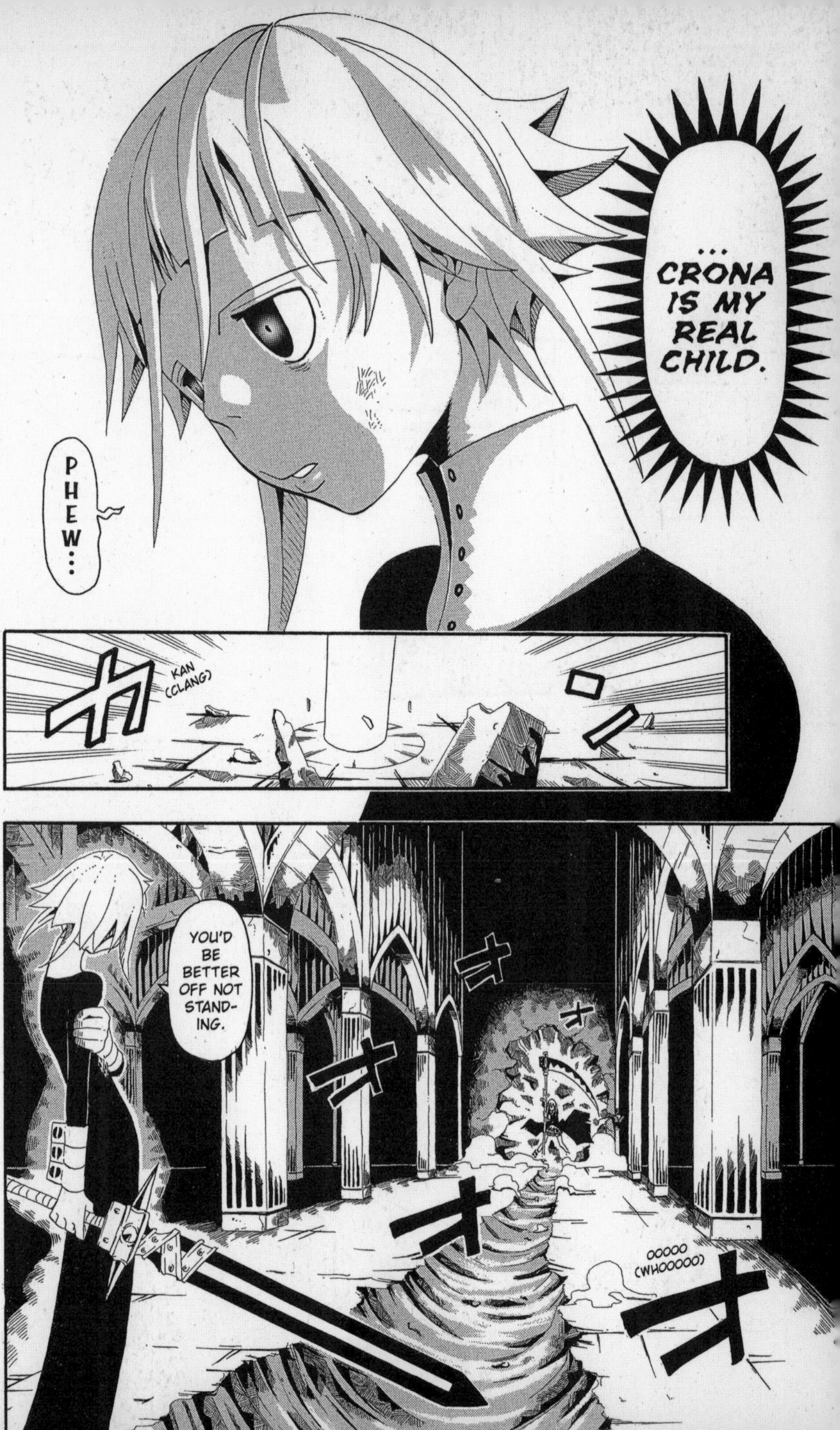

... CRONA IS MY REAL CHILD.
PHEW...
KAN (CLANG)
YOU'D BE BETTER OFF NOT STANDING.
OOOOO (WHOOOOO)

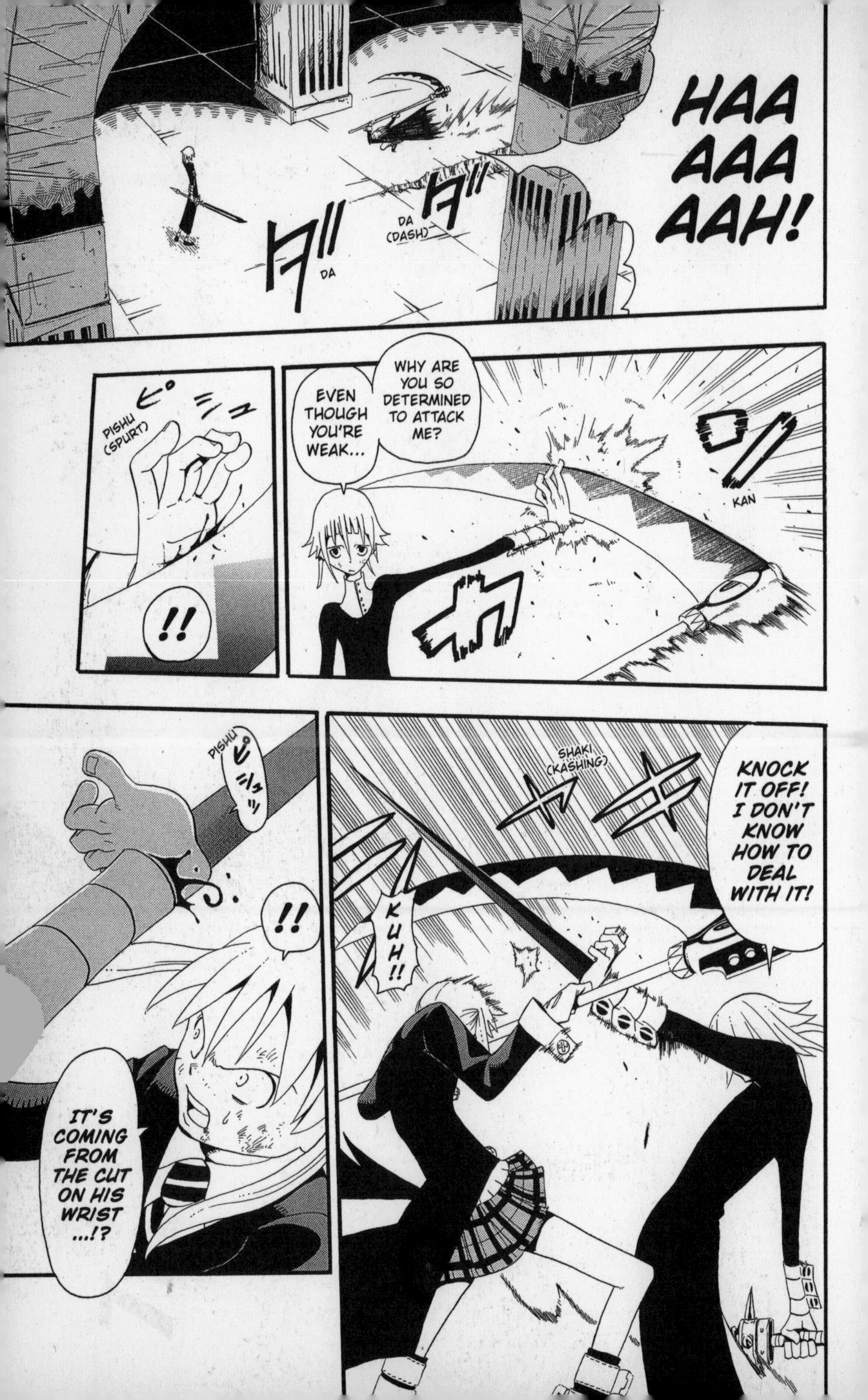
HAAA AAA AAH!
DA (DASH)
DA
KAN
WHY ARE YOU SO DETERMINED TO ATTACK ME?
EVEN THOUGH YOU'RE WEAK...
PISHU (SPURT)
!!
KNOCK IT OFF! I DON'T KNOW HOW TO DEAL WITH IT!
SHAKI (KASHING)
KUH!!
PISHU
!!
IT'S COMING FROM THE CUT ON HIS WRIST ...!?

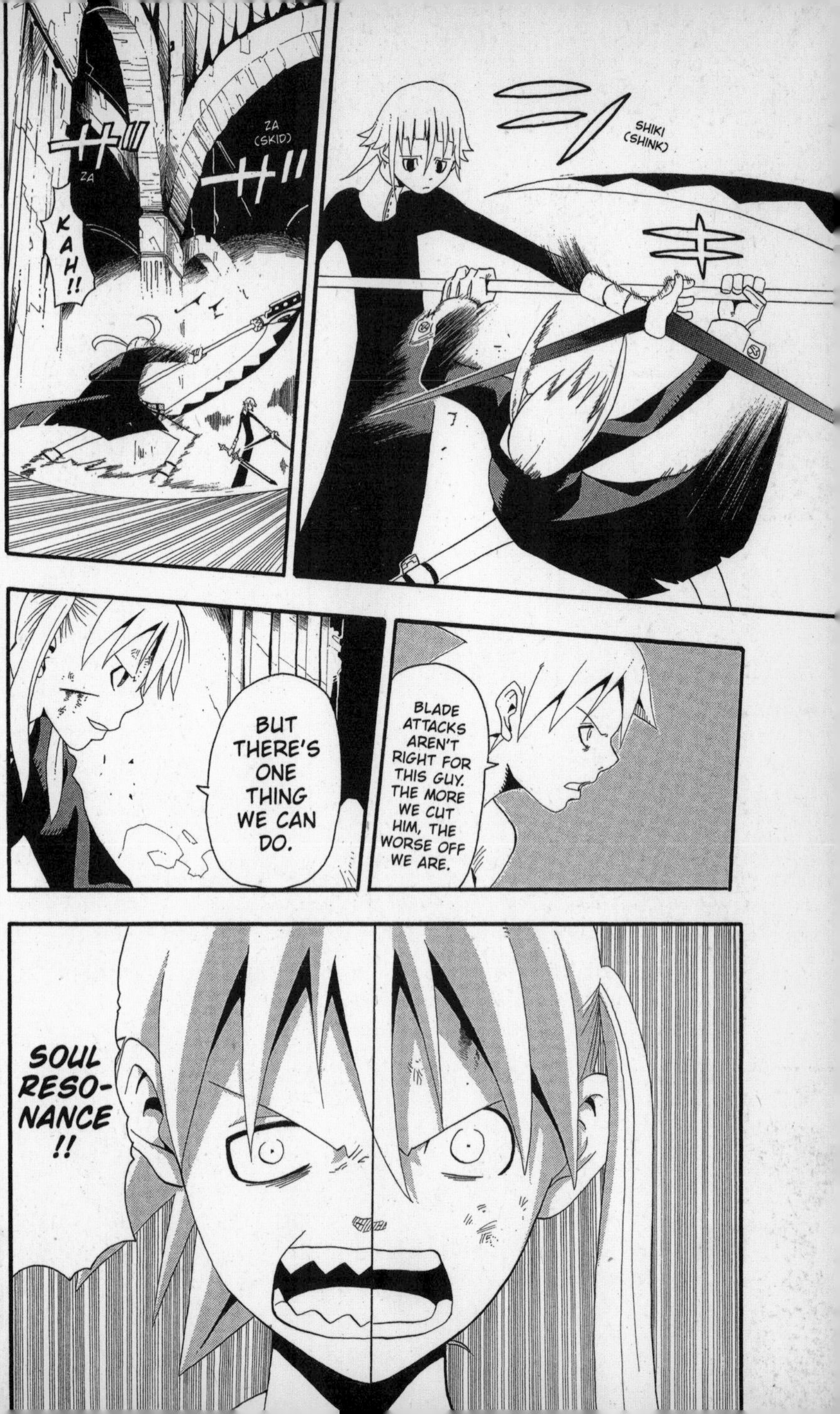
SHIKI (SHINK)
ZA (SKID)
ZA
KAH!!
BLADE ATTACKS AREN'T RIGHT FOR THIS GUY. THE MORE WE CUT HIM, THE WORSE OFF WE ARE.
BUT THERE'S ONE THING WE CAN DO.
SOUL RESONANCE!!

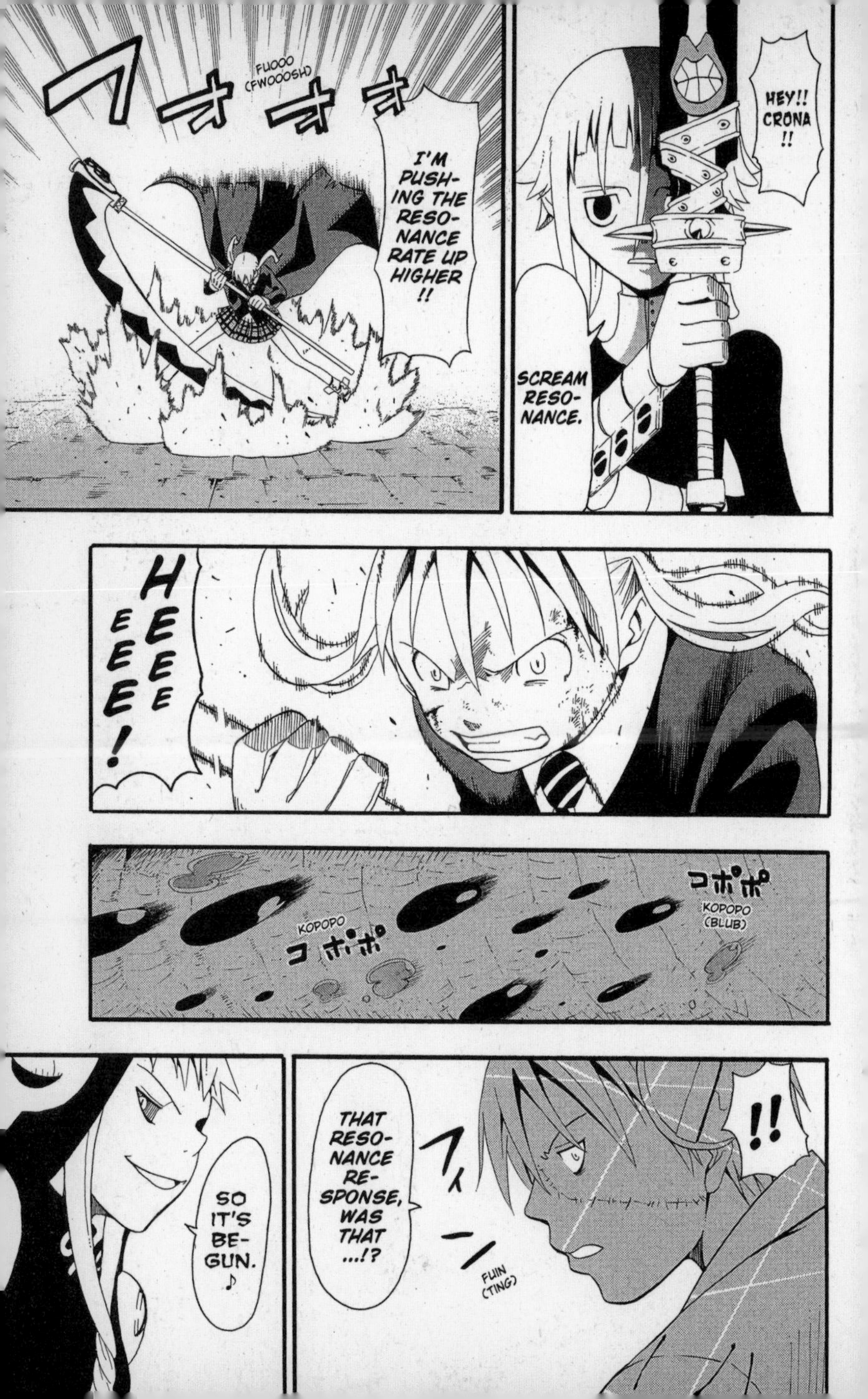

HEY!! CRONA!!
SCREAM RESONANCE.
I'M PUSHING THE RESONANCE RATE UP HIGHER!!
フォォォ
FUOOO (FWOOOSH)
HEEEEEEE!
コポポ
KOPOPO (BLUB)
KOPOPO
コポポ
!!
THAT RESONANCE RESPONSE, WAS THAT...!?
ヘィー
FUIN (TING)
SO IT'S BEGUN. ♪

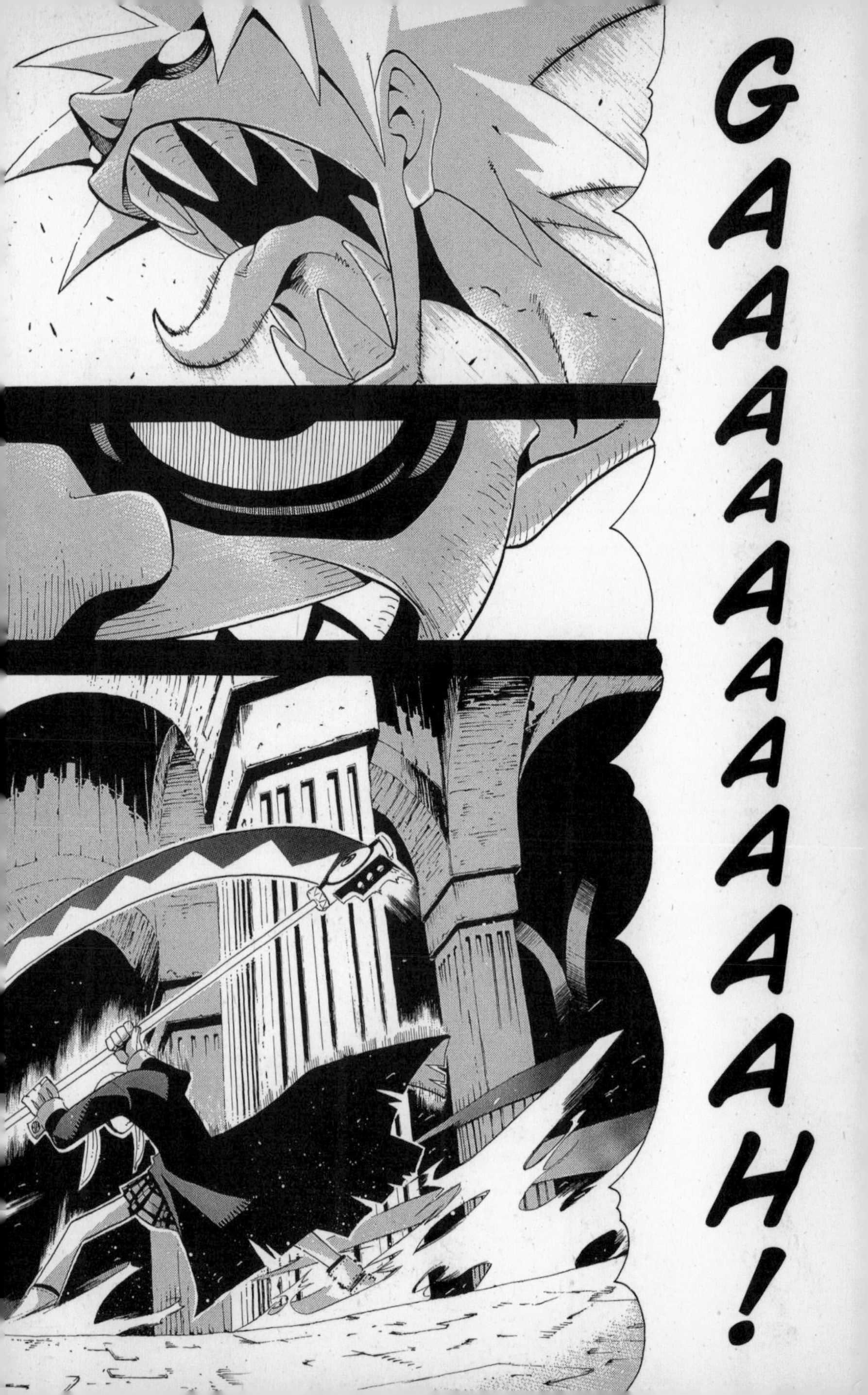
GAAAAAAAAAH!

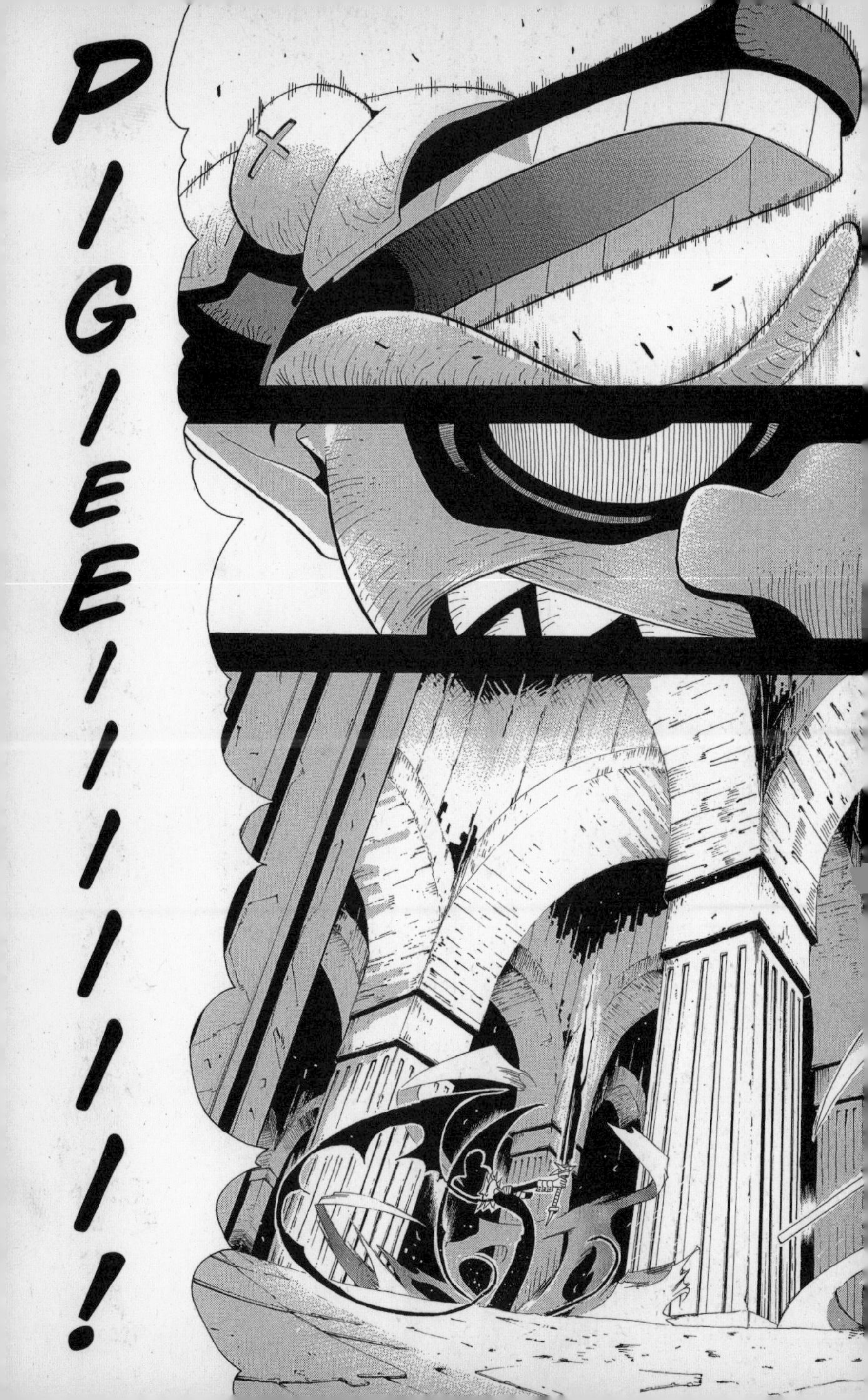
PIGIEEIIIII!

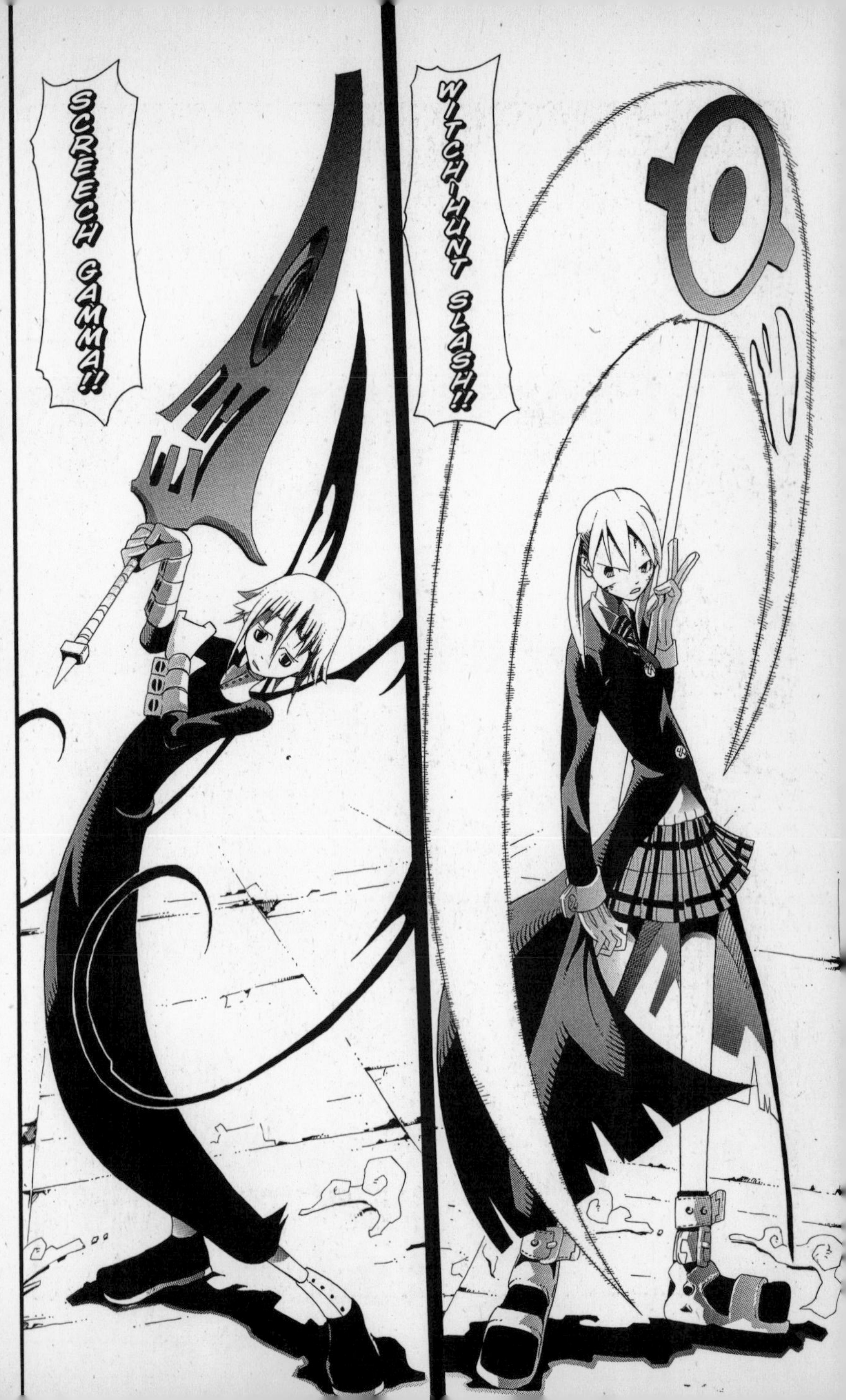
WITCH-HUNT SLASH!!
SCREEECH GAMMA!!

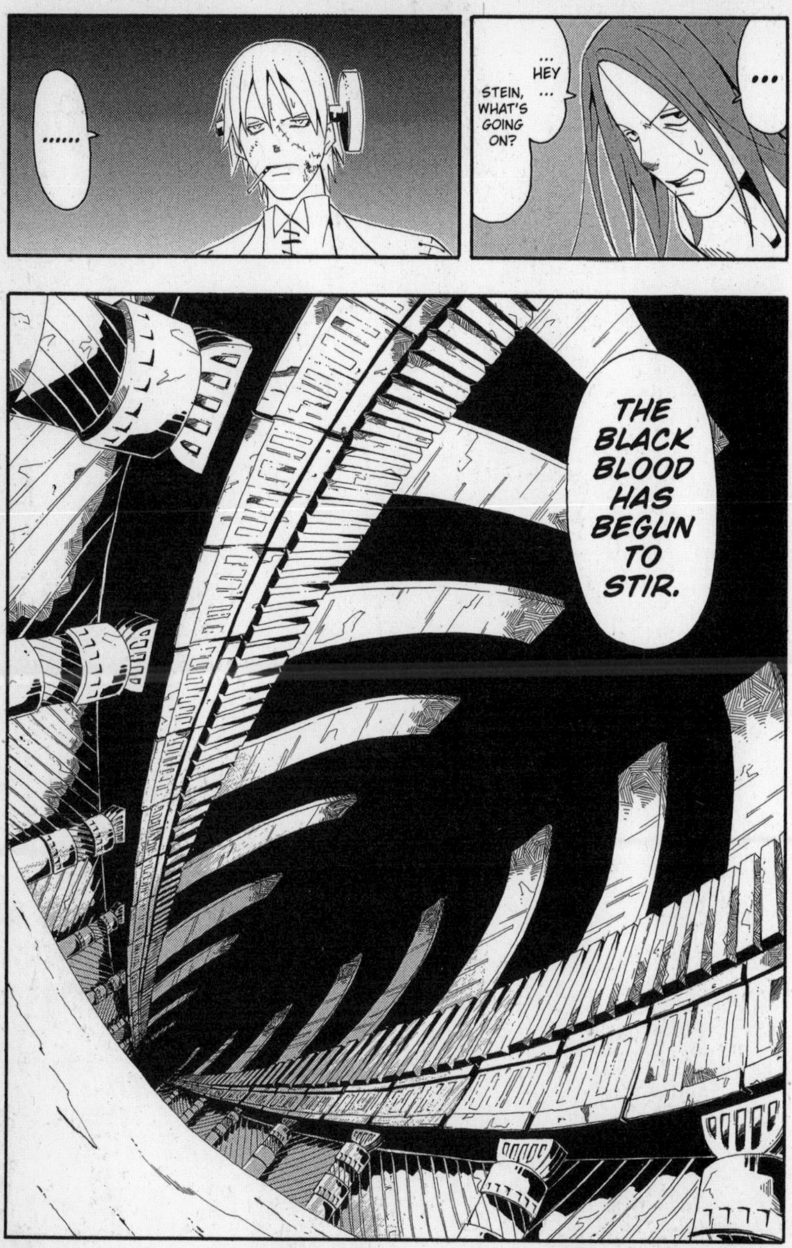
...
... HEY ... STEIN, WHAT'S GOING ON?
......
THE BLACK BLOOD HAS BEGUN TO STIR.

SOUL EATER

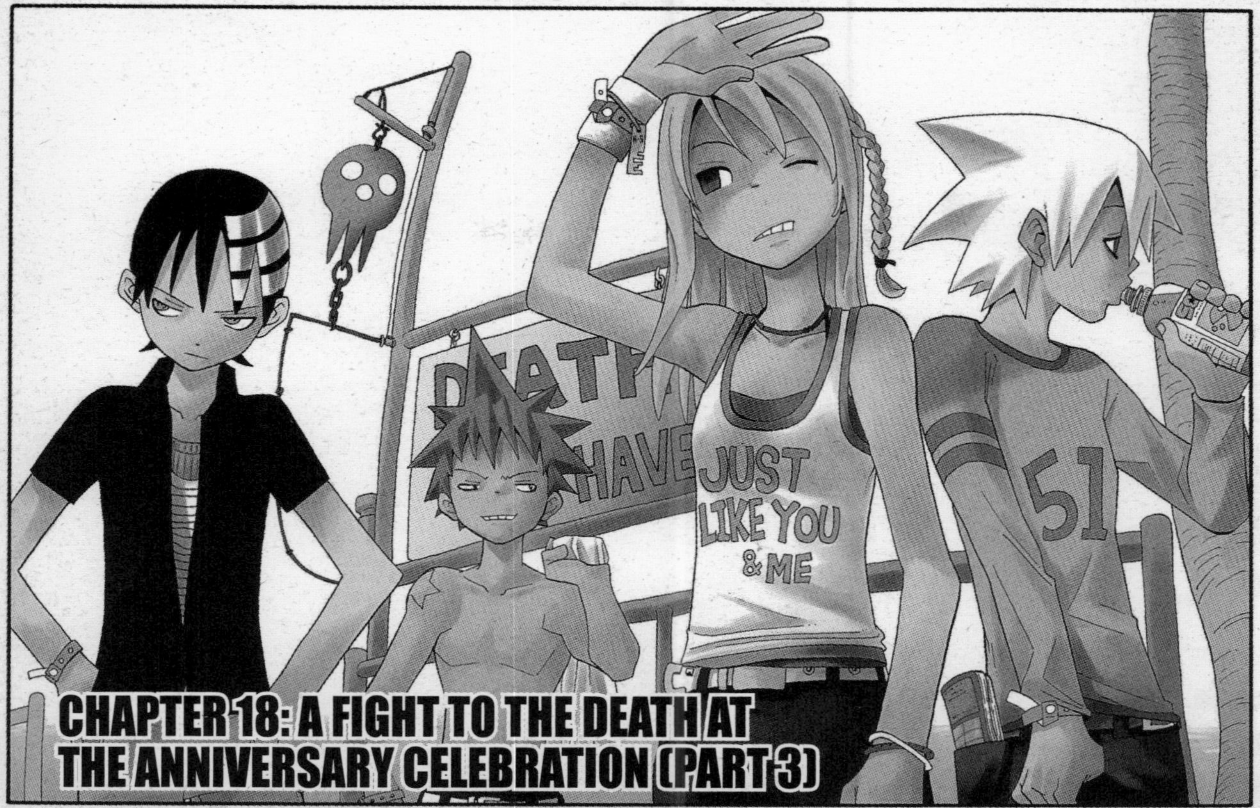
DEATH
HAVE
JUST LIKE YOU & ME
51
CHAPTER 18: A FIGHT TO THE DEATH AT THE ANNIVERSARY CELEBRATION (PART 3)

SOUL EATER

IMAGES FLOW BY LIKE A SHEET OF RAIN.

PLACE, SOUND, AND TIME

PASS OVER ME IN AN INSTANT.

LOOKING FORWARD AND TAKING IT ALL IN,

I MOVE FORWARD...

WITHOUT EVEN NOTICING THE LOUD STATIC

GETTING CLOSER...

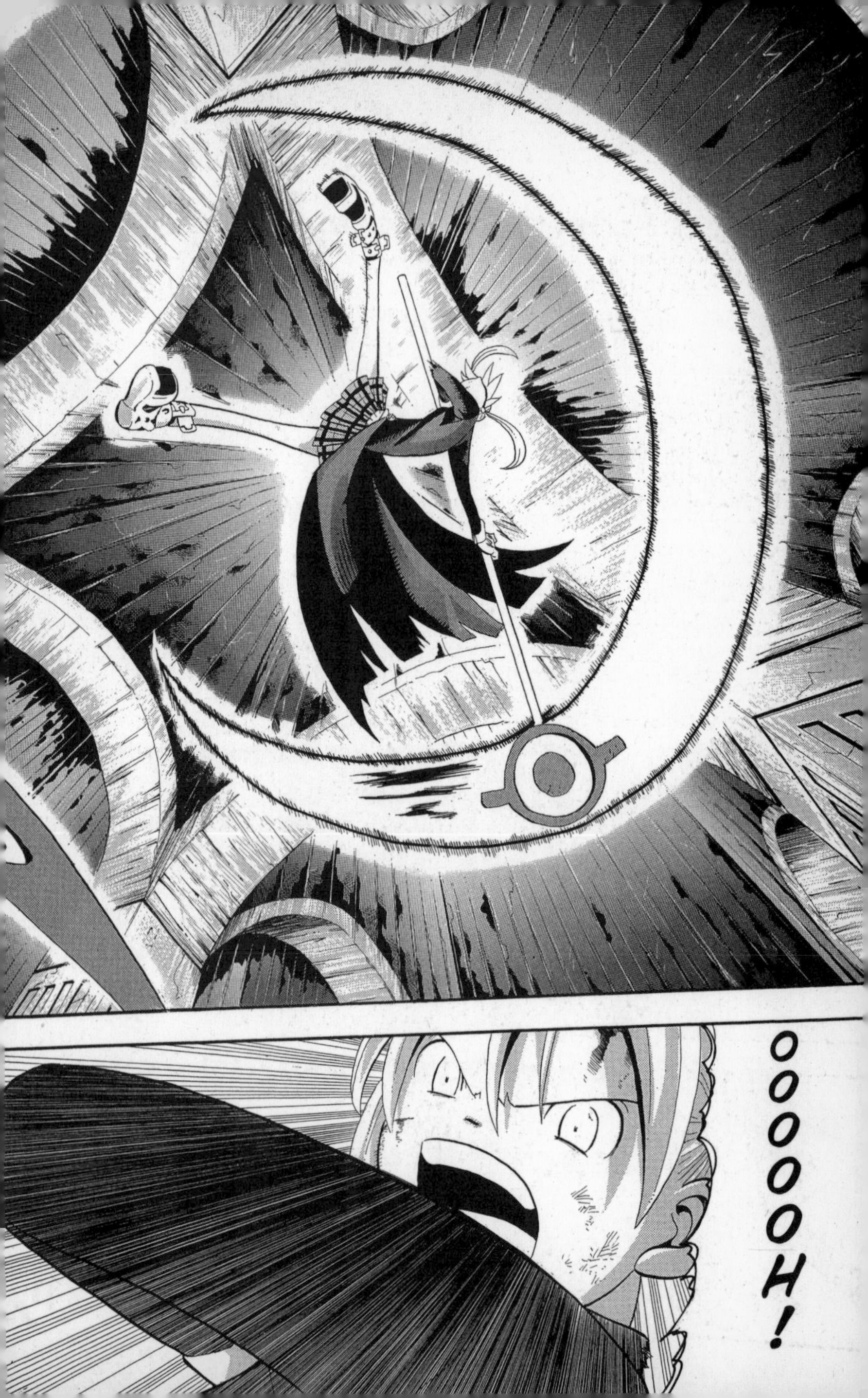
OOOOOOH!

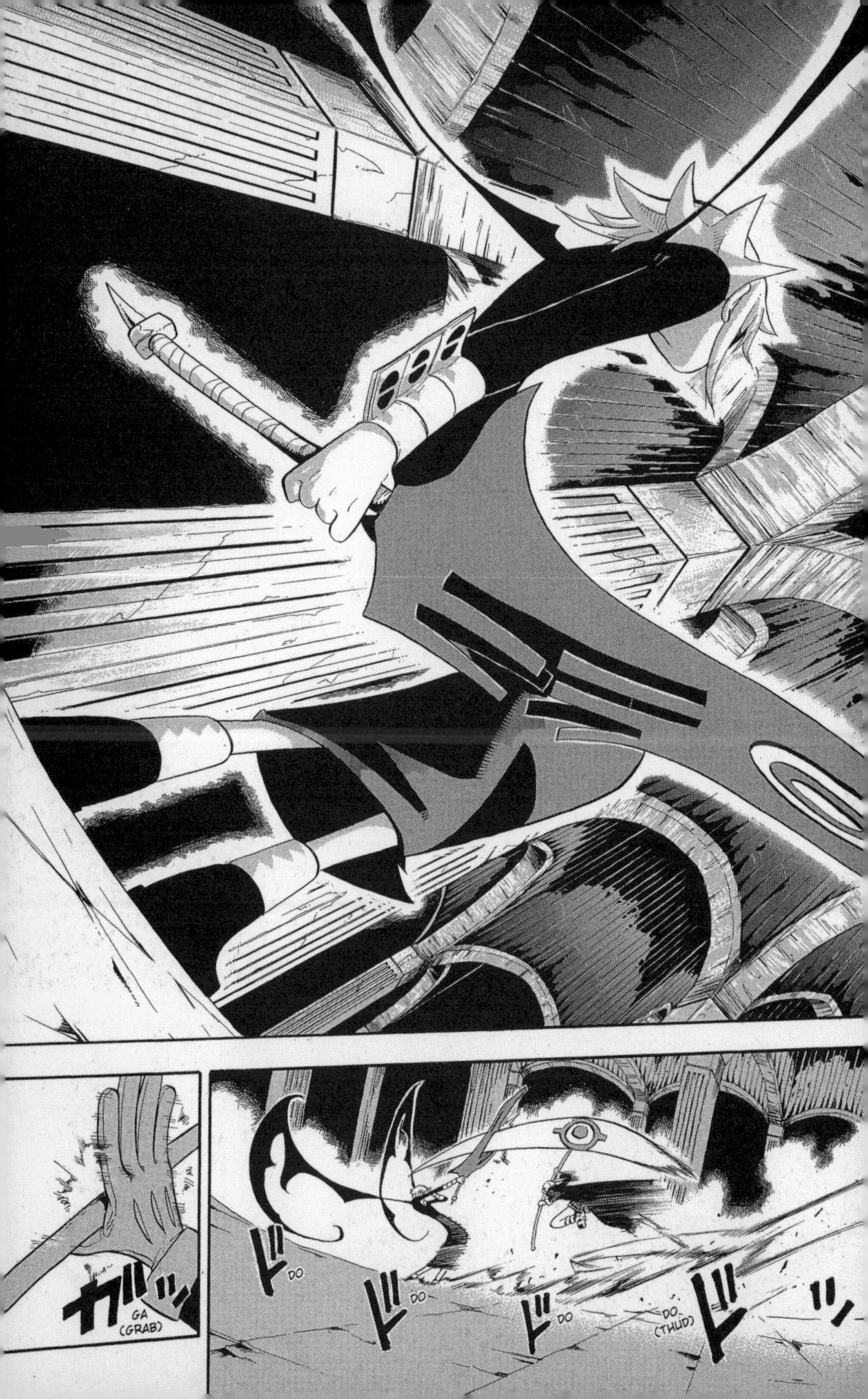
DO
DO
DO
DO (THUD)
GA (GRAB)

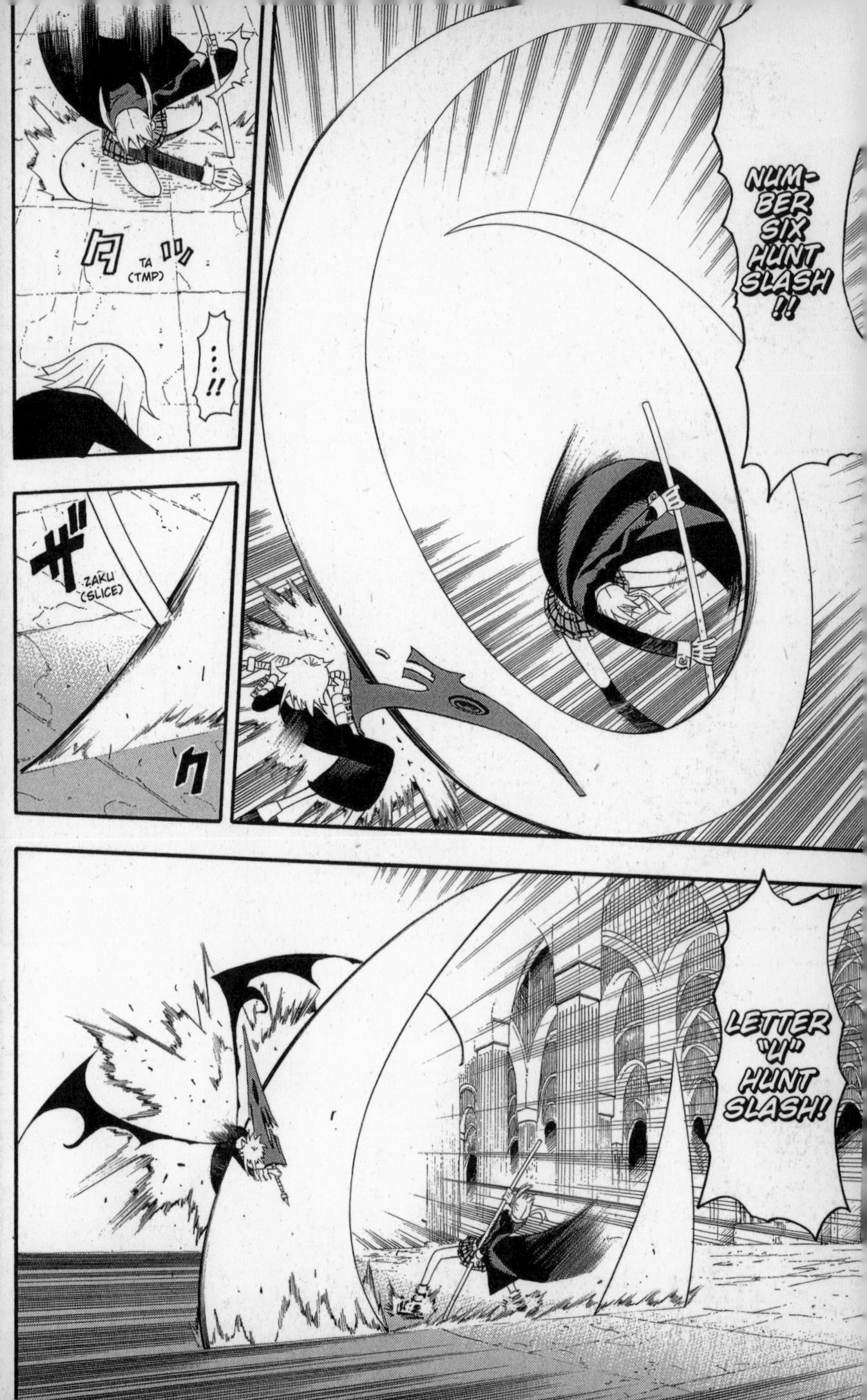
NUMBER SIX HUNT SLASH!!
TA (TMP)
....!!
ZAKU (SLICE)
LETTER "U" HUNT SLASH!

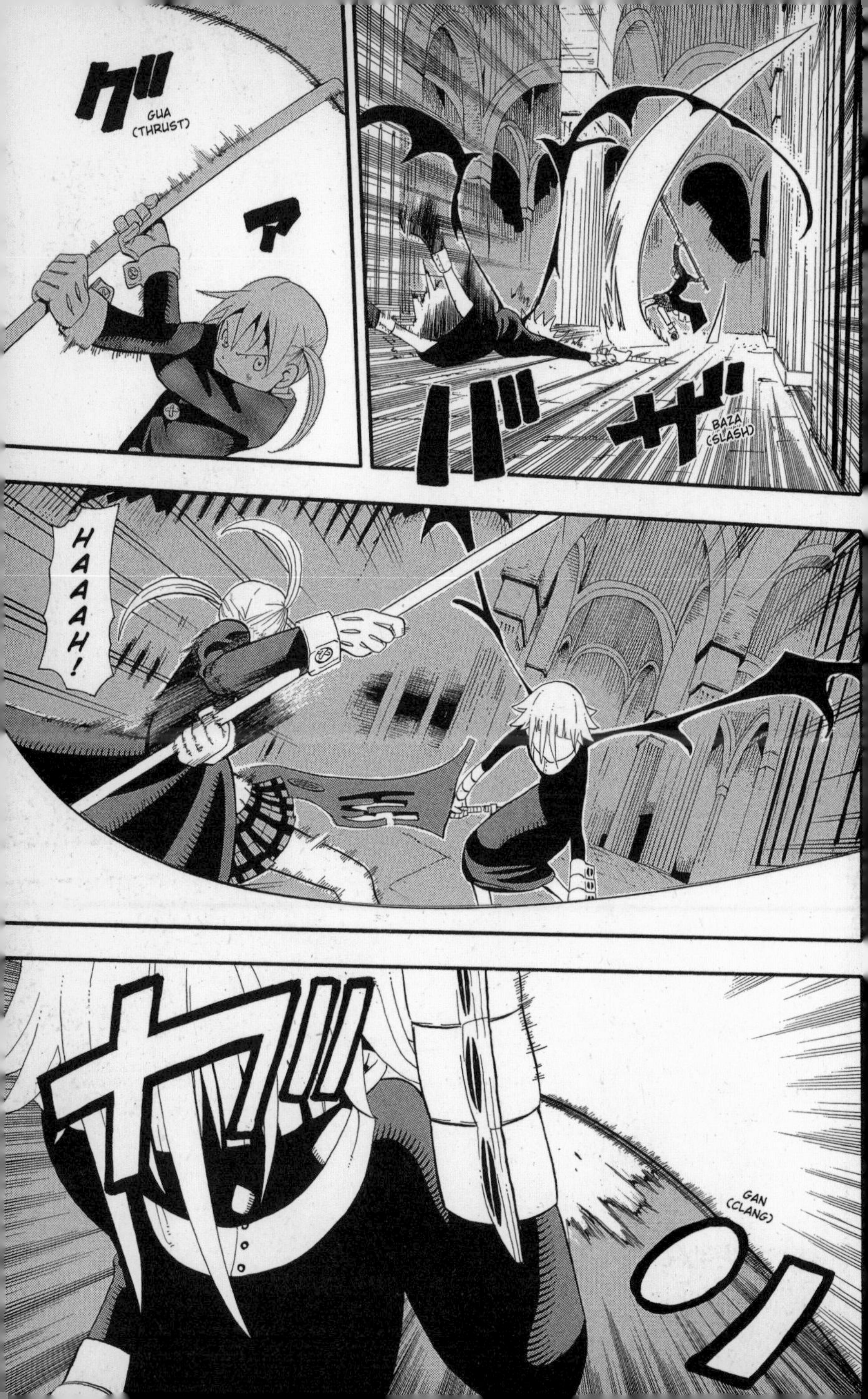

BAZA (SLASH)
GUA (THRUST)
HAAAAH!
GAN (CLANG)

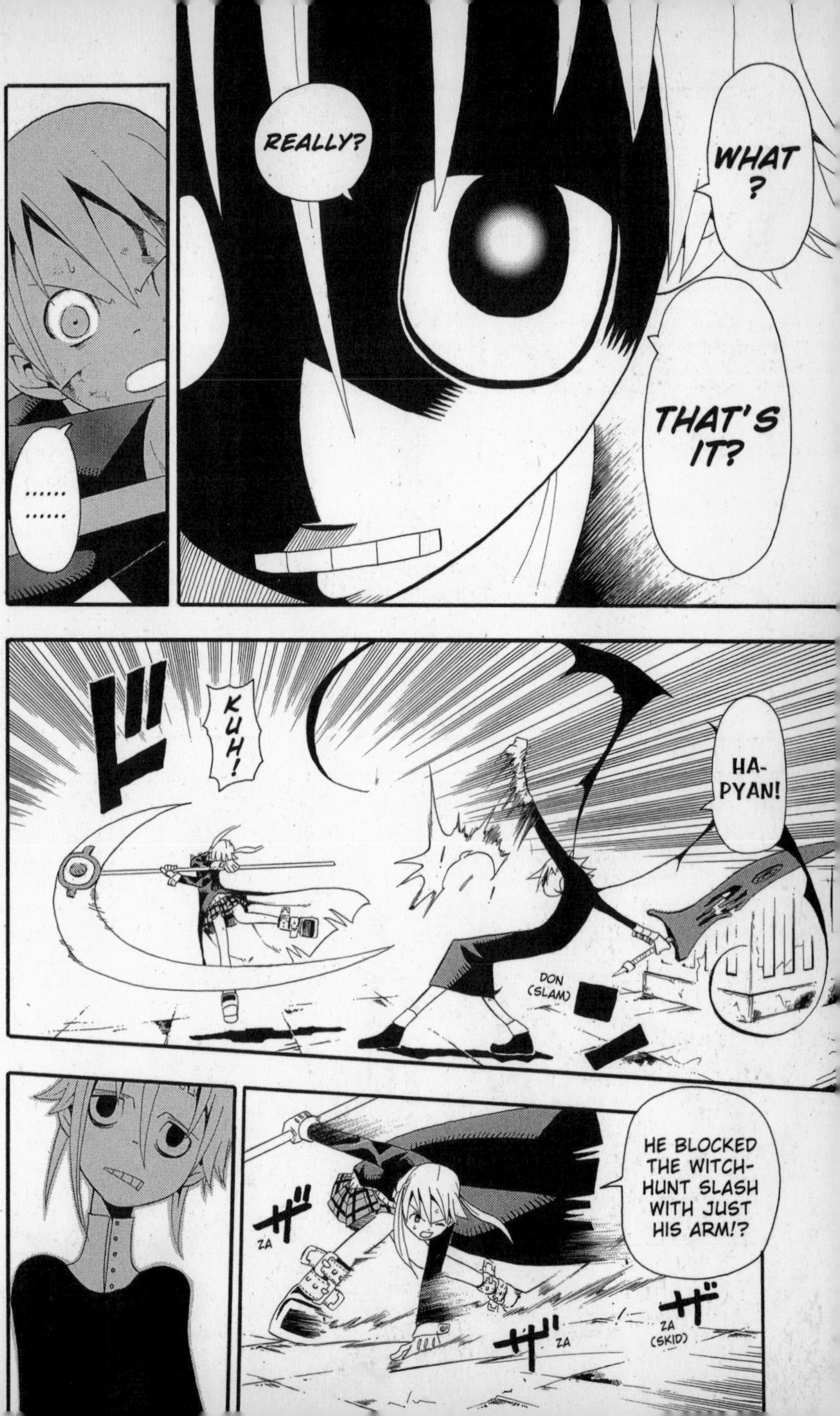
WHAT?
THAT'S IT?
REALLY?
......
......
HA-PYAN!
KUH!
ドッ
DON (SLAM)
HE BLOCKED THE WITCH-HUNT SLASH WITH JUST HIS ARM!?
ザ
ZA (SKID)
ザ
ZA
ザ
ZA

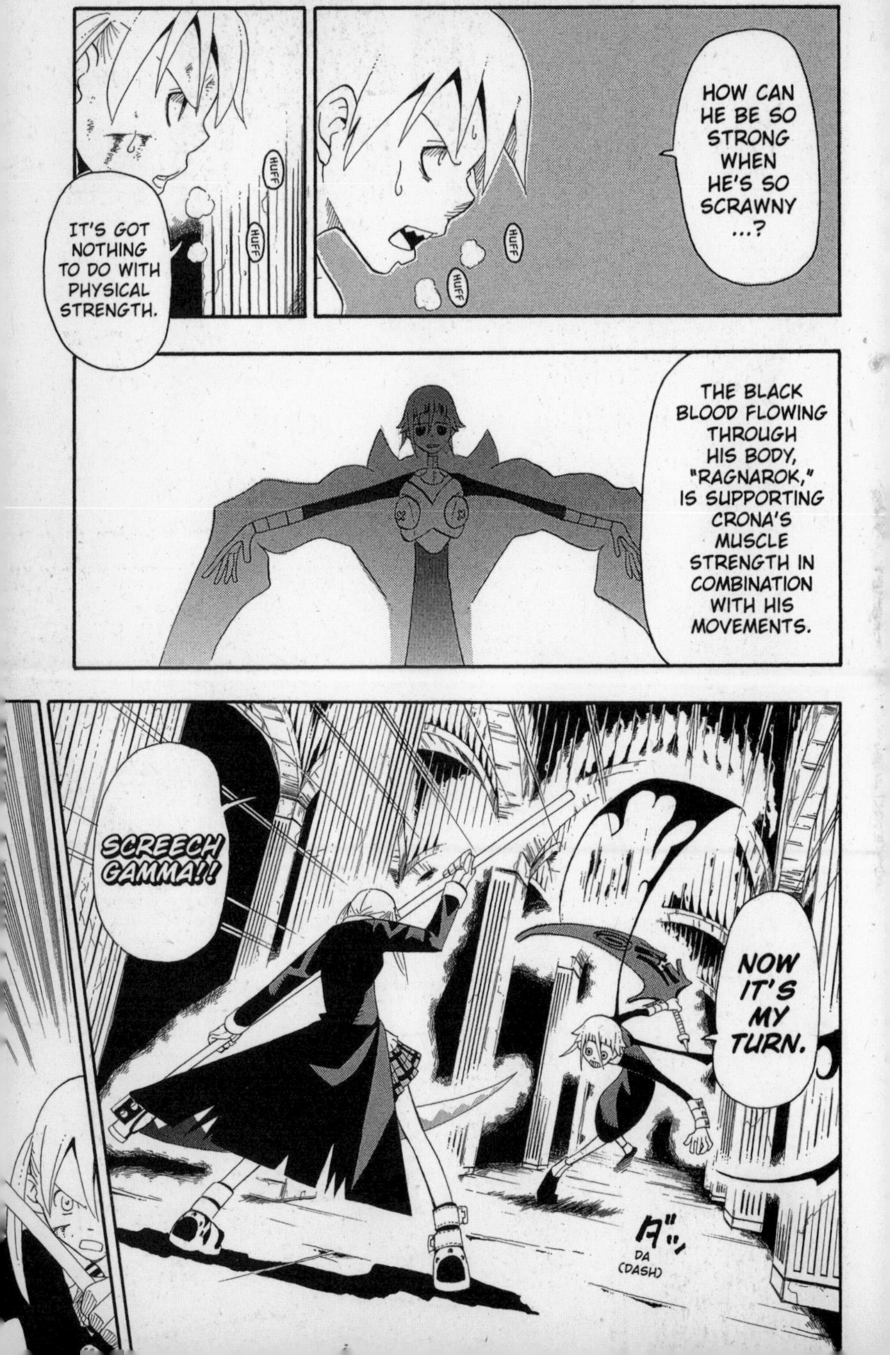
HOW CAN HE BE SO STRONG WHEN HE'S SO SCRAWNY ...?
HUFF
HUFF
HUFF
HUFF
IT'S GOT NOTHING TO DO WITH PHYSICAL STRENGTH.
THE BLACK BLOOD FLOWING THROUGH HIS BODY, "RAGNAROK," IS SUPPORTING CRONA'S MUSCLE STRENGTH IN COMBINATION WITH HIS MOVEMENTS.
NOW IT'S MY TURN.
SCREECH GAMMA!!
DA (DASH)

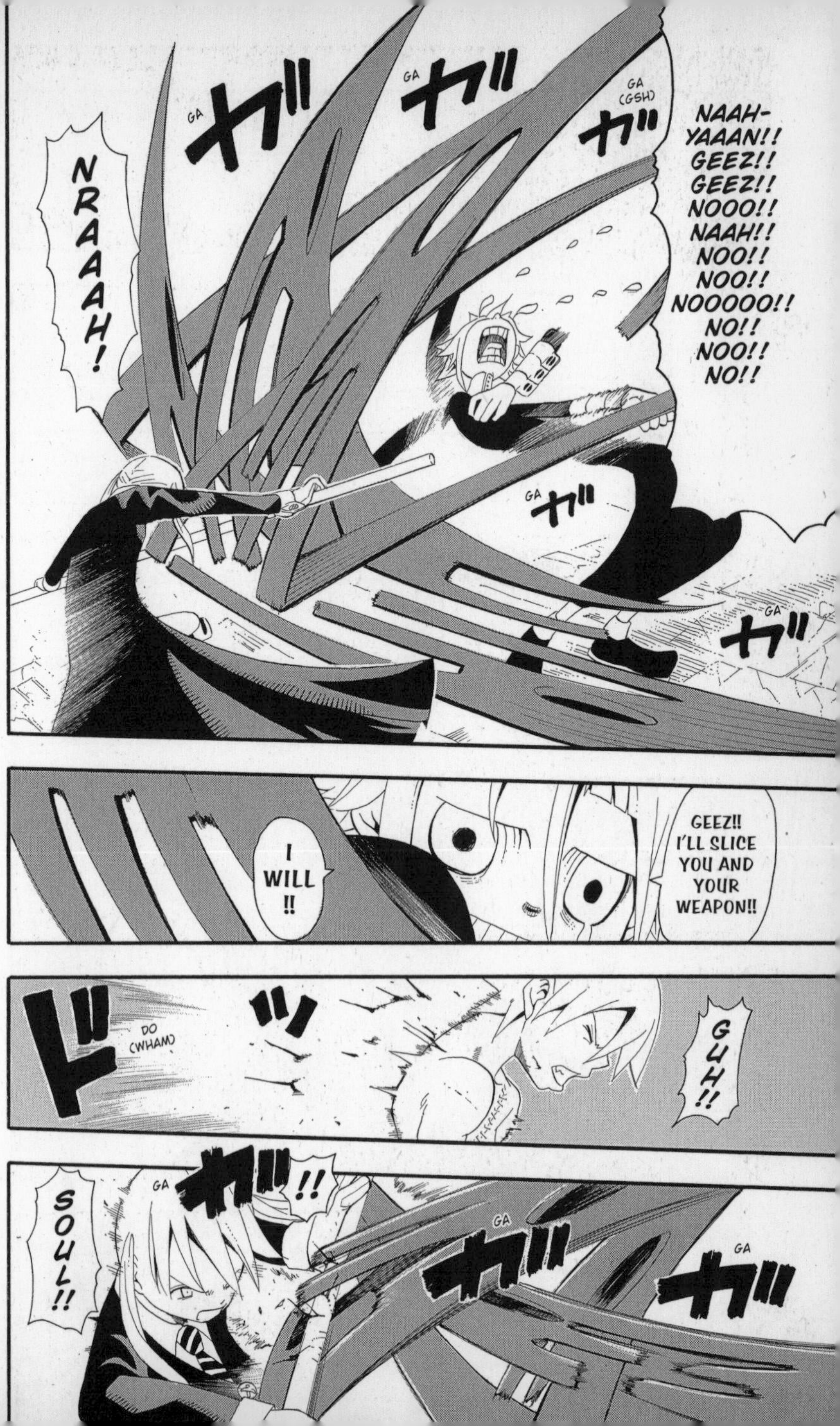
NAAH-YAAAN!! GEEZ!! GEEZ!! NOOO!! NAAH!! NOO!! NOO!! NOOOOO!! NO!! NOO!! NO!!
GA (GSH)
GA
GA
NRAAAAH!
GA
GA
GEEZ!! I'LL SLICE YOU AND YOUR WEAPON!!
I WILL!!
GUH!!
DO (WHAM)
GA
GA
GA
SOUL!!

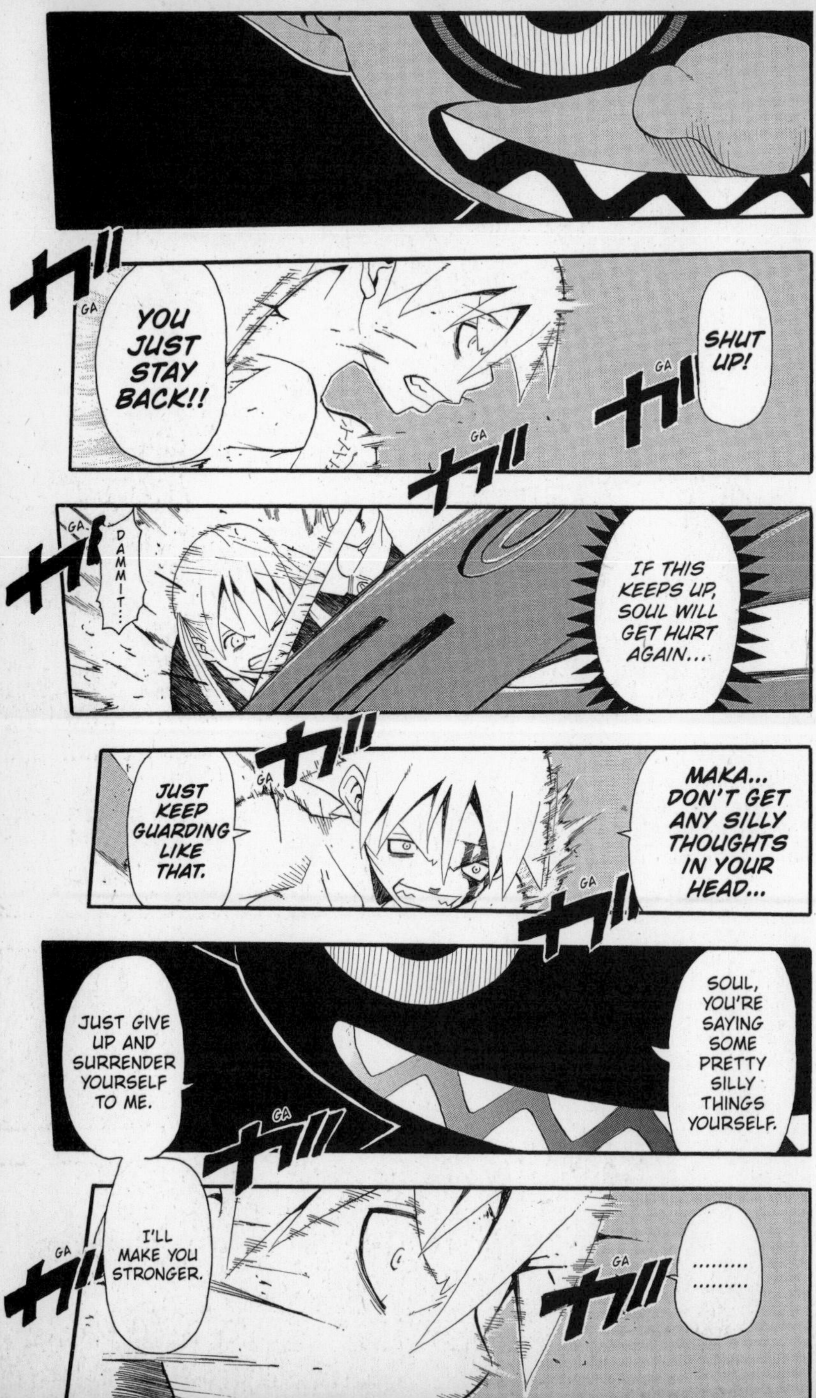
GA
SHUT UP!
GA
YOU JUST STAY BACK!!
GA
IF THIS KEEPS UP, SOUL WILL GET HURT AGAIN...
GA
DAMMIT......
MAKA... DON'T GET ANY SILLY THOUGHTS IN YOUR HEAD...
GA
JUST KEEP GUARDING LIKE THAT.
GA
SOUL, YOU'RE SAYING SOME PRETTY SILLY THINGS YOURSELF.
GA
JUST GIVE UP AND SURRENDER YOURSELF TO ME.
....
GA
I'LL MAKE YOU STRONGER.
GA

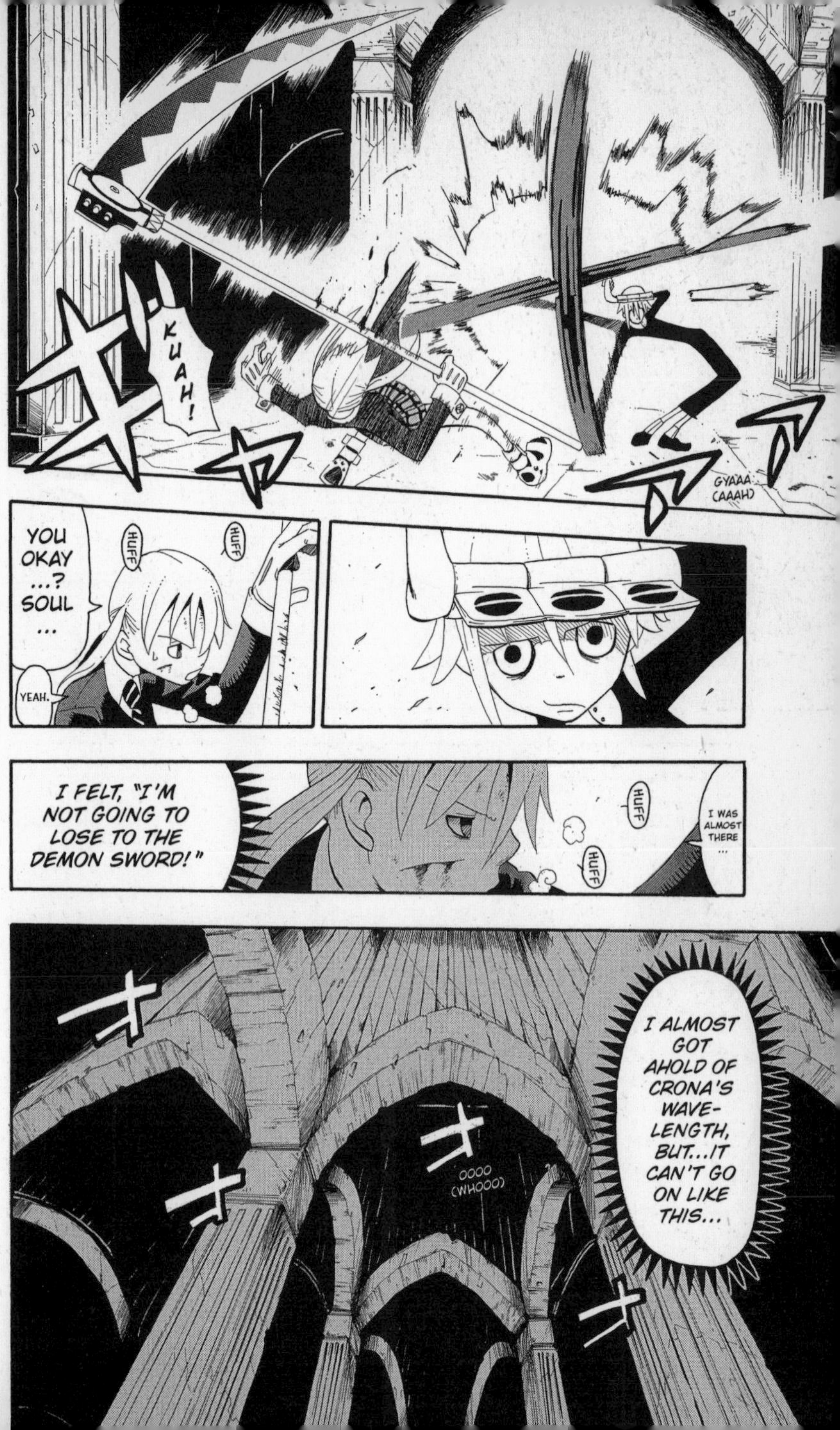
KUAH!
GYAAA (AAAH)
HUFF
HUFF
YOU OKAY ...? SOUL ...
YEAH.
I WAS ALMOST THERE ...
HUFF
HUFF
I FELT, "I'M NOT GOING TO LOSE TO THE DEMON SWORD!"
I ALMOST GOT AHOLD OF CRONA'S WAVE-LENGTH, BUT...IT CAN'T GO ON LIKE THIS...
OOOO (WHOOO)

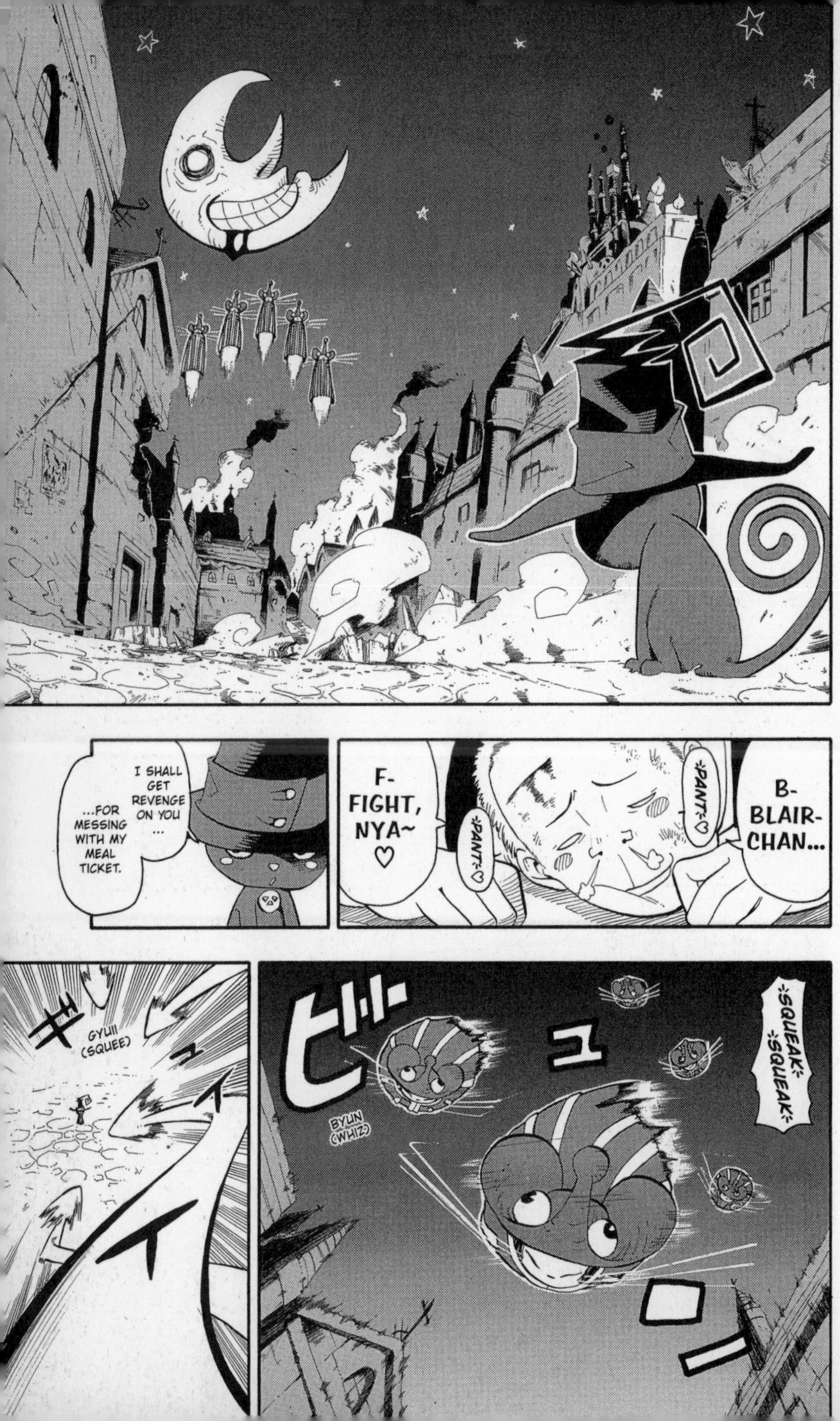
B-BLAIR-CHAN...
PANT ♡
PANT ♡
F-FIGHT, NYA~ ♡
I SHALL GET REVENGE ON YOU ...
...FOR MESSING WITH MY MEAL TICKET.
SQUEAK SQUEAK
BYUN (WHIZ)
GYUII (SQUEE)

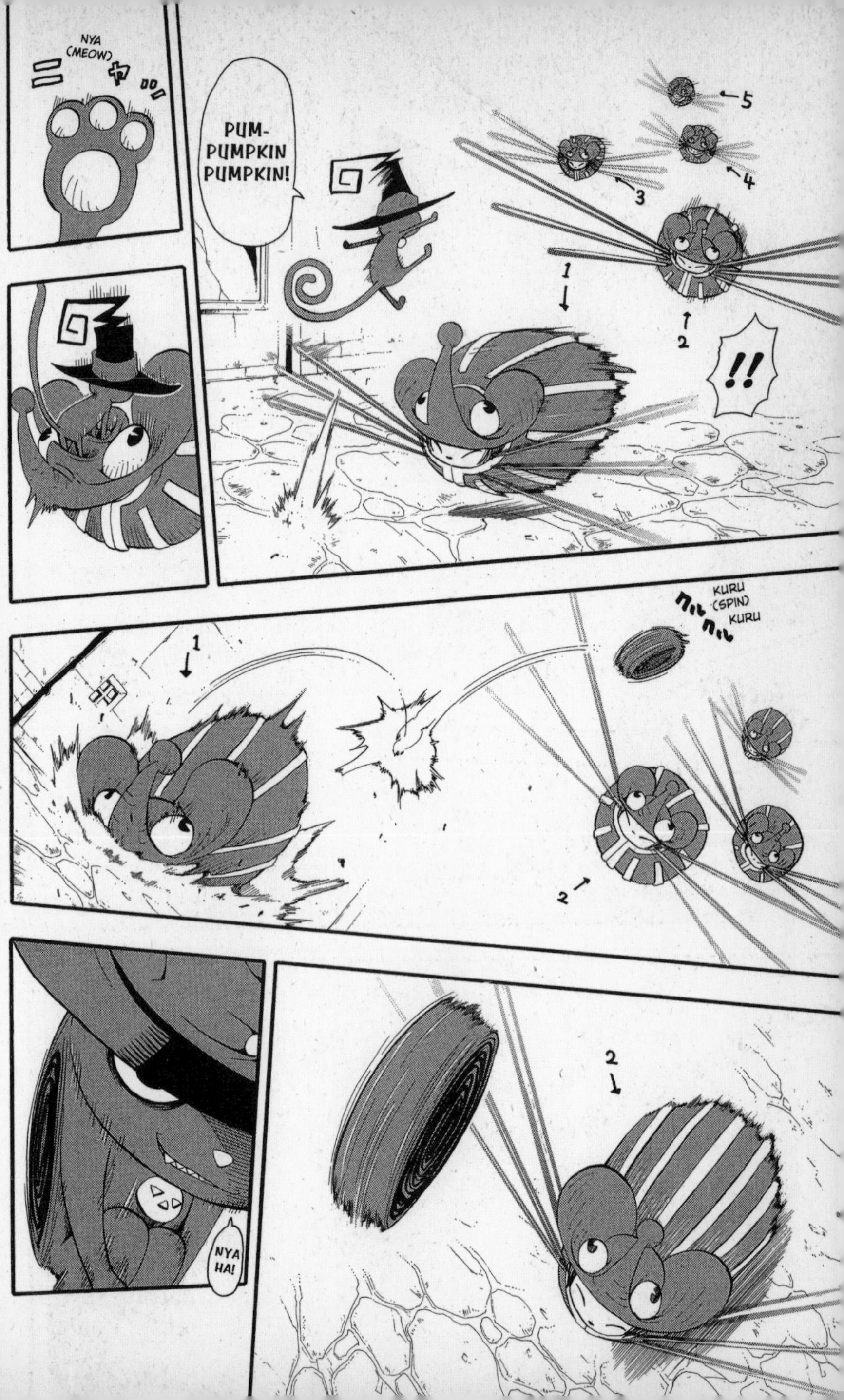
5
4
3
PUM-PUMPKIN PUMPKIN!
1
2
!!
NYA (MEOW)
KURU (SPIN) KURU
1
2
2
NYA HA!

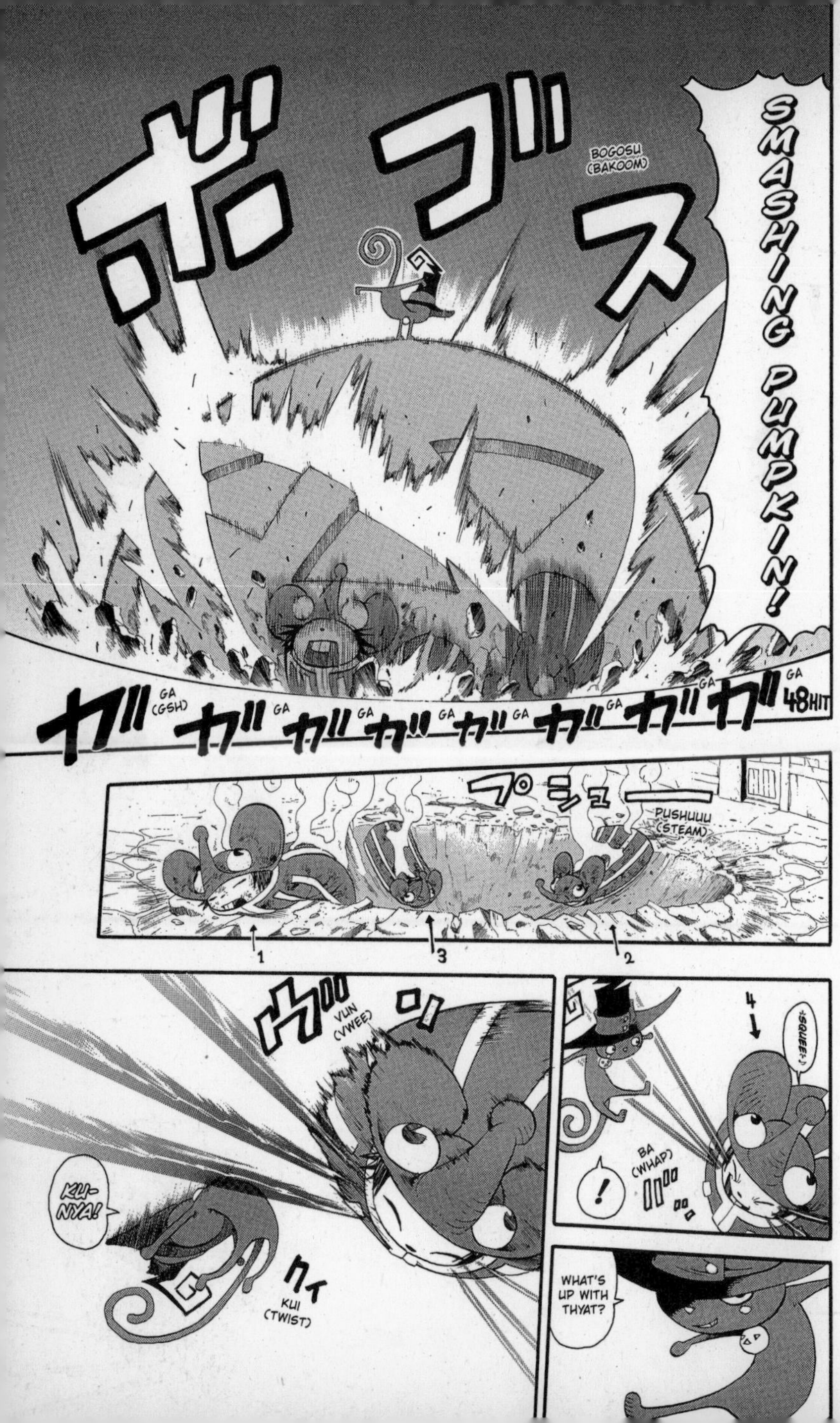
SMASHING PUMPKIN!
BOGOSU (BAKOOM)
GA (GSH) GA GA GA GA GA GA GA
48HIT
PUSHUUU (STEAM)
1
3
2
4
SQUEE
BA (WHAP)
!
WHAT'S UP WITH THYAT?
VUN (VWEE)
KU-NYA!
KUI (TWIST)

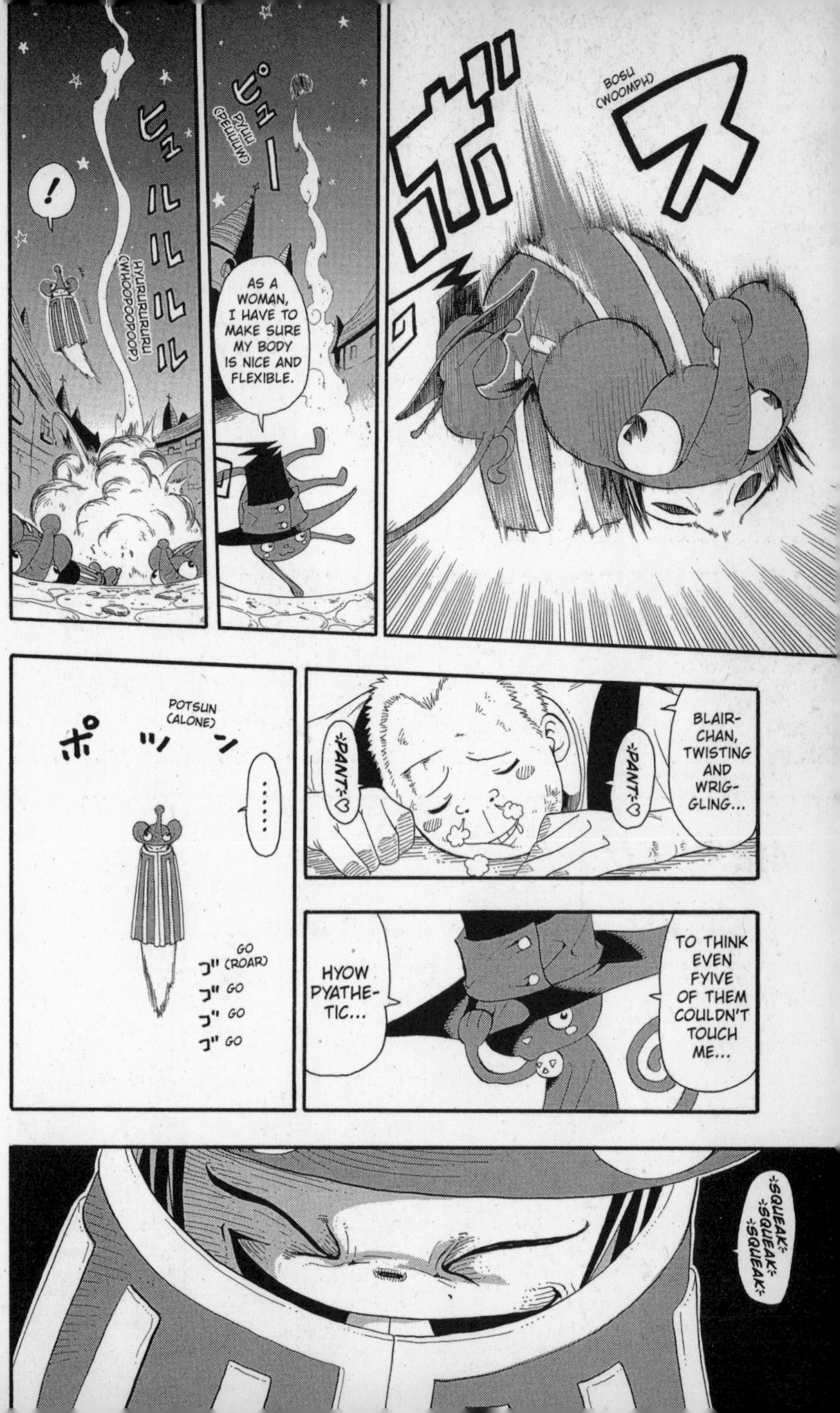
ボスッ
BOSU (WOOMPH)
ピュー
PYUU (PEUUW)
AS A WOMAN, I HAVE TO MAKE SURE MY BODY IS NICE AND FLEXIBLE.
ヒュルルルル
HYURURURURU (WHOOPOOPOOP)
!
BLAIR-CHAN, TWISTING AND WRIG-GLING...
PANT ♡
PANT ♡
TO THINK EVEN FYIVE OF THEM COULDN'T TOUCH ME...
HYOW PYATHE-TIC...
ポツン
POTSUN (ALONE)
......
ゴ" GO (ROAR)
ゴ" GO
ゴ" GO
ゴ" GO
SQUEAK SQUEAK SQUEAK

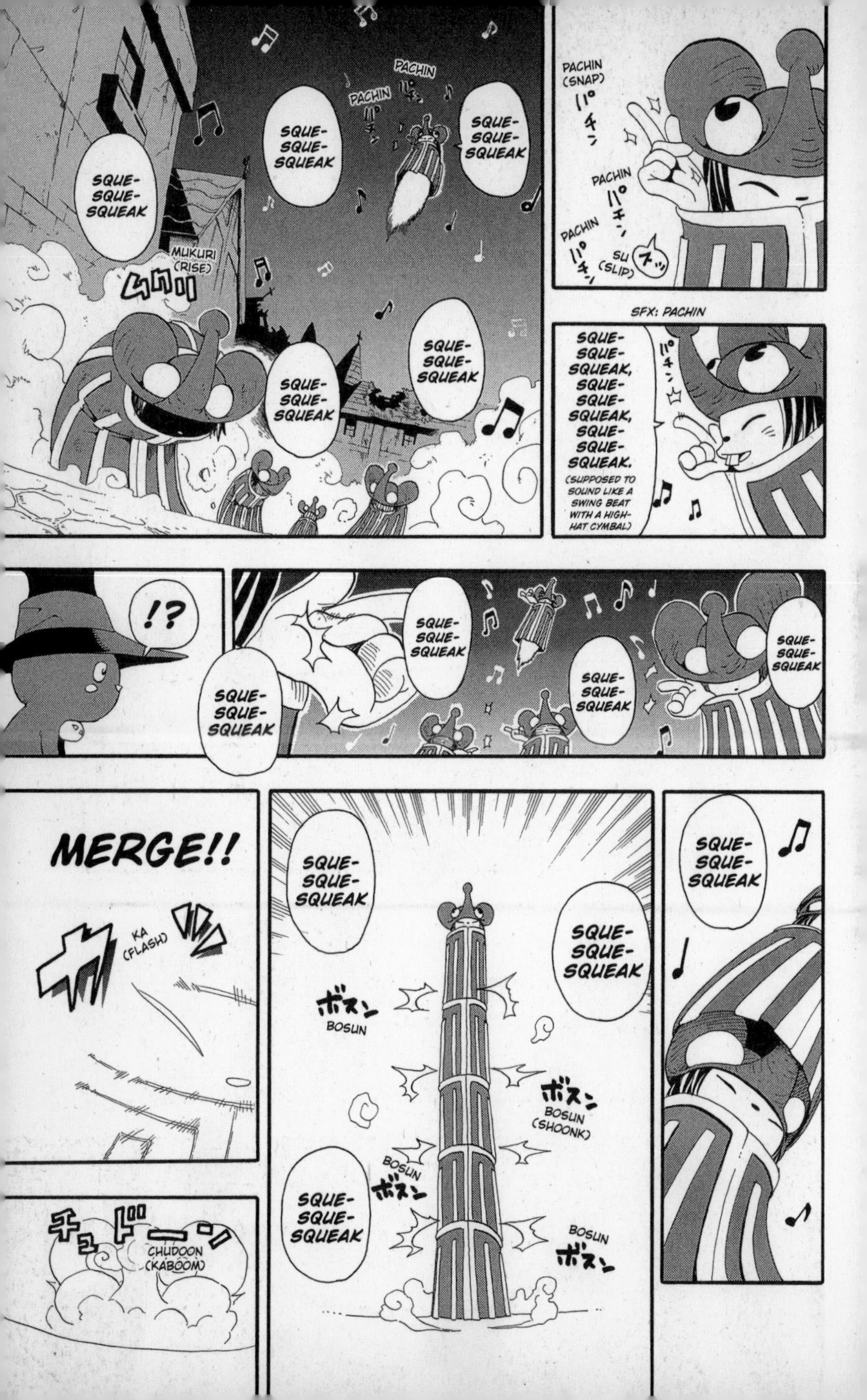
PACHIN (SNAP)
パチン
PACHIN
パチン
PACHIN
パチン
SU (SLIP)
スッ
SFX: PACHIN
パチン
SQUE-SQUE-SQUEAK, SQUE-SQUE-SQUEAK, SQUE-SQUE-SQUEAK.
(SUPPOSED TO SOUND LIKE A SWING BEAT WITH A HIGH-HAT CYMBAL)
SQUE-SQUE-SQUEAK
PACHIN
PACHIN
SQUE-SQUE-SQUEAK
SQUE-SQUE-SQUEAK
MUKURI (RISE)
SQUE-SQUE-SQUEAK
SQUE-SQUE-SQUEAK
SQUE-SQUE-SQUEAK
SQUE-SQUE-SQUEAK
SQUE-SQUE-SQUEAK
SQUE-SQUE-SQUEAK
!?
SQUE-SQUE-SQUEAK
SQUE-SQUE-SQUEAK
SQUE-SQUE-SQUEAK
ボスン
BOSUN
ボスン
BOSUN (SHOONK)
BOSUN
ボスン
SQUE-SQUE-SQUEAK
BOSUN
ボスン
MERGE!!
KA (FLASH)
CHUDOON (KABOOM)

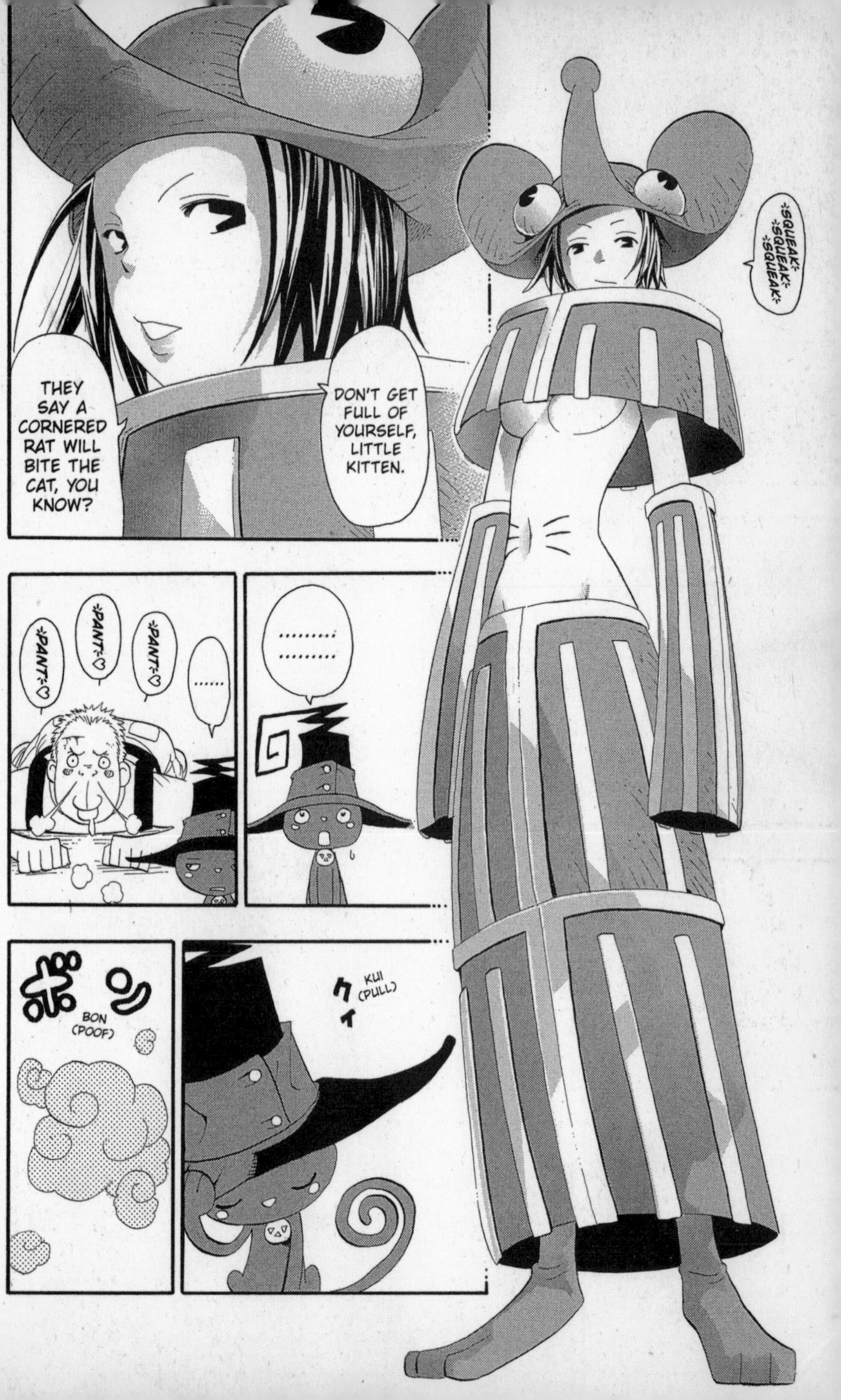

SQUEAK SQUEAK SQUEAK
DON'T GET FULL OF YOURSELF, LITTLE KITTEN.
THEY SAY A CORNERED RAT WILL BITE THE CAT, YOU KNOW?
....
....
......
PANT♡
PANT♡
KUI (PULL)
BON (POOF)

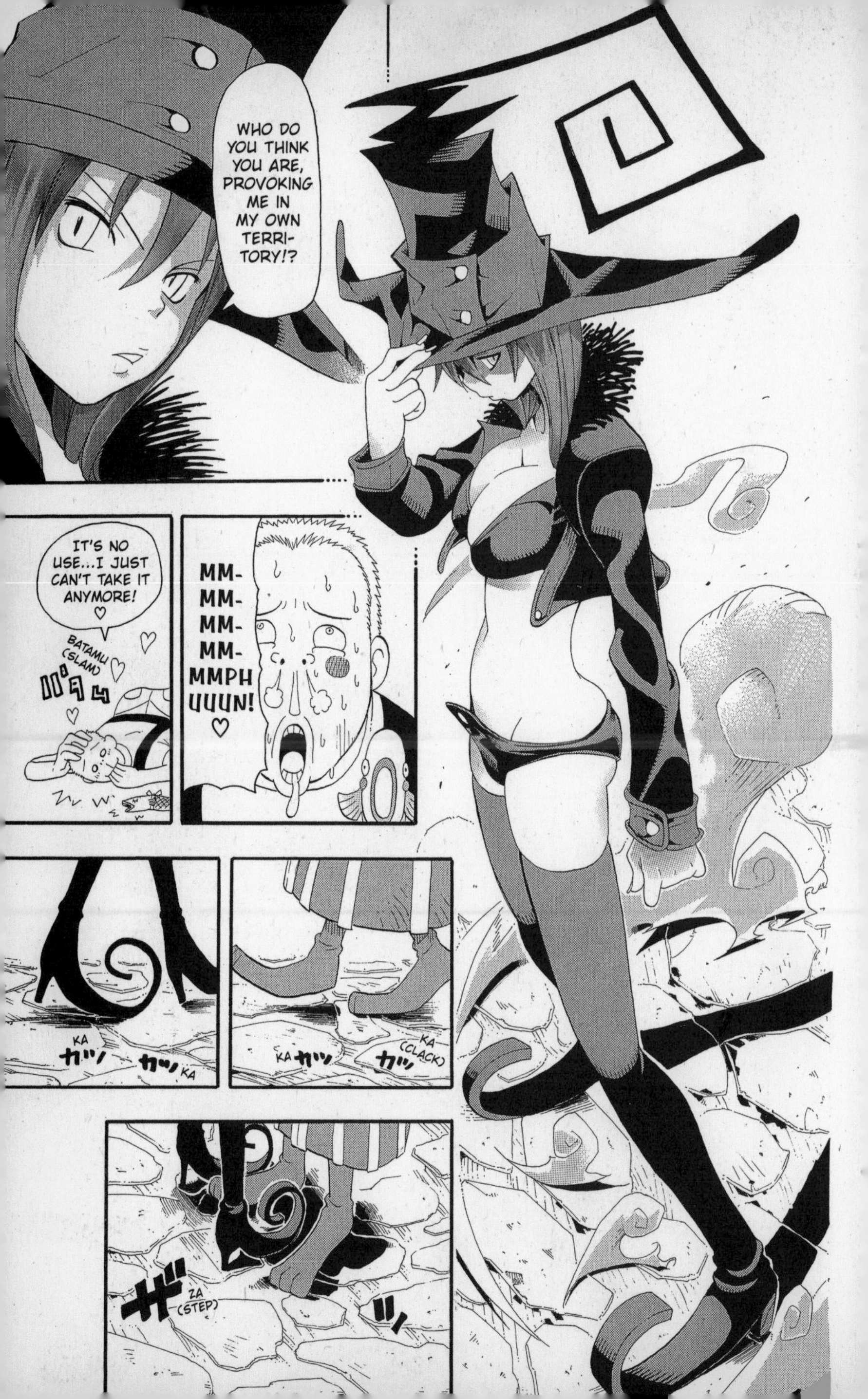
WHO DO YOU THINK YOU ARE, PROVOKING ME IN MY OWN TERRITORY!?
MM-MM-MM-MM-MMPH UUUN! ♡
IT'S NO USE...I JUST CAN'T TAKE IT ANYMORE! ♡
BATAMU (SLAM)
バタム
KA (CLACK)
カツ
KA
カツ
KA
カツ
KA
カツ
ZA (STEP)
ザッ

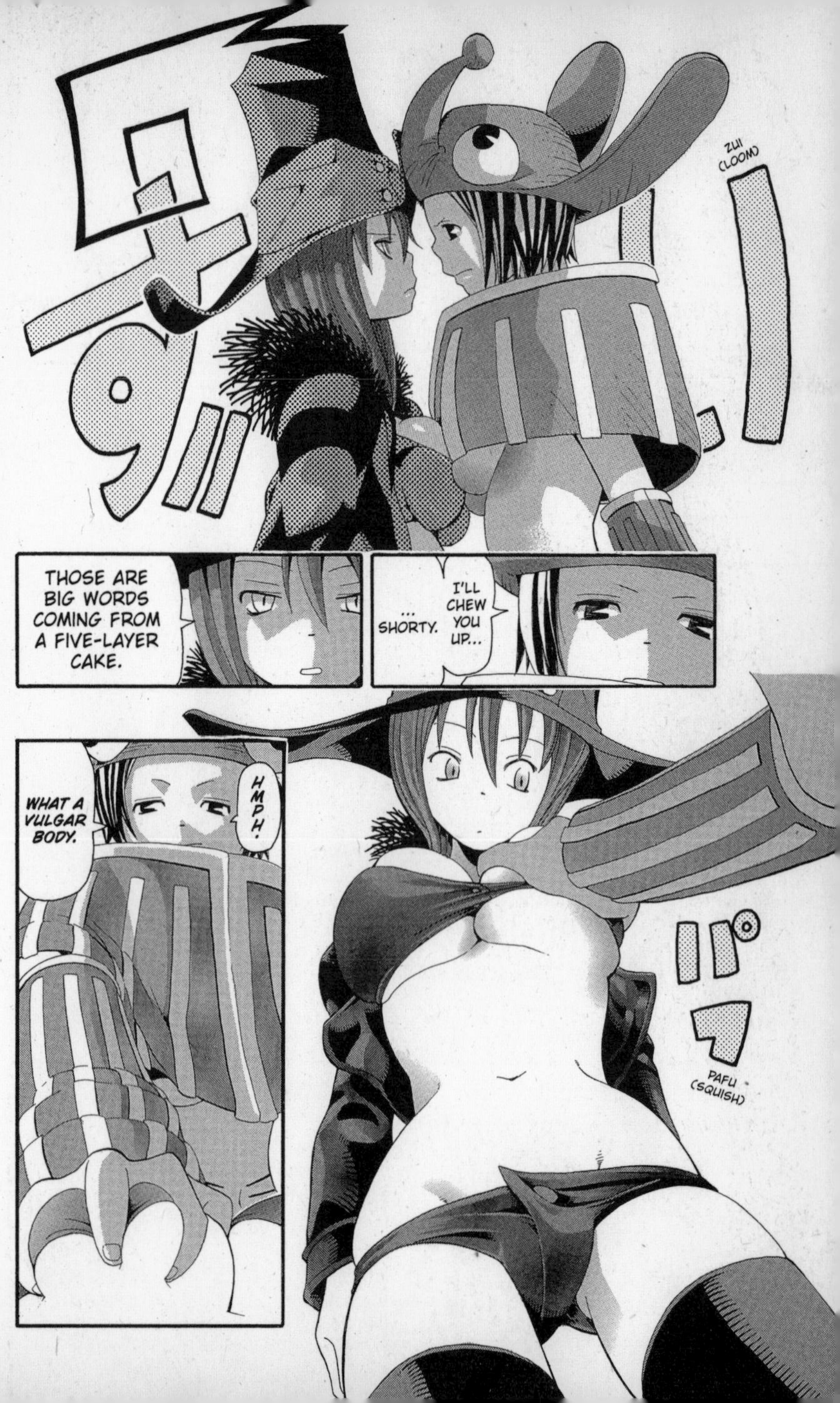
ZUI (LOOM)
I'LL CHEW YOU UP...
... SHORTY.
THOSE ARE BIG WORDS COMING FROM A FIVE-LAYER CAKE.
PAFU (SQUISH)
HMPH!
WHAT A VULGAR BODY.

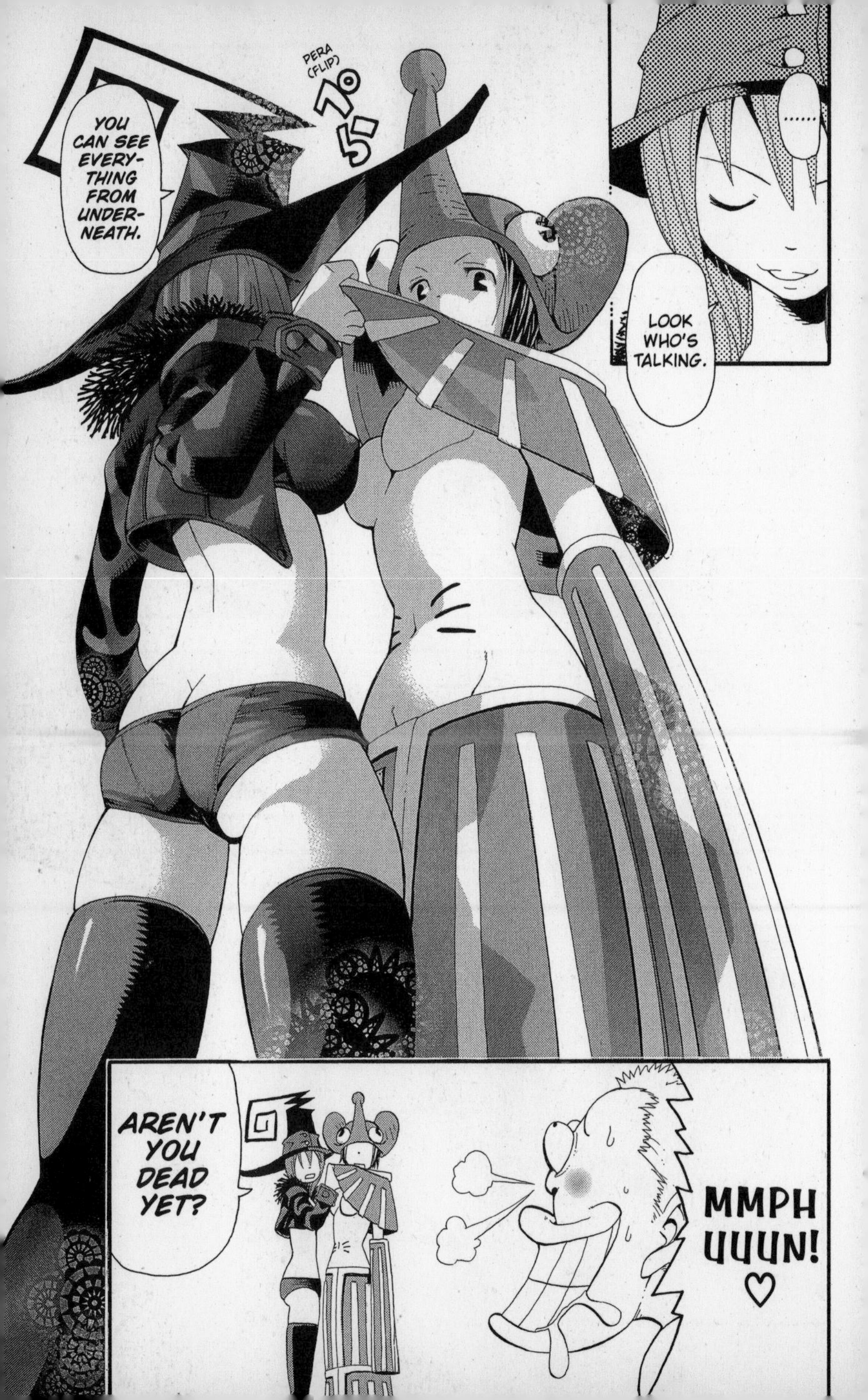
......
LOOK WHO'S TALKING.
PERA (FLIP)
YOU CAN SEE EVERYTHING FROM UNDERNEATH.
MMPH UUUN! ♡
AREN'T YOU DEAD YET?

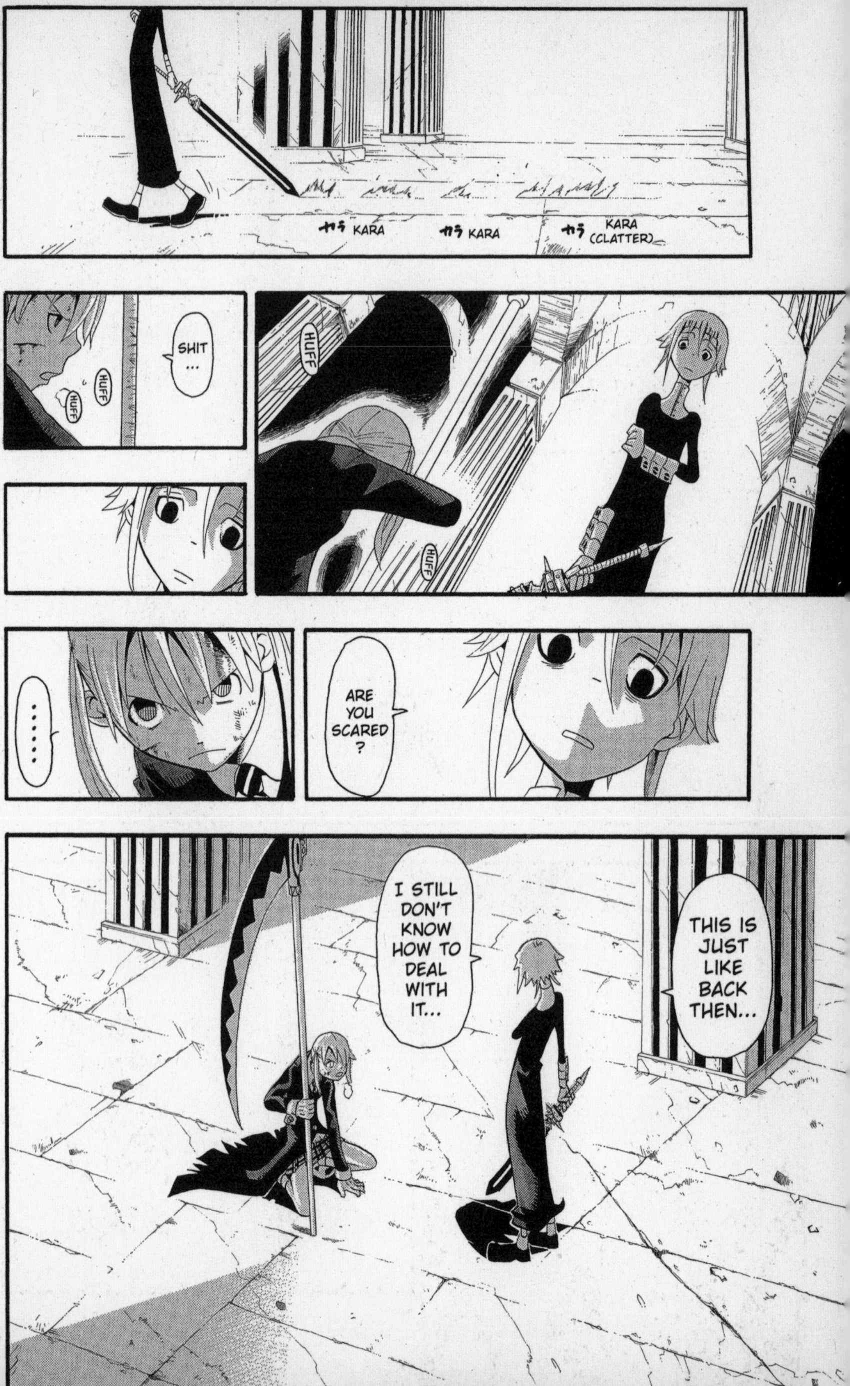
カラ KARA (CLATTER)
カラ KARA
カラ KARA
HUFF
HUFF
SHIT ...
HUFF
HUFF
ARE YOU SCARED?
......
THIS IS JUST LIKE BACK THEN...
I STILL DON'T KNOW HOW TO DEAL WITH IT...

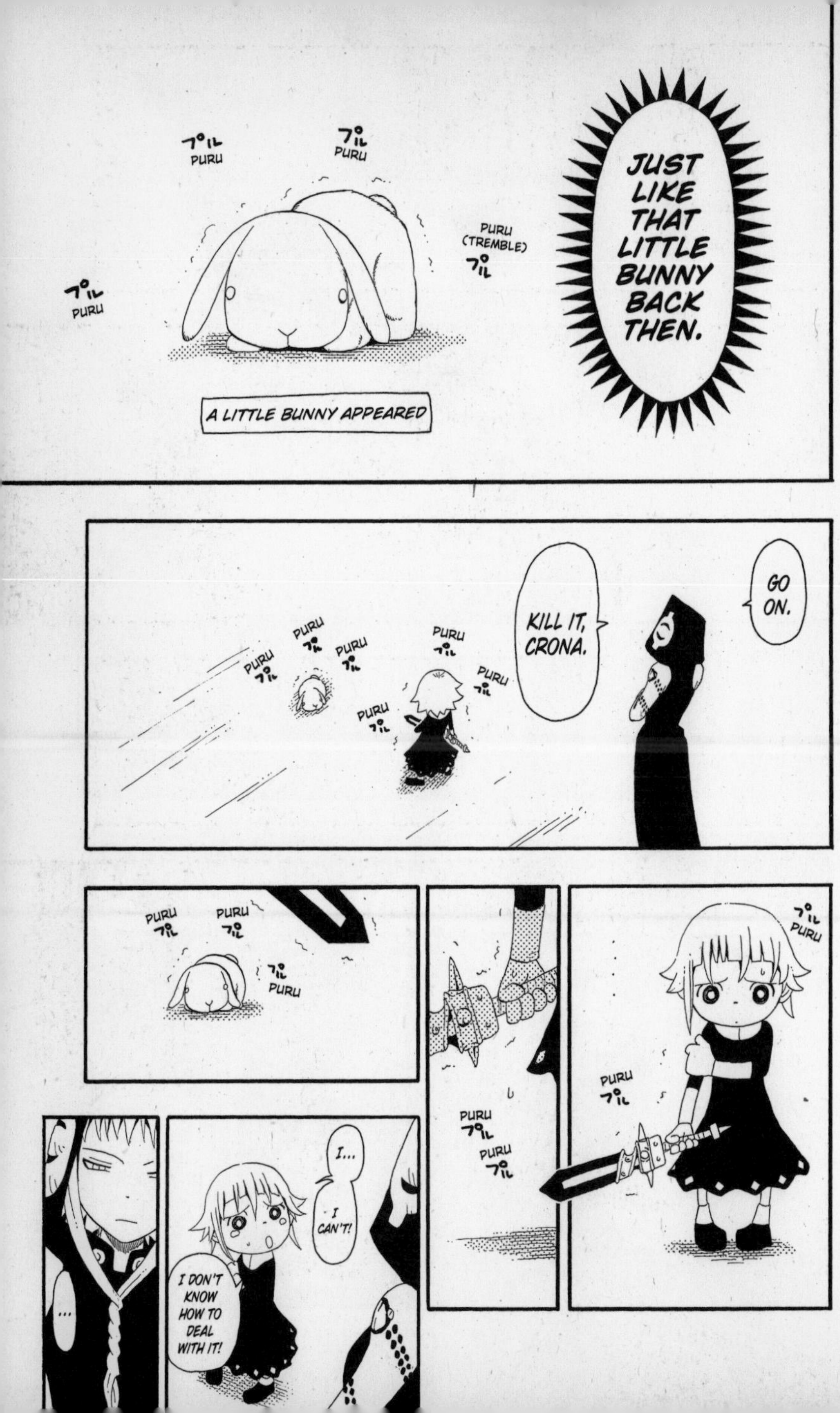
JUST LIKE THAT LITTLE BUNNY BACK THEN.
プル PURU (TREMBLE)
プル PURU
プル PURU
プル PURU
A LITTLE BUNNY APPEARED
GO ON.
KILL IT, CRONA.
PURU プル
PURU プル
PURU プル
PURU プル
PURU プル
PURU プル
プル PURU
PURU プル
PURU プル
PURU プル
PURU プル
PURU プル
プル PURU
I...
I CAN'T!
I DON'T KNOW HOW TO DEAL WITH IT!
...

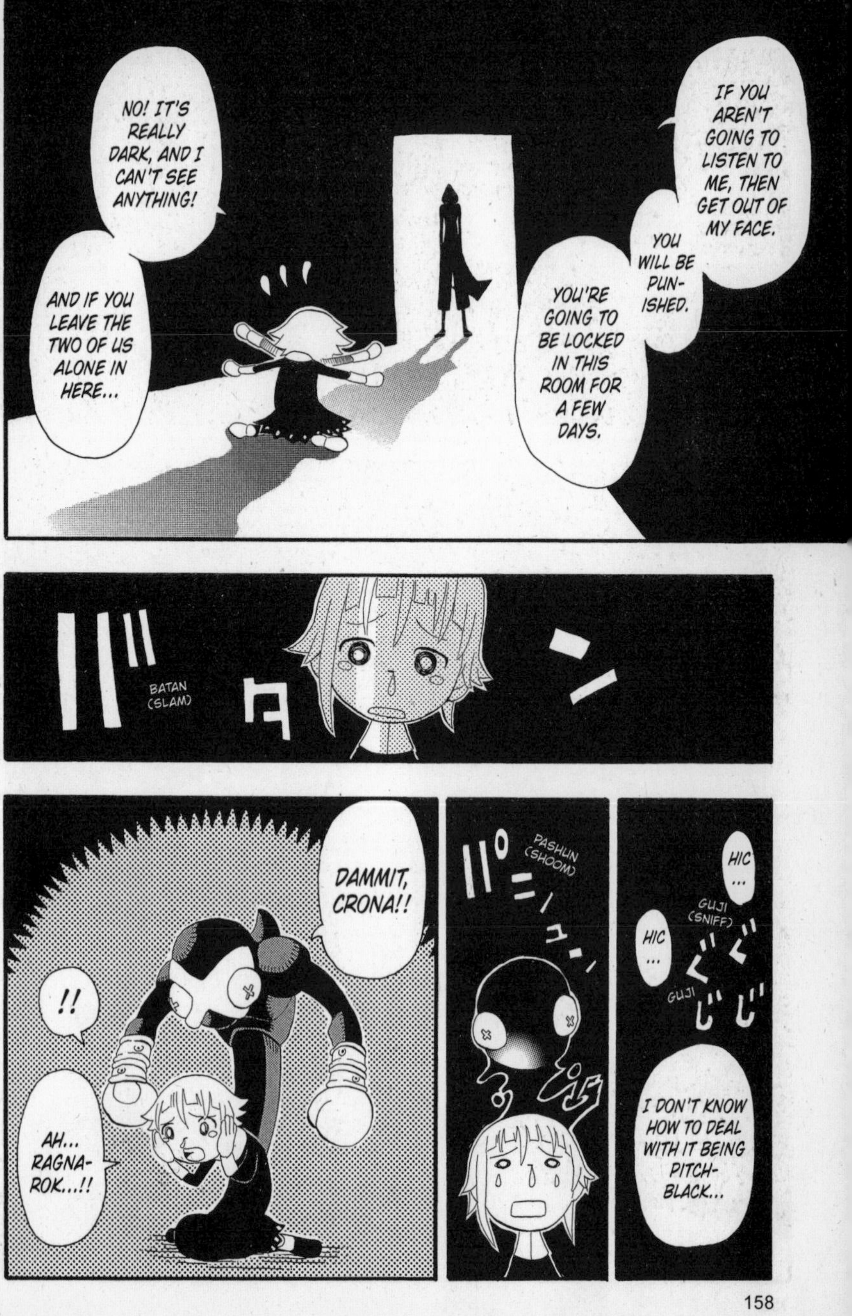
IF YOU AREN'T GOING TO LISTEN TO ME, THEN GET OUT OF MY FACE.
YOU WILL BE PUN-ISHED.
YOU'RE GOING TO BE LOCKED IN THIS ROOM FOR A FEW DAYS.
NO! IT'S REALLY DARK, AND I CAN'T SEE ANYTHING!
AND IF YOU LEAVE THE TWO OF US ALONE IN HERE...
BATAN (SLAM)
HIC...
GUJI (SNIFF)
HIC...
GUJI
I DON'T KNOW HOW TO DEAL WITH IT BEING PITCH-BLACK...
PASHUN (SHOOM)
DAMMIT, CRONA!!
!!
AH... RAGNAROK...!!

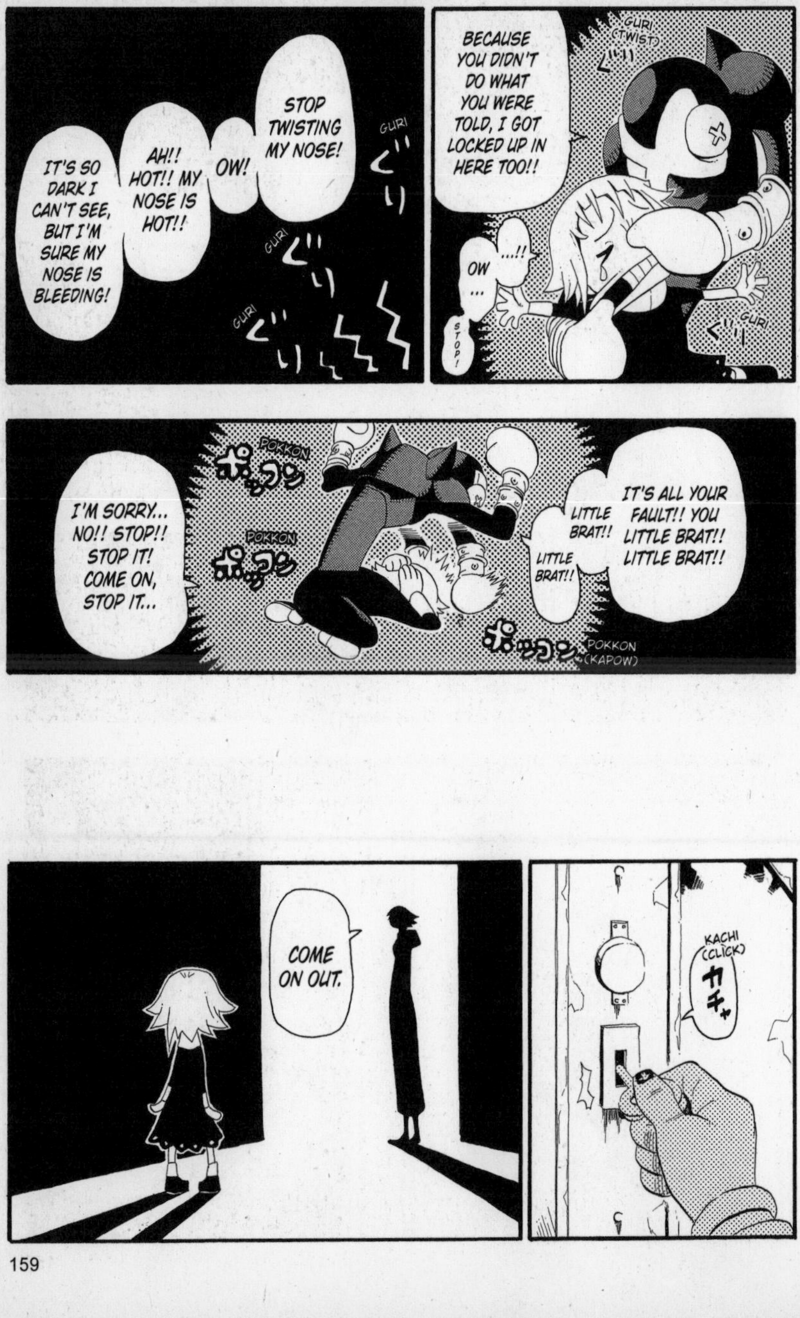
GURI (TWIST)
BECAUSE YOU DIDN'T DO WHAT YOU WERE TOLD, I GOT LOCKED UP IN HERE TOO!!
...!!
OW ...
STOP!
GURI
GURI
STOP TWISTING MY NOSE!
OW!
AH!! HOT!! MY NOSE IS HOT!!
IT'S SO DARK I CAN'T SEE, BUT I'M SURE MY NOSE IS BLEEDING!
GURI
GURI
IT'S ALL YOUR FAULT!! YOU LITTLE BRAT!! LITTLE BRAT!!
LITTLE BRAT!!
LITTLE BRAT!!
POKKON
POKKON
POKKON (KAPOW)
I'M SORRY... NO!! STOP!! STOP IT! COME ON, STOP IT...
KACHI (CLICK)
COME ON OUT.

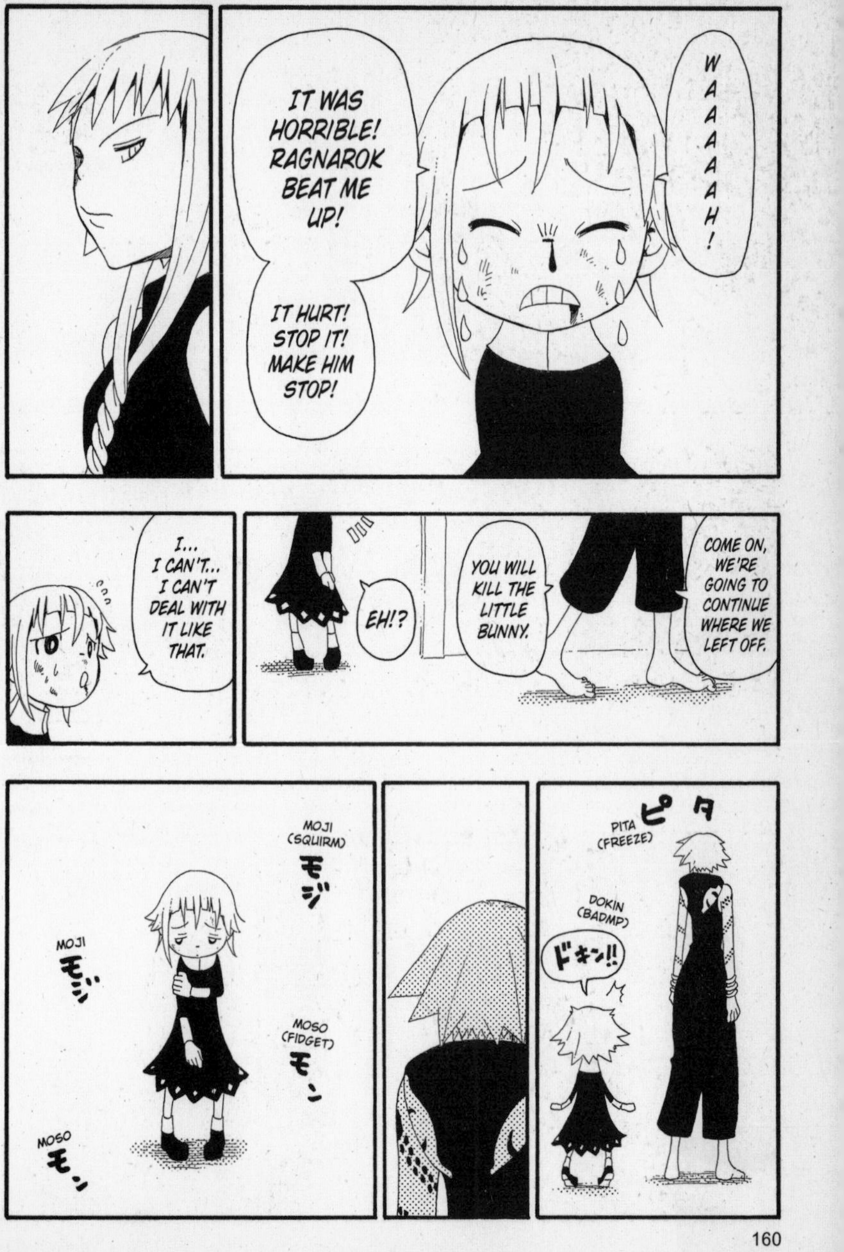
WAAAAAAH!
IT WAS HORRIBLE! RAGNAROK BEAT ME UP!
IT HURT! STOP IT! MAKE HIM STOP!
COME ON, WE'RE GOING TO CONTINUE WHERE WE LEFT OFF.
YOU WILL KILL THE LITTLE BUNNY.
EH!?
I... I CAN'T... I CAN'T DEAL WITH IT LIKE THAT.
ピタ
PITA (FREEZE)
DOKIN (BADMP)
ドキン!!
MOJI (SQUIRM)
モジ
MOJI
モジ
MOSO (FIDGET)
モソ
MOSO
モソ

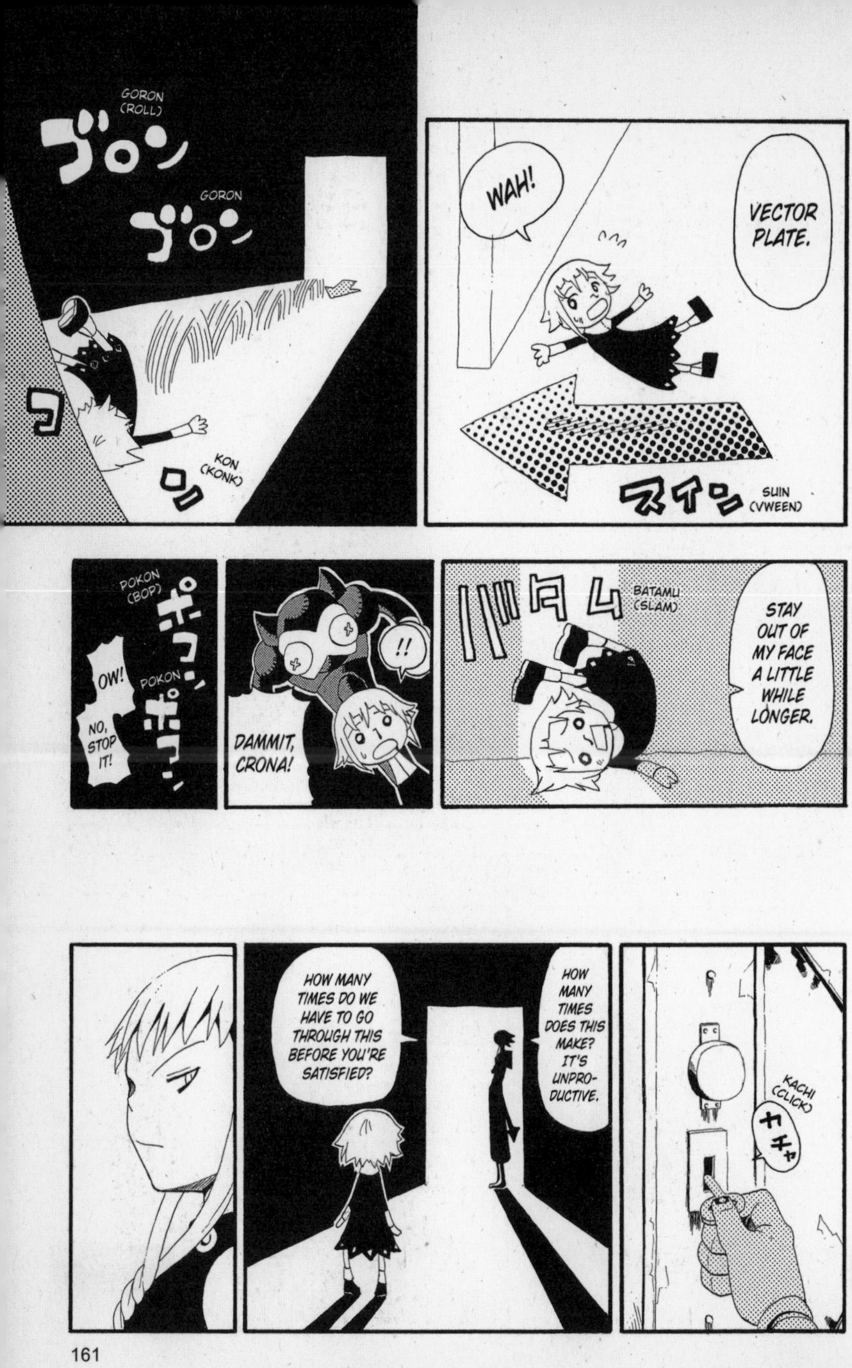
VECTOR PLATE.
WAH!
SUIN (VWEEN)
GORON (ROLL)
GORON
KON (KONK)
STAY OUT OF MY FACE A LITTLE WHILE LONGER.
BATAMU (SLAM)
!!
DAMMIT, CRONA!
POKON (BOP)
OW!
POKON
NO, STOP IT!
KACHI (CLICK)
HOW MANY TIMES DOES THIS MAKE? IT'S UNPRODUCTIVE.
HOW MANY TIMES DO WE HAVE TO GO THROUGH THIS BEFORE YOU'RE SATISFIED?

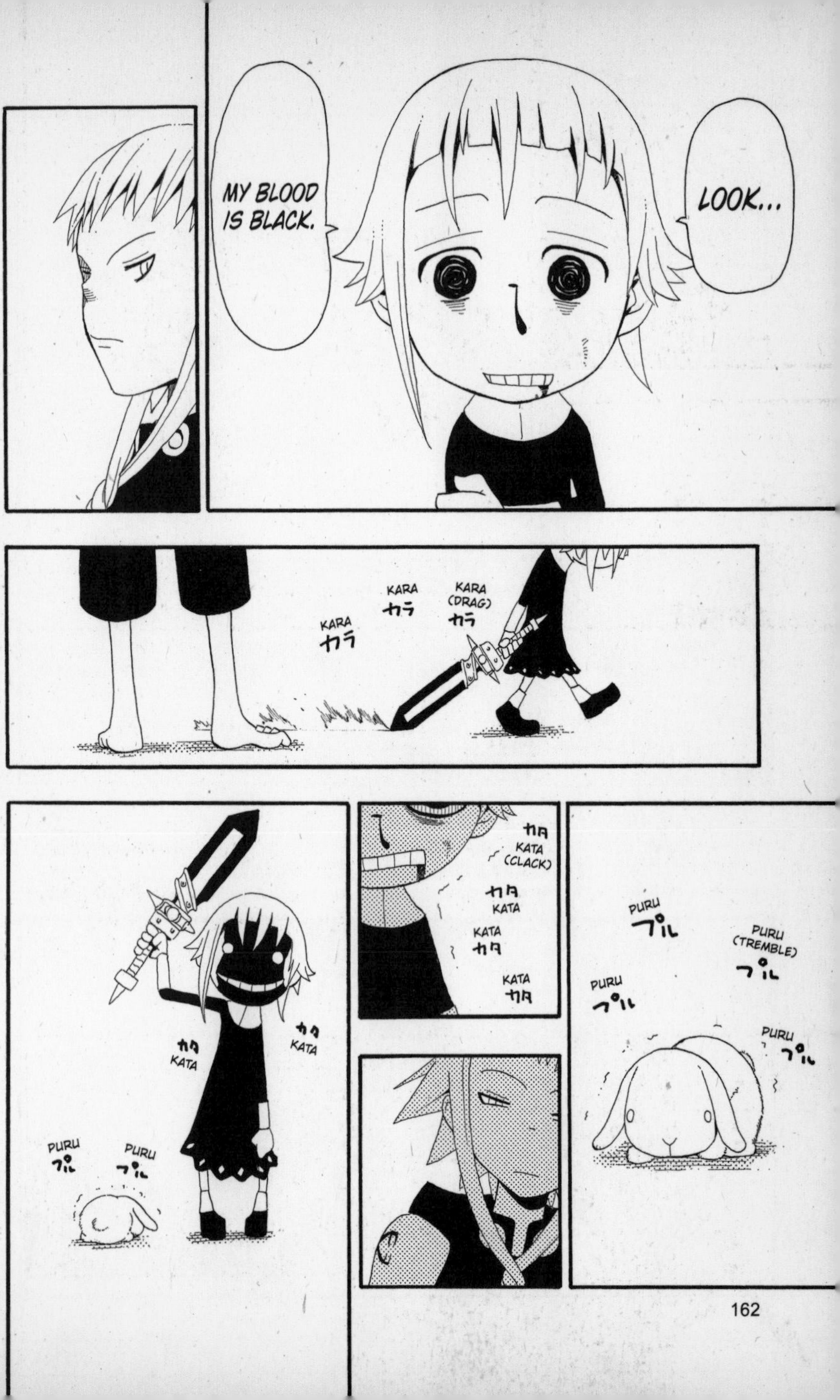
LOOK...
MY BLOOD IS BLACK.
KARA (DRAG) カラ
KARA カラ
KARA カラ
PURU (TREMBLE) プル
PURU プル
PURU プル
PURU プル
カタ KATA (CLACK)
カタ KATA
KATA カタ
KATA カタ
カタ KATA
カタ KATA
PURU プル
PURU プル

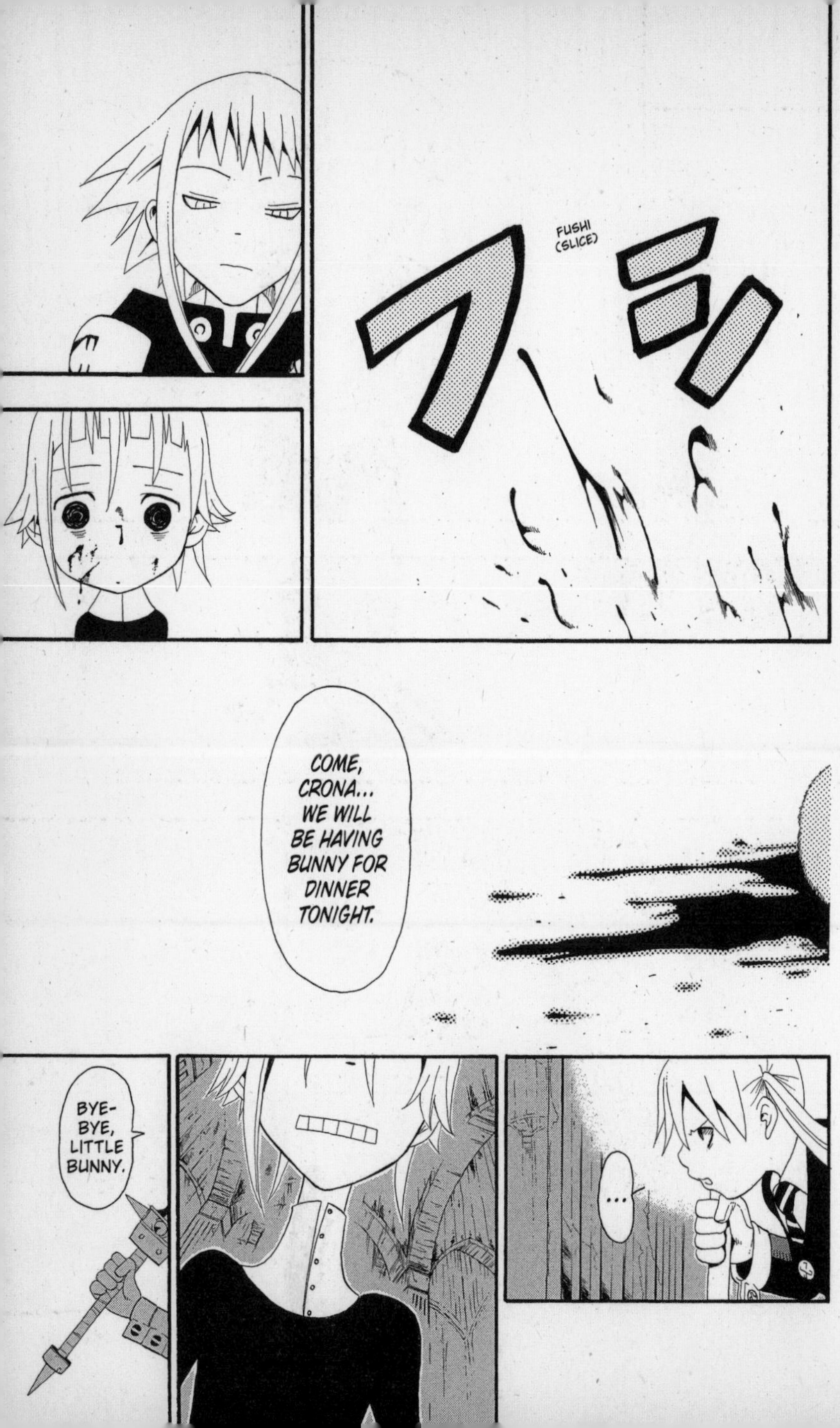
FUSHI (SLICE)
COME, CRONA... WE WILL BE HAVING BUNNY FOR DINNER TONIGHT.
...
BYE-BYE, LITTLE BUNNY.

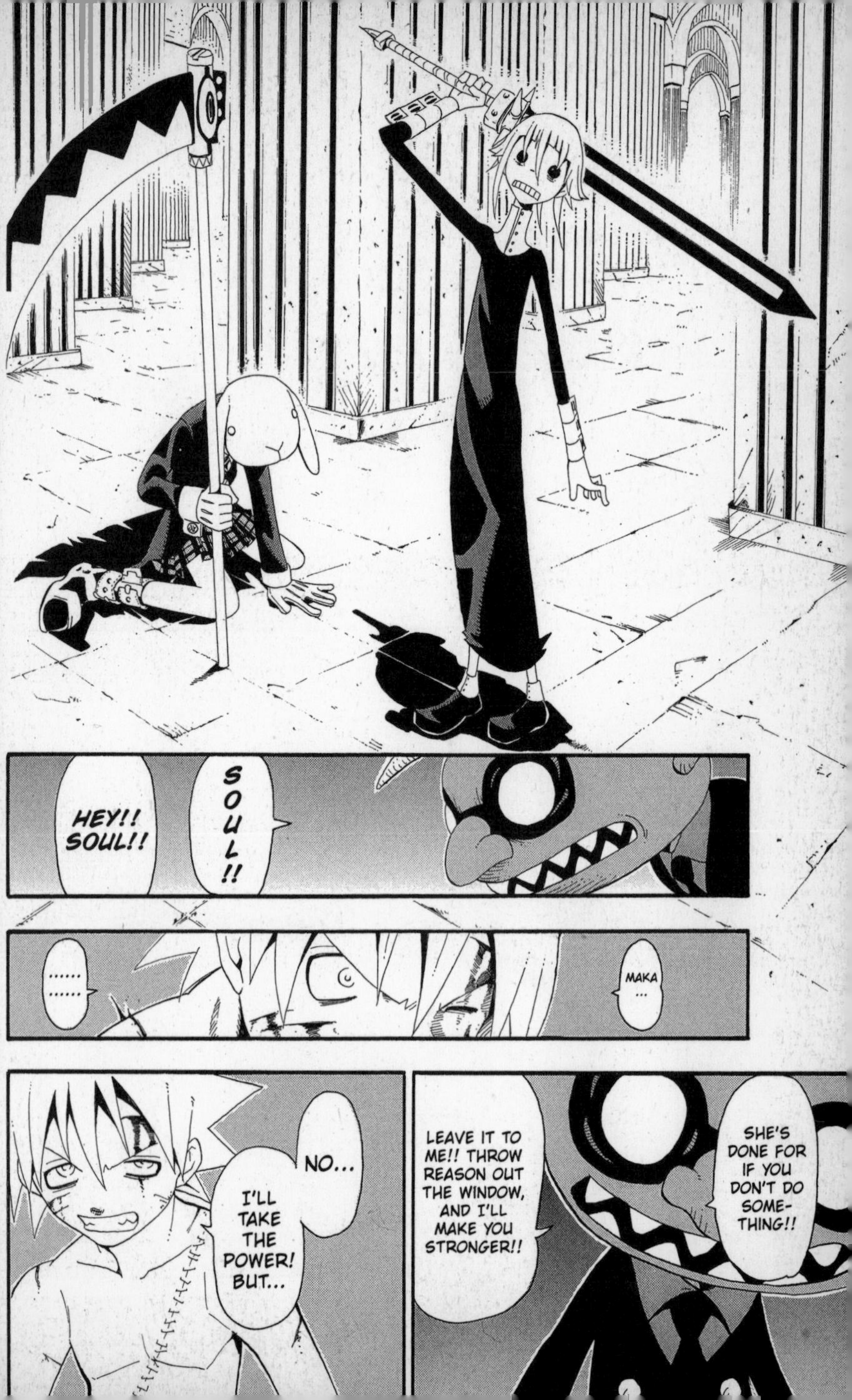
SOUL!!
HEY!! SOUL!!
MAKA ...
....
SHE'S DONE FOR IF YOU DON'T DO SOME-THING!!
LEAVE IT TO ME!! THROW REASON OUT THE WINDOW, AND I'LL MAKE YOU STRONGER!!
NO...
I'LL TAKE THE POWER! BUT...

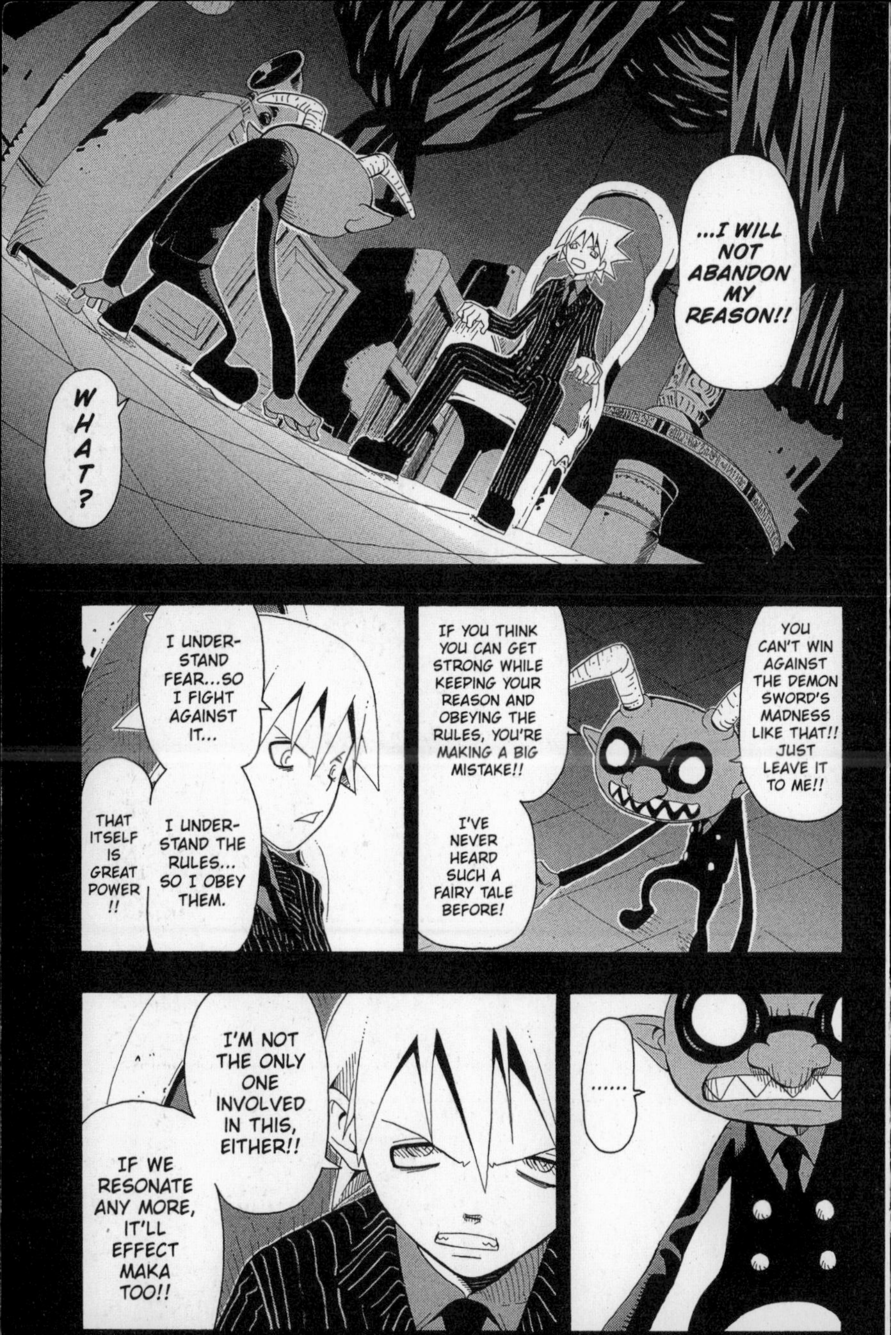
...I WILL NOT ABANDON MY REASON!!
WHAT?
YOU CAN'T WIN AGAINST THE DEMON SWORD'S MADNESS LIKE THAT!! JUST LEAVE IT TO ME!!
IF YOU THINK YOU CAN GET STRONG WHILE KEEPING YOUR REASON AND OBEYING THE RULES, YOU'RE MAKING A BIG MISTAKE!!
I'VE NEVER HEARD SUCH A FAIRY TALE BEFORE!
I UNDERSTAND FEAR...SO I FIGHT AGAINST IT...
I UNDERSTAND THE RULES... SO I OBEY THEM.
THAT ITSELF IS GREAT POWER!!
......
I'M NOT THE ONLY ONE INVOLVED IN THIS, EITHER!!
IF WE RESONATE ANY MORE, IT'LL EFFECT MAKA TOO!!

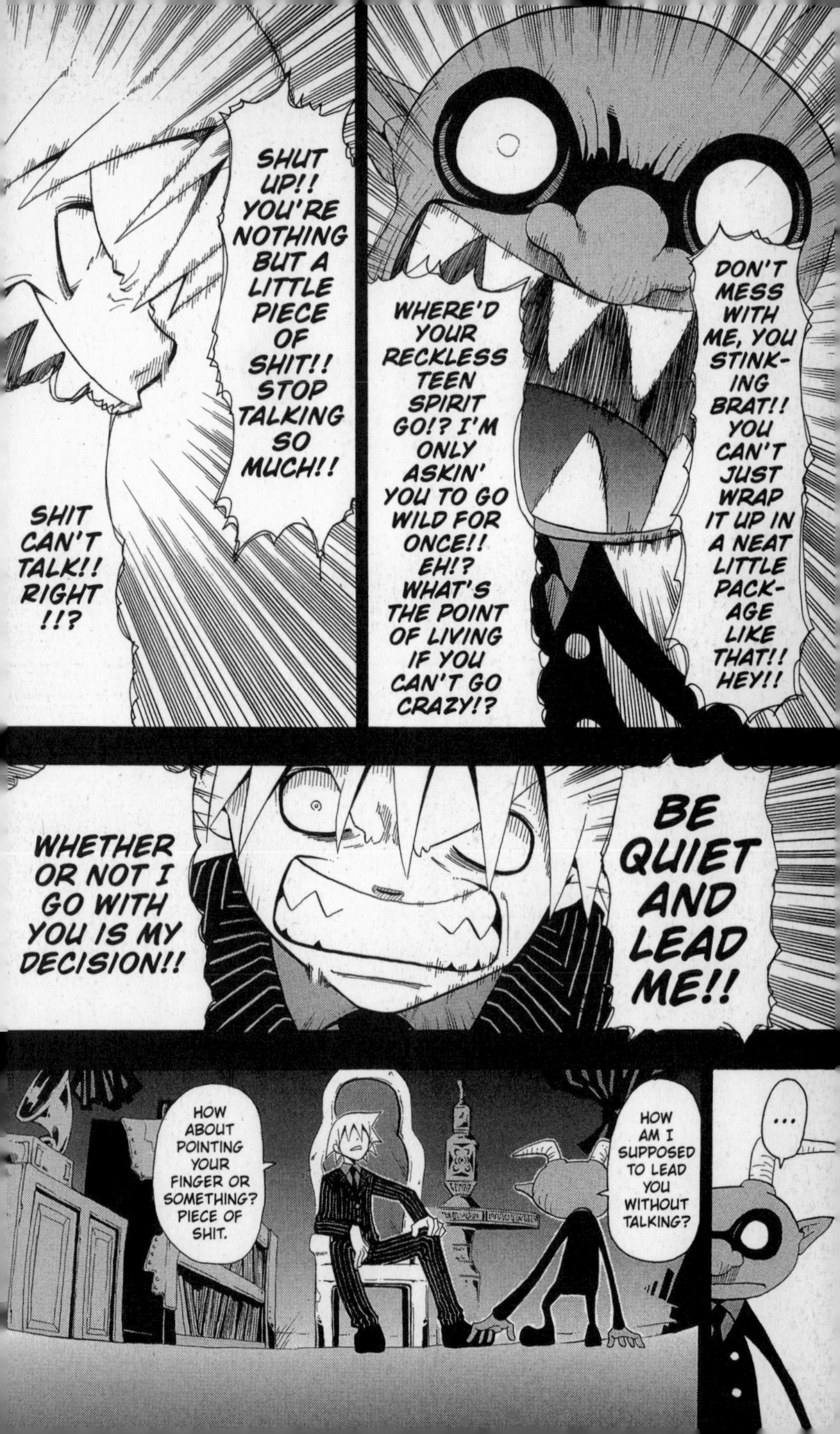
DON'T MESS WITH ME, YOU STINKING BRAT!! YOU CAN'T JUST WRAP IT UP IN A NEAT LITTLE PACKAGE LIKE THAT!! HEY!!
WHERE'D YOUR RECKLESS TEEN SPIRIT GO!? I'M ONLY ASKIN' YOU TO GO WILD FOR ONCE!! EH!? WHAT'S THE POINT OF LIVING IF YOU CAN'T GO CRAZY!?
SHUT UP!! YOU'RE NOTHING BUT A LITTLE PIECE OF SHIT!! STOP TALKING SO MUCH!!
SHIT CAN'T TALK!! RIGHT !!?
BE QUIET AND LEAD ME!!
WHETHER OR NOT I GO WITH YOU IS MY DECISION!!
...
HOW AM I SUPPOSED TO LEAD YOU WITHOUT TALKING?
HOW ABOUT POINTING YOUR FINGER OR SOMETHING? PIECE OF SHIT.

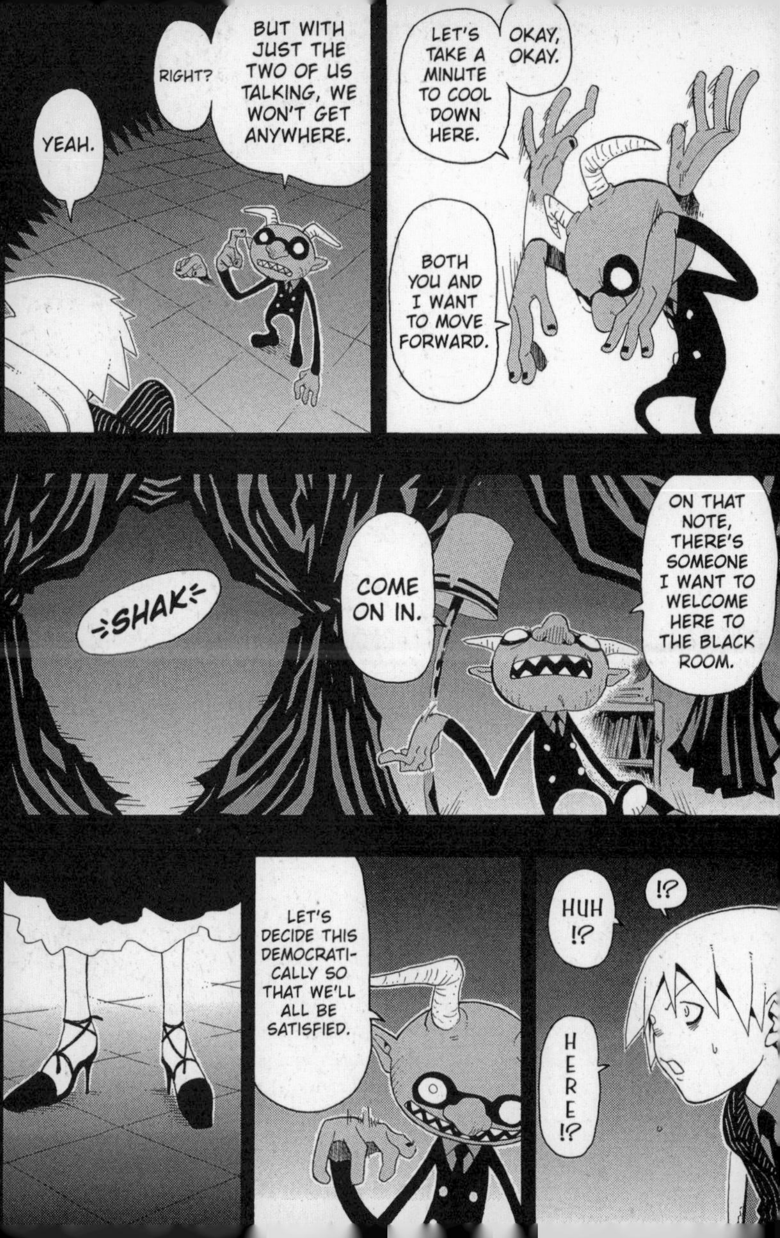
OKAY, OKAY.
LET'S TAKE A MINUTE TO COOL DOWN HERE.
BOTH YOU AND I WANT TO MOVE FORWARD.
BUT WITH JUST THE TWO OF US TALKING, WE WON'T GET ANYWHERE.
RIGHT?
YEAH.
ON THAT NOTE, THERE'S SOMEONE I WANT TO WELCOME HERE TO THE BLACK ROOM.
COME ON IN.
SHAK
!?
HUH !?
HERE !?
LET'S DECIDE THIS DEMOCRATICALLY SO THAT WE'LL ALL BE SATISFIED.

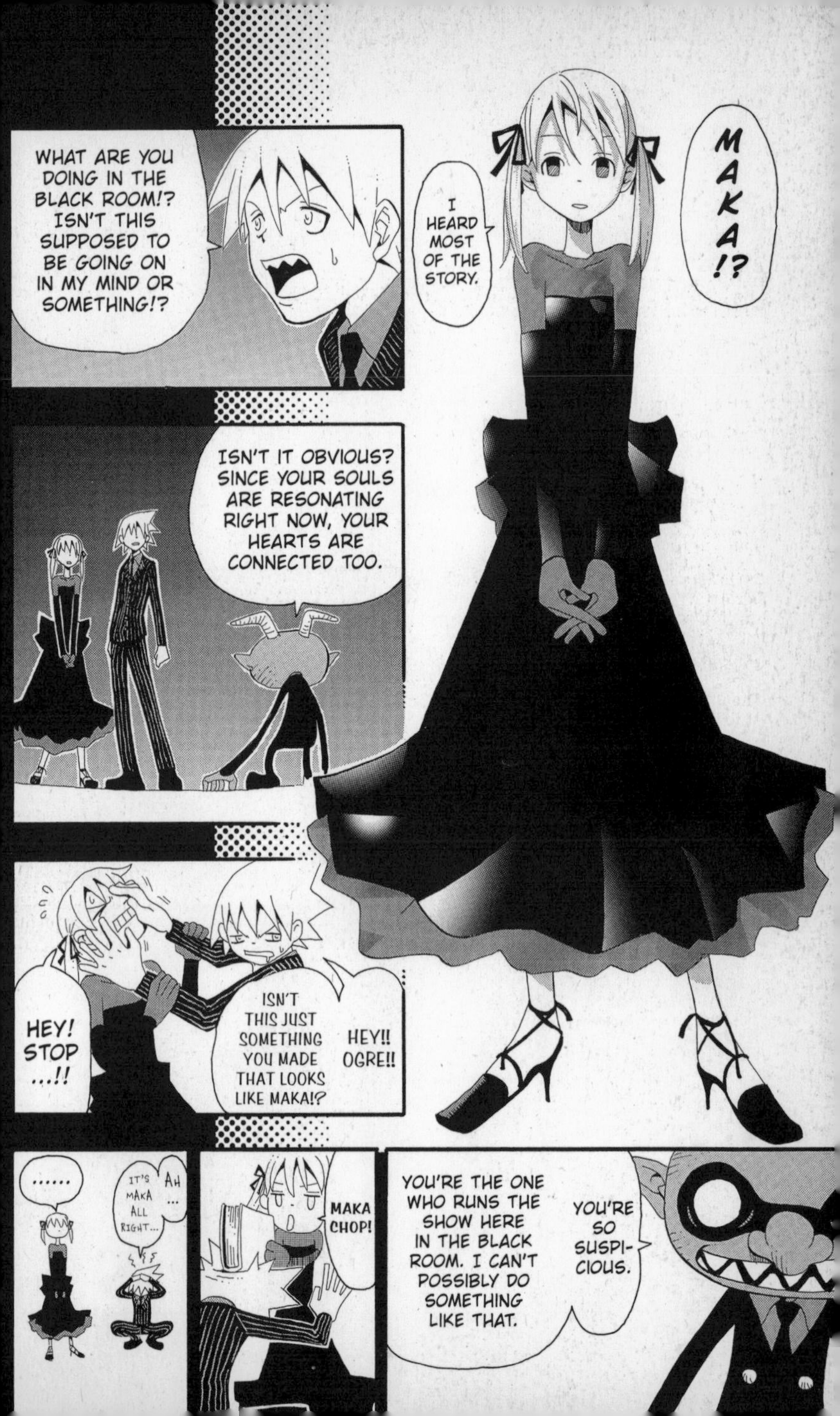
MAKA!?
I HEARD MOST OF THE STORY.
WHAT ARE YOU DOING IN THE BLACK ROOM!? ISN'T THIS SUPPOSED TO BE GOING ON IN MY MIND OR SOMETHING!?
ISN'T IT OBVIOUS? SINCE YOUR SOULS ARE RESONATING RIGHT NOW, YOUR HEARTS ARE CONNECTED TOO.
HEY!! OGRE!!
ISN'T THIS JUST SOMETHING YOU MADE THAT LOOKS LIKE MAKA!?
HEY! STOP ...!!
YOU'RE SO SUSPICIOUS.
YOU'RE THE ONE WHO RUNS THE SHOW HERE IN THE BLACK ROOM. I CAN'T POSSIBLY DO SOMETHING LIKE THAT.
MAKA CHOP!
AH ...
IT'S MAKA ALL RIGHT...
......

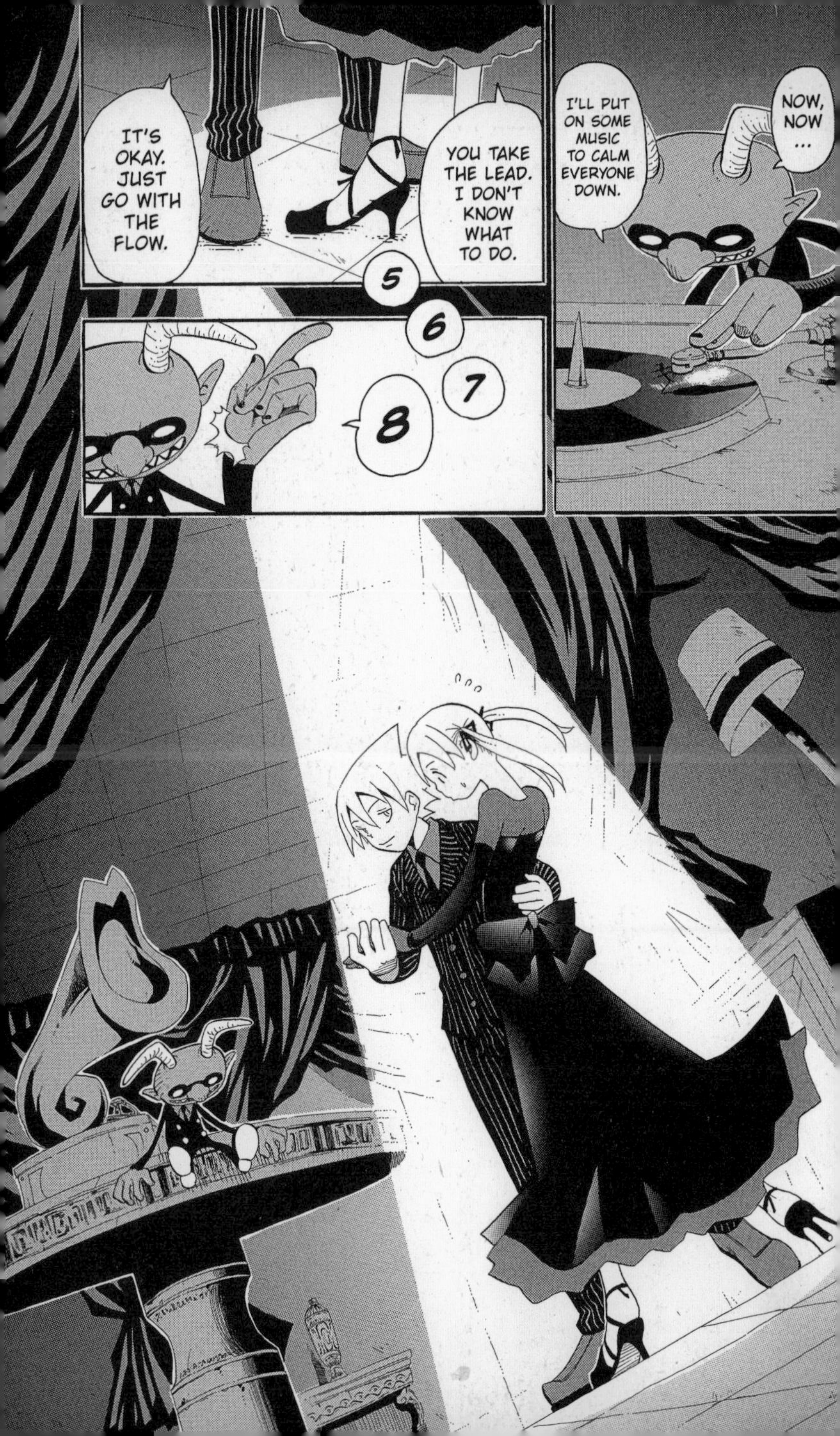
NOW, NOW ...
I'LL PUT ON SOME MUSIC TO CALM EVERYONE DOWN.
YOU TAKE THE LEAD. I DON'T KNOW WHAT TO DO.
IT'S OKAY. JUST GO WITH THE FLOW.
5
6
7
8

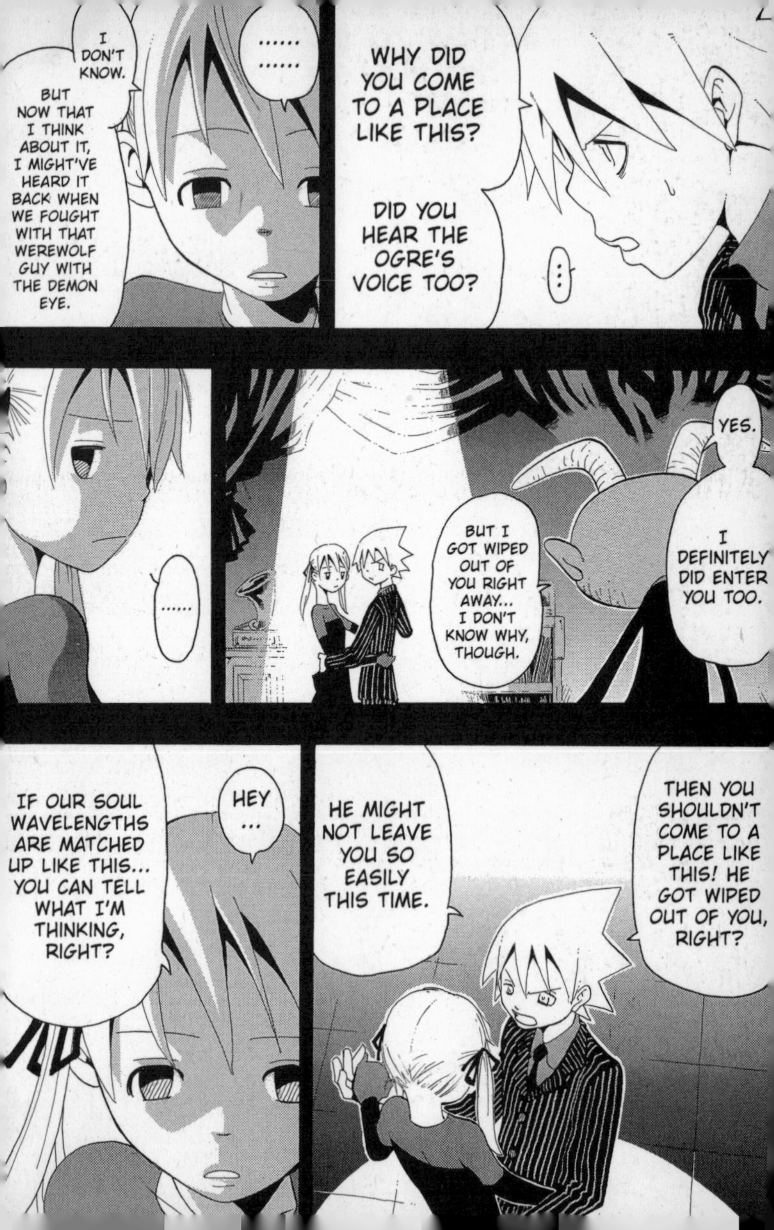
WHY DID YOU COME TO A PLACE LIKE THIS?
DID YOU HEAR THE OGRE'S VOICE TOO?
...
......
......
I DON'T KNOW.
BUT NOW THAT I THINK ABOUT IT, I MIGHT'VE HEARD IT BACK WHEN WE FOUGHT WITH THAT WEREWOLF GUY WITH THE DEMON EYE.
YES.
I DEFINITELY DID ENTER YOU TOO.
BUT I GOT WIPED OUT OF YOU RIGHT AWAY... I DON'T KNOW WHY, THOUGH.
......
THEN YOU SHOULDN'T COME TO A PLACE LIKE THIS! HE GOT WIPED OUT OF YOU, RIGHT?
HE MIGHT NOT LEAVE YOU SO EASILY THIS TIME.
HEY...
IF OUR SOUL WAVELENGTHS ARE MATCHED UP LIKE THIS... YOU CAN TELL WHAT I'M THINKING, RIGHT?

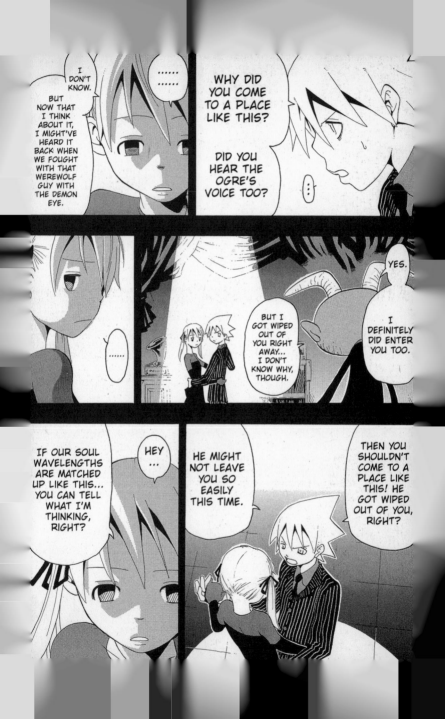

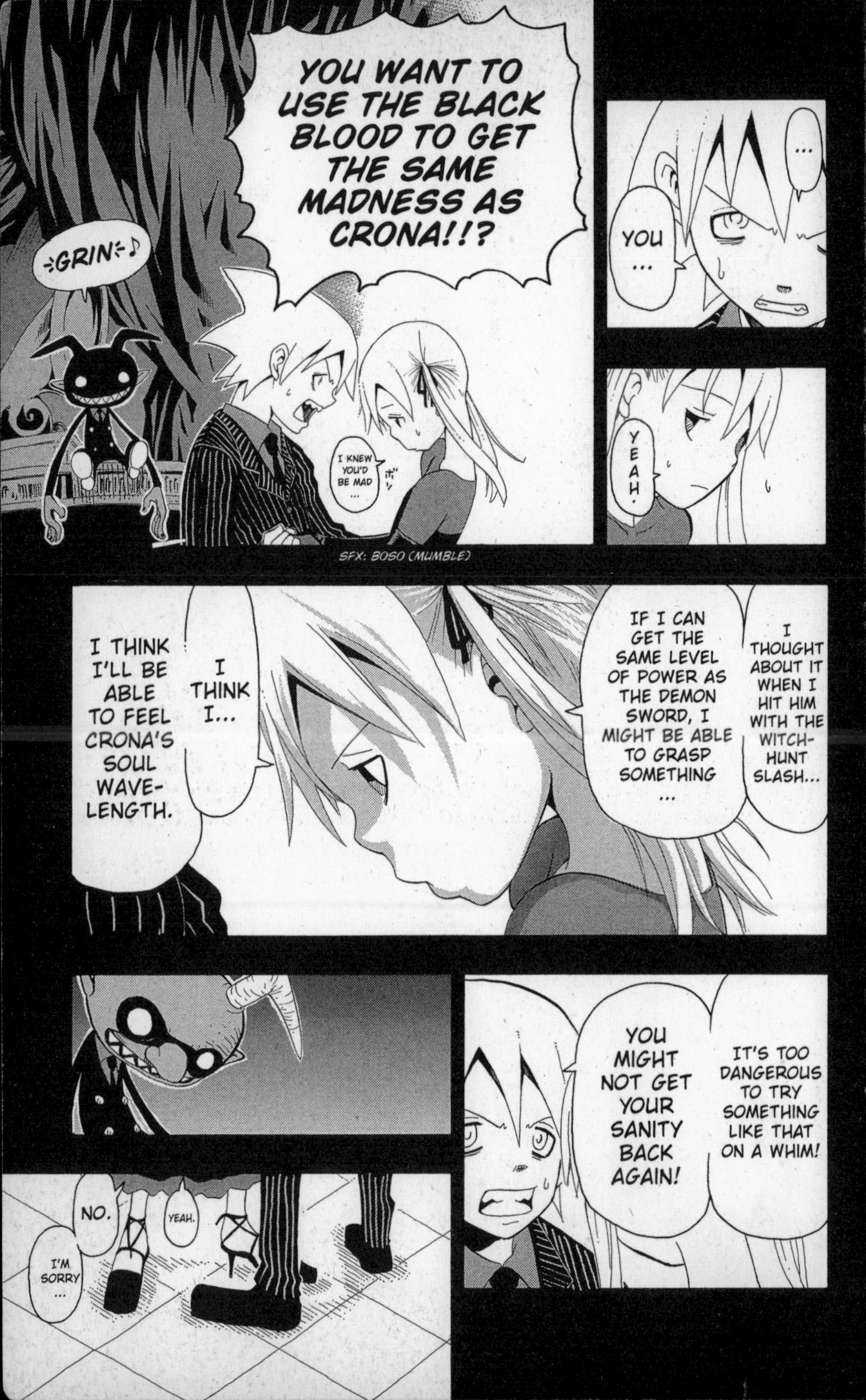
...
YOU ...
YEAH.
YOU WANT TO USE THE BLACK BLOOD TO GET THE SAME MADNESS AS CRONA!!?
GRIN♪
I KNEW YOU'D BE MAD ...
SFX: BOSO (MUMBLE)
I THOUGHT ABOUT IT WHEN I HIT HIM WITH THE WITCH-HUNT SLASH...
IF I CAN GET THE SAME LEVEL OF POWER AS THE DEMON SWORD, I MIGHT BE ABLE TO GRASP SOMETHING ...
I THINK I...
I THINK I'LL BE ABLE TO FEEL CRONA'S SOUL WAVE-LENGTH.
IT'S TOO DANGEROUS TO TRY SOMETHING LIKE THAT ON A WHIM!
YOU MIGHT NOT GET YOUR SANITY BACK AGAIN!
YEAH.
NO.
I'M SORRY ...

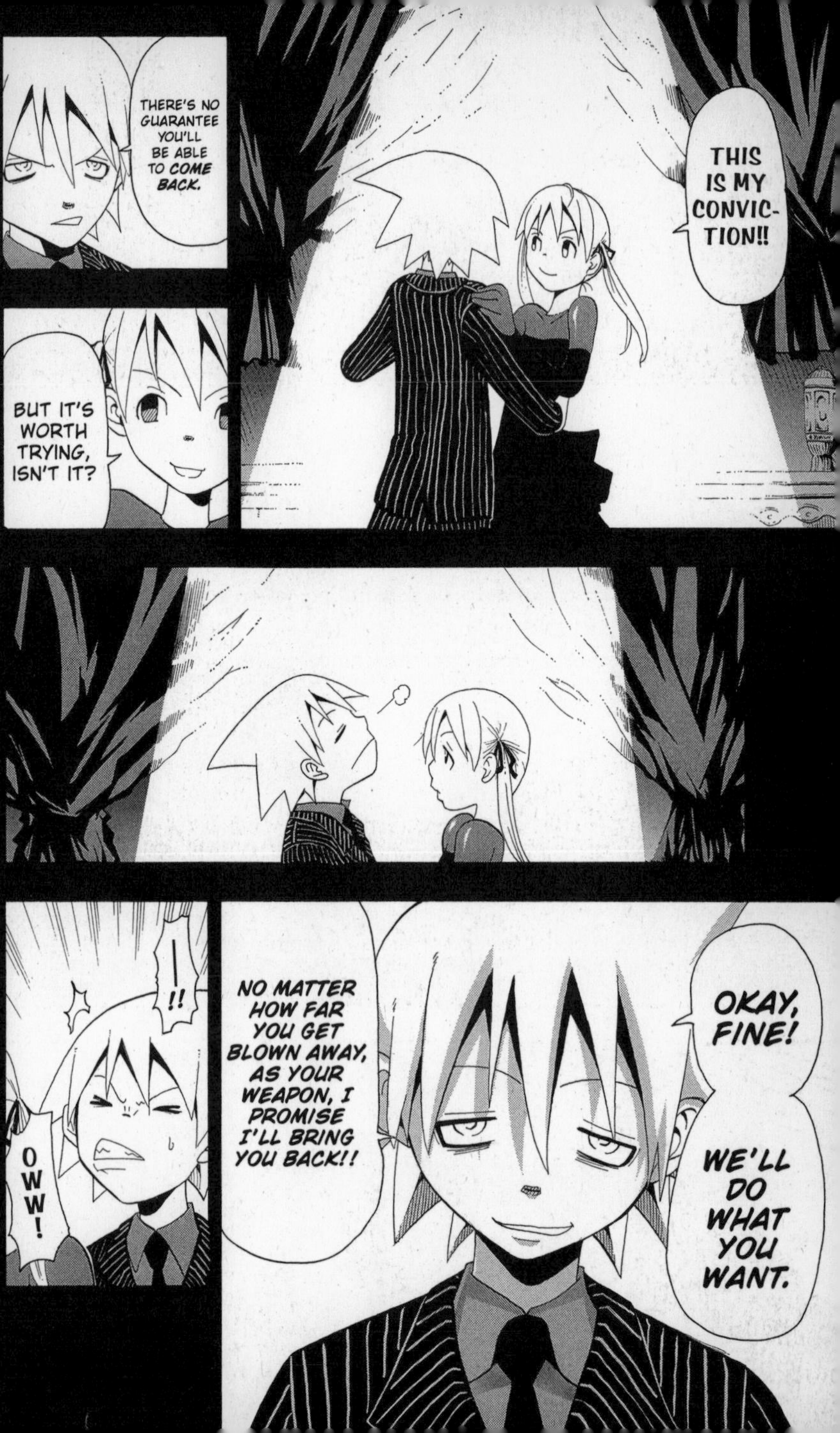
THIS IS MY CONVICTION!!
THERE'S NO GUARANTEE YOU'LL BE ABLE TO COME BACK.
BUT IT'S WORTH TRYING, ISN'T IT?
OKAY, FINE!
WE'LL DO WHAT YOU WANT.
NO MATTER HOW FAR YOU GET BLOWN AWAY, AS YOUR WEAPON, I PROMISE I'LL BRING YOU BACK!!
!!
OWW!

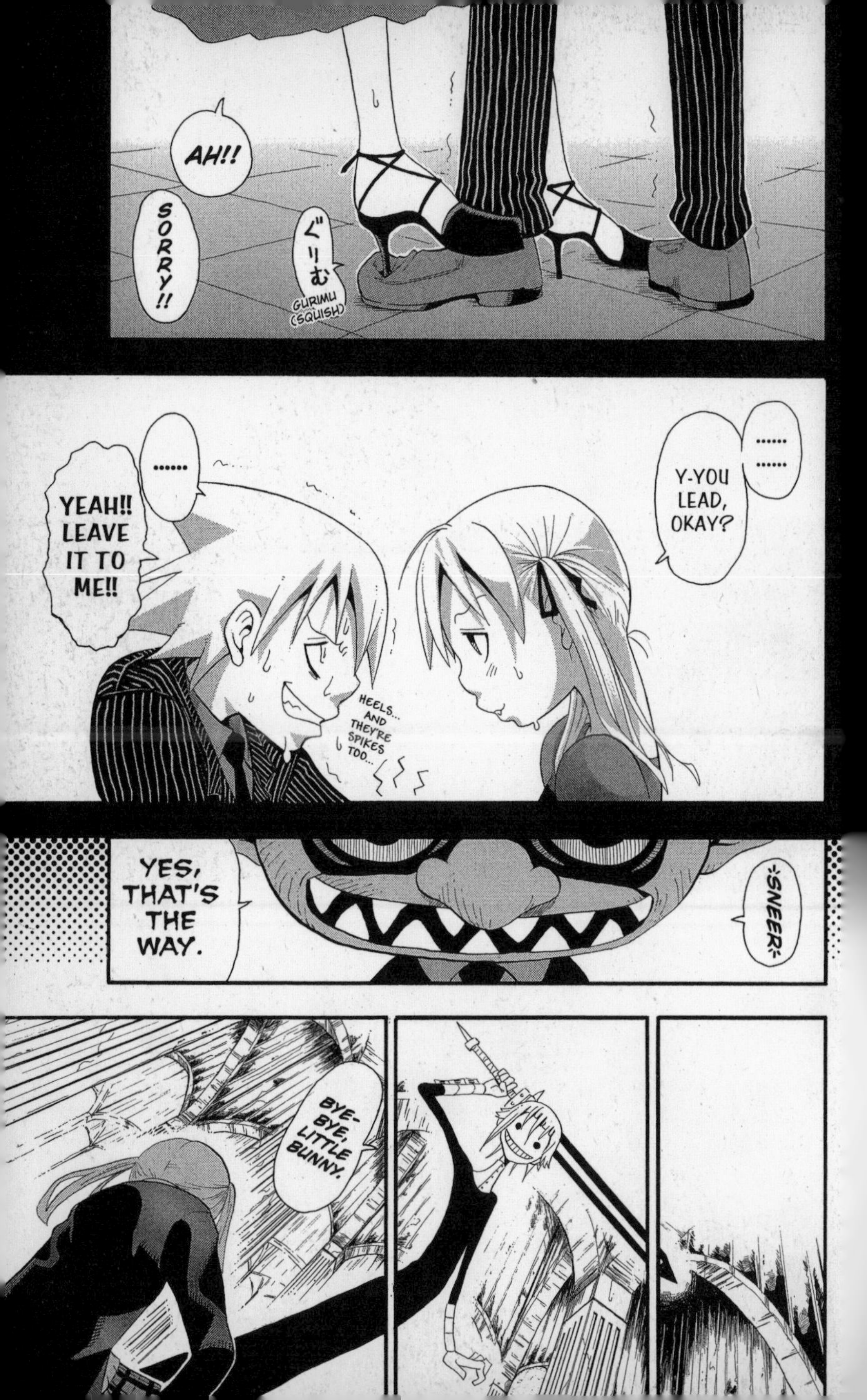
AH!!
SORRY!!
ぐりむ
GURIMU (SQUISH)
......
......
Y-YOU LEAD, OKAY?
......
YEAH!! LEAVE IT TO ME!!
HEELS... AND THEY'RE SPIKES TOO...
SNEER
YES, THAT'S THE WAY.
BYE-BYE, LITTLE BUNNY.

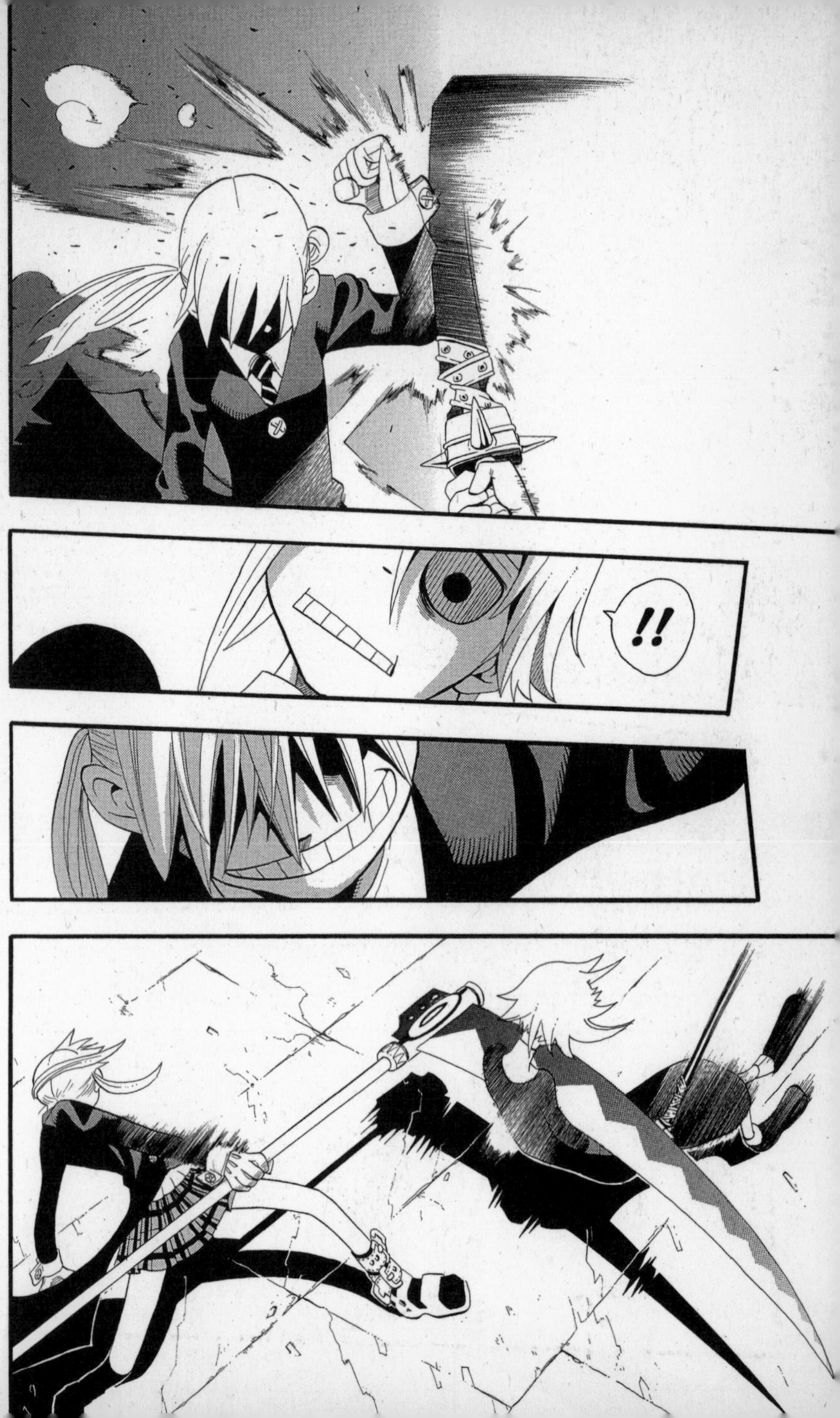
!!

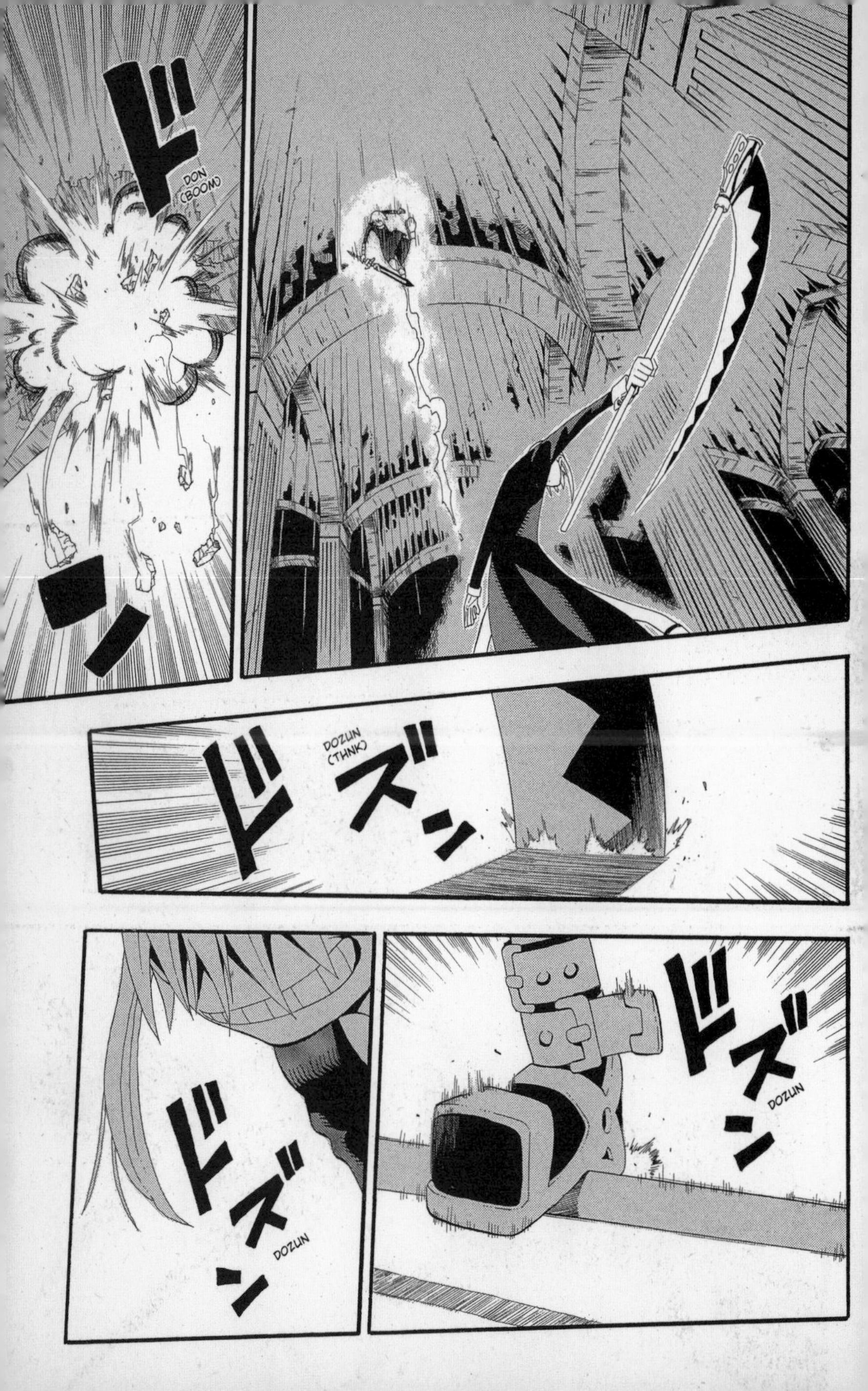
ドン
DON
(BOOM)
ドズン
DOZUN
(THNK)
ドズン
DOZUN
ドズン
DOZUN

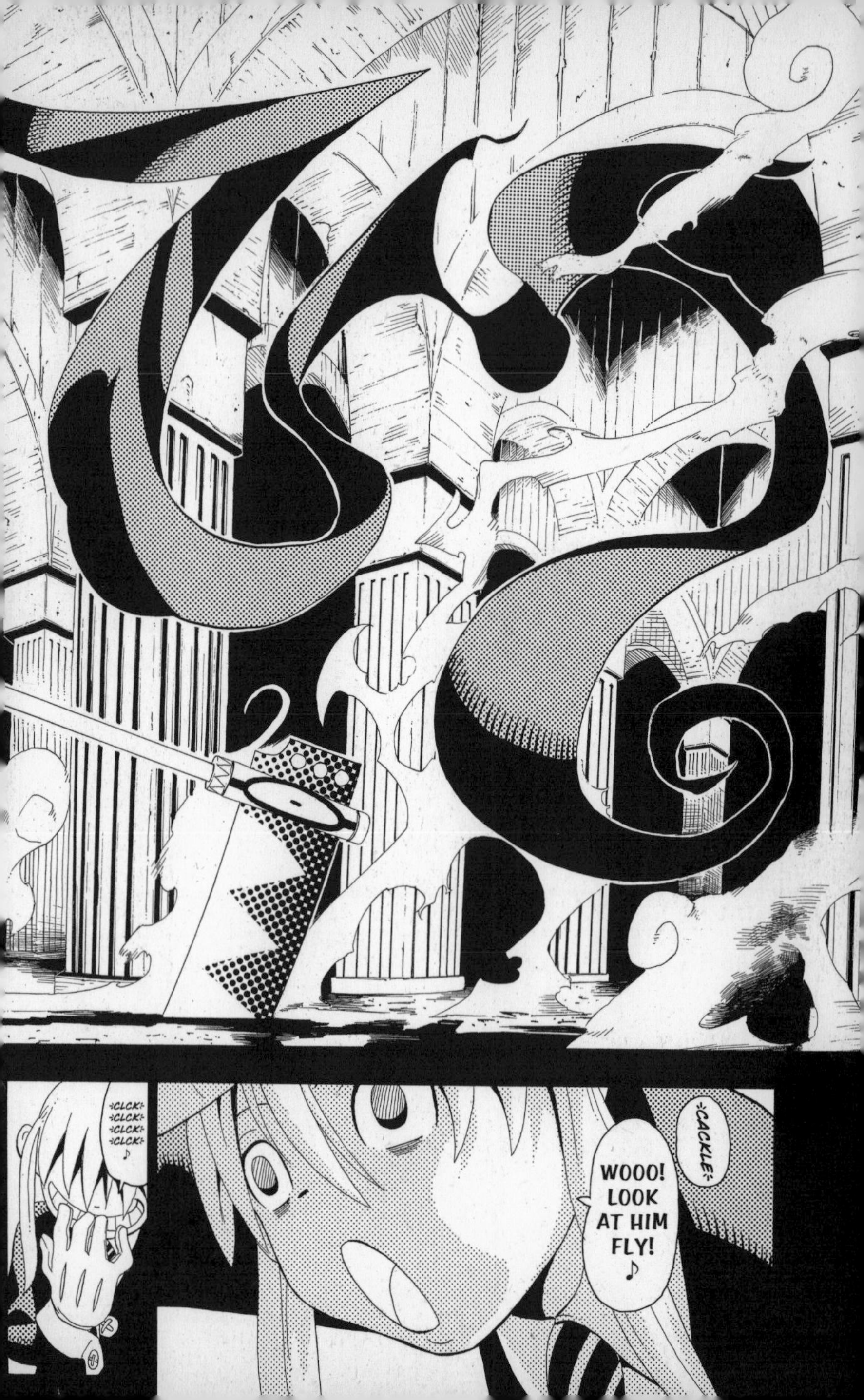
CACKLE
WOOO! LOOK AT HIM FLY! ♪
CLCK CLCK CLCK CLCK ♪

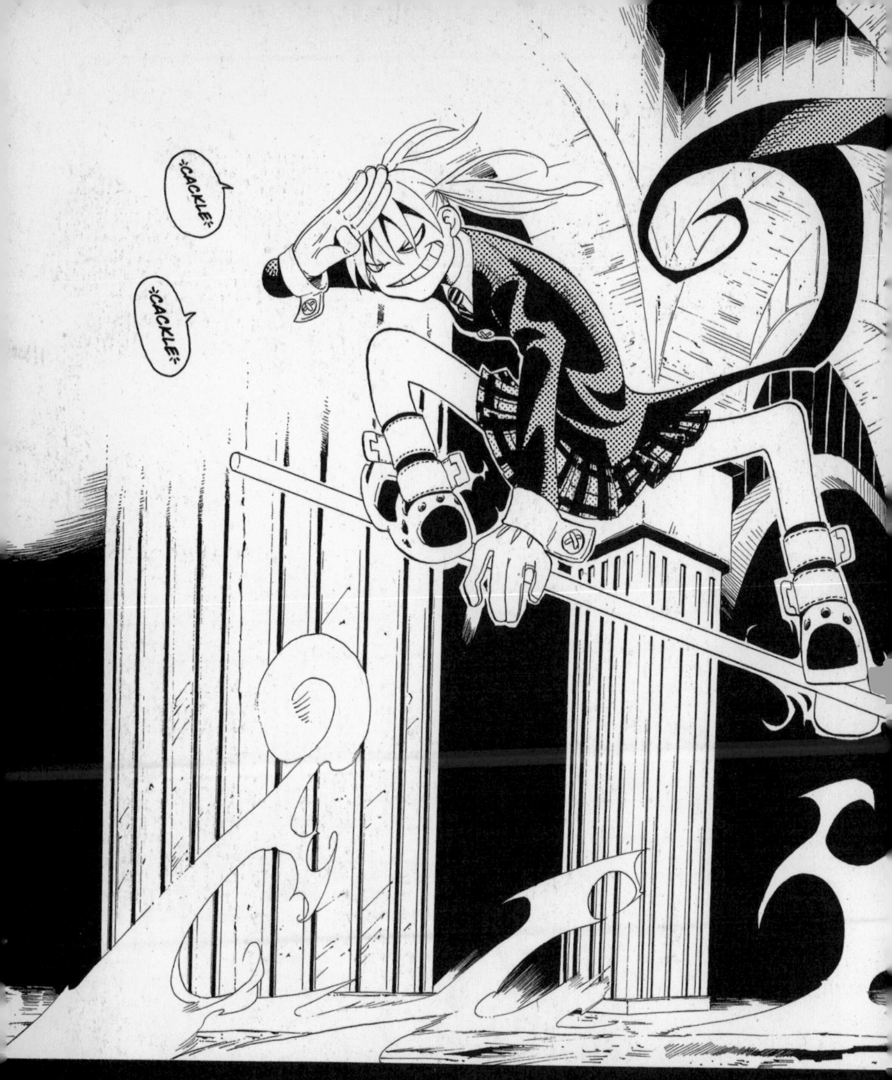
CACKLE
CACKLE

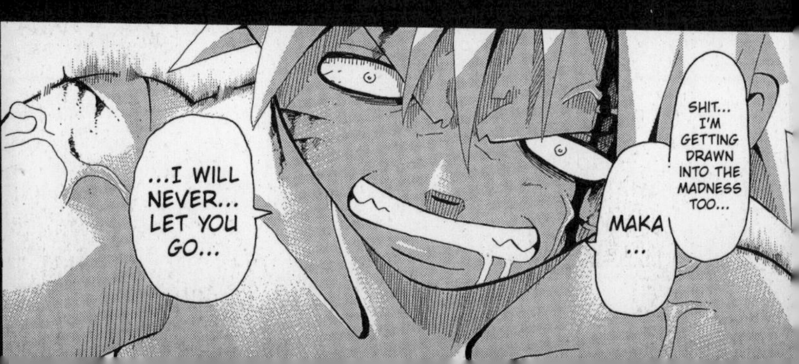
SHIT... I'M GETTING DRAWN INTO THE MADNESS TOO...
MAKA ...
...I WILL NEVER... LET YOU GO...

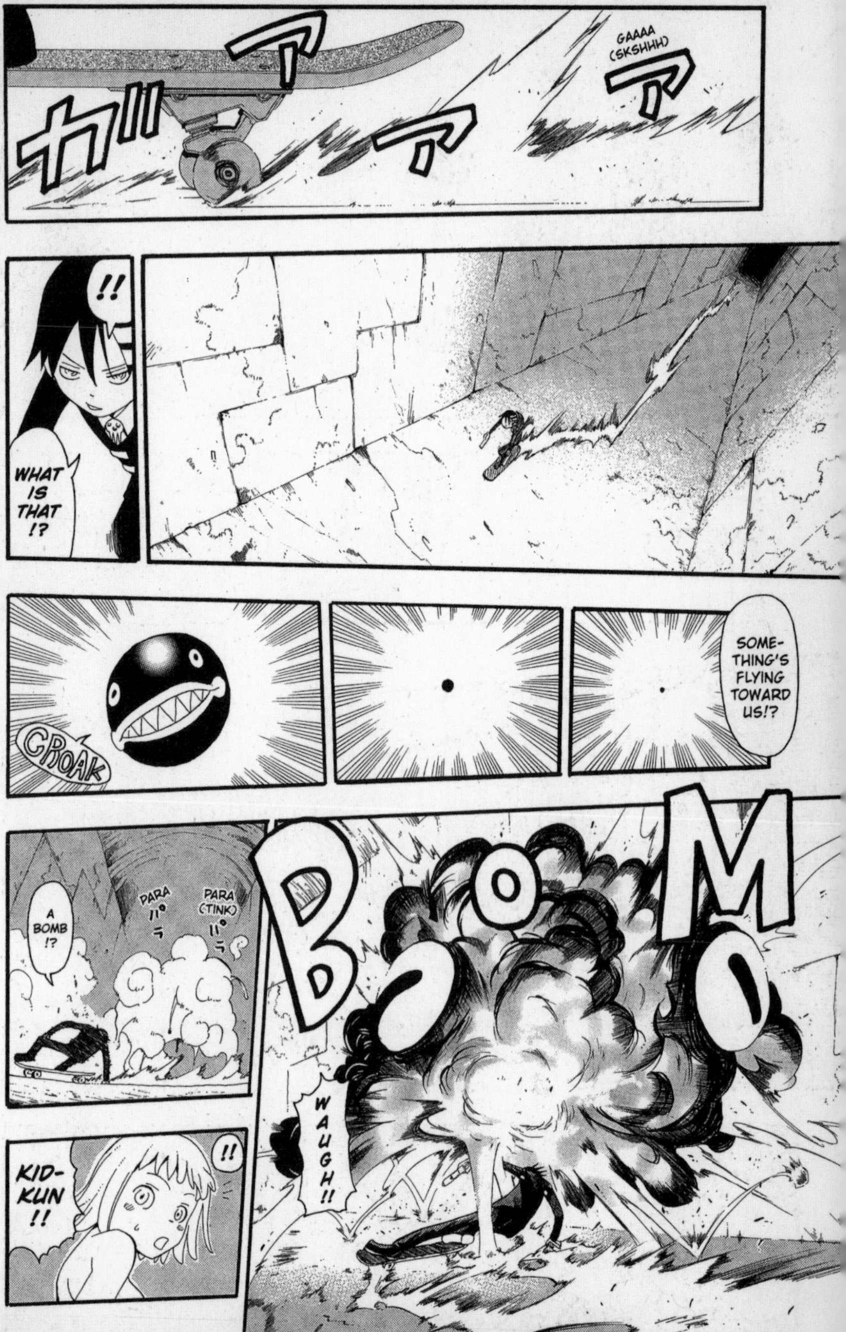
カァァァ
GAAAA (SKSHHH)
!!
WHAT IS THAT!?
SOMETHING'S FLYING TOWARD US!?
CROAK
BOOM
WAUGH!!
PARA (TINK)
PARA
A BOMB!?
!!
KID-KUN!!

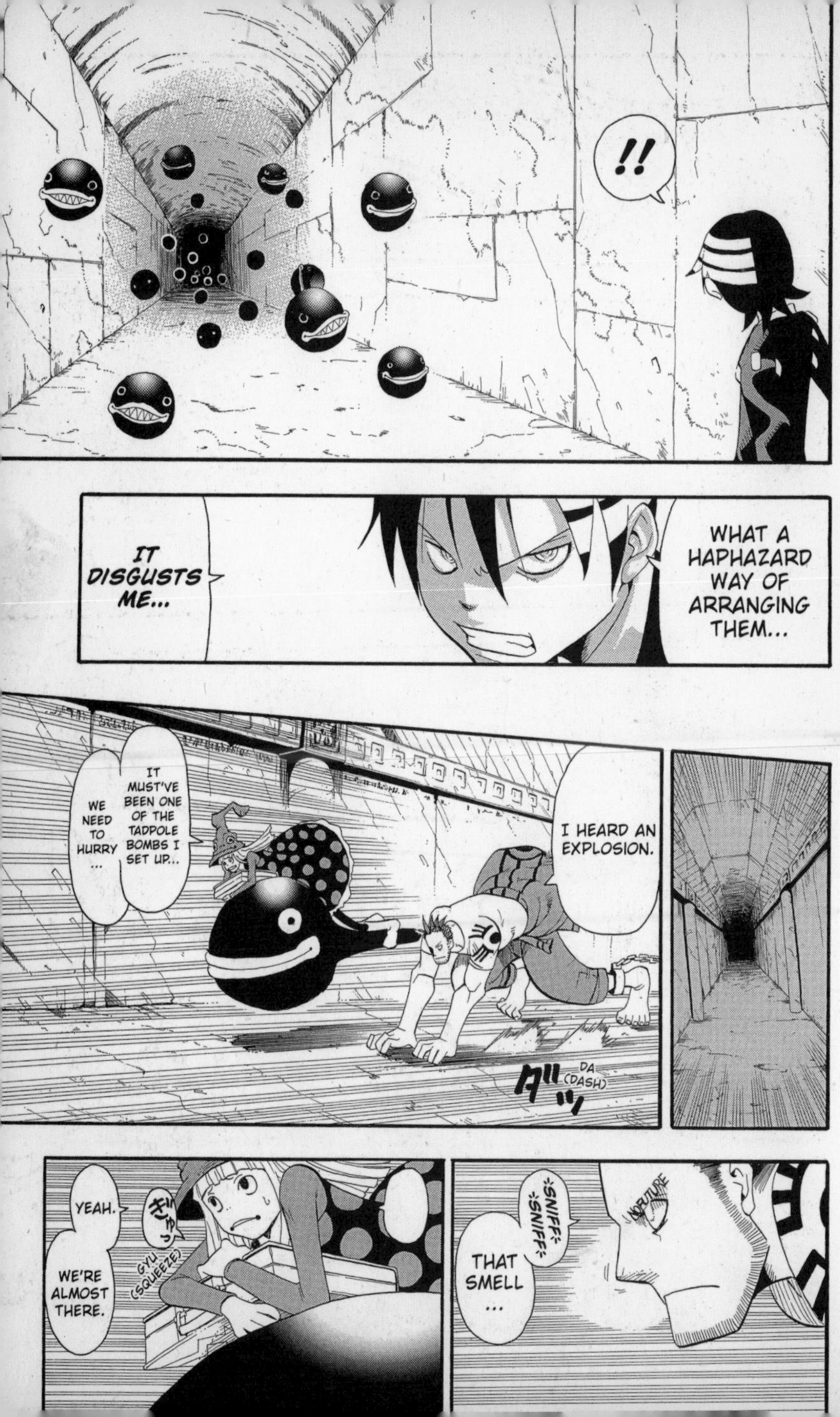
!!
WHAT A HAPHAZARD WAY OF ARRANGING THEM...
IT DISGUSTS ME...
I HEARD AN EXPLOSION.
IT MUST'VE BEEN ONE OF THE TADPOLE BOMBS I SET UP...
WE NEED TO HURRY...
DA (DASH)
NO FUTURE
SNIFF SNIFF
THAT SMELL...
YEAH.
GYU (SQUEEZE)
WE'RE ALMOST THERE.

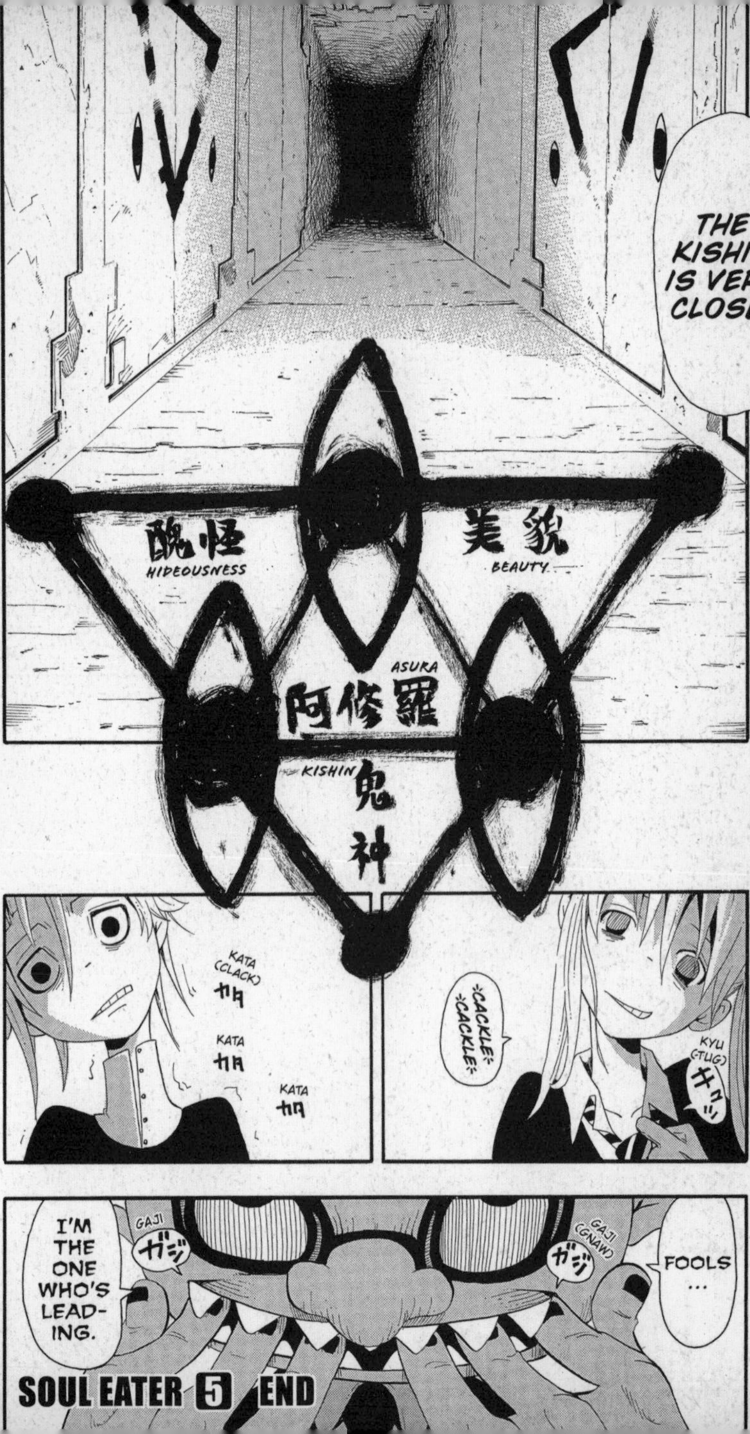

THE KISHIN IS VERY CLOSE.
美貌
BEAUTY
醜怪
HIDEOUSNESS
ASURA
阿修羅
KISHIN
鬼神
CACKLE *CACKLE*
KYU (TUG)
キュッ
KATA (CLACK)
カタ
KATA
カタ
KATA
カタ
FOOLS...
GAJI (GNAW)
ガジ
GAJI
ガジ
I'M THE ONE WHO'S LEAD-ING.
SOUL EATER 5 END

SOUL EATER

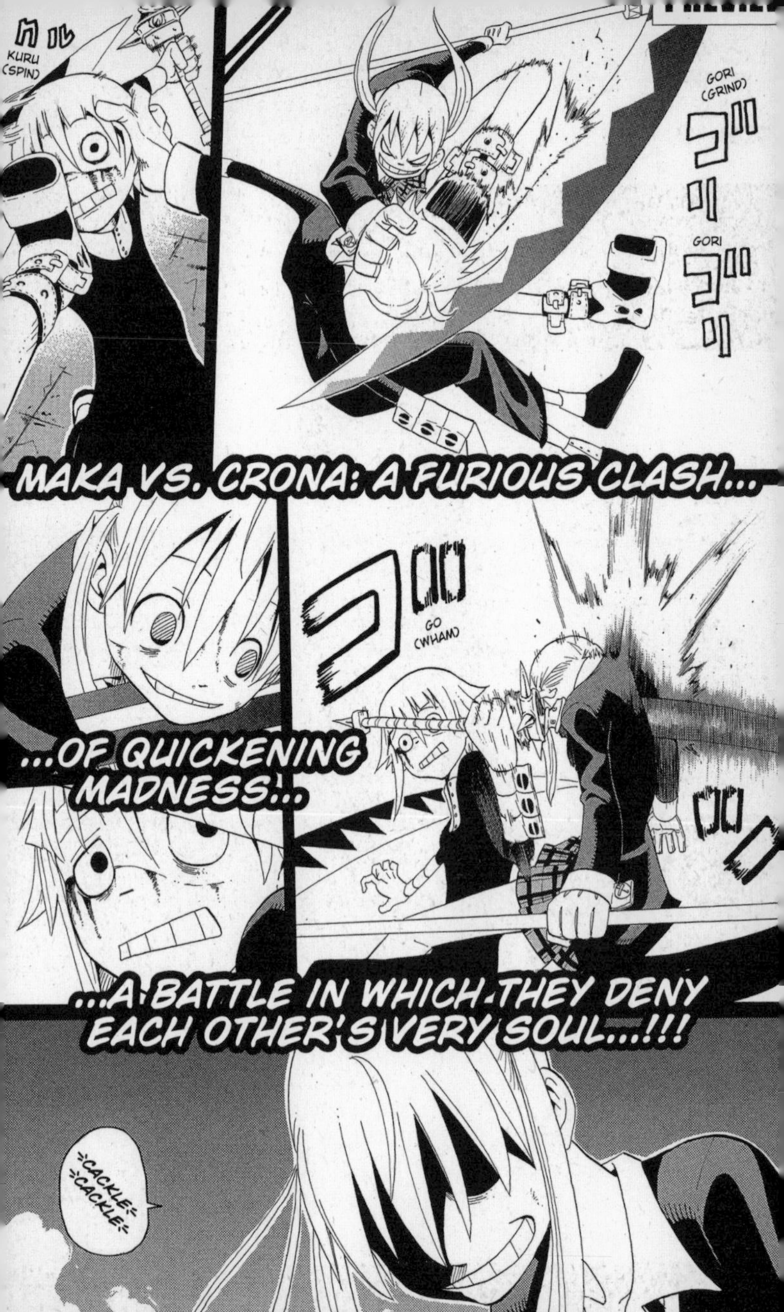
ゴリ
GORI (GRIND)
ゴリ
GORI
クル
KURU (SPIN)
MAKA VS. CRONA: A FURIOUS CLASH...
ゴッ
GO (WHAM)
...OF QUICKENING MADNESS...
...A BATTLE IN WHICH THEY DENY EACH OTHER'S VERY SOUL...!!!
CACKLE *CACKLE*

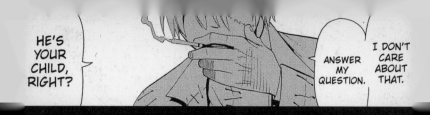

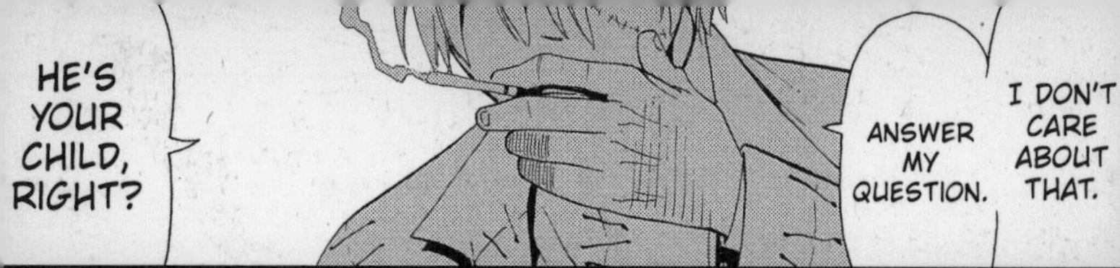
I DON'T CARE ABOUT THAT.
ANSWER MY QUESTION.
HE'S YOUR CHILD, RIGHT?

MEDUSA, THE HEARTLESS WITCH WHO WOULD ABANDON EVEN HER OWN CHILD...

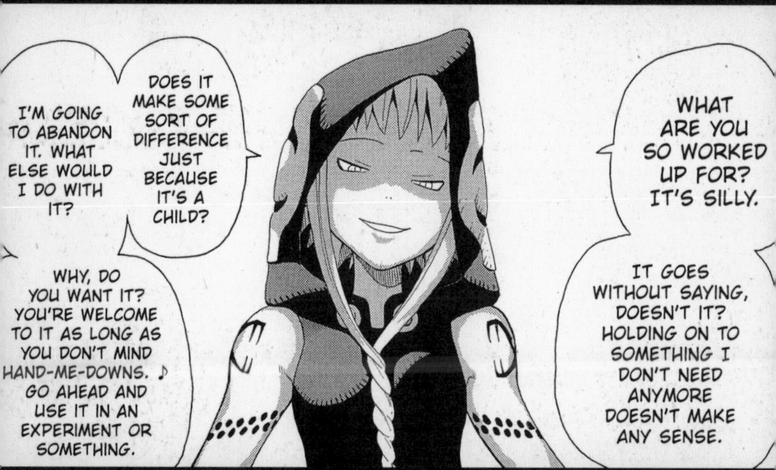
WHAT ARE YOU SO WORKED UP FOR? IT'S SILLY.
IT GOES WITHOUT SAYING, DOESN'T IT? HOLDING ON TO SOMETHING I DON'T NEED ANYMORE DOESN'T MAKE ANY SENSE.
DOES IT MAKE SOME SORT OF DIFFERENCE JUST BECAUSE IT'S A CHILD?
I'M GOING TO ABANDON IT. WHAT ELSE WOULD I DO WITH IT?
WHY, DO YOU WANT IT? YOU'RE WELCOME TO IT AS LONG AS YOU DON'T MIND HAND-ME-DOWNS. ♪ GO AHEAD AND USE IT IN AN EXPERIMENT OR SOMETHING.

WILL LIGHT REACH INTO THE DARKNESS IN CRONA'S HEART...!!?

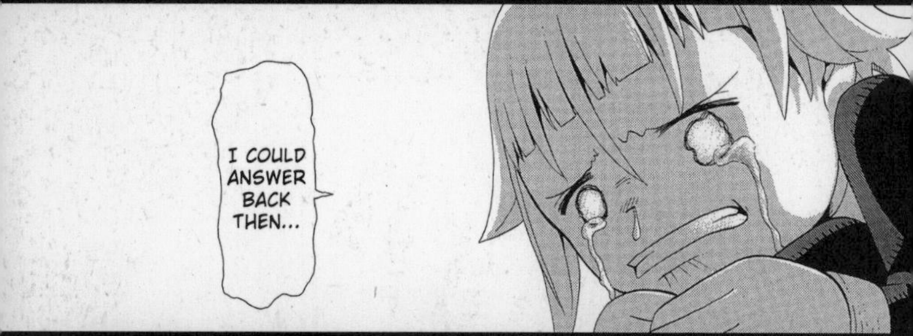
I COULD ANSWER BACK THEN...

Continued in Soul Eater Volume 6!!

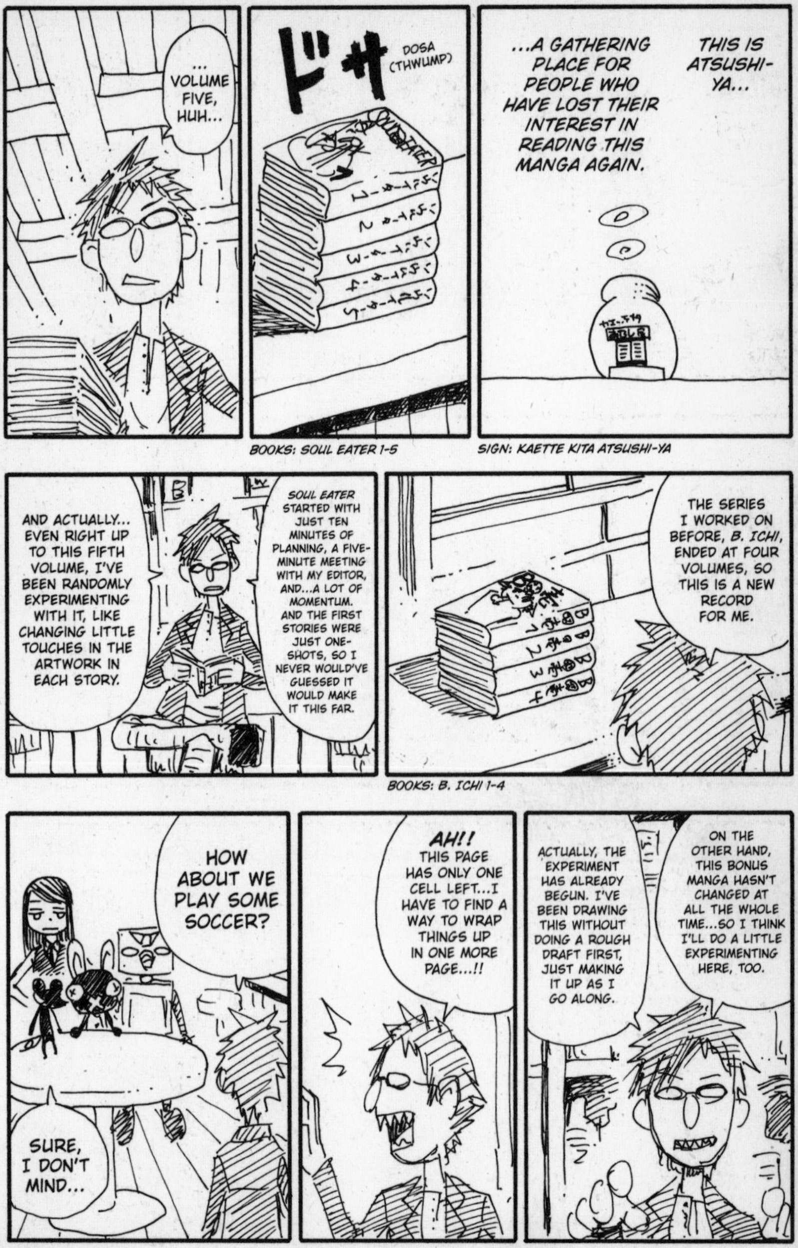
THIS IS ATSUSHI-YA...
...A GATHERING PLACE FOR PEOPLE WHO HAVE LOST THEIR INTEREST IN READING THIS MANGA AGAIN.
SIGN: KAETTE KITA ATSUSHI-YA
DOSA (THWUMP)
BOOKS: SOUL EATER 1-5
...VOLUME FIVE, HUH...
THE SERIES I WORKED ON BEFORE, B. ICHI, ENDED AT FOUR VOLUMES, SO THIS IS A NEW RECORD FOR ME.
BOOKS: B. ICHI 1-4
SOUL EATER STARTED WITH JUST TEN MINUTES OF PLANNING, A FIVE-MINUTE MEETING WITH MY EDITOR, AND...A LOT OF MOMENTUM. AND THE FIRST STORIES WERE JUST ONE-SHOTS, SO I NEVER WOULD'VE GUESSED IT WOULD MAKE IT THIS FAR.
AND ACTUALLY... EVEN RIGHT UP TO THIS FIFTH VOLUME, I'VE BEEN RANDOMLY EXPERIMENTING WITH IT, LIKE CHANGING LITTLE TOUCHES IN THE ARTWORK IN EACH STORY.
ON THE OTHER HAND, THIS BONUS MANGA HASN'T CHANGED AT ALL THE WHOLE TIME...SO I THINK I'LL DO A LITTLE EXPERIMENTING HERE, TOO.
ACTUALLY, THE EXPERIMENT HAS ALREADY BEGUN. I'VE BEEN DRAWING THIS WITHOUT DOING A ROUGH DRAFT FIRST, JUST MAKING IT UP AS I GO ALONG.
AH!! THIS PAGE HAS ONLY ONE CELL LEFT...I HAVE TO FIND A WAY TO WRAP THINGS UP IN ONE MORE PAGE...!!
HOW ABOUT WE PLAY SOME SOCCER?
SURE, I DON'T MIND...

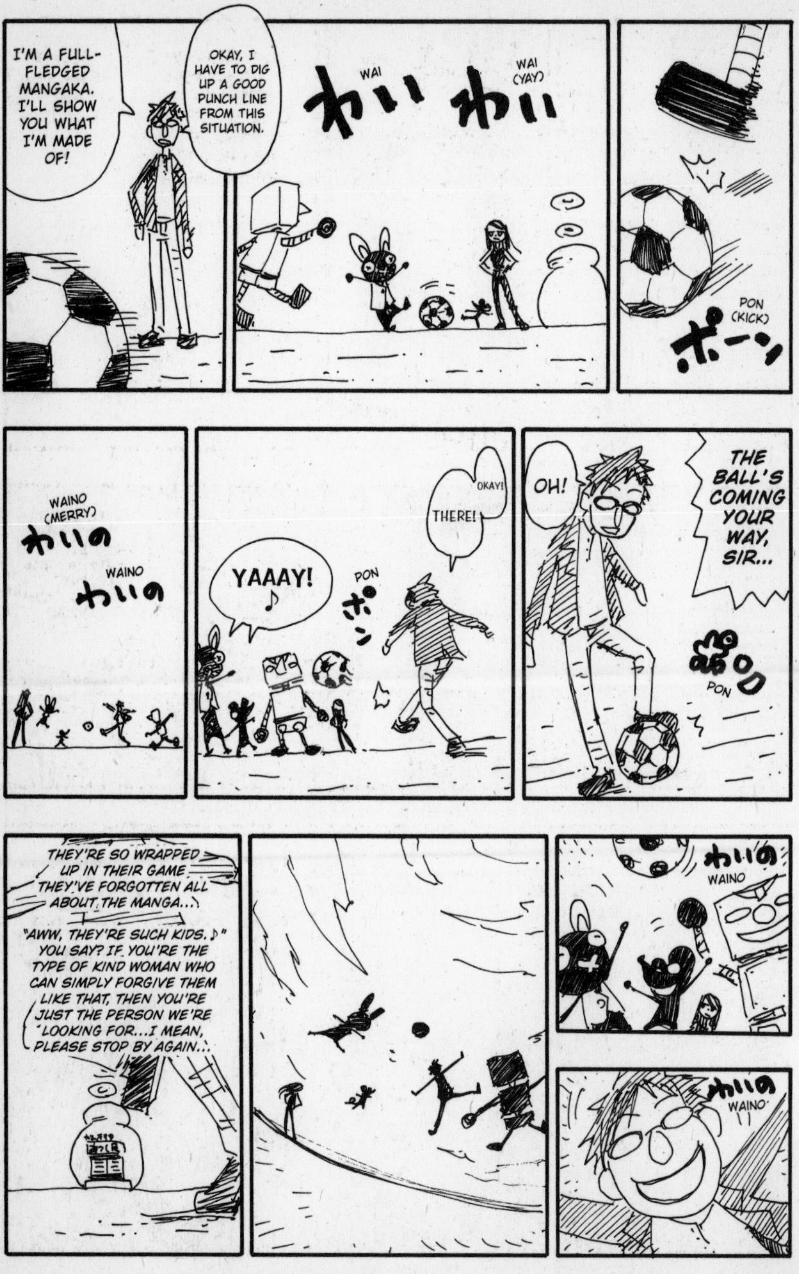
ポーン
PON (KICK)
OKAY, I HAVE TO DIG UP A GOOD PUNCH LINE FROM THIS SITUATION.
わい
WAI (YAY)
わい
WAI
I'M A FULL-FLEDGED MANGAKA. I'LL SHOW YOU WHAT I'M MADE OF!
THE BALL'S COMING YOUR WAY, SIR...
OH!
PON
OKAY!
THERE!
ポン
PON
YAAAY! ♪
わいの
WAINO (MERRY)
わいの
WAINO
わいの
WAINO
わいの
WAINO
THEY'RE SO WRAPPED UP IN THEIR GAME THEY'VE FORGOTTEN ALL ABOUT THE MANGA...
"AWW, THEY'RE SUCH KIDS. ♪" YOU SAY? IF YOU'RE THE TYPE OF KIND WOMAN WHO CAN SIMPLY FORGIVE THEM LIKE THAT, THEN YOU'RE JUST THE PERSON WE'RE LOOKING FOR...I MEAN, PLEASE STOP BY AGAIN...

Translation Notes

Common Honorifics

no honorific: Indicates familiarity or closeness; if used without permission or reason, addressing someone in this manner would constitute an insult.

-san: The Japanese equivalent of Mr./Mrs./Miss. If a situation calls for politeness, this is the fail-safe honorific.

-sama: Conveys great respect; may also indicate that the social status of the speaker is lower than that of the addressee.

-kun: Used most often when referring to boys, this indicates affection or familiarity. Occasionally used by older men among their peers, but it may also be used by anyone referring to a person of lower standing.

-chan: An affectionate honorific indicating familiarity used mostly in reference to girls; also used in reference to cute persons or animals of either gender.

-senpai: A suffix used to address upperclassmen or more experienced coworkers.

-sensei: A respectful term for teachers, artists, or high-level professionals.

Page 22
"**Cheers! Cheers! Jeers!**" Here, Doctor Stein starts out saying "*Kanpai!*" (which means "Cheers!" in Japanese), but the third time, he says "*nanmai*," which sounds roughly similar to "*Kanpai*," but has a totally different meaning ("how many"). This just goes to show how "drunk" Doctor Stein is...or not.

Page 34
Although the name is "**Independent Cube**" in English, the Chinese characters given mean "area of non-interference."

Page 56
Asura is also a term for a low-ranking deity in Buddhism and Hinduism. These dieties are typically portrayed as belligerent, looking for any excuse to get into a fight.

Page 118
Gi, Go, and Shoku are how the Japanese refer to the Three Kingdoms of ancient China: Wei, Wu, and Shu. Also, when Stein says "Three-fold!!" he uses the word "*sangoku*," which is a homonym for the Japanese word for "three countries/kingdoms".

Page 186
Kaette Kita means "returned" in Japanese and is a reference to *Kaette Kita Ultraman* (*The Return of Ultraman*), a short live-action film made by Daicon Films — a company that would eventually develop into Gainax, a major anime production company.

Can't wait for the next volume? You don't have to!

Keep up with the latest chapters of some of your favorite manga every month online in the pages of YEN PLUS!

MAXIMUM RIDE

DANIEL X

YOTSUBA&!

K-ON!

gossip girl

Visit us at www.yenplus.com for details!

YEN+ Plus

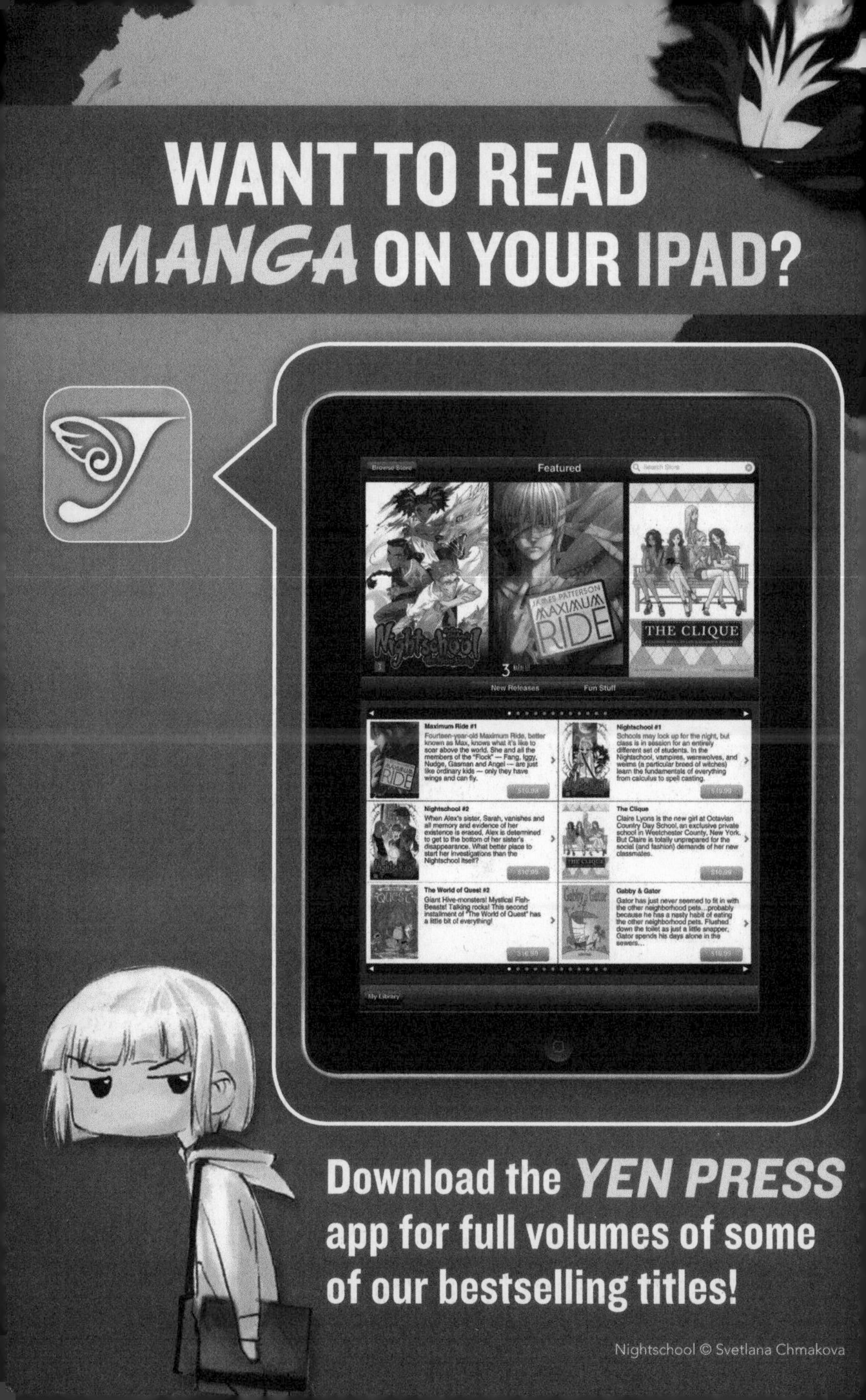
WANT TO READ
MANGA ON YOUR IPAD?
Featured
New Releases
Fun Stuff
My Library
Download the YEN PRESS
app for full volumes of some
of our bestselling titles!
Nightschool © Svetlana Chmakova

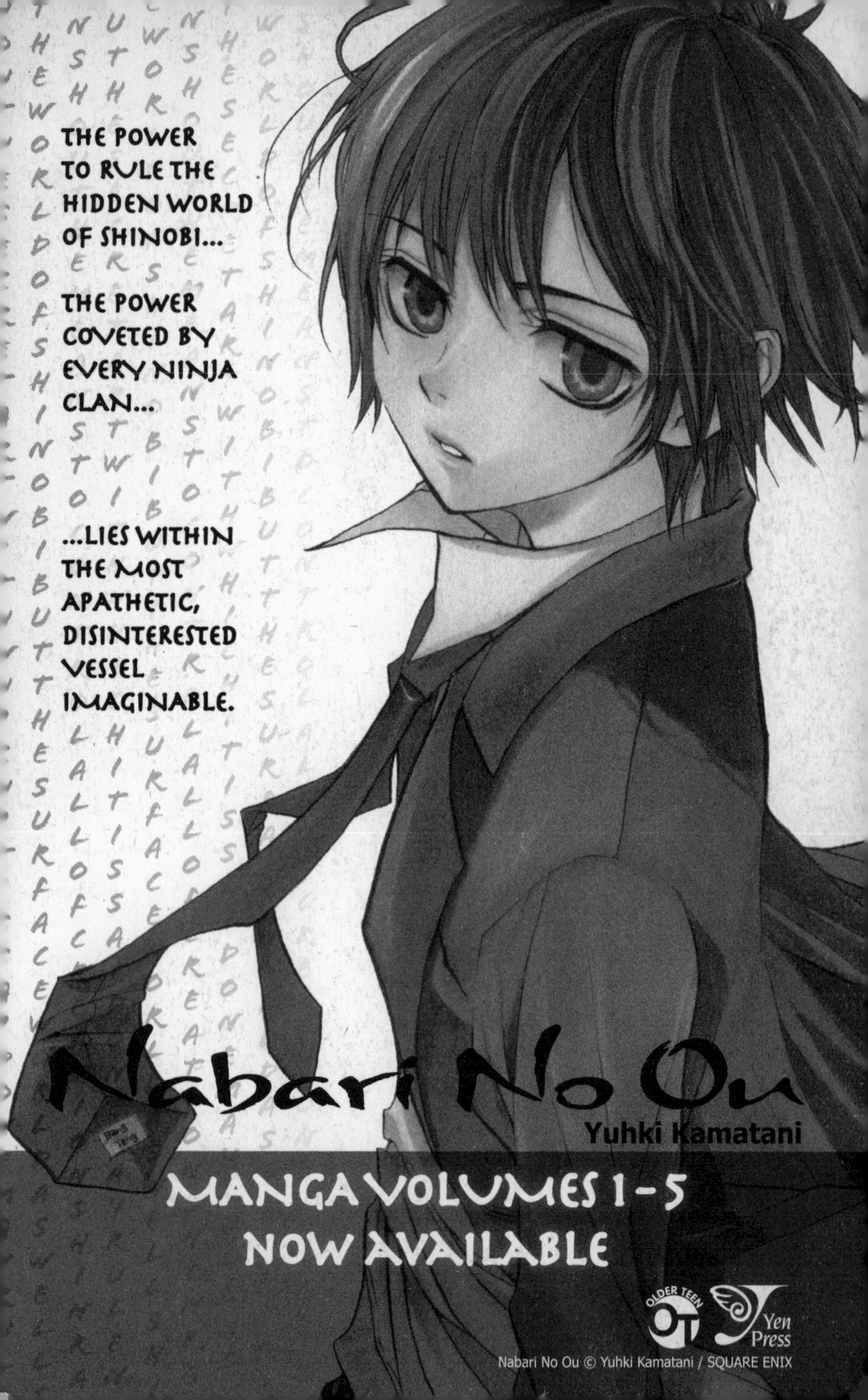
THE POWER TO RULE THE HIDDEN WORLD OF SHINOBI...
THE POWER COVETED BY EVERY NINJA CLAN...
...LIES WITHIN THE MOST APATHETIC, DISINTERESTED VESSEL IMAGINABLE.
Nabari No Ou
Yuhki Kamatani
MANGA VOLUMES 1-5
NOW AVAILABLE
OLDER TEEN
OT
Yen Press
Nabari No Ou © Yuhki Kamatani / SQUARE ENIX

The Phantomhive family has a butler who's almost too good to be true...

...or maybe he's just too good to be human.

Black Butler

YANA TOBOSO

VOLUMES 1-4 IN STORES NOW!

SOUL EATER ⑤

ATSUSHI OHKUBO

Translation: Amy Forsyth

Lettering: Alexis Eckerman

SOUL EATER Vol. 5 © 2006 Atsushi Ohkubo / SQUARE ENIX. All rights reserved. First published in Japan in 2006 by SQUARE ENIX CO., LTD. English translation rights arranged with SQUARE ENIX CO., LTD. and Hachette Book Group through Tuttle-Mori Agency, Inc.

Translation © 2011 by SQUARE ENIX CO., LTD.

Yen Press
Hachette Book Group
237 Park Avenue, New York, NY 10017

www.HachetteBookGroup.com
www.YenPress.com

Yen Press is an imprint of Hachette Book Group, Inc. The Yen Press name and logo are trademarks of Hachette Book Group, Inc.

First Yen Press Edition: February 2011

ISBN: 978-0-316-07107-9

10 9 8 7 6 5 4

BVG

Printed in the United States of America